W9-BGX-110

Criminal Behavior Systems
A Typology

Criminal Behavior Systems

A Typology

Second Edition

Marshall B. Clinard
University of Wisconsin

Richard Quinney

HOLT, RINEHART AND WINSTON, INC.
New York   Chicago   San Francisco   Atlanta
Dallas   Montreal   Toronto   London   Sydney

To Ruth and Valerie

Preface

Criminal behavior covers a great variety of violations of criminal laws. For purposes of explanation this behavior must be broken down into types. In this book, after discussing the construction of types of crime, we formulate and utilize a typology of criminal behavior systems. We believe that continued progress in criminology will depend greatly on the study of types of criminal behavior.

The first edition of this book appeared in 1967. It has been received both as a textbook and as a substantial contribution to criminology. The typology has been reprinted and referred to frequently in other books. Nevertheless, we felt that the book needed considerable revision and were encouraged by others to make some substantive changes. The new edition no longer contains a collection of readings but is a substantive and integrated discussion of a typology of criminal behavior systems. In the original edition, research articles on each type of criminal behavior followed the discussion. In this revision we have increased the discussion of each type and have incorporated the research into our presentation. Those who are interested in the separate research studies may wish to consult the first edition.

In this edition we have developed more fully the dimensions of our typology. In particular, we felt in the original formulation we had not properly considered how certain offenses relating to each type had become defined as crimes nor the differences in the legal processing of each type, a difference that affects each type of behavior. Consequently, we have added to our dimensions, previously consisting of "criminal career of the offender," "group support of criminal behavior," and "correspondence between criminal and legitimate behavior," the dimensions "legal aspects of selected offenses" and "societal reaction and legal processing."

New material has been added to the discussion of each type, particularly those sections on violent personal and political criminal behavior. A new type, *corporate* criminal behavior, has been added to the original eight types of criminal behavior—*violent personal, occasional property, public order, conventional, political, occupational, organized,* and *professional.* We feel that this new type distinguishes between the complex criminal behavior of large corporations and other kinds of occupational criminal behavior. It also relates to the problems inherent in corporate capitalism.

It is our hope that this book will continue to be useful to criminologists in formulating their own theories and research on criminal behavior and to students in the field of criminology.

We are indebted to those who have devoted much time and effort to research on types of criminal behavior. Our typology has grown out of such work.

Madison, Wisconsin   M. B. C.
Chapel Hill, North Carolina   R. Q.
September 1972

Contents

Criminal
Behavior
Systems
A Typology

Types of Criminal Behavior 1

We all attempt to give meaning to our existence. Our common goal is to make the world understandable. A principal way we achieve understanding is by generalizing beyond the unique and the particular. Whether we are entirely participants or sometime observers of the social scene, we understand largely by searching for the recurrent and uniform. We thus comprehend the world of concrete experience by abstraction.

All phenomena, of course, are unique in time and space. Nothing ever recurs. But in order to make our experiences intelligible, we make sacrifices in the infinite variety of life. We construct images or concepts in our attempt to "know" the world around us. These constructs are a reduction of our experiences, a reduction that treats occurrences *as if* they were similar, recurrent, and general. Events are placed into categories. Phenomena become comparable.

Thus, as with all human endeavors, the systematic study of behavior is based on an ordering of the diversified world of discrete phenomena. This is accomplished in the sciences by the development of classifications or typologies. Concrete occurrences are ordered and compared by categorizing observations into classes or types. As abstractions, types necessarily deviate from the concrete in that they accentuate attributes relevant to a particular analysis. A type consists of characteristics that have empirical referents, although they may not be experienced directly in the form of a given type.

Typologies have been used for centuries in the study of physical and human phenomena. For example, an important typology was created by the Swedish botanist Linnaeus two centuries ago when he developed the modern scientific classification of plants and animals. The use of typologies is common today, not only in botany, but in zoology, geography, geology, and other physical sciences. Similarly, in the area of human behavior, the scientist attempts to derive types, whether they be types of social organization, occupational types, or types of deviants. The use of types in the ordering of the diversities of observed phenomena has been instrumental in the development of the social sciences.

Types not only reduce phenomena to more systematic observation; they also assist in the formulation of hypotheses and serve as guides for research. The construction of types may lead to theoretical formulation. The

1

constructed type, in fact, as Hempel notes, can serve as a theoretical system in itself by "(1) specifying a list of characteristics with which the theory is to deal, (2) formulating a set of hypotheses in terms of those characteristics, (3) giving those characteristics an empirical interpretation, and (4) as a long-range objective, incorporating the theoretical system as a 'special case' into a more comprehensive theory."[1]

Thus the construction of types from a broad range of phenomena is a necessary stage in the development of specific theories; it also offers the possibility of formulating a comprehensive theory for the explanation of all the phenomena under observation. And, conversely, a typology can be derived from a general theory of a specified phenomenon. There is, indeed, an interaction between theory construction and typology. While types may emerge from theory, they also are instrumental in the reformulation and expansion of theory. Typology and its relation to theory construction are essential to the further development of general theory.

TYPOLOGIES IN CRIMINOLOGY

A diverse and wide range of behaviors is included in the category of crime. The one characteristic which all the behaviors have in common is that they have been defined as criminal by recognized political authority. Much of the work in criminology has been concerned with crime in general. Because of the increasing realization, however, that crime refers to a great variety of behaviors, criminologists have in recent years turned their attention to the study of particular types of crime. Thus, criminologists are now

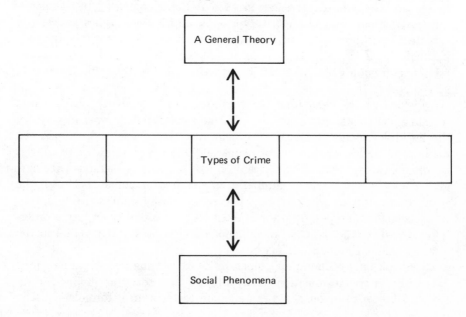

giving greater attention to the identification, classification, and description of types of criminal behavior.

Moreover, efforts are being made to delineate categories of crime and criminal behavior which are homogeneous with respect to a specific explanation. In criminology, considering the wide range of phenomena subsumed under the concept of crime, a general theory may be formulated after specific types of crime have been established. The diagram on the opposite page illustrates a method of theory construction in criminology.

The interdependence of typology and theory construction is clear. Theoretical assumptions are necessary for the formulation of types, and a typology forces the reformulation of general theory. An adequate explanation of crime will show not only how the explanation applies to all crime but how it is specified to explain the various types of crime.

Criminologists in the past have constructed and utilized many different typologies of crime and criminals. The most common typologies have been the legalistic, individualistic, and social.

Legalistic Typologies

The oldest and still the most frequently used forms of classification are based on the legal definition of the offense. A familiar legalistic classification is in terms of the seriousness of the offense as indicated by the kind of punishment provided for the behavior. The most serious offenses are called felonies and are usually punishable by confinement in a state prison or by death. The less serious offenses are called misdemeanors and are usually punishable by fines or by confinement in a local jail. As a classification of crime this is not very useful and is ambiguous because it is difficult to make clear-cut distinctions between the two major types of offenses. For example, many criminal acts classified as felonies in one state are classified as misdemeanors in other states. Also the form of punishment prescribed for a given offense differs from time to time and from place to place.

It is common also to identify the criminal act (or the criminal) in terms of a legal category. Thus, criminals are referred to as murderers, burglars, robbers, embezzlers, and rapists in terms of specific offenses defined in the criminal code. The category of "crimes against the person" includes such illegal acts as murder, assault, and rape; "crimes against property" include burglary, larceny, forgery, and automobile theft; and "crimes against public order" consist of such behavior as prostitution, gambling, drunkenness, disturbing the peace, and the use of narcotics. This method of classifying criminals suffers from a number of disadvantages.[2] For example (1) it tells nothing about the person and the circumstances associated with the offense, nor does it consider the social context of the criminal act, as in the case of rape or the theft of an auto; (2) it creates a false impression of specialization by implying that criminals confine themselves to the kind of crime for which they happen to be caught or convicted; (3) it is a common practice in order to secure easy convictions to allow offenders to receive a reduced sentence by "plea copping" or pleading guilty to a lesser charge that may only slightly resemble the original charge or offense; (4) because the legal definition of a criminal act varies according to time and place, the legal classification of crime presents problems for comparative analysis; and (5) most important of all, the use of legal categories in a classification assumes that offenders with a certain legal label, such as burglars, robbers, auto thieves, and rapists, are all of the same type or are a product of a similar process.

There have been a number of attempts to overcome some of the problems of legalistic classifications, while still utilizing the legal categories. Although the categories of crime defined in the criminal law may not be appropriate for sociological purposes, they may nevertheless be used in various ways in forming types of crime. One possibility is that types may be defined *within* specific legal categories. For example, burglars, depending upon their mode of operation, could be divided into housebreakers, safecrackers, professional burglars, and amateur burglars. Another possibility is that legal categories may be *combined*. Criminologists who favor the strategy of defining types according to legal categories claim that the procedure is desirable because official data concerned with criminal histories exist in terms of legal nomenclature, and because the criminal code contains specific operational definitions of criminal behavior.

Roebuck has constructed a criminal typology based on arrest records of 1155 prison inmates in the District of Columbia reformatory.[3] On the basis of arrest patterns, Roebuck postulates four main types of careers: the single arrest pattern, the multiple pattern, the mixed pattern, and no pattern. The single pattern refers to those situations in which an individual is arrested three or more times for one type of crime such as narcotic violations or burglaries. The multiple pattern refers to those situations in which an individual presents two or more patterns. The mixed pattern refers to those situations in which an individual is arrested three or more times but no single pattern emerges. The fourth type, no pattern, refers to those situations in which an individual is arrested fewer than three times. Employing this scheme, thirteen different patterns of crime emerge: single robbery, single narcotics, single numbers game, single burglary, single sex offense, single auto theft, single confidence game, single forgery, double pattern (larceny and burglary), double pattern (assault and drunkenness), triple pattern (larceny, assault, and drunkenness), mixed patterns, and no patterns. His typology includes such offender types as "Negro drinkers and assaulters," "Negro drug addicts," "Negro armed robbers," and "Negro jack-of-all-trades offenders." The types are then described and compared according to the social and personal characteristics of the offenders in each respective type.

Whereas typologies such as this have been useful in pointing out the error of using a single arrest to type an offender and suggesting instead career patterns, they have a number of limitations. One has been the tendency to categorize offenders by race, as a Negro or Caucasian armed robber, which may not be an especially meaningful distinction. Moreover, such inductively derived typologies could mount up indefinitely by this method of using arrests.

Another possibility regarding the use of legal categories is that sociological types may be constructed that *cut across* some of the behaviors included in a number of legal categories. Cressey, for example, included within "criminal violation of financial trust" some of the behaviors officially handled as forgery, confidence game, embezzlement, and larceny by bailee.[4] As practical as these procedures of using various legal classifications appear, they have largely resulted in innumerable unrelated categories of crime lacking a common frame of reference. They have not generated integrated typological schemes.

An important problem remains in the construction of legal typologies of crime. The problem is in respect to the controversy over what behaviors and what persons should be regarded as criminal.[5] This controversy is relevant to the construction of typologies of crime. Posed in question form: At what stage of the criminal defining process should persons and behaviors be regarded as criminal? Is it at the stage of official detection, at the stage of official adjudication, or at the stage of official disposition? Or, to state the extreme, should a typology of crime include persons and behaviors irrespective of official legal action? Even if the criterion of official legal action is dropped in the construction of a typology, there is still the problem of how long a person remains a criminal after he violates the criminal law. Ultimately the selection of the stage of legal action that is going to be used in defining the persons and behavior to be included in a typology of crime depends upon the purpose of the typology and the kinds of research problems that are anticipated.

The use of legal categories of crime is valid when the purpose is to understand the process by which behavior becomes defined as criminal.[6] Since criminality is not inherent in behavior but is a quality conferred upon individuals and acts by others, the study of the formulation and administration of the law is important to the criminologist. The legal definition of crime is the best indication of how the category of crime is created as a form of public policy. Any typology could incorporate the legal aspects of criminal offenses. The legal category itself is a social phenomenon.

Individualistic Typologies

Several Italian criminologists who rejected the legal definitions of crime over seventy-five years ago were instrumental in turning the attention of criminologists to classification and to the use of criteria other than those found in the criminal law.[7] The early criminologists of the Italian or positivist school delimited types of offenders in terms of a heterogeneous collection of personal attributes. Lombroso (1835–1909), for example, identified, to his satisfaction at least, a "born criminal" with a unique, inferior physique. Later, Lombroso recognized other types of criminals, including (1) the insane criminal, (2) the criminal by passion, and (3) the occasional criminal, a type that emphasized the social aspects of the offender as well as individualistic characteristics.

Garofalo (1852–1934), an Italian jurist, maintained that criminals are characterized by psychological anomalies. He divided these defectives into four categories: (1) typical criminals, or murderers who kill for enjoyment, (2) violent criminals, (3) criminals deficient in pity and probity, and (4) lascivious criminals. In a not too different fashion, Ferri (1856–1929) distinguished between five types of criminals, namely (1) the insane, (2) the born, (3) the habitual, (4) the occasional, and (5) the passionate.

Clinical psychologists and psychiatrists have subsequently attempted to classify criminal offenders by utilizing either a single personality trait or a syndrome or grouping of traits. Accordingly, criminal offenders have been grouped according to whether they are immature, emotionally insecure, dependent, hostile, antisocial, nonconformists, or aggressive. Sometimes a single trait has been used to apply to a variety of criminal careers differing in both the nature and the seriousness of the activity. Consequently, personality trait syndromes by themselves have little meaning for distinguishing either types of criminal careers or the behavior of criminals from noncriminals who also may have these traits.

In terms of individualistic factors, offenders also have been divided according to their sex, age, rural-urban background, and other personal attributes. Sex is not a meaningful criterion for classification for, with the exception of prostitution, women in the Western world now commit as wide a variety of offenses as men, although not as frequently. It is increasingly difficult to distinguish clearly among offenders merely upon the basis of sex. Likewise, age is a somewhat meaningless classification because all types of crime are committed by persons of varying ages. Offenders committing the most overt serious crimes, however, are more frequently under twenty-five years of age, while the so-called white collar crimes of business and professional persons are committed by older persons. Classification of offenders by age has little merit, for the criminal development of an offender may have little relation to his age. An offender may be considered developed criminally if he has unfavorable attitudes toward laws, property, and the police, professional knowledge of techniques to commit crimes and avoid prosecution, and a framework of rationalizations to support his conduct. These qualities can be present in a teen-age offender and be comparatively absent in a middle-aged one.

The individualistic approach to criminal classification employs the questionable assumption that individuals with particular personal characteristics commit certain types of crime. In addition, the individualistic approach implies that persons with these characteristics specialize in particular offenses. Finally, while individualistic classifications may have limited diagnostic possibilities for treatment, they have little utility for the construction of sociological theories of criminal behavior.

Social Typologies

If crime is to be studied as a social phenomenon, it is necessary to delineate types of criminal behavior according to the social context of the criminal offender and the criminal act. A number of such types have been developed. Two European criminologists of the last century, Mayhew and Moreau, proposed criminal types based on the way in which crime is related to the various *activities* of the criminal. Mayhew distinguished between professional criminals, who earn their living through criminal activity, and accidental offenders, who commit criminal acts as a result of unanticipated circumstances. Moreau added one other type of criminal to Mayhew's types. Recognizing that many of the criminals who commit crimes against the person cannot be included in either of Mayhew's types, Moreau designated the *habitual criminal* as one who continues to commit criminal acts for such diverse reasons as a deficiency in intelligence and lack of self-control.

Aware of the Mayhew-Moreau criminal types, Lindesmith and Dunham devised a continuum of criminal behavior ranging from the *individualized criminal* to the *social criminal*.[8] The criminal acts of the individualized criminal are committed for diverse and personal reasons, with the behavior finding little cultural support. The criminal behaviors of the social criminal, on the other hand, are supported and prescribed by group norms. The social criminal through his criminal behavior achieves status and recognition within a group. In addition, although the social criminal uses illegitimate means, the goals he seeks, such as economic gain and security, are valued by the broader culture. The types of criminals found between the extremes share in varying degrees the characteristics of one or the other polar types. In the individualized category is the situational or accidental criminal, for example, a murderer who prior to the crime was a law-abiding person. In the social category is the professional criminal, such as the racketeer or the confidence man. Lindesmith and Dunham also employ a third type, *habitual-situational.* This type is utilized to classify all those criminals who actually are not professional, but are more than situational or accidental offenders. This type of criminal is described as the offender who, while not a profesional, is constantly in trouble with the legal authorities, committing in a somewhat fortuitous and free-wheeling manner such crimes as robbery and larceny, intermixed with legitimate economic activities. A slum juvenile delinquent might be described as *habitual-situational.* This trichotomy, while consisting of rather broad categories, does not, however, appear to be exhaustive. For instance, as Lindesmith and Dunham suggest, white collar crime committed by persons in the upper socioeconomic groups, does not

seem to fit in any one of the three categories. It is not a situational or accidental crime, since in many cases the individual criminal may have committed the crime continuously over a lifetime. It is not a professional crime,
for in many cases (such as embezzlement) the offender may be a situational criminal. Also, it is not a habitual-situational crime, for Lindesmith
and Dunham definitely describe this type as being overt in nature, and
white collar crime is characterized by anything but overtness. More important, research subsequent to the development of this typology has indicated considerable group and social factors in such offenses as murder,
aggravated assault, and forcible rape which they had tended to regard as
of the individual type.

A number of criminologists have stressed vocational aspects of certain forms of crime. They have seen that some crimes are committed by
persons who pursue criminal behavior as a *career*. Reckless has suggested
two types of criminal careers: ordinary and professional.[9] As career crimes,
these three types of crime are similar in that they usually involve property
offenses for the purpose of gain; the criminals tend to specialize in particular violations; the commission of the offenses requires various degrees of
skill and experience; crime is pursued as a way of life; and career criminals
continue in crime for a long period of time, possibly for a lifetime. In
terms of differences among the career types, ordinary criminals represent
the lowest rank of career crime. They engage in conventional crimes, such
as robbery, larceny, and burglary, which require limited skill. Ordinary
criminals lack the organization to avoid arrest and conviction. Professional
criminals, on the other hand, are highly skilled and are thus able to obtain
considerable amounts of money without being detected. Because of organization and contact with other professional criminals, these offenders are
often able to escape conviction. Professional criminals specialize in offenses
that require skill rather than violence, such as confidence games, pickpocketing, shoplifting, sneak thievery, and counterfeiting. Whereas this
distinction is important and valid insofar as it goes, it is limited to those
who make an occupation or career out of crime.

A more comprehensive typology has been developed by Gibbons. His
typology is based primarily on role-careers in which identifiable changes
occur in different offender types.

There are some criminal patterns in which role-performance is begun
and terminated in a single illegal act, and there are others in which involvement in the deviant role continues over several decades or more,
as in the instance of professional criminals. Some delinquent roles lead
to adult criminality, whereas other delinquent roles are terminal ones,
for they do not normally precede or lead to involvement in adult deviation. In turn, some criminal roles have their genesis in juvenile delinquent
behavior, whereas certain other forms of adult criminality develop in
adulthood and are not presaged by delinquent careers. Then, too, some

role-careers involve more changes in the component episodes of the pattern than do others. Semiprofessional property offenders are one illustration. This pattern begins at the onset of minor delinquent acts in early adolescence. Such a career line frequently leads to more serious forms of delinquency with advancing age: repeated police contacts, commitment to juvenile institutions, "graduation" into adult forms of illegal activity, and more contacts with law enforcement and correctional agencies. Over this lengthy development sequence, the social-psychological characteristics of offenders also change. For example, the degree of hostility toward policemen and correctional agents exhibited by the adult semiprofessional criminal is likely to be considerably greater than the antagonism demonstrated by the same person at an early age. The same comment could be made regarding changes in self-image, attitudes, and other matters.[10]

A uniform frame of reference employing the criteria of "definitional dimensions" and "background dimensions" is used by Gibbons. The definitional dimensions consist of: (1) the nature of the offense behavior, (2) the interactional setting with others in which the offense takes place, (3) self-concept of the offender, (4) attitudes toward society and agencies of social control such as the police, and (5) the steps in the role career of the offender. There are four aspects of the "background dimensions" of each type: (1) social class, (2) family background, (3) peer group associations, and (4) contact with defining agencies such as the police, courts, and prisons. On this basis Gibbons sets up fifteen adult types and nine juvenile types.

Adult Types	*Juvenile Types*
Professional thief	Predatory gang delinquent
Professional "heavy" criminal	Conflict gang delinquent
Semiprofessional property criminal	Casual gang delinquent
Property offender—"one-time loser"	Casual delinquent,
Automobile thief—"joyrider"	nongang member
Naive check forger	Automobile thief—"joyrider"
White-collar criminal	Drug user—heroin
Professional "fringe" violator	Overly aggressive delinquent
Embezzler	Female delinquent
Personal offender—"one-time loser"	"Behavior problem" delinquent
"Psychopathic" assaultist	
Violent sex offender	
Nonviolent sex offender—	
nonviolent "rapo"	
Nonviolent sex offender—	
statutory rape	
Narcotic addict—heroin	

Unfortunately, some of his types are not sharply delineated and tend to overlap or be unclear as to their specific characteristics. Other types depart from an essentially general group and cultural frame of reference and present a largely individualistic psychological orientation which is somewhat contradictory to the overall frame of reference.

A somewhat different typology has been developed by Cavan, which gives principal consideration to the public reaction to crime and the criminal's reaction to the public.[11] In an analysis of the interaction between the public and the criminal, seven types of criminal behavior are constructed: (1) criminal contraculture (professional crime, robbery, burglary), (2) extreme underconformity (for example, occasional drunkenness), (3) minor underconformity (for example, embezzlement), (4) "average" conformity (minor pilfering), (5) minor overconformity (exactness in obeying laws and moral codes), (6) extreme overconformity (attempts to reform society by persuasion and legal means), and (7) ideological contraculture (strenuous efforts to remodel society, possibly through the use of illegal means). Because societal reaction is crucial to the criminal's self-concept and subsequent behavior, it is an important variable to be included in a typology of crime.

An indication of the importance of the typological approach in modern criminology can be seen in the attention devoted to the subject in several contemporary criminology textbooks. Bloch and Geis, for example, give considerable attention to types of criminal behavior systems and to the social and cultural structure in which criminal behavior systems arise.[12] Their types of criminal behavior systems include professional crime, organized crime, homicides and assaults, sex offenses, property offenders, white collar crime, and public order offenses.

PRINCIPLES OF CRIMINAL TYPOLOGY

There are several methodological problems in the construction of criminal typologies. These problems serve as the basic principles of criminal typology.

Classification and Typology

While not always followed in practice, a distinction can be made between a classification (composed of classes) and a typology (composed of types). A strict *classification* consists of a set of variables or attributes which are linked to form a number of logically possible classes. A *typology*, in contrast, attempts to specify the ways in which the attributes of observable phenomena are empirically connected in the formation of particular types.

Moreover, in a classification there is the assumption that all cases within a class share the properties of that class to the same extent. The type, however, "acts as a point of reference that determines the extent to which any empirical case conforms to it, the principal consideration therefore being degree of approximation."[13] It is the construction of types rather than classes that interests the criminologist.

Ideal and Empirical Typologies

Another distinction that is commonly drawn is between two kinds of typologies: the ideal and the empirical.[14] Following the lead of Max Weber, an ideal type is an abstraction that does not necessarily describe concrete cases, but represents possible or even extreme cases. An ideal type may be conceived of as a distortion of the concrete. All empirical occurrences can then be viewed in terms of the ideal type.

The empirical typology, on the other hand, is supposedly composed of types that describe exactly the patterns that exist in the real world. While the ideal type is the observer's abstraction, the empirical type is supposed to represent what actually exists.

The distinction between ideal and empirical types is, however, arbitrary. But more than this, the distinction suffers from a faulty epistemology. The problem is related to the age-old controversy between realism and nominalism.

> The question as to whether forms or configurations exist ontologically as the "realist" tradition holds, or whether the form or configuration is merely an abstraction characteristic of the nomenclature as held by the "nominalist" position has persistently been reflected in the argument as to whether types are "real" or merely convenient "fictions." Are types just constructs or are they dictated to observation by some natural arrangement of the phenomena themselves? The literature regarding the "ideal type" has contributed heavily to this controversy. By and large it has been a spurious and fruitless controversy in the social sciences. The question of whether types are real is obviously a metaphysical one and may be of some relevance to philosophers but has little to do with the methodology of the social sciences. The reality of *anything* can be questioned in the same sense that the reality of types is questioned if one wants merely to play the metaphysical game.[15]

Nevertheless, we cannot naively assume that types are "real." But we can dispense with the question of objective reality and the observer's ability to copy it. "There is no reason to believe in the objective reality of anything. Our concern, rather, is with the formulation of constructs that are meaningful for the purposes at hand."[16] Certainly we construct types on the basis of our perceptions and our experiences. Nothing is either totally *a priori* or completely the result of induction. To conceive of types as developing from either source is to ignore the metaphysical problem of the nature of reality. We construct whatever gives meaning to our lives and to the problems that we pose.

First and Second Order Constructs

It is obvious that when social scientists develop constructs, such as criminal types, these constructs are removed from the world of the participants in society. Alfred Schutz has noted this most clearly in his discussion of first order and second order constructs: "The constructs of the social sciences are, so to speak, constructs of the second degree, that is, constructs of the constructs made by the actors on the social scene, whose behavior the social scientist has to observe and to explain in accordance with the procedural rules of his science."[17] And following Schutz, types based on first order constructs are what McKinney calls "existential types," or typifications constructed by participants in society; while the types developed by social scientists, based in part on these data, are "constructed types."[18]

The criminologist is thus engaged in the construction of constructions. By means of types, drawing on the commonsensical world of actors, we are able to understand the social world. But as participants ourselves, it is not always clear whether our constructs are entirely first or second order. They are probably both; but to be concerned solely with the problem is again to fall prey to the unanswerable metaphysical problem.

Moreover, our constructions (our types) are not always based on the common sense of the participants. Rather, our constructions may not at times even take into consideration whether or not they are built on the commonsensical world. But no matter. What we always attempt to do is to make the world understandable at least to ourselves and our audience. And that need not—for better or worse—take into consideration what the world means to those we are describing. But it would probably help.

Theoretical Assumptions and Underlying Dimensions

No matter how implicit, some assumptions about crime and society are always present when we construct criminal typologies. In addition, the particular selection of dimensions is guided by the interests of the criminologist. In other words, the purpose at hand determines how the typology is to be constructed. Also, the level of explanation desired by the criminologist will play a part in the particular selection of dimensions in the typology.

General characteristics for the construction of typologies can be developed in the course of criminological research. With the use of such a technique as factor analysis, for example, common characteristics of offenders can be found. These dimensions in turn can be used in the construction of a typological system. Typologies can also be constructed through the use of findings from other research studies of various kinds of crime and delinquency. Once such typologies are constructed, and with the addition of terms, concepts, and postulates, typologies can serve as axiomatic theories whereby further statements regarding types of crime can be deduced.[19]

Related to the selection of characteristics underlying typologies is the problem of the phenomena to be included in the typology. There has been the tendency in criminology, especially in the development of typologies, to avoid distinguishing between the subclasses of phenomena included in the study of crime. The phenomena associated with crime include (1) the formulation and administration of criminal law, (2) the development of persons and behaviors that become defined as criminal, and (3) the social reactions to crime.

The distinction between these three subject areas is crucial in the construction of typologies in criminology. For example, if a typology is based on *criminal law*, attention is focused on the process by which criminal definitions are imposed on human activity by agents of the law. On the other hand, if the objective is a typology based solely on the *criminal and his behavior*, the emphasis is on the process by which persons who are subject to criminal definition acquire their self-conceptions and their values, and how they associate with others in social and cultural contexts. Or a typology could be constructed on the basis of the nature and extent of *social reaction* to crime.

Yet another typology, a *criminal behavior system*, could be constructed that would consider all three areas of phenomena associated with crime. Such a typology would suggest how persons with certain characteristics and behaviors develop patterns that have a certain probability of becoming defined as criminal and receive a particular reaction from society. The development of a multidimensional and integrative typology is our primary concern.

Comprehensiveness and Homogeneity of Types

There is also the question of whether a typology should include the entire range of crime or be limited in scope. A typology that attempts to be comprehensive must necessarily formulate types at a fairly high level of abstraction. When this is done it is unlikely that many cases will remain outside of the typology. Even cases that exhibit a lack of specific patterning could be included in such a type.[20]

Should a typology incorporate both adults and juveniles? Many of the offenses of juveniles are behaviorally the same as those of adults. Therefore, in constructing types, there may be little reason to create separate types of minors and adults. Instead, various forms of juvenile delinquency can be included in a single typology, as we have done. When an offense committed by a juvenile would be a crime if committed by an adult, it is included within our typology. On the other hand, one could construct a typology based on uniquely juvenile offenses, such as truancy, but this is not our intent.

No typology, unless it is on a very low level of abstraction, can contain purely homogeneous types. For every type, several subtypes could be delineated. The level of abstraction of the typology in general and each type in particular determines the extent to which subtyping may be appropriate. It is always the purpose of the analysis combined with the desired level of abstraction that influences the construction of types. Understandably many of our types could eventually be broken down into subtypes, but this will have to wait further criminological research.

Trends in Criminal Typology

Whatever the nature of typological construction, the trend in criminology is clearly toward further study of types of crime. In the development of typologies we cannot, however, expect to achieve a typological system that all criminologists will agree is the most desirable. To be certain, some classifications will at various times be more popular than others. But there are a number of reasons why we cannot look forward to one typology in criminology.

First, as already mentioned, typologies differ according to the purposes they are to serve. Since there will continue to be a multitude of purposes, including levels of analysis and degrees of generality, there will be a number of typologies. Second, there is the fact that crime is relative. That is, the definitions of crime change from time to time and from place to place. Therefore, the behaviors and persons to be included in a typology will vary according to time and place. It may be that future typologies will be developed which will include the crimes of other historical periods. Third, theory within criminology will continue to develop. As this happens, typologies will be altered. Finally, theories, theoretical frameworks, and the related typologies will change as the orientations of criminologists change. Inevitably, as with all intellectual trends, the interests of criminologists will be attuned to the developments in the larger society.

THEORETICAL DIMENSIONS FOR A TYPOLOGY OF CRIMINAL BEHAVIOR

In the typology presented in this book, types of crime are viewed as *systems* of behavior. As heuristic devices, types are necessarily constructed as *systems*. As one writer noted, "The constructed type is a special kind of concept in that it consists of a set of characteristics wherein the relations between the characteristics are held constant for the purposes at hand. Hence, the type is a pragmatically constructed 'system.' "[21] Our *criminal behavior systems* are constructed types that serve as a means by which concrete occurrences can be described and compared within a system of theoretical dimensions that underlie the types.[22]

The theoretical assumptions of our typology are contained in the five dimensions of the typology. The dimensions are:

1. Legal Aspects of Selected Offenses
2. Criminal Career of the Offender
3. Group Support of Criminal Behavior
4. Correspondence between Criminal and Legitimate Behavior
5. Societal Reaction and Legal Processing

Included in these five dimensions are the diverse phenomena associated with crime, that is, the formulation and administration of criminal law, the development of persons and behaviors that may be defined as criminal, and the social reactions to the behaviors. Together the five dimensions with their specific assumptions form the theoretical basis for our typology of criminal behavior systems.

Legal Aspects of Selected Offenses Crime is a definition of human conduct that is created by authorized agents in a politically organized society.[23] Criminal laws are formulated by those segments of society that have the power to translate their interests into public policy. Criminal laws thus consist of behaviors that are regarded as threatening to the ruling class. The social history of particular criminal laws is a reflection of changes in the power structure of society.

Criminal Career of the Offender The behavior of the offender is shaped by the extent to which criminally defined norms and activities have become a part of the individual's career.[24] The career of the offender includes the social roles he plays, his conception of self, his progression in criminal activity, and his identification with crime. Offenders vary in the degree to which criminally defined behavior has become a part of their life organization.

Group Support of Criminal Behavior The behavior of offenders is supported to varying degrees by the norms of the groups to which they belong. Those who are defined as criminal act according to the normative patterns learned in relative social and cultural settings. Group support of criminal behavior varies according to the associations of the offender with differential norms and the integration of the offender into social groups.

Correspondence between Criminal and Legitimate Behavior Criminal behavior patterns are structured in society in relation to legitimate and legal behavior patterns. Within this context persons develop and engage in actions that have relative probabilities of being defined as criminal. Criminally defined behaviors thus vary in terms of the extent to which they correspond to legitimate patterns of behavior in society. The behavior of the offender is viewed in relation to the norms of the segments of society that have the power to formulate and administer criminal law.

Societal Reaction and Legal Processing Criminally defined behaviors vary in the kind and amount of reactions they receive from the public and from the society in general. The social reactions range from the degree of approval or disapproval to the official sanctioning procedures. Different policies of punishment and treatment are established and administered for each type of criminal behavior. Social reactions are also affected by the visibility of the offense and the degree to which the criminal behavior corresponds to the interests of the power structure of society. Finally, the types of criminal behavior vary in the ways that they are processed through the legal system. Patterns of detection, arrest, prosecution, conviction, sentencing, and punishment exist for each type of criminal behavior.

On the basis of these five theoretical dimensions our typology of criminal behavior systems is constructed.

A TYPOLOGY OF CRIMINAL BEHAVIOR SYSTEMS

Nine types of criminal behavior systems are constructed in relation to the five theoretical dimensions. The types are:

1. Violent Personal Criminal Behavior
2. Occasional Property Criminal Behavior
3. Public Order Criminal Behavior
4. Conventional Criminal Behavior
5. Political Criminal Behavior
6. Occupational Criminal Behavior
7. Corporate Criminal Behavior
8. Organized Criminal Behavior
9. Professional Criminal Behavior

The nine criminal behavior systems can be summarized and diagramed in table form as shown on pp. 18–20.

Violent Personal Criminal Behavior The criminal laws of homicide, assault, and forcible rape are found in most societies, yet the legal categories are qualified and interpreted in their respective social and historical contexts. The offenders do not conceive of themselves as criminals. They are often persons without previous records, but because of certain circumstances commit a personal offense. The offenses are not directly supported by any group, although there may be subcultural definitions favorable to the general use of violence. There is strong reaction to offenses.

Occasional Property Criminal Behavior Criminal laws protect the material interests of the propertied classes, specifically prohibiting forgery, shoplifting, vandalism, and auto theft. The offenders do not usually conceive of themselves as criminals and are able to rationalize their criminal behavior. They are usually committed to the general goals of society and find little support for their behavior in group norms. The behaviors violate the value placed on private property. Societal reaction is not severe in those cases where the offender has no previous record. There is leniency in legal processing.

Public Order Criminal Behavior Specific criminal laws embody the moral sense of particular segments of the community. Such offenses as prostitution, homosexuality, drunkenness, and drug use may be "victimless," but they are disturbing to some community members. The violators may conceive of themselves as criminals when they are repeatedly defined as criminals by others. There is considerable association with other offenders, and some of the behaviors are supported by rather clearly defined subcultures. There is some correspondence between the illegal behaviors of public order offenders and legitimate patterns. Some of the offenses are desired by part of the legitimate society. There is strong social reaction by some segments of society and weak reaction by others. Only a small portion of the offenses result in arrest.

Conventional Criminal Behavior   The laws that protect private property include such crimes as larceny, burglary, and robbery. Offenders begin their careers early in life, often in gang associations. Offenders vacillate between the values of the larger society and those of a criminal subculture. Some offenders continue primary association with other offenders, while others pursue different careers. The behaviors are consistent with the goal of economic success, but inconsistent with the sanctity of private property. There may be a series of arrests and convictions. Rehabilitation programs preserve the status quo without changing social conditions.

Political Criminal Behavior   Criminal laws are created by governments to protect their own existence. Specific criminal laws, such as conspiracy laws, as well as traditional laws, are made to control and punish those who threaten the state. However, government or its officials also violate criminal laws. Political offenders, acting out of conscience, do not usually conceive of themselves as criminals. They receive support for their behavior by particular segments of society. The behaviors of citizens against the government are consistent with the ideal of political freedom and basic human rights. Governmental crimes correspond to the belief in political sovereignty. Public acceptance of political crime depends on the extent to which the policies of the government are regarded as being legitimate.

Occupational Criminal Behavior   Legal regulation of occupations has served to protect the interests of occupational groups. The offenders violate the law in the course of their occupational activity. They are able to rationalize their conduct. Some occupations, or groups within occupations, tolerate or even support these offenses. The behavior corresponds to the pursual of business activity. Because such offenses are committed by "respectable" persons, social reaction has traditionally been mild. Official penalties have been lenient, often restricted to the sanctions administered by the professional associations. Public reaction is becoming less tolerant.

Corporate Criminal Behavior   Criminal laws and administrative regulations have been established to regulate the restraint of trade, false advertising, misuse of trademarks, and the manufacture of unsafe foods and drugs. The laws serve to protect the corporations themselves and to secure

	Violent Personal Criminal Behavior	Occasional Property Criminal Behavior	Public Order Criminal Behavior
Legal Aspects of Selected Offenses	The criminal laws of homicide, assault, and forcible rape are of ancient origin. Yet the legal categories are qualified and interpreted in their respective social and historical contexts. Likewise, the ruling class is able to exclude the forms of violence that enhance its own position.	Criminal laws protect the material interests of the propertied classes. Specific laws prohibit forgery, shoplifting, vandalism, and auto theft.	Specific criminal laws embody the moral sense of particular segments of the community. Such offenses as prostitution, homosexuality, drunkenness, and drug use are disturbing to some community members. Many of the crimes are "victimless" in that only willing participants are involved. Yet it is easier for the power elite to outlaw these behaviors than to either accept them or to change the social arrangements that produced the behaviors.
Criminal Career of the Offender	Crime is not part of the offender's career. He usually does not conceive of self as criminal.	Little or no criminal self-conception. The offender does not identify with crime. He is able to rationalize his behavior.	Most offenders do no regard their behavior as criminal. They do not have a clearly defined criminal career. Ambiguity in self-concept produced in continued contact with legal agents.
Group Support of Criminal Behavior	Little or no group support. Offenses committed for personal reasons. Some support in subcultural norms.	Little group support. Generally individual offenses. Associations tend to be recreational.	Offenses such as prostitution, homosexual behavior, and drug use grow out of, and are supported by, rather clearly defined subcultures. Considerable association with other offenders.
Correspondence between Criminal and Legitimate Behavior	Violations of values on life and personal safety.	Violation of value on private property. Offenders tend to be committed to the general goals of the society.	Some of the offenses are required by legitimate society. Much of the behavior is consistent with legitimate behavior patterns.
Societal Reaction and Legal Processing	Strong social reaction. Harsh punishments. Long imprisonment.	Social reaction is not severe when the offender does not have a previous record. Leniency in legal processing. Probation.	Strong reaction by some segments of society, weak reaction by others. Only a small portion of the offenses result in arrest. Sentences are strong for some offenses, such as the possession of narcotic drugs.

Conventional Criminal Behavior	Political Criminal Behavior	Occupational Criminal Behavior
The laws that protect private property include such crimes as larceny, burglary, and robbery. Since the primary interest is in protecting property, general laws regarding property do not need to distinguish the career nature of many property offenders.	Criminal laws are created by governments to protect their own existence. Specific criminal laws, such as conspiracy laws, as well as traditional laws, are made to control and punish those who threaten the state. Yet the government and its officials often violate criminal laws. Political criminal behavior thus includes crimes against government and crimes by government.	Legal regulation of occupations has served to protect the interests of occupational groups, and in some cases to regulate harmful occupational activities. The legal codes that control occupations and professions tend to be made by the occupations and the professions themselves, representing their own material interests.
Offenders begin their careers early in life, often in gang associations. Crimes committed for economic gain. Vacillation in self-conception. Partial commitment to a criminal subculture.	Political offenders do not usually conceive of themselves as criminals and do not identify with crime. They are defined as criminal because they are perceived as threatening the status quo (as in crime against government), or they are criminal when they violate the laws that regulate the government itself (crime by government).	Little or no criminal self-conception. Occasional violation of the law, accompanied by appropriate rationalizations. Violation tends to be a part of one's work. Offenders accept the conventional values in the society.
Behavior supported by group norms. Early association with other offenders in slum areas. Status achieved in groups. Some persons continue primary association with other offenders, while others pursue different careers.	Support is received by particular groups or by segments of society. They identify or associate with persons who share similar values. Behavior is reinforced by specific norms.	Some occupations, or groups within occupations, tolerate or even support offenses. The offender is integrated into social groups and societal norms.
Consistent with goals of economic success, but inconsistent with sanctity of private property. Gang delinquency violates norms of proper adolescent behavior.	Crimes against government usually correspond to basic human rights. The actions and beliefs, however, are opposed by those who are threatened by these freedoms. Crimes by government correspond to contrary behavior patterns that promote the sovereignty of government rulers.	Behavior corresponds to the pursual of business activity. "Sharp" practices and "buyer beware" philosophy have guided work and consumption patterns.
A series of arrests and convictions. Institutionalization and rehabilitation of the offender. Agency programs that preserve the status quo without changing social conditions.	Official reactions tend to be severe in the case of crimes against government. Considerable harassment may be experienced and heavy sentences may be imposed. Public acceptance of political offenses depends on the extent to which the policies and actions of the government are accepted. Reactions to governmental crime depends on the consciousness of the public regarding the activities of the government.	Reactions have traditionally been mild and indifferent. Official penalties have been lenient, often restricted to the sanctions administered by the professional association. Public reaction is becoming less tolerant.

	Corporate Criminal Behavior	Organized Criminal Behavior	Professional Criminal Behavior
Legal Aspects of Selected Offenses	With the growth of corporations, criminal laws have been created to regulate such activities as restraint of trade, false advertising, fraudulent sales, misuse of trademarks, and manufacture of unsafe foods and drugs. Criminal laws —especially administrative regulations—have been established by the corporations themselves to secure a capitalist economy.	Many traditional laws have been used in the attempt to control organized crime, especially those regarding gambling, prostitution, and drug traffic. The government has more recently enacted special criminal laws in order to infiltrate organized criminal activity in legitimate business and racketeering. But since organized crime is closely tied to the general business economy, these laws tend to invade the privacy of all citizens rather than to control organized crime.	Professional crimes are distinguished by the nature of the criminal behavior rather than by specific criminal laws. Such professional activities as confidence games, pickpocketing, shoplifting, forgery, and counterfeiting are regulated by the traditional laws that protect private property.
Criminal Career of the Offender	The violating corporate official and his corporation have high social status in society. Offenses are an integral part of corporate business operations. Violations are rationalized as being basic to business enterprise.	Crime is pursued as a livelihood. There is a progression in crime and an increasing isolation from the larger society. A criminal self-conception develops.	A highly developed criminal career. Professional offenders engage in specialized offenses, all of which are directed toward economic gain. They enjoy high status in the world of crime. They are committed to other professional criminals.
Group Support of Criminal Behavior	Crime by corporations and corporate officials receives support from similar, even competing, businesses and officials. Lawbreaking is a normative pattern within many corporations. Corporate crime involves a great amount of organization among the participants.	Support for organized criminal behavior is achieved through an organizational structure, a code of conduct, prescribed methods of operation, and a system of protection. The offender is integrated into organized crime.	Professional offenders associate primarily with other offenders. Behavior is prescribed by the norms of professional criminals. The extent of organization among professional criminals varies with the kind of offense.
Correspondence between Criminal and Legitimate Behavior	Corporate crime is consistent with the prevailing ideology that encourages unlimited production and consumption. Only recently has an alternative ethic developed that questions practices that support corporate crime.	While organized crime may be generally condemned, characteristics of American society give support to organized crime. The values underlying organized crime are consistent with those valued in the free enterprise system.	Professional criminal activity corresponds to societal values that stress skill and employment. Some of the offenses depend upon the cooperation of accomplices. The operations of professional crime change with alterations in the larger society.
Societal Reaction and Legal Processing	Strong legal actions have not usually been taken against corporations or their officials. Legal actions have been in the form of warnings and injunctions, rather than in terms of criminal penalties. Public reactions and legal actions, however, are increasing in respect to corporate crime.	Considerable public toleration of organized crime. Offenses are not usually visible to the public. Immunity of offenders, as provided by effective organization, prevents detection and arrest. Convictions are usually for minor offenses.	Considerable public toleration because of the low visibility of professional crime. Offenders are able to escape conviction by "fixing" cases.

a capitalist economy. The criminal behaviors are an integral part of corporate business operations. Violations are rationalized as being basic to business enterprise. Corporate crime involves a great amount of organization among the participants. The offenses are consistent with the prevailing ideology that encourages unlimited production and consumption. Strong legal actions have not usually been taken against corporations and their officials. Public reactions and legal actions are increasing.

Organized Criminal Behavior   Many of the traditional laws have been used in the attempt to control organized crime. Special laws have been enacted to deal with criminal activity in legitimate business and racketering. The offenders pursue crime as a livelihood. In the lower echelons they conceive of themselves as criminals, associate primarily with other criminals, and are isolated from the larger society. In the top levels the offenders associate with persons of legitimate society and often reside in the better residential areas. There is considerable correspondence between the criminal activities of organized crime and legitimate society. Illegal services desired by legitimate society are provided by organized crime. The principles of large-scale enterprise are shared by legitimate society. The public tolerates organized crime, partly because of the services it provides and partly because of the problems in dealing with its operation. Conviction is usually for minor offenses.

Professional Criminal Behavior   Professional crimes are distinguished by the nature of the criminal behavior rather than by specific criminal laws. The laws that protect private property are used to control confidence games, pickpocketing, shoplifting, forgery, and counterfeiting. Professional criminals pursue crime as a livelihood and way of life. They conceive of themselves as criminals, associate with other criminals, and have high status in the world of crime. The extent of organization among professional offenders varies with the kind of offense. There is some correspondence between professional crime and dominant behavior patterns in that professional offenses involve work and skill. The public tolerates many of the offenses because of the low visibility of the behaviors. Many cases of professional criminal behavior are "fixed" in the course of legal processing.

ORGANIZATION OF THE BOOK

The organization of this book is based on the typology of criminal behavior systems constructed above. Each chapter is devoted to one of the criminal behavior systems of the typology. There is a discussion of the type according to each of the theoretical dimensions. Each type is described and previous research and writing on the type are discussed. Each chapter is concluded with a selected bibliography for the particular criminal behavior system.

NOTES

1 Carl G. Hempel, "Typological Methods in the Natural and the Social Sciences," *Proceedings*, American Philosophical Association, Eastern Division (Philadelphia: University of Pennsylvania Press, 1952), Pt. 1, p. 84.

2 See Richard R. Korn and Lloyd W. McCorkle, *Criminology and Penology* (New York: Holt, Rinehart and Winston, 1959), pp. 143–144.

3 Julian B. Roebuck, *Criminal Typology: The Legalistic, Physical-Constitutional-Hereditary, Psychological-Psychiatric and Sociological Approaches* (Springfield, Ill.: Charles C Thomas, Publisher, 1967).

4 Donald R. Cressey, *Other People's Money* (New York: The Free Press, 1953).

5 See Paul W. Tappan, "Who Is the Criminal?" *American Sociological Review*, 12 (February 1947), pp. 96–102.

6 Richard Quinney, *The Social Reality of Crime* (Boston: Little, Brown & Company, 1970), pp. 3–25; Austin T. Turk, *Criminality and Legal Order* (Chicago: Rand McNally & Company, 1969), pp. 8–18.

7 See Hermann Mannheim, ed., *Pioneers in Criminology* (London: Stevens & Sons, Ltd., 1960), Chaps. 1 and 19; Stephen Schafer, *Theories in Criminology* (New York: Random House, 1969), Chaps. 6 and 7.

8 Alfred R. Lindesmith and H. Warren Dunham, "Some Principles of Criminal Typology," *Social Forces*, 19 (March 1941), pp. 307–314.

9 Walter C. Reckless, *The Crime Problem*, 4th ed. (New York: Appleton-Century-Crofts, 1967), pp. 279–298.

10 Don C. Gibbons, *Changing the Lawbreaker: The Treatment of Delinquents and Criminals*, © 1965, Prentice-Hall, Inc., Englewood Cliffs, N. J., pp. 51–52. Gibbons utilizes his typology in his criminology textbook, *Society, Crime, and Criminal Careers* (Englewood Cliffs, N. J.: Prentice-Hall, 1968), pp. 193–433.

11 Ruth Shonle Cavan, *Criminology*, 3d ed. (New York: Thomas Y. Crowell Company, 1962), Chap. 3.

12 Herbert A. Bloch and Gilbert Geis, *Man, Crime, and Society*, 2d ed. (New York: Random House, 1970), pp. 101–106, 167–379.

13 John K. Rhoads, "The Type as a Logical Form," *Sociology and Social Research*, 51 (April 1967), p. 348.

14 Edwin D. Driver, "A Critique of Typologies in Criminology," *The Sociological Quarterly*, 9 (Summer 1968), pp. 356–373; Theodore N. Ferdinand, *Typologies of Delinquency: A Critical Analysis* (New York: Random House, 1966), pp. 41–79; Arthur Lewis Wood, "Ideal and Empirical Typologies for Research in Deviance and Control," *Sociology and Social Research*, 53 (January 1969), pp. 227–241.

15 John C. McKinney, "Typification, Typologies, and Sociological Theory," *Social Forces*, 48 (September 1969), p. 5.

16 Richard Quinney, *The Problem of Crime* (New York: Dodd, Mead & Company, 1970), p. 138.

17 Alfred Schutz, "Concept and Theory Formation in the Social Sciences," Maurice Nathanson, ed., *Philosophy of the Social Sciences* (New York: Random House, 1963), p. 242.

18 McKinney, "Typification, Typologies, and Sociological Theory," pp. 1–3.

19 Clarence Schrag, "A Preliminary Criminal Typology," *Pacific Sociological Review*, 4 (Spring 1961), pp. 11–16.

20 See Clayton A. Hartjen and Don C. Gibbons, "An Empirical Investigation of a Criminal Typology," *Sociology and Social Research*, 54 (October 1969), pp. 56–62.

[21] John C. McKinney, *Constructive Typology and Social Theory* (New York: Appleton-Century-Crofts, 1966), p. 7.

[22] Our typology of criminal behavior systems had its beginnings in Marshall B. Clinard, *Sociology of Deviant Behavior* (New York: Holt, Rinehart and Winston, 1957), pp. 200–209.

[23] This theoretical perspective is developed in Quinney, *The Social Reality of Crime*, pp. 15–23.

[24] For the theoretical background of this perspective, see Marshall B. Clinard, *Sociology of Deviant Behavior*, 3d ed. (New York: Holt, Rinehart and Winston, 1968), pp. 251–256.

Violent Personal Criminal Behavior | 2

Personal crimes involving violence include acts in which physical injury is inflicted, primarily criminal homicide, aggravated assault, and forcible rape, as well as attempts to inflict such injury. Kidnapping involves the element of physical force, and child molesting on occasion also involves the use of force and personal violence. Armed robbery involves violence because of the element of force, such as a gun, knife, or threat of violence in obtaining money.

The use of violence and the reaction of society to it can be viewed in an even wider perspective. The use of personal violence has played an important part in human history from riots to war.

> Not all violence transgresses legal norms, but legal sanctions proscribing many types of violence reflect a general societal opposition to violence, the historical concern with it, and the need to regulate its expression. Murder, rape, aggravated assault, armed robbery, and kidnapping are obvious examples of criminal violence. Labor riots, race riots, lynching mobs, fights among delinquent gangs, and attacks by organized criminal syndicates are all forms of collective violence that have punctuated the history of social change.[1]

Wars, civil riots, and violent demonstrations may involve thousands of individual acts of assault, murder, arson, vandalism, and theft.[2] These are forms of collective violence, however, and, on the whole, their origin and nature are quite different from individual violent personal acts such as criminal homicide, assault, and forcible rape. Collective acts of violence will be discussed in the chapter on political criminal behavior (Chapter 6).

The discussion here will deal only with criminal homicide, aggravated assault, and forcible rape, inasmuch as there is significant research on these offenses. Robbery will not be included as a violent personal crime, primarily because the behavior is generally associated with a career of theft and will thus be discussed as a type of conventional crime. One might include arsonists who set fire to a person's dwelling or property because of a quarrel or general feeling of hatred. Such cases constitute over half of all arson cases and nearly all offenders, like those who commit homicide, assault, and forcible rape, are from lower-class slum areas.[3] This type of offense, however, is more likely to injure the property than to cause personal injury to the victim, and for this reason is excluded from this typology. Also some child molesters could be included, but only 17 percent, one study showed, used force in order to gain compliance, and only 3 percent inflicted actual physical violence upon the child.[4]

LEGAL ASPECTS OF SELECTED OFFENSES

For most of the cultural history of man, generally the murder of or assault on a person was considered to be a private wrong for which the relatives of the deceased either took vengeance or demanded compensation. Such individual acts of violence were, on the whole, of minor concern to the tribal or political state. In fact, it required law enforcement beyond its capacity. Today the minimization of crimes of violence is a matter of primary concern to the legal order.

The distinction between criminal and noncriminal homicides required many centuries of development under English law upon which American law has largely been based. Excusable homicides include killings by misadventure and, under certain circumstances, self-defense. Whereas excusable homicides were never considered felonies in common law, they required the king's pardon and generally resulted in the confiscation of the offender's property, although later this was done away with.

The distinction between murder and manslaughter can be traced to the Norman Conquest. Originally murder (murdrum in Latin) applied both to the killing of a Norman and the fine levied by the king on a district if the offender was not brought to justice. This distinction between the killings of Normans and Englishmen was not eliminated until the fourteenth century when murder acquired the meaning of willful and justifiable homicide. Pardonable homicides were distinguished from those that had "malice aforethought." Early English law did not distinguish between degrees of homicide; all were considered murder. Distinctions in modern law have their origin in statutes enacted in the late fifteenth and sixteenth centuries which excluded "murder upon malice aforethought" from benefit of clergy. Thus two categories were created, the second being all criminal homicides that were not murder, namely, a new category called manslaughter. In the old common law of England one who inadvertently killed another while committing some other felony was guilty of murder.

The type of *criminal homicide* which will be referred to here as "murder" consists of murder, first or second degree, nonnegligent manslaughter, excluding justifiable homicide or attempts or assaults to kill, and negligent manslaughter other than manslaughter arising from motor vehicles. Murder is the unlawful killing of a human being with "malice aforethought."[5] Malice aforethought represents a "guilty mind" but not necessarily premeditation and planning. In many parts of the United States there are degrees of murder, first and second, a legal situation that affects the length of sentence. The concept of malice aforethought eventually took on a meaning under criminal law quite different from its original usage. Today a killing may be said to have malice aforethought when the accused (1) intended to kill either the victim or another, (2) intended to inflict serious bodily injury on the victim, (3) did not intend to kill but engaged in conduct of extreme recklessness, (4) killed another in the course of committing some other felony, or (5) killed a policeman while resisting arrest. Some of these acts are treated as first and others as second degree murder. Under present-day law one may kill an assailant when he believes he is in imminent danger of losing his life or of suffering serious bodily injury. This must be proven to the satisfaction of law enforcement authorities. Generally a person may also use "deadly" force to save a third party who is a member of the actor's household or one to whom the actor has special obligations.

Manslaughter is unlawful or criminal homicide without malice aforethought, that is, without a state of mind that makes a killer a murderer. It covers a wide range of acts, including those which result in accidental death. A person might attack another without the intention of causing death or severe bodily harm but death may be the outcome. The unlawful killing is in a sudden heat or anger and without premeditation. The element of provocation by the victim is often considered an element in manslaughter. All such manslaughter is termed voluntary or nonnegligent manslaughter. Involuntary manslaughter is death arising from unintentional killing, primarily from negligence, that is, death attributable to the negligence of some person other than the victim. In research studies of criminal homicide, deaths arising from negligence in motor vehicle accidents are usually excluded.[6]

In general, murder and aggravated assault are similar, for both involve the use of physical force to settle an argument or a dispute. In aggravated assault there is an attempt to cause a person injury or even deprive him of his life. Nearly all murders thus represent some form of aggravated assault, the chief difference being that the victim died. In fact, serious assaults are invariably considered felonies as they cover such behavior as an attempt to inflict severe injury or to kill, including assault with a deadly weapon, assault to commit murder, or assault by shooting, cutting, stabbing, maiming, and so forth. Whether the behavior results in injury or is only an attempt to cause injury, it is still aggravated assault. In most cases it is probably the element of chance that prevents the offense from sliding over into criminal homicide by the death of one of the parties.

Compared to other crimes, homicide is fairly accurately reported and recorded so that it is possible to make international comparisons. The United States rate is considerably higher than that of most European countries but much lower than most Latin American and African countries. According to United Nations reports, of the twenty-three countries with the highest homicide rates, only Finland, West Germany, Israel, and Czechoslovakia are developed countries, and all of them are near the bottom of the list, which does not include the United States.

The United States rate per 100,000 population is 6.0, Australia 1.5, Canada 1.3, and England and Wales 0.7.[7] Even Finland, which has one of the highest rates in Europe, has a rate of only 2.3. Contrary to many, however, the criminal homicide rate in the United States has moved down and apparently is lower than it was in the 1930s; a national study in 1968 showed that "the wilful homicide rate has decreased somewhat to about 70 percent of its high in 1933."[8] A Philadelphia study, however, indicated that the decline in criminal homicide is misleading.[9] Since rates for aggravated assault and assault with intent to kill have increased, the decline in criminal homicide appears to be the result of better communication with the police to prevent homicides, more rapid transportation to a hospital, and advances in medical technology that have saved seriously wounded persons. Yet, there cannot be complete assurance, for cases of aggravated assault, in turn, may have increased because of more frequent reporting to the police. "Other factors liable to give rise to increased recording of this type of crime include increased reporting by doctors and hospitals, the growth in medical and hospital treatment facilities, and the greater population coverage by medical insurance plans such as Blue Cross which would be likely to step up hospital admissions and recourse to medical treatment. Still only a minority of such assaults, even with knives, are reported; but the proportion may well be increasing."[10]

Forcible rape, the act of having unlawful sexual intercourse with a woman against her will, is to be distinguished from statutory rape, or sexual intercourse with a female under a specific age, generally sixteen or eighteen, with or without consent. Although the actual percentage is not known, it appears that forcible rape constitutes only a small proportion of all arrests and prosecutions for rape. Most arrests for rape are for statutory rape. In the United States, rape involves sexual intercourse accompanied by force and against the woman's consent. If she consents to the intercourse, although the consent may be reluctantly given, and although there may be some force used to obtain it, the offense is generally not rape. In England, on the other hand, the woman's consent is no defense if it is obtained by force.

CRIMINAL CAREER OF THE OFFENDER

Murderers, assaulters, and forcible rapists generally do not have criminal careers. In the case of homicides it is rare to find a person arrested for this crime who has previously committed such an offense, although he may have arrests for other offenses. Approximately two-thirds (60.9), for example, of a sample of homicide offenders in Florence, Italy, had no criminal record.[11] Many had never been arrested before or been incarcerated. People do not make careers out of assaulting people. Of all those arrested in the United States, for example, between 1964 and 1967 for serious crimes, only 35 percent of those arrested for aggravated assault had been arrested previously for this offense.[12] A few persons are exceptions in using actual or threatened violence in the form of assault and even homicide as part of their careers in crime. They are organized criminal offenders who will be discussed in a later chapter.

Most murderers and assaulters do not conceive of themselves as being real "criminals"; they seldom identify with crime, and criminal behavior is not a significant part of their life organizations. To most of these offenders a criminal is one who steals. The situation is different with forcible rapists, since they are reported by some to have a fairly extensive criminal record for other offenses, particularly against property.

Persons who commit assault are unlikely to be involved in other types of crime. In a St. Louis study the majority of the offenders had no prior arrest records, and of those who did, relatively few were for crimes against the person.[13] Two-thirds of the cases in the age bracket of 20–34, however, had a prior arrest record. Contrary to general belief, black assaulters were no more likely than others to have had a prior arrest record. In another St. Louis sample of eighty-eight male offenders, it was found that persons arrested for crimes of violence are rarely arrested for crimes against property and that the reverse holds equally true for property offenders.[14] On the other hand, of those convicted of murder between 1957 and 1968 in England and Wales, between one-half and two-thirds had a criminal record of some type, primarily offenses against property.[15]

A Philadelphia study of criminal homicides found that 66 percent had been previously arrested for offenses against the person (48 percent for aggravated assault) and only 34 percent had any record for property or other offenses.[16] Of these offenders with an arrest record, a larger proportion had a record of aggravated assault involving wife beating and fighting than all types of property offenses combined. In a Wisconsin study, it was found that about half (46.7 percent) of ninety-six Wisconsin prisoners serving time for murder had never been arrested before, whereas only one in three of the sex offenders and only one in eleven of the property offenders had such a record.[17]

A London study of crimes of violence found that the vast majority (eight in ten) of London offenders convicted for a violent offense were convicted for the first time for this type of offense. In fact, the study concluded that "the analysis of crimes of violence according to their factual substance shows that most of the crime is not committed by criminals for criminal purposes but is rather the outcome of patterns of social behavior among certain strata of society."[18] A considerable proportion (nearly half), however, had been convicted of petty offenses, larceny, malicious damage, drunkenness, and, in some instances, breaking and entering. The previous offense history was lowest, however, among those whose offenses arose from a family dispute.

Many of those involved in rape appear to have had a record of arrests for criminal offenses. One study of 1292 forcible rape offenders in Philadelphia showed that 50 percent of them had a past arrest record, and there was little difference in the extent of this past record between black and white offenders.[19] Only 20 percent of those with a past arrest record, however, had previously committed a crime against the person, with blacks far outnumbering the whites in this respect. Approximately one in ten (9 percent) had committed rape in the past. Another study has shown that by the age of twenty-six, 87 percent of forcible rapists had been convicted of some crime; two-thirds had been convicted of a felony, half of them non-sex offenses. For slightly more than half, the forcible rape was their first sex offense, and for about one-quarter, their second. A substantial number had a record of juvenile offenses, 22 percent of the sample, but only 5 percent for sex offenses.[20] In another study aggressive sex offenders showed few sex offenses but many nonsex offenses, a ratio quite different from that of other sex offenders.[21]

GROUP SUPPORT OF CRIMINAL BEHAVIOR

The general cultural and subcultural pattern seems to determine the frequency of crimes of violence. Acceptance of the use of violence varies from country to country, region to region, and state to state. It also varies by neighborhood within a city, by social class, occupation, race, sex, and age.[22] The existence of *subcultures of violence*, normative systems of a group or groups smaller than the total society, has been advanced as a concept, primarily by Wolfgang and Ferracuti, to explain these variations.[23] According to this view, specific populations such as social classes, ethnic groups, and so forth have different attitudes toward the use of violence. The favorable attitudes toward violence are organized into a set of norms that are culturally transmitted. Such subcultural groups exhibit norms about the importance of human life in the scale of values, and the kinds of reactions to certain types of social stimuli in the evaluation of such stimuli and the socialization process in general. A subculture of violence represents values that stand apart from the dominant, central, or "parent" culture or society. It should be pointed out, however, that the proponents of a "subculture" of violence actually base the existence of the theory of differences in *rates* of violence between various groups. This does not, of course, mean that *all* persons in any group share the values supposedly reflected in a subculture of violence or, conversely, in a subculture of nonviolence. A number of propositions about such a subculture of violence have been advanced.

1. *No subculture can be totally different from or totally in conflict with the society of which it is a part.* A subculture of violence is not entirely an expression of violence, for there must be interlocking value elements shared with the dominant culture. . . .
2. *To establish the existence of a subculture of violence does not require that the actors sharing in these basic value elements should express violence in all situations.* The normative system designates that in some types of social interaction a violent and physically aggressive response is either expected or required of all members sharing in that system of values. That the actors' behavior expectations occur in more than one situation is obvious. There is a variety of circumstances in which homicide occurs, and the history of past aggressive crimes in high proportions, both in the victims and in the offenders, attests to the multisituational character of the use of violence and to its interpersonal characteristics. But, obviously, persons living in a subcultural milieu designated as a subculture of violence cannot and do not engage in violence continuously, otherwise normal social functioning would be virtually impossible.
3. *The potential resort or willingness to resort to violence in a variety of situations emphasizes the penetrating and diffusive character of this culture theme.* The number and kinds of situations in which an individual uses violence may be viewed as an index of the extent to which he has assimilated the values associated with violence.
4. *The subcultural ethos of violence may be shared by all ages in a subsociety, but this ethos is most prominent in a limited age group, ranging from late adolescence to middle age.* We are not suggesting that a particular ethnic, sex, or age group all share in common the use of potential threats of violence. We are contending merely that the known empirical distribution of conduct, which expresses the sharing of this violence theme, shows greatest localization, incidence, and frequency in limited subgroups and reflects differences in learning about violence as a problem-solving mechanism.
5. *The counter-norm is nonviolence.* Violation of expected and required violence is most likely to result in ostracism from the group. Alienation of some kind, depending on the range of violence expectations that are unmet, seems to be a form of punitive action most feasible to this subculture. The juvenile who fails to live up to the conflict gang's requirements is pushed outside the group. The adult male who does not defend his honor or his female companion will be socially emasculated. The "coward" is forced to move out of the territory, to find new friends and make new alliances.
6. *The development of favorable attitudes toward, and the use of, violence in a subculture usually involve learned behavior and a process of differential learning, association, or identification.* Not all persons exposed—even equally exposed—to the presence of a subculture of violence absorb and share in the values in equal portions.
7. *The use of violence in a subculture is not necessarily viewed as illicit conduct and the users therefore do not have to deal with feelings of*

guilt about their aggression. Violence can become a part of the life style, the theme of solving difficult problems or problem situations. It should be stressed that the problems and situations to which we refer arise mostly within the subculture, for violence is used mostly between persons and groups who themselves rely upon the same supportive values and norms. A carrier and user of violence will not be burdened by conscious guilt, then, because generally he is not attacking the representatives of the nonviolent culture, and because the recipient of this violence may be described by similar class status, occupational, residential, age, and other attribute categories which characterize the subuniverse of the collectivity sharing in the subculture of violence.[24]

Middle-class norms prohibiting violence often clash with lower-class norms that require violence in certain situations.

The significance of a jostle, a slightly derogatory remark, or the appearance of a weapon in the hands of an adversary are stimuli differentially perceived and interpreted by Negroes and whites, males and females. . . . A male is usually expected to defend the name and honor of his mother, the virtue of womanhood (even though his female companion for the evening may be an entirely new acquaintance and/or a prostitute), and to accept no derogation about his race (even from a member of his own race), his age, or his masculinity. Quick resort to physical combat as a measure of daring, courage, or defense of status appears to be a cultural expectation, especially for lower socio-economic class males of both races.[25]

The greater the degree of integration of the individual into a subculture of violence, in terms of expected reactions to certain types of stimuli and the importance of human life, the more likely that he will resort to violence in a dispute or to gain a sexual objective. Child rearing practices and peer group associations that employ violence are part of this subculture. "Ready access to weapons may become essential for protection against others in this milieu who respond in similarly violent ways, and the carrying of knives or other protective devices becomes a common symbol of willingness to participate in and to expect violence, and to be ready for its retaliation."[26] Thus in the United States violence is often associated by young males with success in a slum world. In this subculture of violence "proving masculinity may require frequent rehearsal of the toughness, the exploitation of women, and the quick aggressive responses that are characteristic of the lower-class adult male. Those who engage in subcultural violence are often not burdened by conscious guilt, because their victims are likely to belong to the same subculture or to a group they believe has exploited them. Thus, when victims see their assaulters as agents of the same kind of aggression they themselves represent, violent retaliation is readily legitimized."[27] Violent crimes are more closely linked to males, particularly young males, partly because of masculinity (or "machismo," as it is known in Latin America), a feeling that maleness is equated with physical aggression.

> Because the young male is better equipped physically than the very young, the middle-aged, or the very old to manifest this form of masculinity; because the youthful male, once having learned this normative value, needs no special education to employ the agents of physical aggression (fists, feet, lithe agility); and because he seeks reinforcement from others for his ego, as do we all, and for his commitment to these values of violence, he comes to play games of conflict within his own subcultural value groups. So does the artist when he competes for a prize, the young scholar for tenure, the financier for new holding companies, and nations for propaganda advantage. But the prescribed rules for street fighting are more deadly quarrels (excepting wars) with weapons of knives, guns, and knuckles instead of the brush, the treatise, or a moon-shot.[28]

Differences between Countries

In general, the homicide rates of the world are related to cultural differences toward the use of violence rather than to laws or individual personality characteristics. On the whole, Latin American countries generally have high rates, whereas most European countries and, in particular, most Scandinavian countries, the United Kingdom, and Ireland have low rates. The United States is about in the middle. South Africa has a very high rate, Turkey and Finland are higher than other European countries, and Ceylon is particularly high for Asia.[29] One study of criminal homicide and assault in Puerto Rico has indicated that the high rates of these crimes in Latin American cultures are related to personal insult or honor. In other words, in some cultures the individual may be expected to use violence in cases of personal vilification or marital triangles.[30] In the Federal District of Mexico City the possibility of death from homicide, it is claimed, is greater than the risk of death from bombing that existed in London during World War II. "The high rates of criminal homicide in Mexico, the convergence of such factors as male sex, membership in the working class and a tradition of employing physical aggression suggest that there exists a subculture of violence."[31]

Regional Differences

Colombia generally has one of the highest rates of violence in the world, having what is probably the most striking example of large-scale cultural violence—called *violencia Colombiana*.[32] While other Latin American countries have always had high homicide rates, Colombia has had a fantastic increase in the cultural use of violence since 1948 when the rate was 11.2 per 100,000, increasing to a high of 51.4 in 1958, and a rate, in 1960, of 33.8. When a popular political leader was assassinated in 1948, violence erupted throughout the country in which Conservatives and Liberals fought bitterly and entire sections of the country fell under armed guerrilla groups. Many of the guerrilla groups eventually became devoid of political meaning and assumed a purely antisocial character. The traditional method was to attack cars and buses or small villages and the killings were carried out in particularly brutal and sadistic manners. Originally rural in nature, violence has permeated the cities and, despite army measures to control it, the homicide rate continues to be high. The homicides during the past ten years in a country of some 10,000,000 persons are estimated to be about 200,000.

Homicides are higher in Sardinia than in any other part of Italy, a fact that prompted an intensive recent study in which Sardinia's violent offenders were compared with Sardinia's nonviolent offenders and, in turn, with violent offenders from other parts of Italy.[33] Psychological tests yielded few attitudes of difference. There were no data that contradicted the hypothesis of a subculture of violence, of the existence of violent, socially learned and reinforced responses of Sardinian offenders. The use of violence, particularly of vendetta (homicides), is regulated by a set of norms or a "code" that takes precedence over Italian criminal law, which is regarded as superimposed. Sardinian offenders exhibited less guilt than other Italian offenders and less rejection by their parents for committing homicides.

> Sardinian violent offenders are reared mostly in a rural milieu that is a subculture of the Italian and even Sardinian legal values and normative culture system. Less educated, occupationally unskilled, farmers or shepherds, they generally are devoid of psychopathologies, resort to violence not within their families but within their residential environment to find targets from an economic nature connected with their honor. Their families seem supportive and understand their use of violence to resolve a problem. Without a sense of guilt, these offenders resort to a reasoned resolution of a conflict through violence rather than seek solace in a civil or criminal court. Reluctant to use the formal authority of the law, which still seems to be imposed from outside the isolationist periphery of his own culture, and supported by all the meaningful groups around him with their same value system as well as dialect, the violent Sardinian offender has significantly different attributes from the violent offenders on the mainland of Italy and from non-violent offenders in general.[34]

The importance of cultural definitions in criminal homicide was revealed several decades ago when wide regional differences in the United States were found.[35] Even today southern homicide rates are considerably higher than those in other regions. This difference is due largely to the facts that cultural definitions demand personal violence in certain situations and that weapons are more frequently carried in some areas than in others. While the high rate of violence in the United States South appears to be a product of a subculture, the explanation of this subculture is not an easy one.[36] For example, some maintain that it is due to the extremely high rates of violence among blacks who constitute a large part of the population. Actually, there is no correlation between these two factors; in fact, states rank lower in violent crimes as the proportion of the black population increases. Another explanation is that the South has a high percentage of lower-class persons, a group prone to violence. Further study, however, actually shows that southern cities with high homicide rates have a higher percentage of the white population in higher status positions. Nor can the pattern of southern violence be explained by the rural nature of the population, relative poverty or backwardness or underdevelopment. After examining this explanation, one writer has suggested it may lie in historical factors such as the influence of slavery as a repressive system on the culture, the type of immigration (Scotch-Irish and fundamentalist) and, above all, "the development of a Southern world view that defines the social, political and physical environment as hostile."[37] Moreover, another study showed that, contrary to the general pattern of other offenses, murder and aggravated assault are negatively correlated with most socio-economic variables whether they occur in rural, urban, or standard metropolitan statistical areas.[38] "Offenses against the person regardless of the population area may become institutionalized and perceived by people in these structures as the most appropriate solutions to interpersonal problems."[39]

The Use of Weapons

The possession of weapons is a part of the subculture of violence as are the norms for their use. The United States, for example, had in its possession in 1968 the tremendous number of 90,000,000 firearms.[40] Of this number, 24,000,000 were hand guns, 35,000,000 rifles, and 31,000,000 shotguns. The United States rate was 13,500 per 100,000 population, while in Canada it was 3000 and in Great Britain under 500. Most European countries have rigorous firearms control laws. Looked at another way, 49 percent of the 60.4 million American households reported firearms ownership or 2.2 firearms per household. Such ownership is highest in the South (59 percent) and lowest in the East (33 percent). Whereas rifle ownership declines sharply with the size of the community, handgun ownership is slightly higher in large cities than in rural areas or in the suburbs.

Firearms, usually handguns, are commonly used in the United States in crimes involving violence—two out of three homicides, one out of five aggravated assaults, and one out of three robberies. Between 1963 and 1968 the number of homicides involving firearms increased 48 percent. Firearms permit greater range, provide more concealment, and permit attacks by persons either unwilling or unable to overpower a victim by other means. When a gun is used the chances of death are five times greater than when a knife is used. In England and Wales, only 18 percent of homicides involve the use of firearms, and only 6 percent of robberies. The percentage of homicides and aggravated assaults involving firearms parallels firearms ownership, except in the South, which lags behind the West and the Midwest in handgun ownership, although it leads in total reported gun ownership. Moreover, a Detroit study showed that firearms violence increased after an increase in handgun acquisition.[41]

There are pronounced differences in the weapons used in aggravated assault and murder. In the United States about one in five of serious assaults were committed with the use of a firearm, as opposed to about two-thirds of homicide cases. About one-fourth of assault cases are committed with hands, fists, and feet, as compared with 10 percent of the homicides.

Local Community, Race, Social Class, and Age

The rates for murder and assault, similar in type, vary a great deal by local area, race groups, social class, and age. An interesting study made in Houston found the characteristics of homicide and aggravated assault offenders to be similar in all aspects, indicating that they represent basically similar behavior.

> Criminal homicide and aggravated assault seem to be similar in all of the analyses. They tend to occur in the same census tracts of the city. The distributions for the hour of the day and day of the week are remarkably similar. They have a very similar age distribution, with regard to both victims and offenders. The race and ethnic proportions in the two categories of offenses are quite similar. So is the representation of the sexes, in both victims and offenders.[42]

Community   That rates of violence vary by local areas and are highest in slums of large cities, primarily where blacks reside, is an indication of the importance of subcultural factors.[43] Slum areas have long been characterized by violence; the explanation lies not so much in the physical characteristics or poverty of the slum but in the way of life, which includes the use of force to settle disputes.[44] In a 1955 study of 489 homicide cases in Houston, Texas, for example, over 87 percent of them occurred in four areas, not far apart, located in certain slum areas near the center of the city.[45] For the most part, other areas within the city had no criminal homicides at all. Nearly all the homicides occurred in areas populated chiefly by blacks and Spanish-Americans. In more than 70 percent of the cases the victim and the murderer lived less than 2 miles apart, and in 32.8 percent of the cases they lived in the same house or on the same block. The conflicts that gave rise to the disputes were chiefly between members of the same social group, and in 87 percent of the cases the

murderer and his victim had known each other before. Some indication of
the relationship between criminal homicides and the pattern of life in certain areas of the city is suggested by the fact that 65 percent of all criminal
homicides in Philadelphia occur during weekends, particularly on Saturday
night.[46]

In Cleveland two-thirds of the homicides studied in the late 1950s took
place in 12 percent of the city, primarily in black areas with slum conditions.[47] In Delhi, India, approximately two-thirds of all murders between
1962 and 1964 occurred in poor or lower middle-class areas.[48] Similarly,
criminal homicides and other crimes of violence in London were found to
be concentrated in slum areas where violence is used to settle domestic disputes and neighborhood quarrels.[49]

As with criminal homicides, most aggravated assaults occur on weekends
and late at night. The spontaneous nature of the offense is indicated by the
fact that most injuries are inflicted by a knife, which is generally the most
accessible weapon. Likewise, assaultive offenders who were members of
juvenile gangs appear to have developed, as a result of social influences, a
higher degree of dependence on the use of force than do property offenders.[50] The gangs to which a group of assaultive offenders belonged, for
example, had as their prime interests gang fighting and rolling drunks
whereas theft was the prime activity of the gangs to which nonassaultive
offenders belonged. The neighborhood factors have been summarized in a
London study.

> The main conclusion is that the vast majority of offenses were com-
> mitted in the poorer areas of London among working-class people. This
> was predominantly so in the cases of domestic strife and neighborhood
> quarrels, but even in the attacks and fights in public houses, cafes and
> streets the victims were involved in fights or attacked by other working-
> class people in the same neighborhood. Social status is to some extent
> reflected in the occupation of the victim and it was found that more
> than two-thirds of the victims were either casual or general laborers, or
> factory workers or in some other unskilled employment, or wives of peo-
> ple so employed.[51]

Race   Racial disparity is greatest in arrest rates for crimes of violence.
The national United States rate per 100,000 in 1966 showed, for example,
a black arrest rate for homicide of 24.1 as compared with 2.5 for whites,
or ten times as great. This is in contrast to crimes against property where
the burglary arrest rate was three and a half times greater. A study of victims and slayers in Philadelphia, between 1948 and 1952, indicated the role
of group factors in defining the use of violence.[52] Murder was found to be
highest among blacks, males, those in the age group 20–24 and 30–34, and
those from the lower social classes. The rate was also found to be related to
certain occupations.

The rate among blacks was found to be four times that of the whites in the Philadelphia study, indicating the role of the subculture of the slum and the isolating effects of segregation from the general norms of society. The highest rate, in fact, was reported among recent black migrants from the South to the city.[53] A Cleveland study showed that while 76 percent of the offenders in homicide cases were black, only 11 percent of the population were blacks.[54] In a Houston study blacks made up only 23 percent of the population but accounted for 63 percent of the offenders.[55] In a Chicago study the criminal homicide rates for nonwhites was approximately ten times that of whites; in fact, the rate for nonwhite females was approximately twice that of white males.[56] Homicides are known to be more common among southern than northern blacks, but the major correlate of the rates of black homicides in the North is the proportion of blacks in a given area who had been raised in the South and this is not a product of the migration itself.[57] A St. Louis study of blacks convicted of carrying weapons showed something of the subcultural definitions of the use of violence in the slum areas from which they came. Approximately 70 percent said that they carried weapons because of fear of attack from others. While other reasons were given, such as to commit a crime or to collect a debt, they generally "felt a concern about being attacked and the need for self-defense and assumed automatically that others in their environment were also carrying weapons, or if not actually carrying weapons 'acted as if they were.' "[58]

Social Class Crimes of violence are found almost entirely in the lower class. Nine out of ten criminal homicides in Philadelphia were in lower-class occupations, laborers, for example, committing far more criminal homicides than did clerks.[59] A London study of crimes of violence, primarily assault, found that the majority of the offenders were unskilled or were casually employed.[60] The higher clerical and professional workers accounted for no more than 5 percent of the total. Of those involved in a sample group of assaulters, four-fifths of the offenders, as well as a like percentage of the victims, were from the working class. "The general neighborhood context is one populated by lower socioeconomic groups—especially Negroes of this class."[61] In Delhi, India, nearly four-fifths of all murderers are from the poorer classes and two-thirds of all victims.[62] Approximately 90 percent of a sample of homicide offenders in Florence, Italy, were from the lower class.[63] The social background of a sample of London persons convicted of assault was not much different from those convicted of criminal homicide; both tended to have a lower-class slum background.[64]

Criminal homicides do occur among middle- and upper-class persons, but they are quite rare, even in countries with high rates such as Colombia, Mexico, Sardinia, or the southern United States. When homicide is committed among such groups it is likely to be more rational and planned. Deterrence probably operates with this group more than with the lower class, for the consequences can be great. In general, however, the life style is such as to abhor the use of violence.

In preparing for the rational, premeditated murder, the middle- or upper-class actor also reasons that he has a considerable portion of his ego-involvement and investment in social life to lose should his blatant, legally antithetic act become detected. In a ponderous assessment of the probabilities of apprehension, this "prudent" and "rational" man is surely more likely than the explosive knife-carrier, prepared for battle, to be inhibited even by the highest of statistical odds against apprehension. We are not suggesting that the "average" middle-class man is primarily deterred from committing homicide by reason of the threat of severe penalty, but neither can we deny such threats some power to restrict and to prevent the commission of these criminal acts. However, our thesis contains principally the notion that the man from a culture system that denounced the use of interpersonal violence will be restrained from using violence because of his positive perspective that conforms to his value system, not because of a negation of it.[65]

Age   Urban violence generally is higher among the younger age groups. Urban arrest rates for homicide in the United States are much higher among the 18–24 male group.[66] In a Philadelphia study of homicides the age group 20–24 predominated for the offenders. While the median age of the offenders was 31.9 years, the median age of the victims was 35.1 years.[67] For aggravated assault and forcible rape the 15–24 year age group is highest. A study of forcible rape cases in Philadelphia revealed that 40.4 percent of the offenders were in the age group 15–19, while if the age range 15–24 were used it would comprise 66 percent of the offenders.[68] Yet it must be remembered that many cases of this type of violence also occur among older age groups, particularly in the cases of homicide and assault.

Group Factors in Forcible Rape

Aggressive sex offenders are generally responding to culturally based patterns of aggression and situational factors. The use of sexual aggression has been shown in one study to be the result of selective socialization experiences of the male which prompt him to aggressive conduct when he encounters females who provide a "sanctioned" stimulus for sex relations.[69] Forcible rape is generally committed by a young unmarried male, aged 15 to 25, who comes from the lower class. In a Philadelphia study, 90 percent of the offenders from both races belonged to the lower part of the occupational scale.[70] Approximately four in ten were from the lower class; if the lower middle is added, the figure is six in ten. One-third were from the lowest part of the lower class. Another study of a sample of forcible rapists showed that this behavior is related to the more aggressive patterns of the lower class, particularly in sexual matters.[71] Offenders of the lower class are those whose behavior included unnecessary violence; for sex to be gratifying it must be accompanied by physical violence or threats. Others came from patterns of gang delinquency where boys with other delinquent records simply wish to have sex relations without considering the wishes of the female. "They are not sadistic—they simply want to have coitus and the females' wishes are of no particular consequence. They are not hostile toward females, but look upon them solely as sexual objects whose role in life is to provide sexual pleasure. If a woman is recalcitrant and will not fulfill her role, a man may have to use force, threat, weapons, or anything else at his disposal."[72] The Kinsey report showed that lower-class males had considerably more frequent premarital sex experiences and were likely to restrict their sexual contacts to the more direct form of sexual union rather than petting and other practices.[73] Moreover, lower-class males are likely to look with disgust on the indirect sexual gratification practices that are sometimes used by other groups.

The role of group factors is also shown by the fact that areas with high rates of forcible rape have been found to correspond to areas having a high rate of crimes against the person generally.[74] The slum areas in Philadelphia where blacks were living had the highest rates of forcible rape. The proportion of black offenders was four times that of the general population, as was the proportion of black victims. The role of group and subcultural factors in forcible rape is also indicated by the high prevalence of multiple rapes in which the victim was raped by more than one male. Of the 646 cases of forcible rape in the Philadelphia study, 43 percent were multiple rapes.[75] Altogether 912 offenders, or 71 percent of the total offenders, were involved in multiple-rape cases. Group factors were also indicated by the fact that black offenders were more likely to be involved in a group rape, the group rape was generally an intraracial affair, and the older the offender the less likely was he to participate in group rape.

The Gusii, a large African tribe in Kenya, are an example of how cultural approval can be given to make forcible rape an accepted form of sex relations for unmarried males.[76] Even the normal forms of sexual intercourse among the married involve the use of male force and female resistance with an emphasis on the pain inflicted by the male upon the female. This aggressive pattern of sexual behavior is not entirely pretense, but represents an extension in marriage of the sexual patterns developed among unmarried Gusii young men because of sexual frustrations resulting from restrictions on interclan sexual contacts, the sexual contacts and provocative behavior of the girls, and the high bride payments which postpone marriage.

Intraracial Nature of Violence

The relation of group factors to crimes of violence can be seen in the fact that in nearly all crimes of violence in the United States both offender and victim are of the same race. This is true of homicide, aggravated assault, and rape. Crimes of violence are *intraracial* rather than interracial. This fact is the result of the tendency for social relations to be still largely with members of one's own race.

The finding of a large-scale study of seventeen large United States cities supports the intraracial nature of violence. "Racial fears underlie much of the public concern over violence, so one of our most striking and relevant general conclusions is that serious 'assaultive' violence—criminal homicide, aggravated assault and forcible rape—is predominantly *intra*racial in nature."[77] The majority of these crimes involve blacks assaulting blacks; most of the rest involve whites victimizing other whites. Where race was known, 24 percent of the homicides were between whites and 66 percent between blacks. Six percent involved blacks killing whites and 4 percent whites killing blacks. In a Houston study 97 percent of the black victims were killed by blacks, 91 percent of the white victims were killed by whites. Eighty-six percent of the Latin-Americans were killed by other Latin-Americans.[78] In Chicago only 6.6 percent of the criminal homicides were interracial, and of this small number 80 percent involved the killing of whites by nonwhites.[79] A larger government survey of 1493 aggravated assault cases in seventeen large cities found that one-fourth of all assaults were between whites, 66 percent between blacks, 8 percent involved blacks attacking whites, and 2 percent involved whites attacking blacks.[80] A study of seventeen large United States cities in 1967 found that 90 percent of all forcible rapes were intraracial; of these 30 percent were both white, 60 percent were both black, 10 percent were whites raping blacks, and less than 1 percent were blacks raping whites.[81]

Situational Interaction and the Use of Violence

Most murder and aggravated assault represent a response, growing out of social interaction between one or more parties, in which a situation comes to be defined as requiring the use of violence. Generally in order for such an act to take place, all parties must come to perceive the situation as one requiring violence. If only one responds in a dispute, it is not likely to become violent; likewise, if only one of the disputants is accustomed to the use of violence, and the other is not, the dispute is likely to end only in a verbal argument. On the other hand, when a cultural norm is defined as calling for violence by a person in social interplay with another who harbors the same response, serious altercations, fist fights, physical assaults with weapons, and violent domestic quarrels, all of which may end in murder, may result. In the process of an argument, A and B both define the initial situation as a serious threat, B then threatens A physically, A threatens B, and B then threatens A. By circular reaction, the situation can then rapidly build up to a climax in which one takes serious overt action, partly because of fear. Consequently, the victim, by being a contributor to the circular reaction of an argument increasing in its physical intensity, may precipitate his own injury or death.

Violence may result from a single argument or dispute. Other cases may result from a series of arguments, extending sometimes over a period of years, between husband and wife, lovers, neighbors, or fellow employees. Increasingly, verbalization in these arguments has declined, while emotional reactions have increased, until, in a final argument, a climax is built up, and with the use of a weapon one of the parties is injured or killed.

Many cases of violence grow out of what some might regard as trivial disputes. What is considered "trivial" by persons is related to their judgments derived from age, social class, and other background factors. To an outside observer of a different social class (psychiatrist, prosecutor, judge, middle-class jury member, researcher), the triviality of such incidents leading to homicide among the lower class may seem to be no reason for such acts of violence. Such homicides may involve the nonpayment of "very small" debts, "minor" disputes, "petty" jealousies, but these may be important to the person involved. From this point of view, "crime and delinquency are sociocultural phenomena, forms of behavior that result from the routine functioning of the normal sociocultural processes. They must therefore be studied in sociocultural terms, and methodologically conceived as existing in their own right."[82] An illustration of how what is "trivial" to one person may not be trivial to another is indicated in the following:

> D was sitting on the bed in his room. V, D's friend of many years, entered the room and headed for the refrigerator. D said: "Where are you going?" V replied: "I'm going to get me a beer out of your refrigerator." D retorted: "Nobody gets no beer out of my ice box unless I tells him to," whereupon V whirled, pulled out a knife, and said: "The Hell with you and your ice box, too." D reached under the mattress, pulled out a pistol, and shot V three times, killing him instantly. D admitted having had "a couple beers." Test of V's blood revealed he had been drinking, but was not intoxicated.[83]

Because of the interplay between two parties that generally exists in a dispute leading to violence, the victim often "causes" his own death or serious injury. Wolfgang's Philadelphia study showed that more than one in four criminal homicides were precipitated by the victim, in that the victim first showed or used a deadly weapon or struck a blow in an altercation.[84] Victim-precipitated homicides were found to be significantly associated with blacks, victim-offender relationships involving male victims of female offenders, mate slaying, alcohol in the homicide situation or in the victim, and victims with a previous record of assault or arrest. Other homicides, not included in this figure, involved the infidelity of a mate or lover, failure of the victim to pay a debt, and use of vile names by the victim in such a manner that the victim contributes to the homicide. In a Chicago study 37.9 percent of the homicide cases were victim-precipitated; of them 80.5 percent of the victims were nonwhite males.[85] Slightly more than half of the nonwhite males precipitated their deaths as compared with one-fifth of the white male victims. Even in robbery the behavior of the victim may incite the robber to kill.

A period of social interaction between the parties takes place before any aggravated assault. In fact, Pittman and Handy, in their St. Louis study, reported that 70.5 percent of the 241 cases studied had been preceded by verbal arguments.[86] Such quarrels included primarily family arguments, but there were also disputes arising in a tavern, as well as other places. Disputes arose primarily from persons of similar age group, sex, and race.

Sex relations generally may be preceded by interplay between two persons, each responding to cues from the other person. The use of force or threat in sexual relations is affected by a number of factors.[87] In the first place, a sexually aroused female may be ambivalent toward sex relations when excited, thus confusing her male partner about the use of more forcible persuasion. Second, some females may actually wish to be overpowered and treated roughly in sex relations. Third, some may wish to justify their own conduct by encouraging force by the male partner. Fourth, the male may interpret the lack of strong verbal or physical resistance by the female as acquiescence to his use of some force.

The victim of forcible rape often appears to have much to do with the fact that she is raped. Amir found that 19 percent of the forcible rapes in his Philadelphia study were victim-precipitated in the sense that the victims actually, or so it was interpreted by the offender, agreed to sexual relations but retracted before the actual act or did not resist strongly enough when the suggestion was made by the offender or offenders.[88] The role of the victim was also crucial when she entered a situation in which sexual stimulation was pervasive or made what could be interpreted as an invitation to sex relations. In over half the rapes the victims displayed submissive behavior. Moreover, 19 percent of the victims had an arrest record and 56 percent of them had been charged with some sort of sexual offense.

Among tribal peoples in most African villages, homicides occur within a traditional setting that defines the social relationships between the killer and the victim.[89] These relationships tend to differ from Western societies; for example, a woman might kill her children rather than her husband in a domestic quarrel. Likewise, altercations over money are rare, but fear of witches or land disputes may be more common reasons for homicide.

Personal Relationships in Violent Crime

Many studies have indicated that close relationships generally exist between the offender and the victim of violence. In fact, a United States government study has concluded that homicide and assault should be looked at within the same frame of reference. They are usually between relatives, friends, or acquaintances; most occur in indoor locations. "The ostensible motives in homicide and assault are often relatively trivial, usually involving spontaneous altercations, family quarrels, jealous rages, and the like. The two crimes are similar; there is often no reason to believe that the person guilty of homicide sets out with any more intention to harm than the one who commits an aggravated assault. Except for the seriousness of the final outcomes, the major distinction is that homicides most often involve handguns while knives are most common in assault."[90] Although people in American cities are often concerned about physical assaults from strangers on city streets, personal violence is far less likely to be perpetrated by a stranger according to a survey of various studies by a Presidential Commission which found that about 70 percent of all willful killings, nearly two-thirds of all aggravated assaults, and high percentages of forcible rapes are committed by family members and others previously known to their victims.[19] The risk of a serious personal attack on any American in a given year is about 1 in 550 (although the risk for slum dwellers of violence is much greater than this); the risk of serious attack from spouses, family members, friends, or acquaintances is almost twice as great as from strangers.[92]

Criminal homicides and aggravated assaults result from domestic quarrels, altercations, jealousies, and arguments over money or property. Most of the offender-victim relationships have been intimate, close, and frequent, primarily involving family members and close friends. The major exception is the small proportion of such homicides occurring in connection with other crimes like robbery. A study of 713 New Jersey murders classified according to victim-offender relationships and the situations in which the murders took place, found that less than one-fourth committed murder in connection with another crime.[93] The largest group (about two-thirds) of the murders grew out of some altercation with male acquaintances, sex rivals, relatives, or among lovers. Wolfgang's Philadelphia study found that approximately a third of 588 male and female criminal homicides resulted from general altercations. Family and domestic quarrels accounted for 14 percent, jealousy 12 percent, altercation over money 11 percent, and robbery, contrary to popular impression, only 7 percent.[94] Close friends and relatives accounted for over half (59 percent) of all homicides and four-fifths of the women victims. In 28 percent of the cases the victim was a close friend of the murderer, in 25 percent a family relative, in 14 percent an acquaintance. In only one out of eight murders was the victim a stranger. As contrasted with men, a much larger proportion of women generally kill someone in their own families. It was concluded that when a woman committed a homicide, the victim was more likely to be her mate, and when a man was killed by a woman, he was most likely to be killed by his wife.[95] A Chicago study showed that 47.4 percent of all criminal homicide victims were slain by a member of the family or a close friend.[96] If one considers only women, 96.1 percent were killed by a family member, close friend, or casual acquaintance. A study of Wisconsin prisoners charged with murder also disclosed a large percentage of cases with a previous history of difficulties with the victim, two-thirds growing out of a long-standing or an immediate quarrel.[97] Many of the Wisconsin murders studied involved difficulties in the marital situation or a long-standing dispute between farmers. Almost half of those who committed forcible rape in Philadelphia were known to each other.[98] A survey of forcible rape cases by the District of Columbia Crime Commission showed the previous personal relationships between victim and offender.

> Almost two-thirds of the 151 (rape) victims surveyed were attacked by persons with whom they were at least casually acquainted. Only 36 percent of the 224 assailants about whom some identifying information was obtained were complete strangers to their victims; 16 (7 percent) of the attackers were known to the victim by sight, although there had been no previous contact. Thirty-one (14 percent) of the 224 assailants were relatives, family friends or boy friends of the victims, and 88 (39 percent) were either acquaintances or neighbors.[99]

A more recent large government survey involving a 10 percent random sample of offense and arrest reports in seventeen large United States cities, found that only a fifth of assaults involved strangers, which was considerably higher even than that for homicide.[100] This study also found that one in four of 668 criminal homicides was between family members and 9 percent involved other primary group relations, 15.4 percent involved an acquaintance, while only 15.6 percent were committed by strangers.[101] Forcible rape, however, was found to be slightly more likely to be committed by a stranger; 53 percent were committed by a stranger, the rest by persons with whom the victim had some acquaintance.[102]

Studies in countries with different cultures have also revealed the significance of personal contacts in criminal homicide. A Danish study revealed that the murderer's victim was a relative or an acquaintance in nine out of ten cases and that strangers were seldom the victims.[103] In an Italian study of eighty persons convicted of criminal homicide in Florence, only fifteen were unacquainted with the victim.[104] Similarly, an Indian study has indicated that most murders occur within the same caste and frequently involve husband and wife.[105] In another Indian study relatives accounted for 26.9 percent of the victims, while friends, acquaintances, neighbors, and coworkers accounted for 50 percent.[106] In a London study, nearly 80 percent of all homicides and "murderous assaults" (an English category of attempted murder) were committed against relatives or victims well known to the attacker. Half the offenses arose from family strife, that is, the offender and the victim belonged to the same family. If close associates, with whom the person lived or worked, are added, the proportion committed by persons intimately associated with their victims increased to 60 percent. A further 20 percent were committed against friends and acquaintances. Arrests in 1960 in London showed that crimes of violence, 90 percent involving felonious assaults, tended to occur in the family between persons who were well known to each other in the neighborhood.[107] More specifically, 13.1 percent involved a family relative, 15 percent a relationship with friends or neighbors of some duration, 15.1 percent acquaintances, and 6.4 percent a business or similar relationship. In 43.1 percent the relationship was slight, but most were not totally strangers, and 7.3 percent involved the police. This study concluded that homicides or murderous assaults on police and on strangers in the street are rare. The dynamics of homicide and aggravated assault are quite different among persons who know each other intimately, relatives, friends, neighbors, than among strangers.

Violence occurs among intimates precisely because they are intimates, and as such, have come to share values and understandings and to develop certain expected reciprocities. When expectations are not met, as they may not be when a relationship begins to sour, it is eminently possible for either or both partners to feel they are being cheated or betrayed. This is a prime situation for the evocation of anger. When the failure of reciprocity is then called openly into question, each one's private history of resentment at previous deficiencies may come to the fore. In the interest of their relationship, intimates often leave unspoken many complaints that might be voiced were they less intimate. Thus the cumulation of intimacy is at the same time likely to be a cumulation of grievance, and anger is thus given considerably greater force when it finally appears. Moreover, because intimates know each other's vulnerabilities and how to offend in an argument, the intensity of arguments is likely to be considerably greater than in one between strangers who are not so knowledgeable. "Many men and a goodly number of women have finally come to the conclusion that homicide is a cleaner, neater solution than the dragged-out, acerbic destruction of ego and dignity that is inherent in breaking off."[108]

CORRESPONDENCE BETWEEN CRIMINAL AND LEGITIMATE BEHAVIOR

Both the criminal law and the religious ideologies of Christianity and Buddhism expressly forbid violence as though all violence is antithetical to organized society. In point of fact, the use of violence on other human beings is often sanctioned by organized society. The killing and other acts of violence of enemy soldiers and even enemy civilians is sanctioned by the political state in wartime. Those persons killed or injured under wartime conditions must exceed by millions all those persons ever killed by civilian murder and assault. For a civilian willfully to kill ten persons may warrant the death penalty or life imprisonment; for a soldier to do the same to the enemy warrants a medal for heroism. The total estimated cost to the principal belligerents during World War I was 17,000,000 men killed or missing in battle, to which must be added 20,000,000 civilian deaths. During World War II 10,000,000 men were killed or missing, and 43,000,000 civilians were killed. If one takes only recorded history, the number of human beings killed in legal warfare must run into the hundreds of millions. All of this makes the civilian killing of other human beings, often in connection with higher moral principles than those involved in war, somewhat of a logical anachronism.

Over the centuries in the name of the political states large numbers of civilians have been killed for reasons of state, religion, class, and ethnic characteristics. Probably the most brutal extermination of this type was the killing and torture deaths of 6,500,000 Jews during the Nazi control of Germany and occupation of Europe. Yet Richard Speck's notorious killing of eight Chicago nurses in 1965 and the sniper killings at the University of Texas by Charles Whitman in 1966 of fifteen persons and the wounding of thirty-one often seem to provoke more horror among many persons. Human life should not be willfully taken; if a state, which represents certain power interests, does it, however, the situation may be regarded as of quite a different nature.

All violence is by no means harmful to a society. As Coser has pointed out, violence in a society may perform a useful function.[109] It may help groups of individuals in a society achieve certain goals that otherwise are difficult for them to achieve, it may serve as a danger signal of political and economic dislocation in a society, and it may serve as a catalyst for change.

Violence has been frequently resorted to, even on a large scale, to achieve certain idealistic moral goals or to reverse the social power of interest groups. For example, the achievement of the right of labor to organize for collective action was a long and violent struggle in most countries. In the United States, "beginning in the 1870's, workingmen attempting to organize for collective action engaged in more than a half century of violent warfare with industrialists, their private armies, and workers employed to break strikes, as well as with police and troops."[110] Even American women used militant action to secure their right to vote in 1920. One historian has referred to this as "positive violence." Surveying the development of the United States he has stated:

> Violence has formed a seamless web with some of the noblest and most constructive chapters of American history: the birth of the nation (Revolutionary violence), the occupation of the land (Indian wars), the stabilization of frontier society (vigilante violence), the elevation of the farmer and the laborer (agrarian and labor violence), and the preservation of law and order (police violence). The patriot, the humanitarian, the nationalist, the pioneer, the landholder, the farmer, and the laborer (and the capitalist) have used violence as the means to a higher end. All too often unyielding and unsympathetic established political and economic

power has incited violence by its refusal to heed and redress just grievances. Thus Governor Berkeley of Virginia ignored the pleas of Virginia
planters and the result was Bacon's Rebellion. Thus the British government in 1774–76 remained adamant in the face of patriot pleas, and the
result was the American Revolution. Thus the tobacco trust scoffed at
the grievances of farmers, and the result was the Kentucky Night Rider
movement. Thus American capitalists ground workers into the dust, and
the result was the violent labor movement. The possessors of power and
wealth have been prone to refuse to share their attributes until it has
been too late. Arrogance is indeed a quality that comes to unchecked
power more readily than sympathy and forbearance.[111]

Historically the United States can be characterized by violence. In general, historical evidence seems to suggest that during the 1960s with riots
based on racial discrimination, the Vietnam war, and other issues, as well
as other forms of violence, that Americans were more violent toward one
another than in the past but probably less violent in total magnitude than
in the latter half of the nineteenth century.[112] In a country of the population diversity of the United States, immigrant and racial groups were
thrown into fierce competition with one another and with the dominant
Anglo-American white Protestant group in their quest for economic security and acceptance. "This scramble for material advantage and for status
has produced violent confrontations, both between the newcomers and the
often nativist Anglo-American establishment and between the economically
competing and status-conscious ethnic minorities themselves."[113] There
have been, for example, bloody anti-Catholic, anti-Irish, anti-German,
anti-Chinese, anti-Italian, and anti-black riots.

America had a long history of violence and vigilantism on the western
frontier. The lack of effective law enforcement agencies invited a degree
of legitimized vigilante justice. But vigilantism was easily adapted to the
urban model—the most famous of which was the San Francisco Vigulaire
Committee of 1856. Such "neo-vigilantism" can be distinguished from the
older frontier model in that it was urban and its victims were different. The
frontier vigilantes mainly dealt with criminals such as murderers, counter-
feiters, horse thieves, and outlaws. The victims of urban neo-vigilantism
were Catholics, Jews, Mormons, blacks, and various ethnic minorities,
union organizers, political radicals, advocates of civil liberties, and nonconformists in general.[114] More recently there have been attacks on nonconformists such as "hippies" and those with different life styles by militant
groups.

The use of violence and counterviolence has long characterized race
relations in the United States. Racial conflict involving slave uprisings and
riots go back to the eighteenth century. The Ku Klux Klan has permeated
the American racial scene with violence for over a hundred years. Lynch
laws involving hanging or killing by an illegal group have existed since the

eighteenth century, and whereas whites have occasionally been victims, the victims were usually blacks; from 1882 to 1903, 1985 blacks were lynched. From 1900 to 1949 there were thirty-three major interracial disturbances or race riots in United States cities in which many were killed or injured. Whites were generally the aggressors and the bulk of the casualties were blacks. Within recent years a pattern of black protest rioting and destruction within black areas developed and more recently there has been militant action by some black groups against whites.

Some forms of violence may be legally approved within a society while others are illegal; some are sanctioned (approved) and some are not.[115] Killing and wounding of another person is approved and sanctioned for a soldier and, in fact, he may be severely punished if he does not use violence when it is expected of or commanded of him. Similarly, the use of force with a club, gun, mace, or other weapon, by law enforcement officers, providing it is not excessive, meets with similar approval. Boxing represents legalized assault of one person by another, largely blows to the head, a sport which for years was banned. Other sports such as football and hockey allow a person to injure another legally. A person may legally use violence in situations of real or perceived self-defense. Even children are legally allowed to be punished physically in a way similar to assault, providing it is not carried to excess.

When it comes to illegal violence there are certain forms that may receive a certain sanctioned response. It is often difficult to secure a conviction where a husband has used violence against someone who has committed adultery with his wife, or where an individual resorts to violence when severely provoked. On the other hand, most all other forms of illegal violence such as criminal homicide and most assaults are not sanctioned.

The social values involved in homicide and aggravated assault among intimates are quite similar to that of nonviolent persons. A study of violence among intimates shows that people assault, and sometimes kill, for the same reasons people live—pride, preservation of honor, to blot out shame, to avenge one's self, to settle an argument, or as a reaction to an insult.[116] Persons who do not use violence utilize other methods to deal with such important values.

SOCIETAL REACTION AND LEGAL PROCESSING

The middle and upper socioeconomic groups in society have codified legal rules that prohibit the use of violence. The middle class denunciation of violence is in part an attempt to discourage attacks against established political power.[117] The criminal laws do not recognize the separate existence of subcultural norms among certain groups that recognize the use of force to settle disputes as legitimate. These same groups would, however, generally not approve of murder, but at the same time in sanctioning violence which may lead to murder there is an inconsistency in their value system.

Middle- and upper-class persons, those in positions of social and political power, react strongly to the use of violence as seen in the severe legal penalties for murder, manslaughter, forcible rape, and child molesting. Moreover, the penalties in the law uniformally do not recognize the close relationship between criminal homicide and aggravated assault. While aggravated assault may result in a short prison sentence or even probation, if the victim dies in some countries the penalty is even death or at least life imprisonment which usually results in serving of a minimum of between 9 and 15 years, which is far greater than for any other criminal offense. Moreover, murder is generally not probationable as some have argued certain cases should be.

Murderers are less likely than nonmurderers to have been previously incarcerated for any type of crime. Because of the nature of murder and the way the public and law enforcement officials react to it, the murderer is more likely to be committed as a first offender than those who commit other crimes. A study of 621 North Carolina offenders in prison for murder and a control group of nonmurderers not only showed this to be generally the case, but this difference was maintained when controlled for race, age, and intelligence.[118] In fact, an inverse relationship was found between the seriousness of the offense (first degree murder, second degree murder, manslaughter, and negligent manslaughter) and having no previous incarceration. "From the data presented in this study, it would seem that the incarcerated murderer has a lower 'criminality level,' and upon his release offers no more threat to society—perhaps less—than other incarcerated offenders."[119]

Likewise, manslaughter and forcible rape are usually punished by an unusually long period of imprisonment. Forcible rape carries the death penalty in three states, while fifteen other states punish it with either death or life imprisonment.[120] Penalties for all offenses with females who are underage are much more harsh than laws prohibiting essentially the same offense with adults.

Such offenses are punished severely not because they constitute a serious threat to the larger political and economic order; rather, the punishment is severe because of the injury to the individual. Severe punishment is thought to work as a deterrent, helps to avoid retaliation by relatives and friends of the victims, and serves to reinstate the religious beliefs held by many in the larger society about the sanctity of life and the sexual conduct of individuals.

In 1970, 86 percent of all criminal homicides in the United States were solved, 67 percent of those charged with murder were prosecuted.[121] Forty-four percent of the adults prosecuted were found guilty and 15 percent were convicted on a lesser charge. The remaining 41 percent won release

by acquittal or dismissal of the charges against them. Of all persons processed for murder, 12 percent were referred to the juvenile courts.

Sixty-five percent of all reported cases of aggravated assault were solved,
and 71 percent of these aggravated assault cases were prosecuted. So many
involve a close family or other relationship that the victim, who may not
have objected to the arrest, is unwilling to testify in court. Consequently,
almost four out of ten cases in 1970 resulted in acquittal or dismissal.
Only 44 percent of adults prosecuted were convicted on this charge, and 16
percent were convicted of a lesser charge. Eighteen percent were referred
to the juvenile courts.

In 1970, 56 percent of all reported forcible rape cases were solved. Of all
persons arrested, 70 percent were prosecuted and of them only 34.6 percent
were found to be guilty. In addition, 18 percent of the adults prosecuted
were convicted of lesser offenses. Problems in prosecution accounted for
acquittals or dismissals in 46 percent of the cases. Juvenile referrals
accounted for a large proportion, 22 percent of the total processed forcible
rape cases.

Contrary to popular opinion, murderers, assaulters, and forcible rapists
generally do not have criminal careers. They do not conceive of themselves
as being real "criminals," they seldom identify with crime, and criminal
behavior is not a significant part of their life organizations. Rather than
being a unique individual phenomena, the basis of most acts of violence
lies in subcultural definitions derived from social class, neighborhood, ethnic group, sex, and so forth. In these terms the victim in many instances
provokes the assault. Despite this, the legal penalties for murder, manslaughter, and forcible rape are much more severe than for other crimes.

NOTES

[1] Marvin E. Wolfgang, "A Preface to Violence," *The Annals,* **364** (March
1966), p. 2.

[2] See, for example, *Report of the National Advisory Commission on Civil Dis-
orders.* Advance Copy of the Commission's Report (New York: E. P. Dutton
& Co. 1968); Thomas Rose, ed., *Violence in America: A Historical and Con-
temporary Reader* (New York: Vintage Books, Random House, 1970); *The
Politics of Protest.* Report of the Task Force on Violent Aspects of Protest and
Confrontation of the National Commission on the Causes and Prevention of
Violence, submitted by Jerome H. Skolnick, Director (New York: Clarion
Books, Simon and Schuster, 1969); Robert H. Connery, ed., *Urban Riots:
Violence and Social Change* (New York: Vintage Books, Random House,
1969); *To Establish Justice, To Insure Domestic Tranquility.* Final Report of
the National Commission on the Causes and Prevention of Violence (Washing-
ton, D.C.: U. S. Government Printing Office, 1969); Charles U. Daly, ed.,
Urban Violence (Chicago: The University of Chicago Center for Policy Study,
1969); James F. Short, Jr., and Marvin E. Wolfgang, eds., *Collective Violence*
(Chicago: Aldine-Atherton, Inc., 1972); and Robert M. Fogelson, *Violence*

as a Protest (Garden City: Anchor Books, Doubleday & Company, Inc., 1971).

[3] James A. Inciardi, "The Adult Firesetter: A Typology," *Criminology*, 8 (August 1970), pp. 145–155.

[4] Child molesting was included in the original edition of this book. See Charles H. McCaghy, "Child Molesters: A Study of Their Careers as Deviants," in Marshall B. Clinard and Richard Quinney, *Criminal Behavior Systems* (New York: Holt, Rinehart and Winston, 1967) and Charles H. McCaghy, "Drinking and Deviance Disavowal: The Case of Child Molesters," *Social Problems*, 16 (Summer 1968), pp. 43–49.

[5] For a discusion in laymen's terms of the issues involved in the concept of murder, see the "Definition of Murder," Chapter 1 of Norval Morris and Colin Howard, *Studies in Criminal Law* (London: Oxford University Press, 1964).

[6] Marvin E. Wolfgang, *Patterns in Criminal Homicide* (Philadelphia: University of Pennsylvania Press, 1958).

[7] *To Establish Justice, To Insure Domestic Tranquility*, p. xiv.

[8] *The Challenge of Crime in a Free Society*. The President's Commission on Law Enforcement and Administration of Justice (Washington, D.C.: U.S. Government Printing Office, 1967).

[9] Wolfgang, *Patterns in Criminal Homicide*, pp. 332–333.

[10] Norval Morris and Gordon Hawkins, "From Murder and from Violence, Good Lord, Deliver Us," *Midway*, 10 (Summer 1969), p. 67.

[11] Mario Simondi, *Dati Su Ottanta Casi Di Omicidio*, Serie Ricerche Empiriche No. 5, Dipartimento Statistico-Metematico, Universita Degli Studi Di Firenzi, 1970.

[12] *Crimes of Violence*. A Staff Report to the National Commission on the Causes and Prevention of Violence, prepared by Donald J. Mulvihill and Melvin M. Tumin with Lynn A. Curtis (Washington, D.C.: U. S. Government Printing Office, 1969), Vol. 12, p. 547.

[13] David J. Pittman and William Handy, "Patterns in Criminal Aggravated Assault," *Journal of Criminal Law, Criminology and Police Science*, 55 (December 1964), pp. 462–470.

[14] Richard A. Peterson, David J. Pittman, and Patricia O'Neal, "Stabilities in Deviance: A Study of Assaultive and Non-Assaultive Offenders," *Journal of Criminal Law, Criminology and Police Science*, 53 (March 1962), pp. 44–49.

[15] *Murder, 1957 to 1968*. A Home Office Statistical Division Report on Murder in England and Wales (London: Her Majesty's Stationery Office, 1969).

[16] Wolfgang, *Patterns in Criminal Homicide*, p. 178.

[17] John L. Gillin, *The Wisconsin Prisoner* (Madison: University of Wisconsin Press, 1946).

[18] F. H. McClintock, *Crimes of Violence* (New York: St. Martin's Press, 1963), p. 57.

[19] Menachem Amir, *Patterns in Forcible Rape* (Chicago: University of Chicago Press, 1971), p. 112.

[20] Paul H. Gebhard, John H. Gagnon, Wardell B. Pomeroy, and Cornelia V. Christenson, *Sex Offenders: An Analysis of Types* (New York: Harper & Row, Publishers, 1965), pp. 192–194.

[21] Albert Ellis and Ralph Brancale, *The Psychology of Sex Offenders* (Springfield, Ill.: Charles C Thomas, Publisher, 1965).

[22] Ronald H. Beattie and John P. Kenney, "Aggressive Crimes," *The Annals*, 365 (March 1966), pp. 73–85.

[23] Franco Ferracuti, Renato Lazzari, and Marvin E. Wolfgang, eds., *Violence in Sardinia* (Rome: Mario Bulzoni, 1970).

24 Marvin E. Wolfgang and Franco Ferracuti, *The Subculture of Violence: Towards an Integrated Theory in Criminology* (London: Tavistock Publications, Social Science Paperbacks, 1967), pp. 158–161.
25 Wolfgang, *Patterns in Criminal Homicide*, pp. 188–189.
26 Marvin E. Wolfgang, "A Sociological Analysis of Criminal Homicide," *Federal Probation*, 25 (March 1961), p. 55.
27 *To Establish Justice, To Insure Domestic Tranquility*, p. 37.
28 Wolfgang and Ferracuti, *The Subculture of Violence*, pp. 259–260.
29 Veli Verkko, *Homicides and Suicides in Finland and Their Dependence on National Character* (Copenhagen: G.E.C. Gads Forlag, 1951); Jacqueline and Murray Straus, "Suicide, Homicide, and Social Structure in Ceylon," *American Journal of Sociology* 58 (March 1953), pp. 461–496; and Arthur Wood, "Murder, Suicide, and Economic Crime in Ceylon," *American Sociological Review*, 26 (October 1961), pp. 744–753. One study found that in general homicide is associated with the degree of urban and industrial development of a country, although there are exceptions. See Richard Quinney, "Suicide, Homicide, and Economic Development," *Social Forces*, 43 (March 1965), pp. 401–406.
30 Jaime Toro-Calder, "Personal Crimes in Puerto Rico," unpublished M. A. thesis, University of Wisconsin, 1950.
31 Wolfgang and Ferracuti, *The Subculture of Violence*, p. 280.
32 German Guzman Campos, Orlando Fals Borda, and Eduardo Umana Luna, *La Violencia en Colombia, Estudio de un Proceso-Social, Tomo Primo*, 2d ed. (Bogota: Ediciones Tercer Mundo, 1962), and Wolfgang and Ferracuti, *The Subculture of Violence*, pp. 275–279.
33 Ferracuti, Lazzari, and Wolfgang, *Violence in Sardinia*.
34 *Ibid.*, p. 12.
35 H. C. Brearley, *Homicide in the United States* (Chapel Hill, N.C.: University of North Carolina Press, 1932).
36 Sheldon Hackney, "Southern Violence," in *Violence in America. A Staff Report to the National Commission on the Causes and Prevention of Violence*, prepared by Hugh Davis Graham and Ted Robert Gurr, Vol. 2, pp. 387–404.
37 *Ibid.*, p. 401.
38 Richard Quinney, "Structural Characteristics, Population Areas, and Crime Rates in the United States," *Journal of Criminal Law, Criminology and Police Science*, 57 (March 1966), pp. 45–52.
39 *Ibid.*, p. 49.
40 *Firearms and Violence in American Life. A Staff Report to the National Commission on the Causes and Prevention of Violence*, prepared by George D. Newton and Franklin E. Zimring (Washington, D.C.: U. S. Government Printing Office, 1969), Vol. 7, p. 6.
41 *Firearms and Violence*, pp. 69–74.
42 Alex D. Pokorny, "Human Violence: A Comparison of Homicide, Aggravated Assault, Suicide, and Attempted Suicide," *The Journal of Criminal Law, Criminology and Police Science*, 56 (December 1965), p. 497.
43 *To Establish Justice, To Insure Domestic Tranquility*, p. 23.
44 Marshall B. Clinard, *Slums and Community Development: Experiments in Self-Help* (New York: The Free Press, Macmillan Company, 1966), Chap. 1, "The Nature of the Slum."
45 Henry Allen Bullock, "Urban Homicide in Theory and Fact," *Journal of Criminal Law, Criminology and Police Science*, 45 (January–February 1955), pp. 565–575.
46 Wolfgang, *Patterns in Criminal Homicide*, pp. 106–107.

[47] Robert C. Bensing and Oliver Schroeder, Jr., *Homicide in an Urban Community* (Springfield, Ill.: Charles C Thomas, Publisher, 1960).

[48] S. Venugopal Rao, *Murder: A Pilot Study of Urban Patterns with Particular Reference to the City of Delhi* (New Delhi: Government of India, 1968), p. 12.

[49] McClintock, *Crimes of Violence.*

[50] Peterson, Pittman, and O'Neal, "Stabilities in Deviance: A Study of Assaultive and Non-Assaultive Offenders."

[51] McClintock, *Crimes of Violence*, pp. 44–45.

[52] Wolfgang, *Patterns in Criminal Homicide.* For a summary, also see "A Sociological Analysis of Criminal Homicide," *Federal Probation*, 25 (March 1961), pp. 48–55; and Franco Ferracuti and Marvin E. Wolfgang, "Design for a Proposed Study of Violence," *British Journal of Criminology*, 3 (April 1963), pp. 377–388. Also see Wolfgang and Ferracuti, *The Subculture of Violence.*

[53] Wolfgang, *Patterns of Criminal Homicide.*

[54] Bensing and Schroeder, *Homicide in an Urban Community*, p. 22.

[55] Alex D. Pokorny, "A Comparison of Homicides in Two Cities," *Journal of Criminal Law, Criminology and Police Science*, 56 (December 1965), pp. 479–487.

[56] Harwin L. Voss and John R. Hepburn, "Patterns in Criminal Homicide in Chicago," *Journal of Criminal Law, Criminology and Police Science*, 59 (December 1968), p. 501. Also see John R. Hepburn and Harwin L. Voss, "Patterns of Criminal Homicide in Chicago and Philadelphia," *Criminology*, 8 (May 1970), pp. 21–45.

[57] Thomas F. Pettigrew and Rosalind Barclay Spier, "The Ecological Structure of Negro Homicide," *American Journal of Sociology*, 67 (May 1962), pp. 621–629.

[58] Leroy G. Schultz, "Why the Negro Carries Weapons," *Journal of Criminal Law, Criminology and Police Science*, 53 (December 1962), pp. 467–483.

[59] Wolfgang, *Patterns of Criminal Homicide.*

[60] McClintock, *Crimes of Violence*, pp. 131–132.

[61] Pittman and Handy, "Patterns in Criminal Aggravated Assault," p. 469.

[62] Rao, *Murder*, pp. 19–21.

[63] Simondi, *Dati su Ottanta Casa di Omicidio.*

[64] McClintock, *Crimes of Violence*, pp. 131–132.

[65] Wolfgang and Ferracuti, *The Subculture of Violence*, pp. 262–263.

[66] *To Establish Justice, To Insure Domestic Tranquility*, p. 22.

[67] Marvin E. Wolfgang, "A Sociological Analysis of Criminal Homicide," in Marvin E. Wolfgang, ed., *Studies in Homicide* (New York: Harper & Row, 1967), p. 19.

[68] Amir, *Patterns in Forcible Rape*, p. 56.

[69] Eugene J. Kanin, "Selected Dyadic Aspects of Male Sex Aggression," *The Journal of Sex Research*, 5 (February 1969), pp. 12–28.

[70] Amir, *Patterns in Forcible Rape.*

[71] Gebhard, Gagnon, Pomeroy, and Christenson, *Sex Offenders: An Analysis of Types.*

[72] *Ibid.*, p. 200.

[73] Alfred C. Kinsey, Wardell B. Pomeroy, and Clyde E. Martin, *Sexual Behavior in the Human Male* (Philadelphia: W. B. Saunders Company, 1948).

[74] Amir, *Patterns in Forcible Rape.*

[75] *Ibid.*, p. 200.

[76] Robert A. Levine, "Gusii Sex Offenses: A Study in Social Control," *American Anthropologist*, 61 (December 1959), pp. 696–990.

[77] McClintock, *Crimes of Violence*, Vol. 11, Chap. 5, "The Offender and His Victim," p. 208.

[78] Alex D. Pokorny, "A Comparison of Homicides in Two Cities."

[79] Voss and Hepburn, "Patterns in Criminal Homicide in Chicago," p. 502.

[80] *Crimes of Violence*, Vol. 11, p. 209.

[81] *Ibid.*

[82] Frank E. Hartung, *Crime, Law, and Society* (Detroit: Wayne State University Press, 1965), p. 147.

[83] *Ibid.*, pp. 145–146.

[84] Wolfgang, *Patterns in Criminal Homicide*, p. 252. Also see T. P. Morris and Louis Blom-Cooper, *A Calendar of Murder* (London: M. Joseph, 1964).

[85] Voss and Hepburn, "Patterns in Criminal Homicide in Chicago," p. 506.

[86] Pittman and Handy, "Patterns in Criminal Aggravated Assault," p. 467.

[87] Gebhard, Gagnon, Pomeroy, and Christenson, *Sex Offenders: An Analysis of Types*, pp. 177–179.

[88] Amir, *Patterns in Forcible Rape*, pp. 259–264.

[89] Paul Bohannan, *African Homicide and Suicide* (Princeton, N.J.: Princeton University Press, 1960).

[90] *To Establish Justice, To Insure Domestic Tranquility*, pp. 25–26.

[91] *The Challenge of Crime in a Free Society*, p. 18.

[92] *Ibid.*, p. 19.

[93] E. Frankel, "One Thousand Murderers," *Journal of Criminal Law, Criminology and Police Science*, **29** (1938–1939), pp. 687–688.

[94] Wolfgang, *Patterns in Criminal Homicide*, p. 191.

[95] *Ibid.*, p. 325.

[96] Voss and Hepburn, "Patterns in Criminal Homicide in Chicago," p. 506.

[97] John L. Gillin, *The Wisconsin Prisoner* (Madison: University of Wisconsin Press, 1946), p. 60.

[98] Amir, *Patterns in Forcible Rape*, p. 234.

[99] Morris and Hawkins, "From Murder and from Violence," p. 70.

[100] *Crimes of Violence*, Vol. 11, p. 219.

[101] *Ibid.*, p. 216.

[102] *Ibid.*, p. 219.

[103] Kaare Svalastoga, "Homicide and Social Contact in Denmark," *American Journal of Sociology*, **62** (July, 1956), pp. 37–41.

[104] Simondi, *Dati su Ottanta Casa di Omicidio.*

[105] Edwin D. Driver, "Interaction and Criminal Homicide in India," *Social Forces*, **40** (December 1961), pp. 153–158.

[106] Rao, *Murder*, p. 23. A Uganda study showed that of 501 homicides, 74.1 percent involved someone with whom the offender was acquainted; 159, or 33 percent, grew out of quarrels involving members of the intimate family, and a fourth of all those killed in an intimate family dispute were wives. Of the remainder, 7.4 percent involved other relatives, and 34.1 percent involved friends, fellow workers, or acquaintances. Musa T. Mushanga, "Criminal Homicide in Western Uganda," unpublished M.A. thesis, Makerere University, Kampala, Uganda, 1970.

[107] McClintock, *Crimes of Violence*, pp. 238, 248. Another study has reported that murders of women in England and Wales between 1957–1968 involved almost entirely persons acquainted with the victim. Of 62 women killed only 11 were by strangers; of 103 male victims, 42 were killed by strangers. *Murder, 1957 to 1968*, pp. 74–75.

[108] *Crimes of Violence*, Vol. 13, p. 516. The quote from this extract appears in William Goode, "Violence among Intimates," *Crimes of Violence*, Vol. 13, p. 958.

[109] Lewis A. Coser, "Some Social Functions of Violence," *The Annals*, 364 (March 1966), pp. 8–18.
[110] *The Politics of Protest*, p. 14.
[111] Richard Maxwell Brown, "Historical Patterns of Violence in America," *Violence in America*. A Staff Report to the National Commission on the Causes and Prevention of Violence, prepared by H. D. Graham and Ted R. Gurr (Washington, D.C.: U. S. Government Printing Office, 1969), p. 55.
[112] "Conclusion," *Violence in America*, Vol. 2, p. 628.
[113] "Immigrant Societies and the Frontier Tradition," *Violence in America*, Vol. 1, p. 80.
[114] Brown, "Historical Patterns of Violence in America," p. 51.
[115] Martin R. Haskell and Lewis Yablonsky, *Crime and Delinquency* (Chicago: Rand McNally & Company, 1970), p. 110.
[116] *Crimes of Violence*, Vol. 12, p. 516.
[117] Wolfgang, "A Preface to Violence," p. 3.
[118] Gordon P. Waldo, "The 'Criminality Level' of Incarcerated Murderers and Non-Murderers," *The Journal of Criminal Law, Criminology and Police Science*, 61 (March 1970), pp. 60–70.
[119] *Ibid.*, p. 20.
[120] Leonard D. Savits, "A Study in Capital Punishment," *Journal of Criminal Law, Criminology and Police Science*, 49 (November–December 1958), pp. 338–341. Also Hugo Adam Bedau, ed., *The Death Penalty in America* (Chicago: Aldine Publishing Co., 1964).
[121] U. S. Department of Justice, *Uniform Crime Reports, 1969* (Washington, D.C.: U. S. Government Printing Office, 1970), p. 9.

SELECTED BIBLIOGRAPHY

Amir, Menachem, *Patterns in Forcible Rape*. Chicago: University of Chicago Press, 1971.
Bensing, Robert C., and Schroeder, Jr., Oliver, *Homicide in an Urban Community*. Springfield, Ill. Charles C Thomas, Publisher, 1960.
Bohannan, Paul, *African Homicide and Suicide*. Princeton, N. J.: Princeton University Press, 1960.
Bullock, Henry Allen, "Urban Homicide in Theory and Fact." *Journal of Criminal Law, Criminology and Police Science*, 45 (January–February 1955), pp. 565–575.
Driver, Edwin D., "Interaction and Criminal Homicide in India." *Social Forces*, 40 (December 1961), pp. 153–158.
Frankel, E., "One Thousand Murderers." *Journal of Criminal Law, Criminology and Police Science*, 29 (1938–1939), pp. 687–688.
Geis, Gilbert, "Violence and Organized Crime." *The Annals*, 364 (March 1966), pp. 86–96.
Gold, Martin, "Suicide, Homicide, and the Socialization of Aggression." *American Journal of Sociology*, 63 (May 1958), pp. 651–661.
Graham, Hugh Davis, and Gurr, Ted Robert, *The History of Violence in America*. New York: Bantam Books, 1969.
Levine, Robert A., "Gusii Sex Offenders: A Study in Social Control." *American Anthropologist*, 61 (December 1959), pp. 696–990.
McClintock, F. H., *Crimes of Violence*. New York: St. Martin's Press, 1963.

Morris, T. P., and Blom-Cooper, Louis, *A Calendar of Murder.* London: M. Joseph, 1964.

National Commission on the Causes and Prevention of Violence, Final Report, *To Establish Justice, To Insure Domestic Tranquility.* Washington, D.C.: U. S. Government Printing Office, 1969.

Peterson, Richard A., Pittman, David J., and O'Neal, Patricia, "Stabilities in Deviance: A Study of Assaultive and Non-Assaultive Offenders." *Journal of Criminal Law, Criminology and Police Science,* 53 (March 1962), pp. 44–49.

Pettigrew, Thomas F., and Spier, Rosalind B., "Ecological Pattern of Negro Homicide." *Journal of Criminal Law, Criminology and Police Science,* 55 (December 1964), pp. 462–470.

Pittman, David J., and Handy, William, "Patterns in Criminal Aggravated Assault." *Journal of Criminal Law, Criminology and Police Science,* 55 (December 1964), pp. 462–470.

Pokorny, Alex D., "A Comparison of Homicides in Two Cities." *Journal of Criminal Law, Criminology and Police Science,* 56 (December 1965), pp. 479–487.

President's Commission on Law Enforcement and Administration of Justice, *The Challenge of Crime in a Free Society.* Washington, D.C.: U. S. Government Printing Office, 1967.

Quinney, Richard, "Suicide, Homicide, and Economic Development." *Social Forces,* 43 (March 1965), pp. 401–406.

Roebuck, Julian, and Johnson, Ronald, "The Negro Drinker and Assaulter as a Criminal Type." *Crime and Delinquency,* 3 (January 1962), pp. 21–23.

Straus, Jacqueline and Murray, "Suicide, Homicide, and Social Structure in Ceylon." *American Journal of Sociology,* 48 (March 1953), pp. 461–469.

Svalastoga, Kaare, "Homicide and Social Contact in Denmark." *American Journal of Sociology,* 62 (July 1956), pp. 37–41.

Verkko, Veli, *Homicides and Suicides in Finland and Their Dependance on National Character.* Copenhagen: G. E. C. Gads Forlag, 1951.

Voss, Harwin L., and Hepburn, John R. "Patterns in Criminal Homicide in Chicago." *Journal of Criminal Law, Criminology and Police Science,* 59 (December 1968), pp. 499–508.

Waldo, Gordon P., "The 'Criminality Level' of Incarcerated Murderers and Non-Murderers." *Journal of Criminal Law, Crimiology and Police Science,* 61 (March 1970), pp. 60–70.

Wolfgang, Marvin E., *Patterns in Criminal Homicide.* Philadelphia: University of Pennsylvania Press, 1958.

Wolfgang, Marvin E., and Ferracuti, Franco, *The Subculture of Violence.* London: Social Science Paperbacks, Tavistock Publications, 1967.

Wood, Arthur, "Murder, Suicide, and Economic Crime in Ceylon," *American Sociological Review,* 26 (October 1961), pp. 744–753.

Occasional Property Criminal Behavior | 3

The characteristics of a fully developed criminal career include identification with crime and a conception of the self as a criminal. There is group support for criminal activity in the form of extensive association with other criminals and with criminal norms and activities. Criminality progresses to the use of more complex techniques and frequent offenses, and ultimately crime may become a sole means of livelihood. Those who have careers in crime generally engage in some type of theft of property or money.

Occasional property criminals are the opposite of career criminals. While they may commit offenses similar in type to those committed by career criminals, they do so only infrequently and irregularly. Likewise, things may be taken, checks forged, and autos stolen, but rather crudely. It has been estimated that three-fourths of all check forgeries, for example, are committed by persons with no previous patterns of such behavior and an even larger proportion of shoplifting is committed by noncareer offenders. Similarly, the destruction of property through vandalism is a sporadic offense; one could hardly visualize a person making a career out of vandalism.

LEGAL ASPECTS OF SELECTED OFFENSES

Any offender who steals or injures property on an occasional basis and whose social behavior fits the criteria of this type would be an occasional property offender. Among the occasional property offenses that have been researched extensively are check forgery, adult shoplifting, vandalism, and auto theft.

Legally, forgery is the false signing of legal instruments which creates a liability. Under the old common law of England forgery was "the fraudulent making, or altering, of a writing to the prejudice of another's rights." In medieval times the clerical or priestly class had a virtual monopoly on writing so other people used seals to authenticate a document. Forgery of seals of other persons was then an offense. Forgery can take many forms such as forgery of wills and other documents, check forgery, and counterfeiting.

Check forgery is extensive in the United States. It seldom involves the formerly popular methods of changing the value of the check, carefully working out facsimile signatures, or the manufacture of false negotiable instruments. Checks are widely used today and are cashed outside of banks, often with only perfunctory methods taken to identify the person. Rather than checks being written on someone else's account, they may be written on a nonexistent account with a nonexistent name or on one's own account without sufficient funds in the bank. For this reason most check forgery is quite simple and is executed by unskilled persons rather than by professionals.

Most shoplifting and employee theft, which are closely related in nature, involve the stealing of relatively small and inexpensive articles; professionals may, however, steal things like furs and jewelry. The total value of such thefts may be quite large. Most large retail establishments, according to a government survey, estimate their overall shrinkage due to shoplifting and employee theft at 1 to 2 percent. Among the 47 percent of neighborhood businesses having a high rate of loss, 60 percent placed it at less than 2 percent and another 28 percent estimated they had lost between 2 and 6 percent.[1]

In retail establishments, managers choose to tolerate a high percentage of shoplifting rather than pay for additional clerks. Discount stores, for example, experience an inventory loss rate almost double that of the conventional department store. Studies indicate that there is in general more public tolerance for theft of property and goods from large organizations than from small ones, from big corporations or utilities than from small neighborhood establishments. Restraints on conduct that were effective in a more personal rural society do not seem as effective in an impersonal society of large organizations.[2]

Some further indication of the extent of shoplifting is revealed by several studies. Store detectives of a single Chicago department store arrested two-thirds as many adult women for shoplifting as were formally charged for all forms of larceny in Chicago.[3] Some investigators believe, however, that theft by employees is an even greater problem than shoplifting, partly because of the difficulty of detection.[4] Of 473 industrial concerns surveyed, 20 percent of all companies and 30 percent with more than 1000 employees reported serious employee thefts of tools, equipment, materials, or company products.

Vandalism involves, legally, "malicious mischief" or the willful destruction, damage, or defacement of property; it can be committed by a juvenile or an adult although most of it is perpetrated by juveniles and youths. More specifically, juvenile vandalism can be defined as "the deliberate defacement, mutilation or destruction of private or public property by a juvenile or group of juveniles not having immediate or direct ownership in the property so abused."[5] It is said that the term "vandalism" was used in

1794 by a writer who, attempting to cast blame for the willful destruction of works of art during the French Revolution, likened such destruction to the behavior of the Vandals who sacked Rome in the fifth century.[6]

Vandalism or the willful destruction of property is widespread in American society. It constitutes one of the largest categories of juvenile delinquency but occurs at all ages. It is associated with affluence for it virtually never occurs in less developed countries (except as a part of rioting) where the destruction of goods in limited supply is inconceivable. Vandalism in the United States is widespread against schools, parks, libraries, public transportation facilities, telephone and electric company facilities, traffic department equipment, and housing. In one year, the public school system of Washington, D.C., reported a loss of 28,500 window panes, replaced at a cost of $118,000. Vandalism includes many kinds of offenses.

> Studies of the complaints made by citizens and public officials reveal that hardly any property is safe from this form of aggression. Schools are often the object of attack by vandals. Windows are broken; records, books, desks, typewriters, supplies, and other equipment are stolen or destroyed. Public property of all types appears to offer peculiar allurement to children bent on destruction. Parks, playgrounds, highway signs, and markers are frequently defaced or destroyed. Trees, shrubs, flowers, benches, and other equipment suffer in like manner. Autoists are constantly reporting the slashing or releasing of air from tires, broken windows, stolen accessories. Golf clubs complain that benches, markers, flags, even expensive and difficult-to-replace putting greens are defaced, broken, or uprooted. Libraries report the theft and destruction of books and other equipment. Railroads complain of and demand protection from the destruction of freight car seals, theft of property, wilful and deliberate throwing of stones at passenger car windows, tampering with rails and switches. Vacant houses are always the particular delight of children seeking outlets for destructive instincts; windows are broken, plumbing and hardware stolen, destroyed, or rendered unusable. Gasoline station operators report pumps and other service equipment stolen, broken, or destroyed. Theater managers, frequently in the "better" neighborhoods, complain of the slashing of seats, wilful damaging of toilet facilities, even the burning of rugs, carpets, etc.[7]

The law generally distinguishes two types of auto theft. One is where there is intent to deprive the owner of the car permanently, in which the car is either kept or "stripped" of many of its parts. The other is borrowing the car for a "joyride" in which the car is eventually returned, although in some cases it is damaged. Since the latter usually involves no intent to deprive the person permanently of the car, the offense is usually designated as "operating the motor vehicle without the owner's permission." The penalty for regular auto larceny is generally about ten years, and operating without the owner's permission, one year or less.[8] It appears that the majority of all auto theft involves joyriding for short-run recreational use.

CRIMINAL CAREER OF THE OFFENDER

Many property offenders commit only an occasional theft of some kind. Such criminal behavior is incidental to their way of life. The offenses are so rare that such offenders in no way make a living out of crime and they do not play criminal roles. Occasional property offenders do not identify with crime or conceive of themselves as criminals. Their offenses show little sophistication in the techniques of crime. Most of them have little real knowledge about criminal activities or of the criminal argot or vocabulary of crime.

Adult occasional shoplifters or pilferers, for example, as contrasted with "boosters" or professional shoplifters, do not, in general, define themselves as being criminals. Generally they are largely "respectable" employed persons or "respectable" housewives.[9]

A study of occasional or naive check forgers showed that they do not conceive of themselves as being criminals. Naive check forgers look upon their offenses as relatively minor acts of crime, because large sections of the public do not think they fit the "criminal" stereotype. This crime has low visibility as a crime because of the peculiar interaction with the victim who accepts the check. As Lemert pointed out, forgery for them emerges "as behavior which is out of character or 'other than usual' for the persons involved."

> Another reason for the congeniality of the check forgery alternative lies in the previously mentioned fact that while it is formally treated as a serious crime, informally it is held to be a relatively minor offense and indeed in some forms not a legal offense at all. Thus when the situation or special variations in the subjective reactions of the person dissociate the more formal business and legal control symbols from the act, it becomes a more attractive or acceptable choice for the crisis-bound individual [who needs money]. It is in this connection that the low social visibility of the crime excludes social clues which otherwise would weight the forgery choice with unpleasant connotations for the self and person considering it.[10]

Nonprofessional adult shoplifters largely steal for their own purposes.

> Amateur shoplifters or "snitches" steal amounts of property which vary in cost, so that some steal petty items and others steal quite costly merchandise. Amateur shoplifters also vary in terms of crime skills, some of them employing "booster bags" and other criminal paraphernalia, while others exhibit only rudimentary techniques of crime. Further, these offenders vary in their degree of involvement in crime, for some steal only once or twice and others are caught up in recurrent acts of deviance. The distinguishing mark of the amateur as contrasted to the professional "booster" is that the former steals merchandise for his own use. The "booster," on the other hand, converts the results of his thievery into cash by selling the stolen goods to other persons.[11]

Naive check forgers commit such offenses in the face of a financial problem when other alternatives are blocked. The offense is a product of certain difficult social situations in which the offender finds himself, a certain degree of social isolation, and a process of "closure" or "constriction of behavior alternatives subjectively held as available to the forger."[12]

Assuming we have established situational isolation as the more general prerequiste for the commission of naive check forgery, it is still necessary to factor out more specific situational factors conducive to the crime. These we believe are found in certain dialectical forms of social behavior, dialectical in the sense that the person becomes progressively involved in them. These behaviors are further distinguished in that they make imperative the possession of money or money substitutes for their continuance or fulfillment. They are objective and identifiable and once a person is committed to them the impetus to "follow through" with them is implicit. A quick example is that of a man away from home who falls in with a small group of persons who have embarked upon a two- or three-day or even a week's period of drinking and carousing. The impetus to continue the pattern gets mutually reinforced by interaction of the participants, and tends to have an accelerated beginning, a climax and a terminus. If midway through such a spree a participant runs out of money the pressures immediately become critical to take such measures as are necessary to preserve the behavior sequence.[13]

The affluence of the more developed countries is associated with vandalism. Such acts are divided into three types: wanton, predatory, and vindictive.[14] The most common is wanton vandalism which involves destructive acts with no utilitarian purpose or gain. Predatory vandalism involves acts of destruction where there are some economic gains, such as the smashing of a telephone booth or parking meter for their coins. Acts of vindictive vandalism are directed at the property of persons of a different race, religion, ethnic background, or social class in which the chief motivation is to express antagonism or hatred toward the group. A large proportion of youths who commit vandalism are likely to have a noncriminal view of themselves and their acts. That often nothing is stolen during acts of wanton or vindictive vandalism tends to reinforce the vandal's conception of himself merely as a prankster and not a young delinquent or criminal.

The juvenile's conception of the act of vandalism is a clue to his self-image. If he construes the event as "just a joke" or "just having fun," it implies that he thinks of himself as a "prankster" and not specifically as a delinquent. This construction, however, does not exclude a conception of his actions as "bad" or "wrong" since concurrently he is able to deny responsibility for his actions by a favorable definition of the situation as an acceptable one for vandalism. This denial of responsibility functions to reduce the disapproval of self and others as a restraining influence.[15]

On the whole, acts of vandalism are committed by persons, therefore, who have no special criminal orientation toward themselves or what they do. They regard their acts as pranks. This conception is reinforced because often nothing is stolen during the acts. Some writers consider this a distinguishing characteristic of the vandal when compared with other property offenders, assuming that since nothing is taken vandalism has a non-utilitarian function. Property destruction does seem, however, to have a function for the adolescent, as he considers it fun and exciting, as well as a protest against his role and status in the social structure of society. The evidence indicates that vandalism is increasing in middle-class suburbia.[16]

Joyriding is not a career type of offense. It is usually done only by teenagers and the offenses committed are sporadic in nature.[17] The usual patterns are quite simple—either stealing a car that has readily accessible keys, using a duplicate key, or jumping the ignition with a wire. The theft of an auto is more like "borrowing" it and does not involve techniques commonly associated with conventional career types of offenders such as selecting a special type of car, finding "fences" for the sale of the car or its parts, or stripping the car. The occasional auto offender, the joyrider, does not necessarily progress in techniques and skills. The car is driven around for a while, then abandoned. This type of illegal behavior is terminated with adulthood.

A similar lack of criminal career characteristics has been noted in a study of young rural offenders who largely commit simple, occasional property offenses.[18] It was found that (1) their criminal behavior did not start early in life, (2) they exhibited little progressive knowledge of criminal techniques and crime in general, (3) crime was not the sole means of livelihood, and (4) they did not conceive of themselves as criminals. The rural offenders did not identify with crime, rather they considered themselves as "reckless" and unattached to traditional ways. They were mobile, referred to their behavior as "fast," and engaged in occasional criminal activity as an adventure.

Of particular significance among occasional offenders is their ability to rationalize their criminal behavior. Adult department store pilferers, for example, tend to take relatively inexpensive items of merchandise just a little above the level of that which they would purchase; therefore, they view their acts as somewhat reprehensible but not really criminal. Other rationalizations include the thought that "department stores are rich" or that many other persons also steal small items.[19]

GROUP SUPPORT OF CRIMINAL BEHAVIOR

The occasional property offender generally has little group support for his criminal behavior. Perhaps one reason why some occasional crimes need relatively little group support is that they are fairly easy to commit in the sense that few skills are employed. This suggests the relative unimportance of criminal associations in crime of this type. Most persons in their everyday lives have occasion to cash personal checks. Likewise, the present-day mass display of merchandise in stores makes training in techniques of theft largely unnecessary. Similarly, most acts of vandalism require little sophisticated knowledge. To some who illegally "borrow" an automobile it involves no more than driving away an unlocked car. Naive check forgeries are committed by persons who have had no previous criminal record and no previous contact or interaction with delinquents and criminals. A study of 1023 naive check forgers showed that one-third had no prior record and almost one-half involved this or other prior forgeries.[20] The remaining offense record was of a type that largely did not involve criminal associations. Naive check forgers are much older than most property offenders, being in their late twenties and thirties and are disproportionately found in the clerical (particularly salesmen), professional, and skilled or craft classes. This type of offender in general does not come from an area with a high delinquency rate.

Similarly, most adult shoplifters have had no present or sustained contact with a criminal subculture. In Cameron's study, approximately 92 percent of the women who were officially charged with shoplifting had never been convicted of an offense.[21] Some may have had such associations when they were younger, however. The behavior of adult shoplifters after arrest indicates how little association with a criminal culture they have generally had.

> Pilferers had no knowledge of arrest procedures, and they had clearly given little or no forethought to the consequences of their arrest. They appeared to have thought about being "caught," but not about being arrested. Not understanding that they would be searched, for example, many attempted to give fictitious names (for a woman, usually her maiden name) while at the same time carrying a billfold or pocketbook with complete identification papers. (They did not realize that arrest implied search.) They consistently offered to pay for the stolen merchandise, failing to understand that they had been arrested and that the merchandise stolen had been impounded as evidence of theft and could not be bought by the thief. They frequently signed a waiver against suit of the store immediately after arrest—tantamount to a confession of guilt—but having signed the waiver, they talked threateningly about suit. (The waiver is simple in appearance, saying that there has been no damage, physical or otherwise, at the hands of store personnel, and detailing possible physical damage. The "otherwise," of course, is the waiver against all suit.) Not infrequently pilferers confessed some of their past thefts to store detectives, detailing the time, place, and objects stolen. Some of these past thefts had been memorable events arousing and continuing to arouse strong feelings of guilt.[22]

Naive check forgery is usually carried out alone. Shoplifting by adults is generally done alone, but shoplifting by juveniles is generally a group activity of quite a different sort. In a Philadelphia study juveniles accounted for 60 percent of all shoplifters, a figure somewhat higher than that found by Cameron in Chicago.[23] Some juveniles in a group act as lookouts. The stealing may or may not be for utilitarian purposes; much of it is done for "kicks." The relation of group factors is indicated by the fact that the highest rates of shoplifting occur in areas of high juvenile crime rates.[24]

In acts of vandalism several persons are usually associated, but what takes place is more the result of the collective interaction of the moment than the product of a criminal subculture or a subculture of vandalism.[25]

Acts of vandalism seldom utilize or even require prior sophisticated knowledge. They grow out of collective interaction of the moment; few are deliberately planned in advance. Participation in acts of vandalism gives status and group interaction to each member; through direct involvement the individual avoids becoming a marginal member of the group. Vandalism is spontaneous behavior and the outgrowth of social situations in which group interaction takes place. Each interactive response by a participant builds upon the action of another participant until a focus develops and the group act of vandalism results. In the typical act of vandalism there are usually five stages: (1) waiting for something to turn up; (2) removal of uncertainty about what to do, resulting in an "exploratory gesture" to the act; (3) mutual conversion of each member of the group to participation; (4) joint elaboration of the vandalism; and (5) aftermath and retrospect.[26]

In his research on juvenile vandalism, Wade has documented these stages. His discussion of the social processes in the act of vandalism follows:

Stage I: "Waiting for something to turn up." Preliminary to the act is the situation from which the suggestion or innovating behavior develops. Much of the juvenile's free time outside school and in other unsupervised contexts is spent in unstructured situations. This free time is characterized by him as "messing around." What is often interpreted as aimless activity by the untrained observer and even the participants themselves has in actuality a subtle pattern. Much of it centers about and emanates from a particular location serving a vital function in the emotional life of the adolescent. These are the kinds of situations utilized by the innovator. The actors are poised, ready for an action-provoking suggestion. As one boy defined a similar situation:

"Well, we were all at the cafe; we didn't have anything to do. We were all sitting, talking. When we didn't have anything else to do, we'd go over there to the cafe and sit down. The guys who were old enough would play the pinball machine."

"An opportunity structure" is present. The aimless talk and "bull sessions" provide the chance for gossip. The talk concerns what other juveniles have done and the escapades of their contemporaries. Such talk might never get started if these seemingly purposeless get-togethers did not occur. One interviewee summed up the situation when he said, "Things get around, boy to boy."

The *play situation* is another general type of context out of which vandalism may develop. The destructive activity may itself be a form of play or it may be a spontaneous outgrowth of the play situation. The two forms are often inextricably bound together by the nature of the play activity itself. The following account illustrates how vandalism may take the form of a play activity:

"There were these lights in the apartment house; they stand on a stand, have a bulb (globe) on the outside. There were three others besides me; we'd been messing around. We went walking around—went down, got a cup of coffee. We came up; we broke that light bulb. Gene picked it up and threw it on the sidewalk. He just acted like he was bowling and threw."

Vandalism as play generally takes the shape of a *game of skill*. As such, either the quantity or the quality of the destruction is stressed. The following account shows how the quantity aspect is emphasized, although not originally intended as the goal of the play activity:

"The first time we did vandalism, me and my brother and another boy down at the garage, we were smoking and playing cards. They had some old cars in the back; we played around there. We cleaned them out one day. Swept out the broken glass—busted windshields—rolled down the windows so we wouldn't cut ourselves. This one guy threw a whiskey bottle up on the roof; threw another. It hit the side of the window. We just started throwing at the windows. When we were through, we had broken twenty-seven of them. We saw who could break out the most. There wasn't anything else to do. We finally got tired and just left. They didn't catch us until the next day. We returned to see what had happened; we were out there playing cards and smoking again."

On other occasions the destruction is subordinate. What primarily counts is one's ability to hit a target with a BB gun, pellet gun, a stone, or some other object. The target chosen is something easily broken since a hit is more visible or audible. A competitive situation ensues with destruction resulting:

"About seven years ago I was shooting out switch lights on a railroad track with an air rifle. There were three of us, and each of us had guns. We were looking for pigeons. One of them said, 'See that switch light up there?' He shot and missed it, and the other boy shot and missed it. I shot and missed it. So we kept on shooting until we hit it.

"Oh, I broke out a few windows—see who was the straighter shot. I had a pellet pistol. See, we'd aim for the center. If you hit the center, then the window wouldn't break, only have a little hole with some small cracks. We tried to shoot through the same hole."

Once the spirit of destructive activity takes hold, massive destruction may result and the "game" quality of the activity heightens. There is a spontaneous eruption of wholesale vandalism:

"This last July my parents were out of town. Me and these other kids went on a hay ride. We got home about eleven o'clock. Well, we were walking around; we were going to stay up all night—just something to keep us awake. We went out and broke windows and ran—just for excitement. We would just walk by and someone would pick up a rock and throw it and everyone would start running. We broke about fifty windows. We went around all night till it got light. We ended up walking quite a ways from our neighborhood."

As the interview data show, vandalism is sometimes the inadvertent result of ordinary play activity. Sometimes it may even be an accidental result. For example, several boys gained entry to a feed mill one weekend in order to play tag on the stacks of feed bags. The original objective soon changed as a number of motorized forklifts were discovered, and the boys began having fun driving them. The resulting destruction was rationalized as accidental:

"Some of us drove the lifts. I found out I couldn't drive, so I didn't drive after about five minutes. I rode with someone else. (Did any of the guys deliberately drive into the feed bags?) They weren't doing that on purpose; sometimes they'd hit them but never on purpose. We didn't know how to drive. They were piled in huge stacks. You'd try to turn around or something; you know the back wheels are supposed to turn. They'd spin too fast; we'd hit the sack. We didn't do all the damage anyway. We weren't the first ones in there."

Stage II: Removal of Uncertainty (the Exploratory Gesture). The unstructured situation as the general context from which vandalism may develop undergoes a significant change when an action-provoking suggestion is made by one of the actors. It is generally in the form of an "exploratory gesture." This is a suggestion, sometimes cautiously, sometimes boldly, broached to effect action from a group. It functions to change the ongoing interaction and to interject a focus to the interest and conversation of the hangers-on. The prevailing boredom begins to disappear as interest develops in the exploratory gesture:

"We were just sitting on the corner talking. Each boy had a different idea, but this boy had a funny idea. He told of wanting to break a window—of about a big crash. I didn't want to do it; I told him that a couple of times. But he called me 'chicken.' Like the Y (another place where he had committed vandalism), just riding around thinking of something to do—get an idea in their heads about causing trouble."

At times the exploratory gesture meets with little or no resistance. This is usually the case when the suggestion involves a play activity having a decided element of excitement. The original suggestion may not be that the group do property damage but that it participate in an activity challenging individual daring. The resulting vandalism is often a by-product of the situation but may also become the substitute activity:

"This one guy came up to us and said, 'Let's go down to the bottom (basement) of Hilliard's (a local new car dealer) and drive around the cars.' So we went and started driving around. I think it was on a Saturday. One of the salesmen came down and chased us out. We went down to this cafe and played the pinball machine. I was telling about it, so one of the guys got the bright idea that we go back there. We drove them around, scratched some of them."

The exploratory gesture may also be in the form of an overt act. In this case the act is an event of vandalism. It may be deliberate or spur-of-the-moment behavior. The episode is taken as a cue by others to commit similar ones, and a series of destructive acts may result. The following interviews illustrate this cue-taking sequence of behavior:

"Well, me and a couple of boy friends and a girl got in a car we had taken. We were going to stay there that night. She asked me if I had a knife. I said, 'Yeah.' So she started cutting up the upholstery, ceiling and everything. After she quit cutting up, Joe got out of the car and went to the drugstore. I locked the door and wouldn't let him back in. So Raymond kicked out the window on the right side of the driver's seat. So Joe put his foot through the same window. Then I bent up the gear shift—took out the speedometer. Joe, he took the glove compartment, took it all apart. If I'd known she was going to cut it up, I wouldn't have given her the knife. I just took it away from her and started cutting up myself. So did Joe and Raymond. I cut up the driver's seat. We didn't want to go home that night—just wanted to stay out."

Obviously, the exploratory gesture that the group participate in an act of vandalism may be rejected. No attempt is made here to determine why, when, or how such a suggestion is refused further elaboration. However, the following stage has implicit propositions considered as suggestive clues to an explanation of why some adolescents will engage in vandalism while others shy away from such behavior.

Stage III: Mutual Conversion. In most instances vandalism is a group type of activity. Some degree of agreement, therefore, must be present among the prospective participants in order for the act to materialize. Prefacing this agreement is a period of mutual exploration as discussed above. As a stage in the ongoing sequence of the act, it may be very incidental and of short duration. On the other hand, a series of exploratory gestures may be made and discarded over a relatively long period of time before the process of "mutual conversion" to the idea takes place. The acceptability of an idea to oneself depends upon its acceptability to others.

A number of pressures operate, causing the individual to accede to the implications of the exploratory gesture. In general, these challenge or threaten the person's self-concept as an acceptable peer. One of the most obvious is the dare to commit the act of vandalism. It functions as a device to measure the boy's courage and manliness before the critical audience of his peers. This form of mutual conversion is illustrated below:

"I came home from doing three lawns, ate dinner. These boys waited for me till I ate dinner. This boy had some BB's and said, 'Why don't you get your gun?' So I got the gun and we walked down the street. Just pointed the gun at it and shot the window. Well, when we started, I thought we were just going over to Larry's house to play cards or mess around. No reason to pick that house (to shoot the window). I think they said, 'Bet you can't hit that window.' It was just about eight by ten inches. After shooting the window we ran."

There are occasions when the dare involves a particularly danger-charged challenge. But one may enhance his status within the peer group if he accepts the dare even though the chances of getting away with the act are negligible. As an example:

"Ronny was stupid for kicking that neon sign in front of the funeral parlor. He knew he was going to get caught. I wouldn't have done it. The cops were standing down the street not more than ten feet away. He was going along; anything he saw he was hitting. One of the boys dared him to do it. Then we tried to run, and we didn't make it."

Usually, the dare is reinforced by an epithet in current vogue among juveniles. The one most often used is "chicken." Whether applied in earnest or in jest, this appellation is taken seriously by the adolescent. It is a threat to his status in the eyes of his peers, especially when it is an overt challenge to test his courage. If the pressure toward conformity is too great, he will react as he thinks others in this reference group would react to a similar challenge. An inner struggle results between what he knows to be the right response in keeping with the internalized norms of the larger social system and the demands of loyalty to the peer group or friendship clique. If he sacrifices the demands of larger society for those of the smaller social group, he does so at the risk of violating the law. When the decision is made in favor of the peer group, the process of mutual conversion has taken place.

Continued peer pressure to conform for the promise of psychological rewards, primarily that of being an accepted member of a favored group, will be too much for some juveniles. They eventually accede, and the act of property destruction is consummated:

"One of the kids I ran around with and I were walking around one night, and we came to the Motor Company. He just picked up a rock and threw it. He didn't tell me he was going to do it. Those were $150 windows, something like that. He picked up a nice, big, juicy rock. He came back and said 'Now it's your chance.' Of course, the guys I ran around with, they call you 'chicken.' One guy dares another—calls him 'chicken.' Some guys can't take that. I took it as long as I could until I got into it. They said if you want to belong to our club, you got to break a window. We broke about eight windows that night. Usually it started by someone calling you 'chicken.' If you get in the gang, you got to break a window if you want to get in our club. So we stopped, found some rocks, and threw them. Happened in a minute and sped off. We thought it was kind of funny."

It was obvious from the story that there is a tendency on the part of these boys to minimize the damage they have done and to excuse their participation in such acts on the basis of an inability to face the scorn of peers if they refuse to commit vandalism. The very fact they do eventually submit to the pressure is indicative of the importance of being accepted as a worthy peer. However, occasionally a boy will find himself included in an act of vandalism without his prior consent. The conversion stage of the act is circumvented as is the preliminary stage of the exploratory gesture. Loyalty to friends prevents him from "ratting" on them:

"Yeah, one of my friends got me in some vandalism. Put a cherry bomb in a toilet stool. We were taking boxing then. A kid came in there where I was, told me all about it. We left and came back there. Police picked us up. He threw the cherry bomb in the toilet stool; I guess to have fun. I was with him when they picked him up. A lady knew he was in the rest room—she suspected him anyway. She called the cops on him. Blew it all to bits. They didn't have any proof that he did it, but he did it. I didn't say anything about it to him, I just said he was crazy (to have done that). I asked him why he came in there (into the gym). He said, 'Be quiet. I'll tell you about it.' He said 'Let's leave.' I said I was fixing to leave. So we left anyway."

The time that it takes before the conversion process reaches fulfillment is dependent upon many factors. The more obvious of these is the seriousness of the proposed action as defined by the prospective participants. Many juveniles who already have a history of delinquencies such as theft are not likely to consider vandalism as a particularly serious offense. Little mutual exploration is necessary preliminary to participation in property destruction by these boys. On the other hand, some juveniles might define vandalism as "kid stuff." No amount of inducement short of financial reward or release from boredom would effect conversion to the idea. But most probably for these boys property destruction would be an incidental and initial phase to the "breaking and entering" of a business establishment for the purpose of burglary.

The mutual conversion process is also effected more quickly in a group in which the configuration of past experiences of the interacting individuals is very similar or strongly related. Little exploration of feelings of fellow members of a delinquent group need be made when past natural histories of their careers indicate predispositions to any behavior hinting of excitement, danger, and even malice.

Stage IV: Joint Elaboration of the Act. In this stage of the social act there is likely to be large-scale property destruction. There is a spontaneous eruption of wholesale vandalism once the spirit of the activity takes hold of the participants. For example, breaking one window may lead to extensive damage to others. Occasionally, the participants become so stimulated by the first few acts of destruction that a veritable orgy of vandalism takes place.

It was indicated in the previous section dealing with the conversion stage in the act of vandalism that the tolerance threshold of some adolescents is much lower than that of others. The effects of family and class socialization patterns need to be temporarily removed in order for some of these boys to participate in such an act. Pressure from peers to conform also makes this condition possible. The pressuring takes place within a group situation in which members interact with each other and upon each other in both direct and indirect ways. Mutual testing with exploratory gestures takes place. Calling each other's bluff through the use of epithets is often the device to complete the process of securing conformity from the individual.

Contributing to the elaboration of an act of vandalism is the element of *mutual excitation.* The play situation is often responsible for generating this type of excitement. This is especially true if there is a competitive event involved. Such a situation may develop into a destructive race between contestants to see who can do the most or the best damage. Underlying the event is a kind of "group psychological intoxication." One participant's behavior serves as the model for another's. Present is a "behavioral contagion" denoted by the spontaneous pickup or imitation by the other individuals of a behavior initiated by one member of the group.

The functional nature of mutual excitation or group contagion is of particular importance in vandalism. A primary function of this element is the tendency for the individual to lose his feeling of self-identity in the prevailing group interaction. This temporary *loss of identity* is especially significant because it helps make possible his participation in vandalism and any resulting elaboration of the act. The very fact that property destruction is generally a group act functions to reduce individual feelings of fear and guilt. The dilution of such feeling in the peer association operates as a sort of "guilt insurance." The peer group inadvertently furnishes a sense of security in numbers which functions to reduce feelings of individuality and responsibility. The belief is present that when the act is committed by a group, the authorities will find it difficult, if not impossible, to single out the specific instigators.

This *feeling of security* is enhanced by the additional belief that vandalism is one of the less serious delinquencies. Particularly is this the case when the adolescent interprets his destructive behavior as a prank or "just being mischievous." This interpretation also functions as a rationalization of the activity and as an attempt to neutralize whatever guilt feelings he may have from participation in vandalism.

There is still another result of the functional nature of the element of mutual excitation. The apparent loss of individuality and responsibility obtained from anonymity operates to bring into the group interaction patterns the more cautious individuals. When this occurs, the range of anonymity is further expanded. An *impression of universality* is created, giving the appearance of group solidarity. On some occasions, especially when the participating group is large, there will be found on the fringes of the group action the supportive individuals who cannot be stampeded into actual participation in the act. Although they do not oppose the group, they tend to draw the line at joining in the "fun." However, these persons are not averse to enjoying the ensuing action. The ultimate effect of these "fringers" is to add to the already created impression of universality, the impression that everyone is "in on the act."

The resulting destructive behavior is extemporaneous. The participants are precipitated into it by the fast-rising events of the situation over which they have had little control. Once the action begins, apparently little can be done to prevent it from gathering momentum. The interview data tend to show that few, if any, of the participants offered strong objections to engaging in vandalism. Group pressure and mutual excitation combined to smother any protestations which arose. Not until the destruction was completed or the participants were chased from the scene did the activity halt.

Stage V: Aftermath and Retrospect. The fifth stage is of particular importance in terms of the meaning of the acts to the participant. The motive for the act will largely determine the evaluation the actor makes of the destructive behavior. The fact that nothing is stolen during most acts of vandalism tends to reinforce the vandal's conception of himself as merely a prankster and not a delinquent. In fact, this would appear to indicate that vandalism is nonutilitarian. Actually, many acts do have some meaning and utility for the participants even though not defined explicitly by them. Some property destruction appears to function for the adolescent as a protest against his ill-defined social role and ambiguous status in the social structure. Other meanings are more specific. If a boy has suffered frustration, he may express his resentment by a revengeful act of destruction:

"Well, he accused us of stealing some stuff out of his joint. He didn't come right out and say it was us, but the way he talked he made it sound like it, particularly us. We were kidding him about an old rifle he had in there, about ninety years old. And he wanted $15 for it, and the stock on it was all cracked up and everything. And we kept kidding his mother—she's in there (the store) with him—and we kept kidding her. And old Gay (the store owner) himself came over there and started raising the devil, blowing off steam and everything. We didn't like it too well. We left and came back later. I told him (his companion), 'Let's go down and break those windows.' He said, 'Okay,' and we went down there and picked up some rocks along the way. We got down there and stood in front of the place till there weren't any cars very close to us, and we threw the rocks and ran."

In his *retrospective view of the act*, the participant sometimes redefines his behavior from the original definition of "fun" to a negative one. There are indications of mixed feelings on the part of these boys as they look back upon such behavior. It is a mixture of rebellion, guilt, and malicious delight. This process of redefinition and revision of self attitudes has been designated by Ellsworth Faris as the "retrospective act." Usually, the apprehension and detention experiences are significant in fostering this change in the definition of the act: "But at the time we thought it was fun until the police came and then that was all."

Another element causing a change in the original definition of the act is the realization that it caused "trouble." This is interpreted in personal terms, that is, being brought down to the police station or to the juvenile court or being involved in a disagreeable family situation. Comments such as these are indicative: "We didn't think about getting caught; we were thinking about having fun. I'm sorry I did it—more trouble than it was fun." "It didn't seem like then that it would amount to this much." "I didn't think it would cause so much trouble."

Although the primary aspect of the guilt is that of apprehension, there is also present a feeling that this kind of behavior might have resulted in something more serious, such as an injury. It is particularly true in cases where damage was done to automobiles by throwing rocks or using slingshots. Attitudes expressive of such guilt feelings are: "I could have hurt someone in the car." "It's bad; it could have caused an accident."

Further indication of the guilt which some held concerning their behavior is a feeling of relief at having been apprehended. This tends to represent how effectively the conventional norms are internalized. The internalization, although not complete enough to forestall deviation from property norms, was still effective enough to provoke guilt feelings. It also led to the realization that vandalism was contrary to parental expectations and "good sense":

"First place, we shouldn't have been over there. Second place, one of us might have got killed. Third place, I'm glad we got caught because we'd do more damage and more damage—be hard on our parents. Fourth place, that was an awful place to go play in, the (feed) mill."

Also present on occasion in the retrospective assessment of the act is the boy's conclusion that vandalism is "senseless." To some extent this represents a feeling of shame with the implication that one's behavior should have reason and utilitarian ends to it. Inherent is the idea that one ought to have good sense to think ahead and weigh the consequences of the act. It also represents a certain amount of chagrin at not having met internalized expectations relative to evaluating consequences before acting.

Although there are these feelings of guilt and shame at having been a participant in vandalism, some express a malicious delight at having been a party to the act. This is especially true if the victim is known to the individual and has been defined in negative terms. In some instances it is an attempt to justify the act to oneself.

By engaging in this kind of retrospective activity the vandal is taking the role of the other. In doing so, a changed conception of self begins to form. It is also conceivable that this same process helps to inhibit certain forms of vandalism as well as encourage still other types. However, whether or not a redefinition takes place will greatly depend upon the individual's "normative reference group." This is especially true of the deviant's choice of behavior responses to begin with in the interactional process.

Since the individual gets much of his self-definition from the way others treat him and talk to him, the roles of law enforcement authorities and other significant adults are important in effecting the retrospective act on the part of the juvenile vandal with the end result of a changed self-image. As mentioned above, his apprehension often leads the boy to re-evaluate the act. This re-evaluation in terms of guilt or shame is probably more true in the case of the boy who has never been arrested before than of the adolescent who is a familiar face to authorities. The adolescent's peers, who also function as significant others, are also highly important in fostering his self-conception, as well as revising it to conform with their perceived expectations of him. Obviously, much depends upon how significantly the actor has identified himself with the normative reference group in question.[27]

CORRESPONDENCE BETWEEN CRIMINAL AND LEGITIMATE BEHAVIOR

Occasional property offenders find little support for their criminal behavior in the legitimate behavior patterns of society. In general, all of the offenses represent a violation of the values placed on private property. The offenders in most cases are attempting to obtain something that they consider to be necessary and important, but due to circumstances are unable to obtain through legitimate channels.

Occasional property offenders tend to be committed to the general goals of society. Naive check forgers "appear to have acquired normal attitudes and habits of law observance."[28] Adult department store pilferers are generally "respectable" citizens with little or no contact with criminal groups.[29] Juveniles involved in joyriding either have no criminal record or none other than for auto theft and are likely to come from conventional middle-class neighborhoods.[30]

On the other hand, the extent to which occasional property crime represents a rejection of legitimate behavior patterns, as incorporated in middle-class norms, is open to question. Much destruction of property through vandalism seems to occur as a way of challenging the complex of values associated with the emphasis placed on private property in our society. In many other cases vandalism appears to be an attempt merely to have some fun. Increasing evidence indicates that middle-class legitimate behavior patterns are not internalized by all persons and groups and that many law violators are involved in a world of their own which is relatively isolated from the behavior patterns of the dominant power segments of society.[31] Others, however, feel that both delinquent and middle-class legal norms are internalized and that delinquency is a product of the delinquent's relations with an inconsistent and vulnerable legal code.[32] With all the forms of vandalism, the behaviors that may become defined as criminal are pursued for a variety of reasons, with variations occurring according to the location of the participants in the social structure. In the study of criminal behavior, the criminologist must be careful not to impute his own motives and values to those that underlie the behavior of the offenders.

SOCIETAL REACTION AND LEGAL PROCESSING

The societal reaction toward occasional crime often is not severe, inasmuch as the offender is unlikely to have any, or at most a minor, previous record. Consequently, the charge is often likely to be dismissed or the offender placed on probation or given a suspended sentence.

In most cases the illegal behavior is carried out in isolation from the supporting values of a criminal subculture or group, and largely in a system of noncriminal relationships. The criminal behavior of the occasional offender is likely to be unstable and when confronted with legal action in the form of an arrest, which defines the behavior as actually being "criminal," the offender is usually deterred from continuing such activity.

The effect of this societal reaction generally holds true whether it is shoplifting, simple check forgery, or vandalism. Persons can behave, for example, as thieves without defining themselves as thieves. Arrests by store detectives or the police are crucial in helping to redefine a shoplifter's conception of his or her behavior as being merely "antisocial" or "bad," to being "criminal." Considerable leniency is thus allowed the occasional property offender by law enforcement and judicial agencies because such offenders are not likely to progress into a career of crime.

Relatively few shoplifters are turned over to the police and prosecuted; juveniles are rarely turned over to prosecution and only about a fourth of the adults are. There are several reasons for this. There is difficulty in getting court action, the suspect often refuses to confess, the thefts are not usually of large items, often the suspects, particularly women, are "respectable middle-class women," and the large companies do not wish to appear to be "picking on" the individual. Losses from shoplifting are frequently figured into the cost of the merchandise. A major factor in the decision to prosecute is the value of the stolen merchandise; those stealing over $50 worth are more likely to be prosecuted.

Another element in the moderate reaction to occasional property crime is the fact that the offenders often come from the same classes that are responsible for the enforcement of the law. In many localities the offenders are an important part of the community. In such communities much criminal behavior of residents is ignored by the local law enforcement agencies. In a study of a rural community, Esselstyn observed that a great deal of discretion operated in the enforcement of the law and that the local sheriff interpreted the law according to the overall interests of the community. The primary functions of the sheriff were to conserve the peace and to provide for the public safety. Reporting of some offenses might have actually threatened those functions. The public also knew of many offenses which were not reported for a variety of reasons. Official reaction to these offenses is increased only when the offenses are engaged in by a large number of persons to such an extent that the behavior becomes a nuisance to the community or exceeds what is regarded as normal for the community.[33] Through legal agencies, communities are able to establish and make viable the limits to which they will tolerate certain forms and amounts of deviant behavior.

There appear to be differentials, however, in the apprehension and prosecution of shoplifters. Black shoplifters are unlikely to be more numerous than the general run of the population, but they are much more likely to be reported to the police.[34] Black offenders are also more likely to receive stiffer penalties. Juvenile thieves are almost never turned over to the authorities for official action, while only about one-fourth of the adult shoplifters are prosecuted.[35]

With repeated offenses "joyriders" often come to the attention of police and courts. Whereas they are more likely to get probation, some end up for a short time in correctional institutions. Most offenders do not define their actions as criminal, although they may consider themselves as "tough," and even though arrested "these contacts do not usually lead the offender to a commitment to adult patterns of criminality. Instead, the joyrider is sufficiently socialized to conventional norms that he ultimately gets a job, gets married, and assumes the behavior of a conventional law-abiding citizen."[36]

NOTES

[1] *Task Force Report: Crime and Its Impact—An Assessment*. The President's Commission on Law Enforcement and Administration of Justice (Washington, D.C.: U. S. Government Printing Office, 1967), p. 84. Figured in dollars this is a huge sum for the country as a whole.

[2] *The Challenge of Crime in a Free Society*. A Report by the President's Commission on Law Enforcement and Administration of Justice (Washington, D.C.: U. S. Government Printing Office, 1967), p. 30.

[3] Loren E. Edwards, *Shoplifting and Shrinkage Protection for Stores* (Springfield, Ill.: Charles C Thomas, Publisher, 1958). Also see Mary Owen Cameron, *The Booster and the Snitch: Department Store Shoplifting* (New York: The Free Press, 1964).

[4] *Task Force Report: Crime and Its Impact*, p. 84.

[5] Marshall B. Clinard and Andrew L. Wade, "Toward the Delineation of Vandalism as a Sub-Type in Juvenile Delinquency," *The Journal of Criminal Law, Criminology and Police Science*, 48 (January–February 1958), pp. 493–499.

[6] S. J. Idzerda, "Iconoclasm during the French Revolution," *American Historical Review*, 60 (October 1954), pp. 13–26. Also see John M. Martin, *Juvenile Vandalism: A Study of Its Nature and Prevention* (Springfield, Ill.: Charles C Thomas, Publisher, 1961).

[7] J. P. Murphy, "The Answer to Vandalism May Be Found at Home," *Federal Probation*, 18 (1954), pp. 8–10.

[8] Jerome Hall, *Theft, Law, and Society*, 2d ed., (Indianapolis: Bobbs-Merrill Company, 1952).

[9] Cameron, *The Booster and the Snitch*.

[10] Edwin M. Lemert, "An Isolation of Closure Theory of Naive Check Forgery," *Journal of Criminal Law, Criminology and Police Science*, 44 (October 1953), p. 305. Reprinted by special permission of the *Journal of Criminal Law, Criminology and Police Science* © 1953 by the Northwestern University School of Law, Volume 44, No. 3.

[11] Don C. Gibbons, *Society, Crime and Criminal Careers* (Englewood Cliffs, N.J.: Prentice-Hall, 1968).

[12] Lemert, "An Isolation of Closure Theory," p. 297.

[13] *Ibid.*, p. 302.

[14] Martin, *Juvenile Vandalism*.

[15] Andrew L. Wade, "Social Processes in the Act of Juvenile Vandalism," in Marshall B. Clinard and Richard Quinney, *Criminal Behavior Systems: A Typology* (New York: Holt, Rinehart and Winston, 1967), p. 108.

[16] Edmund W. Vaz, ed., *Middle-Class Juvenile Delinquency* (New York: Harper & Row, 1967).

[17] Leonard D. Savitz, "Automobile Theft," *Journal of Criminal Law, Criminology and Police Science*, 50 (July–August 1959), pp. 132–143.

[18] Marshall B. Clinard, "Rural Criminal Offenders," *American Journal of Sociology*, 50 (July 1944), pp. 38–45.

[19] The extent to which the size of the victim organization may play a role in rationalization for the offender is indicated in public attitudes toward stealing from large organizations. See Erwin O. Smigel, "Public Attitudes toward Stealing as Related to the Size of the Victim Organization," *American Sociological Review*, 21 (June 1956), pp. 320–327.

[20] Lemert, "An Isolation of Closure Theory."

[21] Cameron, *The Booster and the Snitch*, p. 110.

[22] *Ibid.*, pp. 147–148.

[23] Gerald D. Robin, "Patterns of Department Store Shoplifting," *Crime and Delinquency*, 9 (April 1963), p. 170; and Cameron, *The Booster and the Snitch*, pp. 101–104.

[24] *Task Force Report: Crime and Its Impact*, p. 84.

[25] Wade, "Social Processes in the Act of Juvenile Vandalism."

[26] Marshall B. Clinard, *Sociology of Deviant Behavior*, 3d ed. (New York: Holt, Rinehart and Winston, 1968), p. 268.

[27] Wade, "Social Processes in the Act of Juvenile Vandalism," pp. 98–108 (with some deletions).

[28] Lemert, "An Isolation of Closure Theory," p. 298.

[29] Cameron, *The Booster and the Snitch*, p. xii.

[30] William E. Wattenberg and James Balistrieri, "Automobile Theft: A 'Favored-Group' Delinquency," *American Journal of Sociology*, 57 (May 1952), pp. 575–579.

31 See Bertram Spiller, "Delinquency and Middle Class Goals," *Journal of Criminal Law, Criminology and Police Science,* **56** (December 1965), pp. 463–478.
32 See David Matza, *Delinquency and Drift* (New York: John Wiley & Sons, 1964).
33 T. C. Esselstyn, "The Social Role of the County Sheriff," *Journal of Criminal Law, Criminology and Police Science,* **44** (July–August 1953), pp. 177–184.
34 Cameron, *The Booster and the Snitch*; Robin, "Patterns of Department Store Shoplifting."
35 Robin, "Patterns of Department Store Shoplifting," pp. 169–170.
36 Gibbons, *Society, Crime and Criminal Careers*, p. 301.

SELECTED BIBLIOGRAPHY

Cameron, Mary Owen, *The Booster and the Snitch: Department Store Shoplifting.* New York: The Free Press, 1964.
Clinard, Marshall B., "Rural Criminal Offenders." *American Journal of Sociology,* **50** (July 1944), pp. 38–45.
————, and Wade, Andrew L., "Toward the Delineation of Vandalism as a Sub-Type of Juvenile Delinquency." *Journal of Criminal Law, Criminology and Police Science,* **48** (January–February 1958), pp. 493–499.
Edwards, Loren E., *Shoplifting and Shrinkage Protection for Stores.* Springfield, Ill.: Charles C Thomas, Publishers, 1958.
Lemert, Edwin M., "An Isolation of Closure Theory of Naive Check Forgery." *Journal of Criminal Law, Criminology and Police Science,* **44** (September–October 1953), pp. 296–307.
Martin, John M., *Juvenile Vandalism.* Springfield, Ill.: Charles C Thomas, Publisher, 1961.
Matza, David, *Delinquency and Drift.* New York: John Wiley & Sons, 1964.
President's Commission on Law Enforcement and Administration of Justice, *Task Force Report: Crime and Its Impact—An Assessment.* Washington, D.C.: U. S. Government Printing Office, 1967, pp. 48–49.
Robin, Gerald D., "Patterns of Department Store Shoplifting." *Crime and Delinquency,* **9** (April 1963), pp. 163–172.
Savitz, Leonard, "Automobile Theft." *Journal of Criminal Law, Criminology and Police Science,* **50** (July–August 1959), pp. 132–145.
Schepses, Erwin, "Boys Who Steal Cars." *Federal Probation,* **25** (May 1961), pp. 56–62.
Smigel, Erwin O., "Public Attitudes toward Stealing as Related to the Size of the Victim Organization." *American Sociological Review,* **21** (June 1956), pp. 320–327.
Vaz, Edmund W., ed., *Middle-Class Juvenile Delinquency.* New York: Harper & Row, Publishers, 1967.
Wade, Andrew L., "Social Processes in the Act of Juvenile Vandalism," in Marshall B. Clinard and Richard Quinney, *Criminal Behavior Systems: A Typology.* New York: Holt, Rinehart and Winston, 1967, pp. 94–109.
Wattenberg, William E., and Balistrieri, James. "Automobile Theft: A 'Favored-Group' Delinquency," *American Journal of Sociology,* **57** (May 1952), pp. 575–579.

Public Order Criminal Behavior | 4

Crimes against public order outnumber other recorded crimes, although Sutherland and Cressey have remarked that "if all cases of fraud could be recorded, fraud would rank close to drunkenness and disorderly conduct in frequency."[1] Public order crimes include prostitution, homosexuality, drunkenness, the use of narcotics, gambling, traffic offenses, disorderly conduct, vagrancy, and exhibitionism.

There are obviously some striking differences in the behavior systems of the more important public order offenses of prostitution, homosexual behavior, drunkenness, and drug use. Still, because of many similarities, all the offenses in this group will be discussed together under each of the topics: the criminal careers of the offenders, group support of criminal behavior, correspondence between criminal behavior and legitimate behavior patterns, and societal reaction. In each case, when pertinent information exists, the differences between these types of offenses will also be indicated.

LEGAL ASPECTS OF SELECTED OFFENSES

The acts involved in crimes against public order are quite different from crimes committed against a person, such as murder, forcible rape, or the theft or destruction of a person's property. In fact, many public order crimes do not involve a real injury to another person. Rather, they disturb the community, as in the case of prostitution, homosexual acts, and drunkenness; they may be thought to be injurious to the individual, as in drunkenness or drug addiction. Since the partners in homosexual behavior are willing associates and the act of taking drugs is voluntary, one writer has used the term "crimes without victims."[2] The same might be said for acts of prostitution in which the customer is a willing partner.

Prostitution

In the Middle Ages prostitution was widespread and regarded as a necessary evil; it was not usually considered a criminal act. The demand for prostitution from all classes was great; therefore, in Europe, it was often not merely tolerated but protected and regulated by law, and was a source of public revenue. Even the Catholic church was involved in the maintenance of some houses of prostitution, particularly in France. The Protestant Revolution, with its extreme concern for personal morals, initiated a reaction against extramarital relations of any type. At the same time many were concerned about the increasing spread of syphilis, brought from the New World, in which prostitutes were heavily involved. Consequently, statutes enacted in the fifteenth and sixteenth centuries against prostitution were enforced to a considerable degree. In England, when prosecution passed from the ecclesiastical courts to the common law after 1640, prostitution as such was not regarded as a criminal offense but rather as a public nuisance.

Although some prostitutes may be selective on the basis of race, age, economic status, or physical attractiveness of the customer, generally she "sells" her sex relations to almost anyone. So emotionally indifferent are most prostitutes that they rarely experience an orgasm with the customer. Prostitutes vary according to their methods of operation. A common form of prostitution in the United States is the "call girl" who does most of her work in response to phone calls and other contacts. The client may come to her room or apartment or she may go to his. This type allows for greater urban mobility and individualization. The streetwalker, or common prostitute, procures her customers as she can, on the street, in parks, in bars, or hotel lobbies.[3] She takes him to a prearranged cheap hotel or rooming house. Often she must pay protection "fees" to the police or through an organized crime syndicate. Organized houses of prostitution are not as common as they once were. Finally, there is the independent professional prostitute who lives in her own apartment or other dwelling, often in an expensive part of the city, and caters to middle- and upper-class persons.

Homosexual Behavior

Homosexual behavior represents sex relations with members of one's own sex, behavior which may be carried out physically in a number of ways, sodomy (anal), fellatio (mouth-genital), and mutual masturbation. Homosexuality is never a crime; it is simply a social psychological state in which one is favorably disposed toward sex relations with a person of one's own sex. Only certain homosexual acts are crimes.

Laws forbidding homosexual behavior come from the ancient Jewish sex codes which were formalized by the Christian church into the Ecclesiastical laws that governed medieval Europe and later provided the basis for English common law. For hundreds of years homosexual acts were punished by the church, often with death or torture. As late as the mid-eighteenth century, homosexuals were burned at the stake in Paris. Liberalization of legal attitudes came in Europe with the French Revolution and later Code Napoleon, which left homosexual acts out of the legal structure, a standard which still exists in many European countries. These laws, however, were later changed to permit homosexual acts only between consenting adults over twenty-one years of age. Whereas many societies seek to protect young persons and "public decency" from homosexual acts, England, France, Spain, Italy, Denmark, and Finland do not consider homosexual acts, committed in private by adults, to be a criminal matter; West Germany is almost the only exception in Europe.

In England homosexual acts first became a matter of the secular courts in 1533 when a statute, with religious implications, was introduced under Henry VIII making sodomy punishable by death. It so remained until the nineteenth century when it was reduced to life imprisonment. Even offenses against an act passed in 1861, which remained in force until 1956, provided life imprisonment for sodomy by two men or by man and wife. Under the law of 1956, sodomy with a person under age was still punishable by life imprisonment, but the sentence for adults was reduced. Penalties of misdemeanor were also provided for certain public homosexual acts. After long parliamentary commission studies and debates, penalties for homosexual acts in private between adults over twenty-one were removed. Penalties are maintained for acts with those younger and for those who procure for homosexual acts.

The legal effect of the French Revolution did not reach largely Protestant puritanical United States. Here antihomosexual felony laws are found in every state except Illinois, California, and Connecticut, where it is legal between consenting adults twenty-one years of age and older. While some of these laws apply equally to male homosexuals and lesbians, in practice only the former are prosecuted. Even acts carried out in private are illegal. The felony statutes usually refer to sodomy or "crimes against nature," for which the maximum penalty in seven states is life imprisonment and in most states up to ten years. Sodomy has been expanded to include mouth-genital contacts and often mutual masturbation. Most states also have misdemeanor statutes covering homosexual acts. In addition, some states have ill-conceived sex deviate laws where a homosexual offender may be committed for so-called treatment in excess of the period provided by the criminal statutes. What this actually represents is usually holding a person in custody.

Drunkenness

Under English common law, intoxication itself was not a crime; it was tolerated whether in a public place or not, unless it resulted in some breach of the peace or disorderly conduct. It was not until 1606 that intoxication in public first became a criminal offense, an act which still remains a criminal offense in most jurisdictions of the United States.

Laws against public drunkenness have their origin in church attitudes, particularly Protestant, towards personal morality, particularly moral ideas about the individual's lack of moral control and his inability to carry out effectively the will of God in his work and family relationships. Such laws against public drunkenness reflect the power structure in that largely lower-class persons are likely to be drunk in public places.

About 2 million persons are arrested annually for public drunkenness in the United States, or about one out of every three arrests excluding those for traffic. Drunkenness is a crime punishable under a variety of statutes and ordinances. Some state "drunk in a public place," while others say "unable to care for his own safety." Others use laws stating that drunkenness that causes a breach of peace is punishable, while others deal with drunkenness under a disorderly conduct provision. Although the laws provide maximum jail sentences ranging from five days to six months, generally it is thirty days. Some states punish habitual drunkenness as a felony with a two-year sentence of imprisonment. Drunkenness under certain conditions, such as while driving a motor vehicle, is severely punished in most countries.

Drug Use

Drugs have been used for centuries; only within recent years have laws been invoked for their control and to make use or possession of some of them a crime. Drugs of various types are used as stimulants or depressants.[4] The most important depressant drugs are marijuana (marihuana), morphine, and heroin, the latter two being derived from opium. These drugs decrease mental and physical activity in varying degrees, depending upon the dosages. The more important drugs can be classified as heroin, morphine, marijuana, cocaine (the best-known stimulant drug) barbiturates or sedatives such as tranquilizers, amphetamines or "pep pills" which stimulate the central nervous system, and hallucinogens or the consciousness expanders such as LSD-25, a chemical synthetic derived mainly from lysergic acid. Methadone, an inexpensive, long-acting synthetic drug which is used in therapy as a substitute (methadone maintenance) for heroin is also used by some illegally for its own effects as a drug.

Although habit-forming narcotic drugs include many types, addiction is generally from morphine, heroin, and cocaine. The physiological and psychological dependence on drugs makes the drug addict a problem both for himself and often for society.[5] As tolerance for the drug is developed and more and more of it must be taken to relieve the physiological and psychological symptoms of withdrawal distress, the habit becomes well established and costly to maintain. Addiction to marijuana is not physiological but is more psychological in nature. This means that a marijuana habit may be broken in much the same way as cigarette smoking. "Contemporary opinion on marijuana dependence, then, is that it has no pharmacologically addicting properties whatsoever, that, indeed, the chemical and pharmacological properties of marijuana are less relevant in understanding its role in drug dependence than are the psychological characteristics of the indi-

viduals using it. For the great majority of the marijuana-smoking population, marijuana is probably less dependence-producing than coffee is for
the coffee-drinking population."[6] A government report has also concluded
that marijuana is not a prelude to addicting drugs.

> The charge that marihuana "leads" to the use of addicting drugs needs
> to be critically examined. There is evidence that a majority of the heroin
> users who come to the attention of public authorities have, in fact, had
> some prior experience with marihuana. But this does not mean that one
> leads to the other in the sense that marihuana has an intrinsic quality that
> creates a heroin liability. There are too many marihuana users who do
> not graduate to heroin, and too many heroin addicts with no known
> prior marihuana use, to support such a theory. Moreover there is no
> scientific basis for such a theory.[7]

Likewise, there is no evidence that marijuana use is associated with crimes
of violence. A government report has concluded that there is no proven
relation:

> Given the accepted tendency of marihuana to release inhibitions, the
> effect of the drug will depend on the individual and the circumstances.
> It might, but certainly will not necessarily or inevitably, lead to ag-
> gressive behavior or crime. The response will depend more on the in-
> dividual than the drug. This hypothesis is consistent with the evidence
> that marihuana does not alter the basic personality structure.[8]

During the nineteenth century opium smoking was found among large
segments of the so-called fringe society of prostitutes, drifters, and so
forth. Morphine and heroin, however, were widely used in the nineteenth
century in America by members of conventional society, particularly by
women, who took them in patent medicines for "female disorders." At that
time many of the drugs now prohibited could be easily and legally pur-
chased. Under the position that the government has a responsibility to protect the citizen from harming himself, the Harrison Act, passed in the
United States in 1914, strictly regulated the opiates and cocaine. This
legislation, and subsequent statutes, made the sale of these drugs illegal
without a doctor's prescription. Marijuana was only added to the prohibited drug list as late as 1937. Within recent years additional federal and
state legislation has been passed. The Federal Narcotics Act of 1956 imposed more severe penalties for possessing, selling, bartering, or transfer-
ring any narcotic drug or marijuana, particularly to a person under eighteen. The sentence was not less than two nor more than ten years on a *first*
offense for illegal *possession* of narcotics or marijuana, five to twenty years
for the second offense, and ten to forty years on the third or later offenses.
In the case of illegal sale, the penalty for the first offense is not less than
five years nor more than twenty, and for subsequent offenses ten to forty
years. Probation or parole was forbidden after the first offense in either

possession or sale. The sale, or conspiracy to sell, heroin, to a person under eighteen is punishable by imprisonment from ten years to life. In 1970 these laws were further strengthened, including a "no-knock" by agents provision, to make narcotic raids easier. In addition, the force of the United States narcotic agents was doubled. Possession on first offense was reduced to a misdemeanor or sentence of under one year. All states also have severe laws regulating drug possession and sale. The severity of these drug laws has not to date been very successful in controlling illegal drugs. Actually, these laws have made drug users into "criminals" and drugs something mysterious and evil. The story of how marijuana came to be illegal is instructive of the role of certain interest power groups in making the criminal law.

Marijuana, or "grass" as it is popularly termed, is derived from the leaves or tender stems of the marijuana plant and is inhaled by smoking specially prepared cigarettes. The usual effect produced is euphoria, a state of "dreaminess," an intensification of feelings, loquacity, inappropriate laughter, and a distorted sense of time and space, all with few unpleasant aftereffects.[9] As late as 1930, only sixteen states had passed laws preventing the use of marijuana. In 1937 Congress passed the Marihuana Tax Act designed to stamp out its use by criminal law proceedings. Becker maintains that there was little public concern, but the passage of the criminal act was the result of the almost single-handed efforts of the Federal Bureau of Narcotics, which produced public awareness of the problem based on rather limited cases and data. This was the result of a number of factors.

> While it is, of course, difficult to know what the motives of Bureau officials were, we need assume no more than that they perceived an area of wrongdoing that properly belonged in their jurisdiction and moved to put it there. The personal interest they satisfied in pressing for marihuana legislation was one common to many officials: the interest in successfully accomplishing the task one has been assigned and in acquiring the best tools with which to accomplish it. The Bureau's efforts took two forms: cooperating in the development of state legislation affecting the use of marihuana, and providing facts and figures for journalistic accounts of the problem. These are two important modes of action available to all entrepreneurs seeking the adoption of rules: they can enlist the support of other interested organizations and develop, through the use of the press and other communication media, a favorable public attitude toward the proposed rule. If the efforts are successful, the public becomes aware of a definite problem and the appropriate organizations act in concert to produce the desired rule.[10]

The influence of this federal legislation has been great. All states punish by criminal law the simple *possessor* of marijuana on the *first* offense. Compared with penalties for conventional crimes such as larceny and burglary, many states have very severe laws. In 1971 in Alabama and Minnesota it was five to twenty years; Missouri up to twenty years; New Jersey, Ohio, and Rhode Island up to fifteen years; and California, Idaho, Indiana, Kentucky, Michigan, and Oregon up to ten years. Other states had penalties ranging from six months, as in Iowa, Vermont, and Washington, to six years. Nebraska was the only state with a modest sentence, where the penalty is seven days in jail (if in possession of less than eight ounces or less than twenty-five marijuana cigarettes), and where an offender must complete an educative course on drugs.

Some European countries take a different approach; most of them regard drug and marijuana use more as a medical than a criminal problem. In nearly all European countries the use of the hard drugs (heroin, cocaine, and morphine) is not a crime but a medical problem in which medical authorities are permitted to prescribe legally the drugs a person requires. While there are laws on the statute books in England, prison terms for marijuana use are virtually never imposed for first or second offenses, and they are almost routinely treated as misdemeanors meriting only token fines.

CRIMINAL CAREER OF THE OFFENDER

Most public order offenders do not regard their behavior as criminal nor do they believe that criminal behavior is part of their life organizations. The ambivalence of general social norms toward much of this behavior accounts, in part, for the fact that most offenders do not have a clearly defined criminal career.

Prostitution

The extent of prostitution and the reaction of society to it has fluctuated over many years, but its definition has remained the same. Prostitution is sexual intercourse, with emotional indifference, on a promiscuous and mercenary basis. In some countries, as well as in many of our states, prostitution itself is legally not a criminal offense; rather, the prostitute is punished for soliciting. Mere sexual experiences do not make the prostitute, for prostitution is largely a product of playing a certain social role.[11] Generally most girls who enter prostitution have lived in local communities, such as slums, where sexual promiscuity has been approved or at least condoned.[12] Prior to entering into prostitution most call girls have had personal contact with someone professionally involved in call girl activities, such as pimps or other call girls.[13] Quasi-prostituting experiences may lead to prostitution as in the case of waitresses who accept money from customers after hours in return for sexual intercourse.

The process of development of a career as a call girl involves three stages: the entrance into the career, the apprenticeship, and the development of contacts. The mere desire to become a call girl is not enough;

rather systematic training in being one and arranging contacts is necessary. After having entered the profession through personal contacts with others also involved, most call girls serve an apprenticeship. When a call girl has agreed to aid a novice she assumes responsibility for her training, usually for a fee; girls who are solicited by a pimp with offers of love or marriage may be trained by him or referred to a call girl by him. Her apprenticeship consists of learning the call girl subculture, a major characteristic being how to develop a sizable and profitable clientele.[14]

The content of the training pertains both to a general philosophical stance and to some specifics (usually not sexual) of interpersonal behavior with customers and colleagues. The philosophy is one of exploiting the exploiters (customers) by whatever means necessary and defining the colleagues of the call girl as being intelligent, self-interested and, in certain important respects, basically honest individuals. The interpersonal techniques addressed during the learning period consist primarily of "pitches," telephone conversations, personal and occasionally sexual hygiene, prohibitions against alcohol and dope while with a "john," how and when to obtain the fee, and specifics concerning the sexual habits of particular customers. Specific sexual techniques are very rarely taught. The current sample included a considerable number of girls who, although capable of articulating this value structure, were not particularly inclined to adopt it.[15]

An important aspect of training in prostitution is the development of contacts. Most frequently names of customers are secured during the apprentice period. For a fee the call girl supervising the trainee refers customers to the apprentice. The nonverbal skills required of a call girl are not as complex as those required of a streetwalker prostitute. "The tasks of avoiding the police, soliciting among strangers for potential customers, and arrangements for the completion of the sexual contract not only require different skills on the part of the streetwalker, but are performances requiring a higher degree of professional 'know-how' than is generally required of the call girl."[16]

A different process was found in an Israeli study of prostitutes where stigma within the family, growing largely out of sexual promiscuity, led to expulsion from the family, a process particularly true of those girls from North African Orthodox homes.[17] Processes of differential identification and association then led the girl into a career of prostitution, being picked up by pimps or other prostitutes and inducted into prostitution. "First, because she is subconsciously favourably predisposed to this process by her stigmatization at home and her identification with images of deviant behavior, in this case sexual promiscuity; second, she is isolated and lonely in town, and any company, pimps and other prostitutes inclusive, would be quite welcome."[18]

Prostitution requires a new monetary relationship with males and a new conception of self. Sexual talk in terms of preferences and money come to replace dating and a degree of preliminary courtship before a sex act. This verbalization must become learned.[19]

Girls who become prostitutes tend to develop attitudes and behavior patterns which are part of their social role. They develop an argot, their own professional language, special acts and services, patterns of bartering with customers and an impersonal relationship with them, as well as a large number of rationalizations for their activities.[20] The earnings of most prostitutes, even allowing for payments to a pimp or for "protection" from the police, are higher than the earnings of most working women.[21] The prostitute is paid for her loss of esteem through negative societal reaction. In fact, Davis concludes that "since the occupation is lucrative, the interesting question is not why so many women become prostitutes, but why so few of them do."[22]

The prostitute is sustained in her profession not only by the ideology but by various supporting relationships. The pimp offers her a more stable emotional relationship with men. In a world of changing male figures he can offer a degree of love and affection. It provides a way of satisfying the self-concept in a world of private depersonalized sexual experience. Lesbian relationships offer much the same support but being without the money tie of the pimp they are less demoralizing.

It is difficult to generalize about the self-attitudes of prostitutes. Because the prostitute encounters a duality of social values there is a tendency to justify or rationalize commercial sex behavior by emphasizing certain legitimate values of society, such as financial success or taking care of persons who are financially dependent on them. One study found that the stated ideology of those who had been call girls for an average length of twenty-seven months included the beliefs that customers are exploitative, that other women are hypocrites about the use of sex to gain advantages, that prostitution provides a valuable social service by providing necessary sexual outlets and psychological comfort to customers, and that call girls' relationships are close and honest.[23] However, when the individual opinions of prostitutes were studied many of the ideologies were generally not supported. The conclusion is that although professional ideology is learned and may serve a function during the apprentice period of prostitution, it does not remain of equal importance throughout a call girl's career. For the apprentice the ideology is important in counteracting a negative self-image and reducing moral conflict during the initial period of prostitution.

Self-concept as a prostitute is one role open to a prostitute; she may sustain her role through interaction with others and an emphasis on the accepted values of sex and commercial exploitation of the general society. Undoubtedly, arrests strengthen the self-concept of a prostitute, as do the attitudes of other persons associated with her. Certainly those who are employed in other occupations, such as a secretary or a model, or those whose customers are from the upper socioeconomic groups, are less likely to conceive of themselves in these terms. One study found that the more socially isolated individuals were more likely to define their behavior as acceptable than were those who were less isolated.[24]

Many prostitutes are able to leave the occupation for marriage or for employment as waitresses, domestic servants, or salesgirls. A few others are able to achieve and maintain a high standard of living. Previous arrest records, however, may make leaving the profession more difficult, and for many, some of whom are eventually affected by venereal disease, alcoholism, and drug addiction, the end is a derelict life, punctuated more or less regularly by arrests and jail sentences. From there it is an easy step to petty stealing and shoplifting. Law enforcement measures fail to reduce prostitution since they confine many persons in the profession. The illegality of prostitution forces the prostitute into a world of police, courts, and correctional institutions. Her contacts with legal authorities often become complicated by arrests for alcoholism, drugs, and petty theft. Her position makes her vulnerable to blackmail by the police and other political and legal corruption. Often she is forced by the police into the role of an informer on thefts and drug use.

Homosexual Behavior

Sex is but one aspect of a person's total life. Generally, it is not independent of a total life pattern and seldom is it the dominating one. Thus the term homosexual is somewhat misleading. Labeling a person a homosexual tends to make a single aspect of his life cover his entire life pattern. One is unlikely to speak of a nonhomosexual as a "heterosexual." There are homosexuals in business and the professions and in lower and upper classes. Some are married, and, like the heterosexual person, have various interests and avocations.

Sex roles are learned. Behavior patterns associated with masculinity and femininity are learned as part of one's sex role. Homosexuality and heterosexuality may therefore be understood within three concepts: sex-role adoption, sex-role preference, and sex-role identification.[25] The first refers to the "actual adoption of behavior characteristic of one sex or the other not simply to desire to adopt such behavior." Sex-role preference is the desire "to adopt the behavior associated with one sex or the other or the perception of such behavior as preferable or more desirable." Finally, sex-role identification, which is crucial in homosexuality, is the incorporation of the role of a given sex and the unthinking reactions characteristic of that role.

There are various types of homosexuals: the overt versus the secret,[26] the adjusted and the maladjusted,[27] the jailhouse turnout and the true homosexual,[28] and the primary and the secondary.[29] It is important to distinguish between those who play a homosexual role under a variety of circumstances and those whose behavior is more likely to be the result of a situation. Behavior of the latter may be regarded as primary or situational and may occur frequently, for example, in one-sex communities, prisons, prisoners-of-war camps, the armed forces, and boarding schools. There are also those who commit occasional homosexual acts, particularly in their adolescence, and persons who perform homosexual acts only for money.

Most persons who commit homosexual acts are not homosexuals in the full sociological sense and are therefore primary deviants; they are not secondary deviants. Secondary deviants seek sexual gratification predominantly and continually with members of the same sex. They develop a self-concept and play a homosexual role in connection with these acts. Such persons come to have the feelings of a homosexual. Goffman has limited the term *homosexual* to "individuals who participate in a special community of understanding wherein members of one's own sex are defined as the most desirable sexual objects and sociability is energetically organized around the pursuit and entertainment of these objects."[30]

The learning of a social role results from having been socialized into the homosexual subculture. One must recognize oneself as a homosexual and enter into the stream of homosexual life. One important research study defined a homosexual not by his homosexual experiences but as any adult who "regards himself as a homosexual and is prepared to say so to the interviewer."[31] This self-conception as a homosexual is derived largely from the reaction of others which results in the homosexual's seeking more and more associations within the homosexual subculture. One study found that the development of a homosexual identity is dependent on the extent and type of information about homosexuals and homosexuality that is available to an actor who has sexual desires towards persons of the same sex.[32] Homosexual identity grows largely out of participation in one-sex environments rather than public labeling. Pressures from society tend to push individuals along a four-stage progression although some individuals do not progress beyond the second stage and others become members of homosexual groups without losing interest in other activities in the community.

The first stage usually occurs in the late teens or early twenties. As his friends start to go out with girls and eventually marry, the homosexual finds other interests and drifts away from their company. Sometimes he is scarcely aware of his homosexual tendencies or has not come to terms with them, but gradually he becomes conscious of his isolation. Many young homosexuals have described their dismay when they have discovered that the sort of things which interest their friends hold no appeal for them.

Thus the young homosexual finds he is driven away from the company of ordinary men and women at just the time when he most needs their help. As he loses his friends he begins to regard himself as an outcast. He finds to his dismay that will-power and self-control are not the answer to his problem. The more extrovert homosexual will soon pass through this second stage and quickly make friends with other homo-sexuals. But others lead lonely lives, plagued by feelings of guilt and accepting the role of the social isolate.

At the third stage the young man meets other homosexuals and begins to go to their meeting places and joins a homosexual group. Some of them soon tire of this opportunity to mix in a group of like-minded in-dividuals, but others accept the chance eagerly. Here a homosexual can feel at ease because he does not have to hide his true inclinations. Indeed, this is such a relief that much of the talk in these groups is about sex. It is here that the two worlds conflict. He must make sure that his friends from the other world do not meet his friends from the homosexual group. He has to explain his absences from the other world, think up con-vincing stories, and learn to lead two lives. Some homosexuals resolve this dilemma by moving on to the fourth stage.

At this last stage the homosexual way of life monopolizes his interests and absorbs all his time. He gives up his efforts to resolve the conflicts between the outside world and the homosexual way of life. He moves exclusively in a homosexual group and adopts a hostile attitude towards all those not in the group. He has, in fact, adopted all the characteristics of an introverted minority group.[33]

For some persons the homosexual relation may be quite stable; the sex-uality is integrated among such "married" couples into long-standing affec-tional, personal, and social patterns of behavior. Most homosexuals, how-ever, are highly promiscuous; the relationships of such homosexuals with others are short-lived and relatively anonymous. Many become acquainted in public places such as public toilets, bars, parks, clubs, cafes, baths, hotels, beaches, and movie theaters.[34] A large part of these sex relations are highly impersonal and may be carried out in a "tearoom,"[35] the homosexual name for a public toilet. Tearooms are readily accessible to the male population—being located near public gathering places—department stores, bus stations, libraries, hotels, YMCAs, and particularly those located in isolated parts of public parks. Usually a third person may act both as voyeur and lookout. In cases of more promiscuous homosexuality "not only are permanent relationships infrequent but even less affectional-sexual links tend to be overshadowed in homosexual life by the predominant pat-tern of 'cruising' and relatively impersonal one-night stands."[36] Because of this pattern of temporary sex relationships, there are some male homosexual prostitutes and some exploitation particularly by juveniles who make themselves available to homosexuals for a monetary reward.[37]

Married persons may engage in homosexual and heterosexual relations. Sometimes marriage may serve as a "cover-up"; in other cases, both types of sex relations may be enjoyed. The homosexual relations may serve when the home situation is unsatisfactory or sex relations are too infrequent. Many such persons, while engaging in impersonal sex relations, cannot sociologically be called "homosexuals." A study, for example, of those who participate in the "tearoom trade," that is carry out sex relations in public toilets, showed the largest group (38 percent) were married or previously married men, largely truck drivers, machine operators, or clerical workers.[38] Most of them did not want a homosexual experience, but rather a quick orgasm that was more satisfactory than masturbation, less involved than a love affair, and less expensive than a prostitute. The second group were "ambisexuals," mostly highly educated members of the middle and upper classes, many of them married or otherwise heterosexual who like the "kicks" of such unusual sex acts. The "gay" group, or openly confessed homosexuals, amounted to only 14 percent, and the last group of "closet queens" was even a smaller proportion. Closet queens are those, unmarried or married, who keep their homosexual acts secret.

Promiscuous homosexuals are more likely to be arrested or go to psychiatrists for treatment because their way of life exposes them to arrest or they have ambivalent feelings about such sporadic activity if they are also heterosexual. A large group of homosexuals, however, consists of those who tend to have more stable homosexual relationships and do not come to the attention of authorities or psychiatric agencies. These are the confirmed homosexuals. In a study of equal groups of fifty homosexuals (1) who had been arrested, (2) who had not been arrested but had been under psychiatric treatment, or (3) who had never been arrested or been under treatment, the latter group was found to be quite different.[39] Members of the latter group more often started homosexual relations with other boys before the age of seventeen; they were more likely to have long-standing relations with men and to have lived with other homosexuals. Over four-fifths (84 percent) had so arranged their lives that homosexual acts generally took place in the privacy of their homes. Most studies find that for homosexuals the later years of life and growing older generally are often highly unsatisfactory. Lack of permanent personal sexual ties and loss of physical attractiveness are common difficulties.[40]

On the other hand, another study of over 1500 male homosexuals found that those over forty-five years of age were better adjusted to a heterosexual world than were those younger.[41] While there was, with aging, less association with homosexuals and with the homosexual "gay" world, as well as a lower frequency of homosexual sex, the older homosexual did not appear to be more lonely or depressed. Part of this is due to the process of aging more than to homosexuality.

Drunkenness

Alcohol, a chemical substance, has been produced in most countries for centuries, either through a process of fermentation or distillation, in the form of distilled spirits such as whiskey or gin, or in the form of fermented beverages such as wine or beer. It is not psychologically habit-forming in the sense that certain narcotics are. As alcohol is consumed, it increasingly acts as a depressant and an anesthetic; it is not a stimulant as is commonly believed. Under the influence of alcohol a person may become aggressive, silent, or even fall into a stupor as a result of the reduction of cortical control rather than as a result of stimulation. With increasing drunkenness there is a dulling of sensory and motor functions, a blunted judgment of oneself and one's activities, and an impairment of functions such as walking. With "the presence of a pint of whiskey in the body, sensory perception is so dulled that the drinker has little comprehension of what he sees, hears or feels; he is stuporous."[42]

Alcohol drinkers may be classified as the social or controlled drinker, the heavy drinker, and the alcoholic; arrests for drunkenness come from the latter two groups.[43] A *social or controlled drinker* drinks for sociability, conviviality, and conventionality. If he chooses, he can refrain from using intoxicating beverages. There are two types of social drinkers, the occasional and the regular drinker. The former drinks sporadically and may have only a few drinks a year, whereas the regular social drinker may drink three or more times a week. Not only does the *heavy* drinker make more frequent use of alcohol than the regular social drinker; he may become frequently intoxicated as a result of consuming large quantities of alcohol. The excessive drinker, in common with social drinkers but with greater difficulty, may be able to curtail or to cease drinking completely on his own volition. Depending upon circumstances, he may continue drinking in this manner for the rest of his life, may later reduce the frequency and quantity of his alcoholic consumption, or may become an alcoholic.

There is considerable evidence that a large proportion of those arrested for drunkenness are alcoholics with a lengthy history of prior drunkenness arrests. In Los Angeles in 1964 about two-thirds of the total arrests for drunkenness were accounted for by one-fifth of the persons arrested. In Portland, Oregon in 1963 there were 11,000 drunkenness cases, but only 2000 persons accounted for them. Some may be arrested as often as twenty times a year.

Alcoholics are those whose frequent and repeated drinking of alcoholic beverages is in excess of the dietary and social usages of the community and to such an extent that it interferes with health or social or economic functioning. The alcoholic is unable to control consistently, or to stop at will, either the start of his drinking or its termination once it has started. Among alcoholics there is (1) a reliance on alcoholic beverages, (2) repetitiveness or chronicity of the drinking in the sense that the drinking does not take place on rare occasions, and (3) ill effects that derive from the drinking and not from other causes. The drinking affects the drinker's life and not just society. The ill effects may be either definite ill health, social or interpersonal ill health, social or interpersonal ill effects, such as disruption of the family or ostracism, which would not occur if the drinking were stopped, or economic effects, such as inability to keep a job, work efficiently, or take care of one's property as well as one could without drinking. While the drinking of alcoholic beverages and heavy drinking are the necessary prerequisites, alcoholism should be regarded as a behavioral phenomenon and not as a biological or psychological entity.

Shifts from the stage of excessive drinking to that of chronic alcoholism, with its social and often physical deterioration, are often imperceptible. The alcoholic process usually extends over a period of ten to twenty years of drinking; one is never a full-blown alcoholic after a few experiences with the effects of liquor. Alcoholism means more than sporadic intoxication. It implies changes in the nature of interpersonal relations with others, attitudes toward drinking, social roles, and conceptions of the self, including increasing dependence on drinking, attitudes which are at variance with those held by others and which were developed through a marginal social existence, numerous rebuffs, arrests, social isolation, and physical deterioration.

Excessive drinking, in itself, does not make the alcoholic. If continued over a long enough time, he may increasingly become involved in difficulties that arise from the drinking itself. He may lose his job, his friends, and his wife due to his drinking, and he may even be arrested and jailed. Drinking may become a way of getting away from problems caused, in turn, by the drinking. He is "involved in a circular process whereby his excessive drinking creates additional problems for him which he can only face with the aid of further excessive drinking. The condition of true alcoholism has been established."[44] The Protestant ethic appears to play a role here, as drunkenness is regarded as a lack of moral strength, will power, and devotion to the goals of personal discipline and work. The societal reaction to drunkenness may be expressed through the husband or wife, employer, work associates, parents, in-laws, neighbors, or church members. In particular, repeated arrests and incarcerations for drunkenness actually serve to reinforce the deviance rather than correct it.[45]

> An excessive drinker who confines his drinking to weekend bouts (a pattern not uncommon in the middle classes), but who does not drink secretively, may find himself frequently arrested and perhaps incarcerated. If this happens often enough, he may be conditioned by the enforcement, the judicial, and the correctional processes in such a way as to contribute to his drinking problem. Where before he confined his drinking to weekends and managed to hold a job and be a breadwinner, he now finds these roles increasingly difficult and harder to maintain, and crises arrive which encourage his drinking. Instead of arresting his excessive drinking, the social policies have modified his deviant behavior and contributed to the development of a more serious deviancy— alcoholism.[46]

Persons arrested for drunkenness tend to be older; of 1,313,063 persons arrested in cities in the United States in 1969, 72.9 percent were over twenty-five years of age. A study of a group who had been arrested at least twice for drunkenness showed that they were 47.7 years old or over twice the age of persons typically arrested for property offenses.[47] Other characteristics in this study showed a disproportionate number to come from the lower class and of Irish or black ethnic status and Protestant background. A disproportionate number had either not been married or were separated or divorced.

Excessive drinking and alcoholism may be perceived by others as extreme deviation, and these persons are often frequently arrested. Excessive drinkers may come to conceive of themselves as problems, and even as alcoholics, but not as criminals even though their drinking may result in frequent arrests. They may come to refer to themselves as "drunks" and "drunken bums" but not as criminals; increasingly the more persistent excessive drinkers come to conceive of themselves as alcoholics or "sick" persons.

Drug Use

Opiate addiction is learned just as other behavior is learned, primarily from association with other addicts or through knowledge of its use. An addict must learn the techniques of drug use and how to recognize and appreciate its effects. The reasons and motivation for the initial use of an opiate may be quite different from the motivation to continue to use it.

> Beyond this, one must have some motivation for trying the drug— whether to relieve pain, to produce euphoria, to please a loved person, to achieve acceptance in a group, or to achieve some other goal. The goal need have little to do with the specific effects of the narcotic. Moreover, the motivation or goal of initial drug use must be sharply distinguished from the motivation to maintain a drug habit. The latter is a product of learning which seems to depend on the interaction between drug effects, especially in the first experience of withdrawal, and the self-conception of the drug user.[48]

The use of opiates is one thing; addiction is another. Addiction is distinguished by "an intense, conscious desire for the drug and by a tendency to relapse, evidently caused by the persistence of attitudes established in early addiction. Other correlated aspects are the dependence upon the drug as a twenty-four hour necessity, the impulse to increase the dosage far beyond bodily needs and the definition of oneself as an addict."[49] Many persons may use heroin over long periods of time and not become addicted; others become addicted in a brief time. Addiction to opiates is a product of the physical qualities of the drug and the recognition of the association of the drug with the distress that accompanies sudden cessation of its use.

> If the individual does not receive daily supply, however, clearly characteristic symptoms, referred to as *withdrawal distress* or the abstinence

syndrome, will appear within approximately ten to twelve hours. He may become nervous and restless, he may develop acute stomach cramps, and his eyes may water and his nose run. Later, he stops eating; he may vomit frequently, develop diarrhea, lose weight, and suffer muscular pains in the back and legs. During this period the "shakes" may develop and if the addict cannot get relief by obtaining drugs he is in for considerable mental and physical distress. . . . Once the drugs are obtained, he appears normal again within about thirty minutes.[50]

Addiction to opiates, therefore, appears to be impossible without recognition of the withdrawal stress.

The sheer physiological or biological effects of drugs are not sufficient to produce addiction although they are indispensable preconditions. The effect which the biological events associated with using drugs has on human behavior is seen as one that is mediated by the manner in which such events are perceived or conceptualized by the person who experiences them. Persons who interpret withdrawal distress as evidence of the onset of an unknown disease act accordingly, and, if they are not enlightened, do not become addicted. Persons who interpret the symptoms of opiate withdrawal as evidence of a need for the drug also act accordingly and, from using the drug after they have understood, become addicted. As the user applies to his own experiences and behavior the attitudes, symbols, and sentiments current in his society, he is faced with a problem of adjusting himself to the unpleasant implications of being an addict in a society that defines him as an outcast, pariah, and virtual outlaw. In his efforts to rationalize his own conduct, which he cannot really understand or justify, and to make it more tolerable to himself, he is drawn to others like himself.[51]

A study of drug users around the University of California, Berkeley campus indicated the drug process begins with a sense of disillusionment about life and society.[52] Trying illegal drugs usually involves feelings of exhilaration and the discovery of a "New World" at the same time that there are initial fears of exposure and arrest. "Commonly a person becomes aware of the possibility of using drugs when it comes to light that a friend is using them. If the novice is a girl, this person is likely to be a boyfriend; if a boy, a roommate or relatively long-time intimate. That a person standing in such a relationship to a novice takes drugs at all is a strong argument for the novice to take them as it dispels prior ideas that only 'dope fiends' and 'derelicts' of one kind or another would ever consider doing so."[53] Rationalizations or neutralizations for using the drugs are learned from others. Using drugs becomes "natural." Some may stay at a pattern of limited use; they might be called "recreational users." Others move on to a more systematic pattern, the "heads," including street-level pushing or selling of drugs, with increased techniques and rationalizations about drug use.

The life cycle of heroin addiction has been described as going through four phases.[54] In the first place, there is tolerance for potential addiction, with experimentation and irregular drug use moving to regular use and addiction. This is followed by a tolerance of the addiction system with the individual interacting with a sociocultural drug culture. The third phase involves a tolerance for potential abstinence in which the individual relapses. Through the use of chemotherapy or drug substitution with methadone, he is heroin-free with supports. The last stage is tolerance of abstinence or nondrug use with no need of supports.

In becoming an opiate addict the individual changes his conception of himself and of the behavior he must play as a "drug addict." The more he associates with other drug addicts and the drug subculture and finds he cannot free himself from dependence on drugs, the more he comes to adopt the self-concept and play the social role of an addict.[55]

Use of marijuana requires availability; and there must be testimony as to its positive values as well as an ability to maintain situations for its use without detection by social control agencies.[56] A person using marijuana for pleasure must learn to conceive of the drug as something which can produce pleasurable sensations.[57] He must learn three things; (1) to smoke the drug in a way that will produce certain effects, (2) to recognize the effects and connect the drug with these effects; and (3) finally, to enjoy the sensations he feels. When a person first uses the drug he does not ordinarily "get high" because he does not know the proper technique of drawing on the cigarette and holding the smoke. Even after learning the technique he does not form a conception of the smoking as being related to pleasure. Even though there are pleasurable sensations, the new marijuana user may not feel that they are enough, or he may not be sufficiently aware of their specific nature to become a regular user. He learns to feel the sensations of "being high" as defined by others. With greater use he begins to appreciate more of the drug sensations. Finally, a further step is necessary to continue the use of marijuana. The person must learn to enjoy the sensations he has experienced. Feeling dizzy, being thirsty, misjudging distances, or a tingling scalp may not of themselves be pleasurable experiences. He must learn to define them in this way. Associations with other marijuana users help to turn sensations that were frightening into something pleasurable and to be looked forward to. In a general way it is like learning to define the medicinal taste of whisky as a pleasant tasting beverage.

There are many who feel that heroin addiction is facilitated by marijuana use. So far this relationship has not been substantiated and as one writer has concluded, "while heroin addiction may imply a one time use of marihuana, marihuana need not imply eventual use of heroin among all groups."[58] Heroin addicts from the lower class often live in a slum world where the two drugs exist in the same milieu, where both are acceptable, and where one's friends use both. One may start with marijuana and then shift to heroin. Among college students and middle-class persons, where heroin is less available, the likelihood is to stick with marijuana. A study of 200 marijuana users, primarily college students and those in higher occupational levels, concluded that most of those who have tried marijuana do not use any other illegal drug and that the characteristics of marijuana itself have little to do with a given individual progressing to more potent drugs. The proportion who had taken heroin was only 13 percent.[59] A study of college drug use reported that generally heroin and opiates are rejected by those who use marijuana because it is perceived as addictive, expensive, difficult to get, requiring a hypodermic needle, and having desensitizing effects.[60] On the other hand, "the empirical and cultural connection between marihuana and the psychedelic drugs, e.g. LSD, is much more powerful and meaningful than heroin."[61] The relationship is even more complicated by regional patterns; among metropolitan residents of the high addiction eastern and western states opiate use is commonly preceded by the smoking of marijuana, but in the southern and rural areas marijuana generally does not precede heroin.[62] This study found that there was a general positive relation in sixteen states, the District of Columbia, and Puerto Rico; in twelve other states there was no relation. Moreover, older heroin addicts generally had not used marijuana; the younger ones had.

Most drug users, whether of the hard drugs or marijuana, do not think of themselves as criminals, for they deny the validity of drug laws and consider as inhumane and cruel the punishment of what should be a matter of individual choice. Widespread support for their views is found among fellow users of the drug and even among segments of the population of nonusers, particularly in the case of marijuana. Persons who use the opiates seldom think of themselves as real criminals because they tend to regard themselves as being in a unique situation whenever they are "hooked" on a drug. They feel it is because of necessity that they violate the law by using the drugs or committing offenses to "support" their habit. Some indication that drug addiction need not be associated with self-regarding criminal attitudes is the fact that in virtually all Western nations there is a high incidence of drug addiction among doctors and, to a lesser extent, among nurses.[63] This is because of the relative availability of the drug and the knowledge of its effect. Performers in the entertainment world, such as jazz and "rock" musicians, also have high rates.[64]

Addicts may engage in petty thefts or prostitution in order to support their habit. Even when criminal activities become associated with securing funds to maintain the drug habit, crime does not become an end in itself. Those addicts, juvenile or adult, who engage in other crime do so chiefly to obtain funds with which to purchase illicit drugs. There is little evidence to indicate that crimes of violence are associated with addiction.

Once addicted to a narcotic drug like morphine or heroin, an individual must depend upon a continuous supply and this demand usually becomes the most important single aspect of his daily life. While originally these addicts took the drug for pleasure or an effect, most of them soon take it to ward off the pain of withdrawal symptoms. As tolerance is built up and larger and more frequent dosages are needed, the cost may be as high as from $15 to $40 or more a day to support the addiction. Such a daily expenditure is generally greater than the addict earns, which forces him to engage in theft or other illegal activities simply to maintain an adequate supply.

Many crimes or other law violations associated with drug addiction involve direct or indirect violations of narcotic laws. Drug addicts may engage in petty stealing, burglary, or "rolling drunks," occasionally even robbery, to get enough money to buy their drugs. They may break into hospitals and doctors' offices to steal drugs, turn to prostitution, or sell drugs and become drug peddlers or "pushers" to get enough drugs for their own needs. Drug addicts also may purchase a small supply of a drug from a peddler and then "water" down the powder with the addition of milk sugar before selling it to the next in line.

GROUP SUPPORT OF CRIMINAL BEHAVIOR

Public order offenses such as prostitution, homosexual behavior, and drug use grow out of, and are heavily supported by, rather clearly defined deviant subcultures. Others, such as drunkenness, have group support in the drinking behavior of certain social classes and ethnic groups and in the general norms of society which support the drinking of alcoholic beverages.

Prostitution

Prostitutes can generally be classified according to their methods of operation.[65] There are individual common prostitutes, organized houses of prostitution, call girl and similar arrangements, and "high class" independent prostitutes. One type is the girl who works in an organized house or brothel. New girls are "broken in" to the rules and regulations and each new prostitute soon learns various sex techniques. She learns how to handle a large number of customers without running the risk of losing them as patrons, how to deal with certain types of men, and how to protect herself against venereal disease. Another type of prostitute is the call girl, who has contributed greatly to the elimination of street soliciting and red-light houses. The call girl often depends upon some organization for recruiting her patrons, although she may operate independently and have her own list of patrons who call upon her directly. More frequently, patrons are secured through the intermediary services of a bellhop, a hotel desk clerk, a taxi driver, or other agent who, for a fee, will give the patron the telephone number used by the girl or arrange for a hotel or motel room. Prostitution is usually associated with panderers or pimps who solicit for the girls and often live off their earnings.

Some prostitution is not strictly organized as such, but is knowingly permitted and may even be encouraged through legitimate, but often shady, businesses, such as burlesque shows, night clubs, or amusement parks. Taxi dance halls particularly afford opportunities for the dancers to make engagements with their patrons, either in a room hired for the occasion or in the dancer's own room or apartment.[66] Through a variety of techniques performers in go-go places, cabarets, or burlesque shows may recruit patrons for later dates.

Prostitutes are often indoctrinated into the profession by someone closely associated with prostitution. Usually from a lower-class background of more freedom in sexual norms, they seldom develop a high degree of organization within their profession. Its very nature is competitive, each prostitute attempting to build up and keep her own clientele; hence such personal group solidarity that exists is mainly for protection from the police or from others who threaten their profession. Prostitutes have a limited argot or special language of their own, which is a mark of a degree of association and group cohesiveness.[67]

Homosexual Behavior

Homosexual behavior appears to be a product of the adoption of certain homosexual subcultural norms and a conception of self. Homosexual experience itself does not make one a homosexual; one research study concluded that "homosexual behavior when young is neither a sign that a boy will grow up to be a homosexual, nor is the absence of such behavior a guarantee that a boy will make a successful heterosexual adjustment."[68] A study of three groups of homosexuals—those who had been imprisoned, those only under psychiatric treatment, and those who had not been imprisoned or treated—showed that nearly all these in the three groups had been introduced into homosexual activities by other boys before the age of sixteen.[69] Only a small proportion in each group had a homosexual initiation by an adult. The channeling of sexual expression into homosexual patterns must come through some cultural or subcultural definitions, just as do heterosexual relations. The very first homosexual experience among 127 homosexuals studied in Great Britain was usually with a schoolboy of the same age and generally constituted sex play, often in a school situation.[70] These experiences, however, did not necessarily lead to homosexuality as a pattern of sex behavior. The first "significant homosexual experience" can be defined as one carried out with an adult or repeated acts carried out with the same boy over a year or so. Over two-thirds of such experiences were with another boy. Only 18 percent were first introduced to homosexuality as boys by adults; another 11 percent had no experience of any sort until they were adults, and in all such cases their partner was an adult.

Another study, however, showed that homosexuals are likely to have had sexual experiences with adult males even before puberty; in one study a third had been approached by men and 27 percent had had physical contact with men.[71]

In a local community secret and overt homosexuals may be linked together through sex and friendship. These homosexual groups, often cutting across class and occupational lines, serve to relieve anxiety and furnish social acceptance. Within such groups narration of sexual experiences and gossip about sexual exploits of others give some unity to the group. An additional function is the provision of a situation that can dramatize adherence to homosexual values.

> The homosexual community thus consists of a large number of distinctive groups within which friendship binds the members together in a strong and relatively enduring bond and between which the members are linked by tenuous but repeated sexual contacts. The result is that homosexuals within the city tend to know of each other, to recognize a number of common interests and common moral norms, and to interact on the basis of antagonistic cooperation. This community is in turn linked with other homosexual communities in Canada and the United States, chiefly through the geographical mobility of its members.[72]

The subcultural world of the homosexual has its own special language. This special vocabulary, with words such as "gay," "straight," and "queen," is "similar in some respects to that of the underworld; in others to that of the theater."[73] There are also subculturally defined ways in which homosexual relations are established. Many communities have special meeting places where homosexuals gather, usually at certain street corners, parks, bars, clubs, or lavatories.[74] Recognition by other homosexuals appears to involve particular gestures, clothes, a way of walking, and a special vocabulary.[75] Consequently a homosexual group as a subcommunity comes to have its "own status symbols and mythology, and may provide the same kind of social and psychological support that a family group provides for other people."[76]

> The organization of the homosexual world outside of the bars, but linked with it by members common to both, is a loosely knit extended series of overlapping networks of friends. The forms of these networks vary greatly. The three most common are: (1) tightly knit clique structures formed from pairs of homosexually "married" persons, or singles, many of whom are heterosexually married; (2) larger groups with one or more loose clique structures as sociometrically central and a number of peripheral members; and (3) loose networks of friends who may meet only on the occasion of parties. Clique structures and pairs, as well as loose networks of friends, cut across occupational and socio-economic levels, although particular professions or occupations such as teaching, medicine, interior decoration, and antique dealers may form association in-groups which have social gatherings.[77]

A particularly important group mechanism of the homosexual world is the "gay" bar.[78] Specialized homosexual bars are associated with larger cities and communities where homosexuals are numerous; the goods and services provided by the bar are adapted to the needs of the homosexual community. Such gay bars are sexual markets where agreements are made for the exchange of sexual services without commitment—the "one night stand." Gay bars also serve as gathering places for friends who want to exchange gossip and enjoy a congenial evening together. In these bars, members are inducted, trained, and integrated into the homosexual community. The homosexual learns a body of knowledge and a set of common understandings about sex activities.

The young man who may have had a few isolated homosexual experiences in adolescence, or indeed none at all, and who is taken to a "gay" bar by a group of friends whose homosexuality is only vaguely suspected or unknown to him, may find the excitement and opportunities for sexual gratification appealing and thus begin active participation in the community life. Very often, the debut, referred to by homosexuals as "coming out," of a person who believes himself to be homosexual but who has struggled against it, will occur in a bar when he, for the first time, identifies himself publicly as a homosexual in the presence of other homosexuals by his appearance in the situation. If he has thought of himself as unique, or has thought of homosexuals as a strange and unusual lot, he may be agreeably astonished to discover large numbers of men who are physically attractive, personable, and "masculine" appearing, so that his hesitancy in identifying himself as a homosexual is greatly reduced. Since he may meet a wide cross-section of occupational and socio-economic levels in the bar, he becomes convinced that far from being a small minority, the "gay" population is very extensive indeed. Once he has "come out," that is, identified himself as a homosexual to himself and to some others, the process of education proceeds with rapid pace. Eager and willing tutors—especially if he is young and attractive—teach him the special language, ways of recognizing vice-squad officers, varieties of sexual acts and social types. They also assist him in providing justifications for the homosexual way of life as legitimate, and help to reduce his feeling of guilt by providing him with new norms of sexual behavior in which monogamous fidelity to the sexual partner is rare.[79]

Some indication of the group support for homosexual behavior are the recognized and organized homosexual clubs that exist in various parts of the United States and particularly in the Netherlands. There is also a national association in the United States, The Mattachine Society, and many magazines, particularly *The Homosexual Citizen*. The magazine articles deal with matters that concern homosexuals such as civil discrimination, police practices, and law reform. They also have reviews of books and plays, love stories, and personal columns.

Drunkenness

The evidences for group components in the excessive use of alcohol are great. There is evidence that alcoholism is associated with a culture where there is conflict over its use, where children are not introduced to it early in life, and where drinking is largely done outside meals for personal reasons and not as part of a ritual, ceremony, or part of family living. The general pattern of drinking in the United States seems to support this relationship as do variations in excessive drinking shown in studies of Irish, French, Italian, and Jewish drinking patterns.[80]

Social drinking is common in most Western countries such as the United States. The excessive use of alcohol leading to arrests for drunkenness appears to be learned from others, group associations and cultural factors playing an important role. Differences exist not only in the drinking customs of societies but in those of subgroups within a society. People learn to drink excessively because of the type of drinking behavior of their companions, social class, occupation, or ethnic status.[81] Group associations determine the kind of beverage and the amount used, the circumstances under which drinking takes place, the time of drinking, and the individual's attitude toward excessive drinking. Of white and black males, for example, appearing before Atlanta courts nearly all drank in company of others rather than alone. In fact, 80 percent of the whites and 65 percent of the drinking companions of the blacks had served similar time in jails.[82]

The drinking norms of an individual appear to conform closely to those of age contemporaries, particularly of friends or marital partners.[83] In industry, drinking patterns are influenced by fellow employees.[84] Drinking customs and attitudes toward drinking vary in terms of class structure; in both the upper and lower classes there are more permissive attitudes toward excessive drinking. Social patterns also call for more immoderate drinking in certain occupational categories. Heavy drinking is found, for example, among certain types of businesses and occupations, merchant seamen, migratory workers, and all-male institutional living.[85]

Such institutional patterns of living have been found in a study using a control group to be related to heavy drinking and residence on skid row.[86] Likewise, heavy drinking is more frequent among Protestants than among Catholics or Jews in the United States. There is less heavy drinking among those of Italian origin than Irish. Excessive drinking appears to be generally higher among American blacks than whites, although the excessive differential shown in arrests may be more a product of discrimination[87]

The role of group factors in creating and perpetuating chronic drunkenness is seen, for example, particularly in skid row, whose members are frequently arrested for drunkenness. Here there are group definitions of behavior in drinking practices; the financing of a bottle is often a group enterprise. Members of skid row protect each other from the police and offer each other the mutual social support that is particularly important for those who have descended from higher positions of social status.[88] In fact, contrary to the stereotyped view that skid row heavy drinkers are unattached persons, the life histories of heavy drinkers show that they are characterized by a higher degree of attachment to others than skid row abstainees and moderate drinkers.[89] Skid row drinking is done in association with small groups who mutually support each other in their drinking habits and offer necessary companionship. A study of 187 chronic police case inebriates, most of them from lower-class backgrounds, showed that their drinking occurred in small intimate groups, less than 8 percent being usually solitary drinkers.[90]

> The major function of these drinking groups . . . is in providing the context, social and psychological, for drinking behavior. In reality we have subcommunities of inebriates organized around one cardinal principle: drinking. The fantasies concerning the rewards of the drinking experiences are enforced in the interaction of the members, who mutually support each other in obtaining alcohol and mutually share it.[91]

> To be fully integrated and acculturated on skid row is to be a drunk since skid rowers place strong emphasis on drinking, and the acculturated person is, by definition, a conformist. . . . Heavy drinking on skid row is a product of group norms rather than the result of individual, addictive craving for alcohol. . . . Characteristic skid row drinking does not take place alone, in the privacy of one's flophouse cubicle, or in secret. The typical skid row heavy drinker (be he "wino," "lush" or "rubbydub") is the member of the group, the bottle gang, and it is the bottle gang not only with whom he drinks but whose controls he observes and through whom he relates to his total social world, the world of skid row. It is the bottle gang which decides on the time, the place of meeting, the amount of alcohol consumed, and the conduct of the drinkers, to say nothing of who shall "go in on the bottle"—i.e., round up necessary funds for the purchase in the first place. The code of sharing—funds and bottle— and membership in the group, mark the skid row heavy drinker even more incontrovertibly than does his predictable appearance in court from time to time following arrest for public drunkenness. It is admittedly hard to live on skid row and not become a heavy drinker—and a more or less chronic police offender. It is not the alcoholic, therefore, but the drunk whose sacrifice of everything to the group's need marks him a totally committed member of a deviant group. The only fully integrated and acculturated member of skid row, the drunk is the true skid row derelict.[92]

Drug Use

The use of drugs, including marijuana, is learned primarily from association with others who are addicts. Most persons are started in the use of drugs by friends and marital partners. Rarely does the use of drugs during illness lead to addiction. Addiction to opiates and drug use in the past was largely among young urban males in slum areas but, more recently, also among youth in certain high school and college populations or dropouts from these groups.

Persons not only learn how to use drugs and appreciate them but they also learn a series of positive beliefs about the benefits of drugs, beliefs that others help to reinforce constantly.[93] The new addict learns about the sources of supply and how he must remain part of the group in order to assure this supply. Even the spread of the intravenous technique of administering opiate drugs with a needle from 1935 to 1965 is an example of the individual's involvement in the drug subculture.[94] Almost all adolescents are introduced to heroin, for example, by boys of similar age or in a group of adolescents.[95] Once an adult or adolescent becomes part of a group using drugs and becomes addicted, it is difficult for him to withdraw from this group. His friends tend to be other users; his sources of supply become important to him. Where a delinquent group is associated with drugs, it is difficult to resist pressures not to participate or to continue in the face of derisive taunts of "chicken," "yellow," "punk," and "square."

The use of marijuana is a group activity, lending itself to friendships and participation in a group setting. It is smoked in intimate groups which, in turn, has a relation to its impact on the individual. This group nature, according to Erich Goode, is reflected in the following:

> (1) it is characteristically participated in a group setting; (2) the others with whom one smokes marijuana are usually intimates, intimates of intimates, or potential intimates, rather than strangers; (3) one generally has long-term continuing social relations with the others; (4) a certain degree of value consensus will obtain within the group; (5) a value convergence will occur as a result of progressive group involvement; (6) the activity maintains the circle's cohesion, reaffirms its social bonds by acting them out; (7) participants view the activity as a legitimate basis for identity—they define themselves, as well as others, partly on the basis of whether they have participated in the activity or not.[96]

Goode, in his study of marijuana smokers, provides an extensive description and analysis of the social context of marijuana use:

> Group processes operate at the very inception of the individual's marijuana using experience. Being "turned on" for the first time is a group experience. Only three percent of my respondents were alone when they had their first marijuana experience. And four percent were in the company of at least one other individual, each of whom was also experiencing marijuana for the first time. All of the remainder—93 percent—had their first marijuana experience in the company of at least one individual who had already smoked marijuana. It is clear, then, that the neophyte marijuana smoker, at the point of his first exposure to the drug, is subject to group definitions of the desirability of the experience, as well as the nature of its reality. Marijuana use, even at its

very inception, *is simultaneously participation in a specific social group.* This generalization holds equally as strong for the *continued* use of marijuana. Marijuana is characteristically smoked in groups, not in isolation. In the sample, only five percent claimed to smoke at least half of the time alone, and almost half—45 percent—said that they never smoked alone. Marijuana cannot be understood apart from the web of social relations in which it is implicated.

Moreover, the *nature* of the group character of marijuana use also significantly determines its impact. Marijuana is not merely smoked in groups, but it is also smoked in *intimate* groups. The others with whom one is smoking are overwhelmingly *significant* others. One rarely smokes with strangers, with individuals whom one does not care for, or is indifferent to, or whom one does not expect to like in the future. Even at large parties where marijuana is smoked, small cliques will form, oases of compatibles, wherein all will share the same activity. Smoking marijuana is symbolic in ways that more accepted behavior is not; it resembles communal eating in civilizations for whom eating well is a rare or intermittent festivity. Brotherhood is an element in the marijuana ritual, as is the notion of sharing something treasured and esteemed. Emphasis is placed on passing a given "joint" around to all present, thus completing a circle; this procedure is generally preferred to that of each participant lighting up his own "joint" and smoking it by himself, without any group continuity. And of course, the clandestine nature of the activity, the fact that it is legally "underground," lends an air of excitement and collective intrigue to marijuana smoking which would be absent in a context of licitness, as with drinking. All of these factors make marijuana use a highly significant (to the participants) and emotionally charged activity. (This is one of the reasons why smokers are so horrified and offended when it turns out that an undercover agent who had been smoking with them later arrests them; he has violated the sanctity of the activity.) All of these factors, some ideological, and some inherent in the nature of the act itself, conspire to link marijuana smoking powerfully to group influences; to make those who participate in it highly susceptible to the group's definitions of reality, of right and wrong, of good and bad, of true and false.[97]

Extensive usage of drugs has been demonstrated among physicians, jazz musicians, prostitutes,[98] juveniles in the slum, and, more recently, among high school and college students. All of them have in common the ready availability or accessibility to a supply of illegal drugs. The high addiction rate, for example, among blacks is largely a product of the fact that the "concentration of the traffic in Negro ghettos made the drug particularly available in these areas and, as time passed, the number of Negroes experimenting with drugs such as marihuana and heroin apparently increased steadily."[99] A more recent study confirmed a similar concentration of high rates of heroin addiction among areas of low socioeconomic groups with a high percentage of minority group members.[100]

A study of southern opiate addicts showed that factors leading to addiction are quite different from those in large United States metropolitan areas and, therefore, quite different from the general pattern of addiction.[101] The largest group become addicted because of medical treatment with drugs, an individual pattern more common twenty-five to fifty years ago. Second in importance is the use of drugs in treating alcohol excesses and the last is pleasure seeking through associations with others. Moreover, the median age of over thirty is much older.

Most persons start taking drugs out of curiosity as to the effects or because of association with persons already addicted. Some adolescents and others take drugs for the "kick," as something tabooed by "squares," and to heighten and intensify the present moment of experience as opposed to the routine way of daily living.[102] Attempting to acquire status among their peers, some adolescents in certain areas often appear to be willing to explore socially unacceptable areas of behavior. The chain-reaction process of addiction has often been called a "sordid and tragic pyramid game" in which the average addict introduces several friends into the habit, often to help solve his own problems of supply. Some are initiated at parties where the first several marijuana cigarettes or "shots" are "on the house" in order to initiate the beginner.[103]

Drug addiction involves participation in an elaborate subculture supported by group norms which one writer has called a "survival system."[104] This involves the justification of the ideology for drug usage and the "reproductive" system: that addicted persons must continually recruit new members in order to sell them drugs to support their habit. There is also defensive communication with its own argot for drugs, suppliers, and drug users, which must be learned by the initiates, and the "neighborhood warning systems" by which addicts are protected by others. The support of the habit requires a complex distribution network of the illegal drugs. This has been termed the "circulatory" system of the drug subculture, namely, the system by which addicts learn to secure illegal drugs.[105] Drugs are imported and wholesale distribution is made largely through organized crime syndicates or other highly organized groups.

All studies indicate a high rate of relapse among drug addicts, varying from 70 to 90 percent in a period of six months to five years. This is, in part, a product of the strong societal reaction on the part of many against the use of drugs which may, in turn, lead to a deviant career.[106] To secure drugs many persons resort to stealing and prostitution; such behavior fulfills the criminal image held by others thus making the rejection of the drug culture difficult. Moreover, recidivism in drug usage is a product of long experience with drugs, the conception of oneself as an addict, association with other addicts, and the recognition of the effects of drugs.[107] Because frequently he is isolated from the conventional world, a drug addict who has stopped using drugs often returns to the company of friends and acquaintances who are still addicted. Drugs are readily available at all times to persons who live in slum areas. Sometimes even the boredom of being a nonaddict is a factor in relapse.

CORRESPONDENCE BETWEEN CRIMINAL AND LEGITIMATE BEHAVIOR

It is difficult to differentiate the goals and general life orientation of homosexuals and heterosexuals except in the means of sex gratification. Likewise, except for those who are highly involved in their way of life, prostitutes, users of drugs, and excessive drinkers are probably not much different in their attitudes toward the general goals of society from those who are not so engaged. Where the behavior becomes more fully an important part of the individual's life organization and there is a degree of isolation from conventional society, however, such offenders may become more committed to the goals of a deviant subgroup, such as the subculture of drug addicts or homosexuals, and less to the larger society.

Much of the behavior of public order offenders is consistent with legitimate behavior patterns. The prostitute's behavior is simply one way of satisfying legitimate male heterosexual needs and is a commercial occupation with the same goal of many other occupations. The homosexual, while deriving satisfaction in a different way, is engaging in what is widely practiced sex behavior. He is involved in a local community of friendships, some of which are as lasting as heterosexual marriages. A drunken person is participating in approved behavior for adults, that is, the drinking of alcoholic beverages.

The use of drugs such as heroin and marijuana, while disapproved, has its counterparts in the frequent use of alcohol, cigarettes, tranquilizers for relaxation, barbiturates for sleeping and relaxation, and other minor drugs such as aspirin. In a sense coffee and tea are also drug stimulants that can have considerable effect when consumed regularly in large quantities. Some idea of the widescale use of the more accepted drugs is indicated by the fact that over 1,000,000 pounds of barbiturate derivatives are manufactured each year in the United States, or the equivalent of twenty-four half-grain doses for each person in the country, enough to kill each twice.[108] In 1957 it was estimated that 7 percent of the adult population was regularly using tranquilizers, sedatives, and drug stimulants; in 1967 one out of every four, or 27 percent, were doing so.[109]

Vold indicated that in many of these public order offenses, as in the United States, there are economic and cultural considerations common to the general society.[110] In such offenses as drunkenness, narcotic addiction, and prostitution, commercial gain plays a prominent part. Prostitution is an economic commodity, the sale of sex. A large economic interest enters the production and sale of alcoholic beverages, and there are large financial gains resulting from the illegitimate sale of narcotics. The illegal behavior represents an occupation for many of the offenders in this group. Prostitution is a "job" as much as any other. There are even opportunities to develop a degree of professional skill with resulting status among one's associates.

Prostitution is linked, for example, with many values of normal society. The general culture stimulates the importance of sexual values and the adequate satisfaction of these values may be difficult for many of the married and unmarried. Prostitution becomes a needed commodity, where other sex arrangements are unavailable or unsuitable. The price of the service may vary from $2 to over $500, depending on the supply and the characteristics and appeal of a particular prostitute. Prostitution is closely allied to normal economic forces. "Our laissez-faire economy and its integration through a price system allows the relatively free operation of supply and demand whether it be commerce in grain futures or sex service."[111] The culture also generally makes it possible for women to exploit sex commercially in other ways besides prostitution, such as the "femininity" displayed to a male customer by a salesgirl, secretary, or waitress. The sex act may also play a part in premarital courtship and even in some marriages that is analogous to commercial exploitation in prostitution.

SOCIETAL REACTION AND LEGAL PROCESSING

Public order offenses are numerous. They constitute behavior considered by law to be contrary to the system of morals or the standards of proper conduct for an individual. Yet the condemnation for the most part is not strong, and one writer consequently has referred to certain offenders of this type as the "petty offender," one who is defined as a criminal because he breaks criminal laws which are chiefly misdemeanors. The petty offender is "arrested on such charges as being drunk in public view, committing a public nuisance, disturbing the peace, loitering, trespassing, vagrancy, family disturbance, and so on."[112]

The behavior involved in these offenses reflects, in part, the changing definitions of what is and what is not proper in behavior and also the extent to which the political state can intervene to protect private morals or do things for the individual's own good. As Vold has pointed out, blasphemy and heresy were regulated in the interest of private and public morality and were once severely prosecuted as criminal offenses. "Both of these have disappeared from the categories of crimes calling for police control in the world of today, though both types of behavior persist in the community. But ideas and events in the world at large have changed and we no longer seek to make men religious by law and police action. Could it be that we may be in the process of a similar transformation in the matter of control of personal habits and morality represented by these categories of petty crime, as they appear in the American world of today?"[113] In other parts of the world many of these public order offenses are not considered to be crimes.

Public order crimes represent efforts to control certain moral and personal behavior through laws, often without attempts to mold public opinion to support the legislative and police activity. Undoubtedly, only a small proportion of these offenses actually committed are ever apprehended. Indeed, there is a dilemma between criminal action as opposed to no action at all against such behavior as prostitution, drunkenness, the use of drugs, and homosexual behavior.

> After many years of penalizing these areas of behavior as crime, we still have the problem behavior with us, and we have as well a large number of officially designated criminals convicted under such procedure. Furthermore, there is widespread recognition of the fact that the behavior is much more prevalent than that reached by criminal prosecution and conviction. Penalizing behavior in these areas as crime does not seem to have been particularly successful in controlling or eliminating the problem behavior. It is entirely possible that we have a larger proportion of our population involved in these behaviors than is the case in some of the countries that do not include them under the criminal law. Behavior in these several areas is criminal because we so define it, but if we should not penalize it as criminal, would the behavior become rampant and without control? That is the dilemma confronting present-day thinking and practices in the United States.[114]

Prostitution

Attitudes toward prostitution have varied historically, and today they differ widely by country. The attitude toward, and the social status of, the prostitute, as Davis has suggested, vary according to three conditions: (1) if the prostitute practices a certain discrimination in her customers, (2) if the earnings are used for some socially desirable goal, and (3) if the prostitute combines with her sexual role others which are more acceptable.[115] Some persons tolerate it as necessary. They feel if certain urban areas were set aside for prostitutes, they could, they naively believe, be regularly inspected for venereal diseases. To those in the women's liberation movement the prostitute is a symbol of woman's enslavement to men.

Arrests for prostitution usually fall under three headings: (1) arrest and prosecution for accosting and soliciting, (2) arrest and prosecution on a charge of "common prostitute" which may fall under disorderly conduct or vagrancy, and (3) arrest and detention under health regulations.[116] Law enforcement directed at prostitutes is sporadic, responding to public attitudes and police-prostitute relations. Most of it is simply to "contain" prostitution through police activity by exercising some control or "harassment."[117] Sometimes there is little enforcement; at other times there are police drives. They are more directed at streetwalkers in conspicuous places and at blacks. Girls who are arrested are more likely to be the inexperienced or those who practice when high on alcohol or drugs.[118]

Law enforcement in prostitution cases is often a sordid business. The demeanor of a prostitute to a police officer has much to do with whether she is arrested; "an obstreperous prostitute symbolizes an affront to a policeman's competence."[119] The prostitute is frequently arrested as the result of solicitation by the police or a "lure" provided by the police. Sometimes informers are used to locate the rooms being used. In order to "buy" her way out of an arrest she may offer to serve as an informant in the apprehension of her pimp or a narcotic peddler. Even the threat of a "quarantine hold" for venereal disease medical examinations is used to control the behavior of a prostitute during arrest and to provide sources for apprehending more serious criminals.

Prostitution is opposed because of: (1) the degradation of the women who engage in it; (2) the effect on general law enforcement through police protection; (3) the effect on marital relations where recourse is had to prostitutes; and (4) the patronage of prostitutes by young persons, soldiers in particular, and its effect on national values. In France prostitution is illegal but condoned, as it is in many other parts of the world, particularly in Latin America. Prostitution, particularly soliciting, is strongly disapproved under Anglo-American law. Prostitution, or the act of solicitation, is generally regarded as a misdemeanor and punished with a fine or a jail sentence of under one year. While punishments are usually not severe, repeated apprehensions may be treated as felonies with a longer sentence. England revised its statutes in 1960 to provide a graduated system of fines for prostitutes who loiter or solicit for prostitution in a public place: £10 for the first offense, £25 for the second, and for the third £25 or three months' imprisonment, or both. The Wolfenden Report in which this legislation was proposed stated rather clearly the reasons for the English public attitude toward prostitution, much of which would be applicable in the United States.

> If it were the law's intention to punish prostitution *per se*, on the ground that it is immoral conduct, then it would be right that it should provide for the punishment of the man as well as the woman. But that is not the function of the law. It should confine itself to those activities which offend against public order and decency or expose the ordinary citizen to what is offensive or injurious; and the simple fact is that prostitutes do parade themselves more habitually and openly than their prospective customers, and do by their continual presence affront the sense of decency of the ordinary citizen. In doing so they create a nuisance which, in our view, the law is entitled to recognize and deal with.[120]

The recently revised penal codes of Illinois and Wisconsin as well as a 1965 statute in New York made the customers as well as the prostitute subject to prosecution. A study in New York City showed, however, that of 508 convicted dispositions only 0.8 percent were for patronizing a prostitute.[121] The police generally ignored the patrons, whose names when arrested were rarely put in the newspapers. Most arrests were of streetwalkers and the high priced call girls and their patrons were generally ignored. It appears that streetwalkers and their customers rank lowest in social prestige. Many call girls work individually and serve the upper classes, particularly corporation customers. "Because such behavior is generally not regarded as offensive, political groups do not exert pressure upon the police and city hall to 'clean it up.' "[122]

Laws against prostitution are efforts to control private moral behavior by punitive social control. In most countries the enforcement of these laws has been sporadic and largely unsuccessful.

> It has persisted in many civilizations throughout many centuries, and the failure of attempts to stamp it out by repressive legislation shows that it cannot be eradicated through the agency of the criminal law. It remains true that without a demand for her services the prostitute could not exist and that there are enough men who avail themselves of prostitutes to keep the trade alive. It also remains true that there are women who, even when there is no economic need to do so, choose this form of livelihood. For so long as these propositions continue to be true there will be prostitution, and no amount of legislation directed towards its abolition will abolish it.[123]

Homosexual Behavior

Attitudes toward homosexual behavior have differed from one period in history to another and from one culture to another. This behavior was prevalent, for example, in Greek and Roman times and in some societies homosexual practices were related to certain religious rites. Some of the negative attitudes in parts of Western society toward homosexuality can be explained by certain aspects of the Christian tradition.[124] The early Christians preached that homosexual behavior was a sin and in the Middle Ages the ecclesiastical courts imposed severe penalties. Certainly much of contemporary public opposition to homosexual acts is that they are "unnatural" in the sense that they do not lead to procreation.

The reactions of people in the United States today to homosexuality are conditioned by subcultural and situational factors. The processes by which persons come to be defined as homosexuals are contingent upon the varying interpretation of others and the treatment as a result of this definition. Interpretation of homosexuality may result in several different societal reactions by nonhomosexuals.[125] These may be explicit disapproval and immediate withdrawal of relationships, explicit disapproval and subsequent withdrawal, no disapproval and relationship sustained, or a "live and let live" response to homosexuals.

In actuality a relatively small proportion of persons are arrested for these acts and the courts and juries tend to be lenient toward the offenders. Considerable reliance is put on the shame or stigma that will result from the apprehension. Apprehension is difficult because there is generally no complaining witness and because such acts occur largely in private. A study of police practices in arresting homosexuals found that:

> Private homosexual conduct between consenting adults is not in practice a matter of major concern to law enforcement agencies. Detection of such conduct is extremely difficult, and it is generally assumed that enforcement resources are better applied to other forms of criminal conduct. . . . As with prostitution, however, there are aspects of homosexual conduct which are of concern to the police because of the nuisance to the public which is created. Solicitation by homosexuals in public places often causes complaints from persons who have been accosted and from the proprietors of reputable places in which such conduct occurs. The police respond to these complaints by dispatching plainclothes officers to these locations to see if they are solicited. These tactics are frequently successful in identifying those persons who are engaging in public solicitation, although the police have encountered some judicial hostility to such enforcement practices.[126]

The political activity of the police in the form of raids on "gay" bars or other homosexual groups or in arrests for sex acts in public toilets tends to unify homosexuals. Homosexual publications, for example, give maximum coverage to police activities.

> The homosexual's relationship to the law and the police, however, may be viewed as latently functional for the group, and this may explain why the group is often reluctant to express its resentment in action as well as words. The homosexual's legal status enables him to see himself as wronged and persecuted, which relieves his own feeling of guilt. The police are a target upon which he may center his hostility; they are the enemy and he is the underdog. It is in large part due to the police that the homosexual can, and often does, regard himself as a member of an unfairly treated minority group. In addition to the latent functions they provide for the homosexual group, police "brutality" and "persecution" rally some support from the larger society on behalf of the group. Reports of brutality against any group, even if they are exaggerated, tend to stimulate the traditional American spirit of "rooting for the underdog."[127]

The police more frequently charge a homosexual with a misdemeanor than a felony because homosexuals are more likely to plead guilty to those than sodomy and juries are reluctant to convict if the penalty seems too severe. New York has, in fact, recently reduced the crime of consenting homosexuality from a felony to a misdemeanor. Broad statutes covering "outrages to public decency" can be used for homosexual acts in or loitering around public toilets. Some states make the "public nuisance" aspects apply only to public acts, meaning that private acts, such as sodomy, can then be punished as felonies. These can even be invoked against heterosexual couples, married or unmarried. The change in felony laws, such as in England, regarding private acts, is not likely to affect prosecutions there and elsewhere because most have always been for indecency in public places and offenses with minors. In fact, few persons are charged under sodomy laws for private acts, unless there is some unusual situation, despite the fact that most such acts occur privately.

The detection of homosexual acts often requires invasions of privacy, paid informers, decoys, provocative agents, interception of mail and telephone calls, and examination of private records. This potential threat of harassment is real to homosexuals even though not carried out often. Police vice squads may "persuade" arrested men to give away the names of their homosexual friends. Harassment may include police raids on homosexual parties, raids about which they feel less compunction than if it were another type of party.[128] To apprehend for acts committed in toilets, parks, and other public places, police may be used in plain clothes and dress, talk, and act in a provocative manner to entrap persons. A California study has described some of these practices. "Decoys may wear tight pants, act effeminately, jingle coins in their pockets, eye men suggestively and enter into conversations, while loitering around toilets or using the urinals. If a man responds with an immoral proposition or lewd gesture, the decoy usually suggests going elsewhere. If the man agrees to this, a second police officer moves in to make the arrest when they leave the toilet. The policeman may provoke the offending sex act, but is not supposed to initiate it himself."[129] American policemen in large cities have on occasion made considerable money by accepting bribes from homosexuals for protection. The threat of exposure has also been a source of frequent blackmail of homosexuals.

A study of law enforcement against homosexuals in Los Angeles County found that of 493 felony arrest cases only 24 acts took place in a private residence. All others were in public or semipublic places. Two hundred seventy-four were in rest rooms, 108 were in cars, 18 in jails, 17 in parks, 15 in the baths, and 11 on the beach. Of the 475 misdemeanor arrests, only 6 occurred in private locales (homes, hotels, apartments). One hundred thirty-nine were in rest rooms, 98 were in cars, 83 in parks, 62 in theaters, 49 in bars, 14 in streets, and 5 in the baths.[130] Of the arrests 457 were for oral copulation (fellatio), probably in part because other acts are difficult in a public place. Of the 493 arrested only 11 asked for a jury trial, primarily because most wished to avoid publicity. Over 95 percent of the convictions were by the judge and for misdemeanors.

Actually the possible civil disabilities imposed on homosexuals by becoming known are probably more feared than the possibility of arrest or conviction. For this reason homosexuals are sensitive to the threat of employer investigation into their private affairs. Knowledge of homosexuality may interfere with citizenship applications. If an American serviceman admits or is diagnosed as having homosexual tendencies, he is discharged without honor, forfeiting his veteran's rights and benefits and making future employment difficult.

Once convicted, or once their condition becomes known to the relevant authorities, male sex deviants (like the leprous or the insane) must expect some legal and social restrictions. If they work in certain fields, such as teaching, or government posts involving security risk, they will lose their jobs. If they belong to a profession with strict disciplinary rules, like solicitors and medical men, they may have their licence to practice taken away. They will not be accepted for admission to the armed forces or the merchant navy, they will be found unsuitable for a wide range of employments such as police, prison service, youth workers and so forth. They will never be considered for important posts in politics or public life. They may even encounter difficulties if they want to enter as students at a university. They will be rejected if they apply to immigrate to another country.[131]

Drunkenness

If excessive drinking is continued over a long enough period of time the individual may increasingly become involved in difficulties that arise from the drunkenness itself. He may lose his wife and job and be ostracized by neighbors and friends. The Protestant ethic may play an important role in the attitudes of others because drunkenness is regarded as a lack of moral strength, of devotion to the goals of personal discipline, of will power, and of dedication to work. Societal reaction is experienced through family members, employers, neighbors, church associates, and the police representing the larger community.

The excessive drinker who becomes an alcoholic is often the chronic drunkenness offender before the courts. He may, with increasing frequency, be arrested and jailed. Drinking may become a way of getting away from the societal reaction to problems caused by the drinking. His drinking problems can be faced only by more excessive drinking, which in turn leads to more arrests for public order disturbances. Final rejection is taking up his life on skid row.

The proportion of arrests for drunkenness vary from city to city. New York City, for example, with a population of almost 8,000,000 averages only 30,000 drunk arrests annually in recent years, as contrasted with Los Angeles, with a much smaller population, where there are nearly 100,000 annual arrests. Officers may use informal means such as calling a taxi, escorting the person home, or asking friends to help him home.[132] This seems to be particularly the case if the person is better dressed and appears to be more well to do. Arresting officers have a great deal of discretion;

when it appears he has no home or family ties he is most likely to be arrested. Some cities have "bum squads" that cruise skid rows and nearby areas making wholesale arrests by apprehending inebriates who are unable to take care of themselves or who are likely to annoy other persons. There may also be other considerations, as one officer in a skid row precinct reports:

> I see a guy who's been hanging around; a guy who's been picked up before or been making trouble. I stop him. Sometimes he can convince me he's got a job today or got something to do. He'll show me a slip showing he's supposed to go to the blood bank, or to work. I let him go. But if it seems to me that he's got nothing to do but drink, then I bring him in.[133]

The administration of public intoxication laws does not affect most middle- and upper-class excessive drinkers and alcoholics who have a home and can drink in private and semiprivate conditions. It discriminates against the homeless and poor. Evidence also suggests, tentatively, that some persons in the lower class feel the brunt of the law more than do others. Pittman and Gordon, and later Benz, found that in one northern community blacks were disproportionately arrested and incarcerated. Pittman and Gordon, in 1958, found in their sample of chronic police case inebriates a high proportion of blacks, 18 percent, as compared to their representation in the general population of the county in which the jail was situated (2 percent).[134] In 1962 Benz found that the jail population, for both alcohol- and nonalcohol-related offenses, still reflected the differential negative treatment accorded blacks. In Monroe County, New York, in 1962, for example, the ratio of nonwhite prisoners to nonwhite population was 1:16, while the comparable white ratio was 1:27.[135]

A Seattle study has traced the cycle of the drunk through the courts: action on the street, the police call box, paddy wagon or police car, booking, padded drunk tank, mug and print shop, cement drunk tank, court docket, courtroom, holding tank, doing time tank, and the street again.[136] Regardless of how or for what reason they are arrested, drunks are usually placed in a barren cell called a "tank" that may hold as many as 50 to 100 persons. They may be places where there is no room to sit or lie down, and where there are inadequate sanitary facilities and ventilation; a stench of vomit and urine is common. "The drunken behavior of some of the inmates is an added hazard. It is questionable whether greater safety is achieved for the individual who is arrested for his safekeeping."[137]

Drunkenness offenders are usually brought before a judge the morning after arrest, often appearing with groups of fifteen to twenty other drunks. There are few due process safeguards and they are hurried through the court process. Persons arrested and held for prosecution for drunkenness almost never have legal representation; they are almost always found guilty. Of all persons charged with public drunkenness in cities reporting to the FBI in 1970, 91.5 percent were found to be guilty.[138] Many of them are alcoholics who may have been arrested 100 to 200 times in a year and who may serve, in their lifetimes, 10 to 20 years in prison. The courtroom procedure has been described as follows:

> "You men have all been charged with drinking in public, being drunk in public or begging which are in violation of the ordinances of the city of Seattle. The maximum penalty for these crimes is $500 fine and/or 180 days in jail. You have a right to plead guilty or not guilty. You have a right to consult a lawyer before you enter a plea of guilty or not guilty. If you want to consult a lawyer you must pay for your own attorney. The court does not have provisions for this. If you wish a continuance, please indicate when you return to court. On a plea of guilty you waive your rights to appeal to a higher court. On a plea of not guilty your case will be continued for trial at a later date. Now return to the court docket and when you are called in you will enter a plea of guilty or not guilty. If you wish to make a statement you may do so." The "rights spiel," as one man fondly dubbed it, takes less than a minute to complete. The group of men are then hurried back into the court docket to listen for their names again. When a man hears his name, he returns to the courtroom alone. He faces the judge's bench, separated by the railing and the prosecuting attorney for the city of Seattle who says, "You have been charged with the crime of public drunkenness, how do you plead?" If a man enters a plea of guilty, and over 90 percent of them do so, the prosecutor reads his prior record to the judge who will sentence him according to a present formula based on his record. A man may plead guilty or not guilty, ask for a continuance, make a statement or request he be sent to the alcoholism treatment center.[139]

Since most drunkenness offenders receive short sentences, they are simply fed, sheltered, and given some recreation; there is little or no treatment. After serving the sentence the drunken offender, probably an alcoholic, returns to his former haunts with no money or job and is often rearrested within days, perhaps even hours. A government report has concluded that the "criminal justice system appears ineffective to deter drunkenness or to meet the problems of the chronic alcoholic offender. What the system usually does accomplish is to remove the drunk from public view, detoxify him, and provide him with food, shelter, emergency medical service, and a brief period of forced sobriety. As presently constituted, the system is not in a position to meet his underlying medical and social problems."[140]

Recidivism rates are extremely high among chronic drunkenness offenders. A District of Columbia study in 1965 showed of approximately 27,000 persons arrested for public intoxication, 56 percent had been arrested five times or more, 29 percent had been arrested twenty or more times, and 12 percent fifty or more times.[141] A large proportion of those frequently arrested were from skid row areas. A Baltimore study of the period 1964–

1965 showed that 966 defendants were convicted two times within twelve months, 369 three times, 175 four times, and 263 were convicted five or more times.

Drug Use

Prior to the passage of the Harrison Act in 1914 outlawing the use of certain drugs without a physician's prescription, there was considerable public tolerance for the use of drugs, which was regarded as a personal problem. By this law and others passed by the states, drug users became "criminals" and drugs something mysterious and evil. The public attitude toward drug addicts represents largely a stereotype toward what has been termed the "dope fiend" myth. That many drug addicts become unproductive is disapproved, as is drunkenness, by the work-oriented Protestant ethic of American society. State penalties have become more severe in recent years, and the possession, sale, or transfer, of narcotics, for example, has often been made a felony instead of a misdemeanor.[142] The enforcement of laws against so-called drug peddlers, in fact, makes "criminals" out of users, for they too are "in possession" of the drug.

> Another interesting feature of our anti-narcotics legislation is that, whereas it purports to be aimed at the peddler of the drug rather than at the user and does not specifically define the use of drugs as a crime, it does in fact make every addict in the United States a criminal unless he happens to be so old and infirm that withdrawal of the drug would cause death or unless he has an incurable disease. It is possible for a man to be a chronic alcoholic and to drink himself to death without violating the law. It is not possible for an addict to use drugs without violating the law or causing someone else to violate the law. As a consequence of the drug user's vulnerability to arrest, much of the punishment for the violation of the drug laws is handed out to the user of the drug rather than to the peddler. The federal institutions and prisons are filled mainly with the victims of the drug traffic, not with those who profit from the traffic.[143]

Reports covering about half the population of the United States in 1969 showed 182,909 arrests for violation of drug laws. Of these, 55 percent were under twenty-one years of age. In the case of marijuana, 63 percent involved arrests of persons under twenty-one, and 27 percent under eighteen. Arrests for marijuana (27.5 percent of the total) were least common in the northeastern states and most common in the north central states (51.6 percent). The effect of such drug-related crimes and imprisonment is to make a career for many out of what was originally addiction to the drug. A study of former heroin addicts from Puerto Rico revealed that:

> More than three-fourths of these Puerto Rican addicts remained more or less continuously addicted over their average 16-year period since the onset of drug use. They had been frequently arrested on felony charges,

many of which were related directly to narcotics. While on drugs their probability of arrest was more than five times greater than when abstinent. A substantial number of these individuals had spent more of their adult lives in prison than out. The majority of these years of incarceration were drug related. Most of these opiate users were following criminal careers, either on a permanent or a sporadic basis. While it cannot be concluded that heroin *caused* their criminality, it is clear that it figured heavily in their illicit activities. The selling of narcotics in particular was a frequent violation. Overall, this study of the long-term correlates of addiction presents a dismal picture of the life patterns of the majority of these human beings. For the most part, they have remained continuing problems to their society and to themselves.[144]

The Fourth Amendment to the Constitution deals with the right of people to be secure in their persons, houses, papers, and effects "against unreasonable searches and seizures." They can be legalized through the issuance of a warrant if the searches involved "probable cause." The latter, in the enforcement of drug laws, often goes beyond the real legal interpretation to illegal search and seizure.[145] Some of these involve frequent routine searches on the street and the search of private premises. In fact, in 1970 Congress adopted a "no knock" provision to facilitate drug apprehension. Intrusions may be made to gain evidence for prosecution procedures; in others they are for investigation, harassment, or the collection of contraband.

Various methods are used to entrap drug sellers, particularly the use of other drug users and prostitutes as informants, various "inside" and "outside" buying situations, and the use of marked money.[146] By being informants individuals protect their own drug supplies or avoid arrest. Methods such as these are used to protect the identity of the informant.

DECRIMINALIZATION OF PUBLIC ORDER OFFENSES

The problem of public order crimes has become so difficult that there has been serious discussion of eliminating or "decriminalizing" public drunkenness, gambling, the use of drugs, homosexual offenses, and even prostitution, on the grounds that these crimes constitute an "overreach of the criminal law." In fact, some professors of criminal law and others have gone even further, recommending the abolition not only of these offenses but similar ones such as abortion, all sex offenses including statutory rape when committed with a girl over fourteen years of age, incest, and bigamy.[147] These offenses, however, would remain crimes if committed against persons under a certain age, if more than a certain quantity of drugs were possessed, and if an injury had been committed in connection with intoxication. On the same grounds, all criminal laws prohibiting disorderly conduct, vagrancy, pornography, and obscenity would be eliminated.

1. *Drunkenness.* Public drunkenness would cease to be a criminal offense.
2. *Narcotics and Marijuana.* Neither the acquisition, purchase, possession nor the use of any drug would be a criminal offense. The sale of some drugs other than by a licensed druggist and on prescription would be prohibited; proof of possession of excessive quantities would constitute a criminal offense.
3. *Gambling.* No form of gambling would be prohibited by the criminal law; certain fraudulent and cheating gambling practices would remain criminal.
4. *Abortion.* Abortion performed by a qualified medical practitioner in a registered hospital would cease to be a criminal offense.
5. *Sexual Behavior.* Sexual activities between consenting adults in private would not be subject to the criminal law. The criminal penalty should be removed from adultery, fornication, illicit cohabitation, bigamy, incest, homosexual offenses, prostitution, pornography, and obscenity.

The arguments for the elimination of public order offenses can be summarized as (1) that such acts should not be the concern of the state, (2) that the interference of the political state makes the matter worse, as in the illegal use of drugs, for "where the supply of goods or services is concerned, such as narcotics, gambling, and prostitution, the criminal law operates as a 'crime tariff' which makes the supply of such goods and services profitable for the criminal by driving up prices and at the same time discourages competition by those who might enter the market were it legal,"[148] (3) that little is accomplished by such crime control as it is ineffective against the behavior of people who are favorably disposed to the behavior, and (4) that the legal processing of the offenses seriously interferes with a justice system that is already insufficient and overburdened. Arrests for these offenses amount to about half of all nontraffic arrests; the 6,000,000 arrests in the United States, many of which then enter the judicial system, could be reduced to 3,000,000. This would make for the more effective criminal administration of the more serious offenses.

The inclusion of public order offenses in the criminal code has other important consequences. Many persons are driven into associations with others who are already well established in the subculture of criminality. It is particularly in the areas of prostitution, illegal drugs, and gambling that police are corrupted. Organized criminals gain enormous profits from gambling, drugs, and, to a certain extent, prostitution which, in turn, is frequently invested in legitimate businesses. The civil rights of individuals involving illegal search and surprise are often violated.

The legalization of prostitution can be approached simply on the ground that whether a woman has sex relations with someone is a private arrangement. Whether she wishes to set some condition for these arrangements, such as a dinner, show, weekend holiday, or a cash fee is also a private and not a public matter. Only where there is a question of age, as under fifteen, or where solicitation might become a public nuisance might the state intervene. In Sweden prostitution is a woman's own affair unless she is physically abused or becomes a general public nuisance. It is against the law, however, to have intercourse with a girl under the age of fifteen, to be a pimp, or for a person to promise monetary compensation for sex relations to someone under eighteen. The Swedish view is that the initiation of sex relations by an adult woman is in line with the idea of the women's liberation movement.

The legalization of homosexual acts has moved rapidly in recent years with the repeal of punitive legislation in Great Britain, Illinois, and Connecticut. There is widespread pressure from professional and homosexual groups for other legislative repeal. In most countries it has not been an offense for many years. Commenting on the need for the elimination of this behavior as a crime two legal writers have stated:

> As far as the police are concerned, a great deal has been written both about corruption in this area and the degrading use of entrapment and decoy methods employed in order to enforce the law. It seems to us that the employment of tight-panted police officers to invite homosexual advances or to spy upon public toilets in the hope of detecting deviant behavior, at a time when police solutions of serious crimes are steadily declining and, to cite one example, less than one-third of robbery crimes are cleared by arrest, is a perversion of public policy both maleficent in itself and calculated to inspire contempt and ridicule.[149]

Arrests for public intoxication take up a great deal of the time of the police and courts which should be employed for more serious offenses. They interfere with effective police law enforcement and the judicial process. There is little indication that the criminal justice system is effective in dealing with the chronic drunkenness offender. One study concluded: "We thus reach a conservative national estimate of annual expenditure for the handling of drunkenness offenders (excluding expenditures for treatment or prevention) of $100 million. In addition, the great volume of these arrests places an enormous burden on the criminal justice system; it overloads the police, clogs the courts, and crowds the jails."[150]

There are indications that the drunkenness of chronic alcoholics, the most common drunk cases and some of whom may have been arrested over a hundred times, may, in the near future, not be treated as crimes. The District of Columbia's highest court ruled in 1966 that a chronic alcoholic cannot be convicted of the crime of public drunkenness and should be handled as a public health problem. In a unanimous decision, known as the Easter decision, the United States Court of Appeals for the District of Columbia said that proof of chronic alcoholism is a sickness and a defense to a drunkenness charge because the defendant "has lost the power of self-control in the use of intoxicating beverages." Since such a defendant lacks the necessary criminal intent to be guilty of a crime, he cannot be punished under the criminal law, the court ruled.

A Presidential commission has recommended that "Drunkenness should not in itself be a criminal offense. Disorderly and other criminal conduct accompanied by drunkenness should remain punishable as separate crimes."[151] As an alternative, the Commission recommended that communities establish civil detoxification units as part of a comprehensive treatment program. They would replace the police station as an initial detention unit for inebriates. Under the authority of civil legislation drunken persons would be brought to the public health facility and detained there until sober. If the person desired, various after-care programs would be provided. Similar conclusions were reached by a recent study done under the auspices of the American Bar Association called *Two Million Unnecessary Arrests.* [152]

Greater understanding of the problem is probably emerging about the role that repressive legislation plays in drug abuse such as heroin. By making such hard drugs difficult to secure, and at a high price, it has encouraged the development of a drug subculture and consequent influences leading to addiction. Efforts are being made to consider drug addiction as a health and not a criminal or police problem. In order to deal more effectively with the drug problem by prevention, that is, curing addicts of their habits, to eliminate the exploitation of drug addicts for mercenary gain, and to reduce the number of crimes committed by addicts as a consequence of their habits, Lindesmith, a leading authority in the field, has made the following proposals:

1. Anti-narcotic laws should be so written that addicts do not have to violate them solely because they are addicts.
2. Drug users are admittedly handicapped by their habits but they should nevertheless be encouraged to engage in productive labor even when they are using drugs.
3. Cures should not be imposed upon narcotics victims by force but should be voluntary.
4. Police officers should be prevented from exploiting drug addicts as stool pigeons solely because they are addicts.
5. Heroin and morphine addicts should be handled according to the same principles and moral precepts applied to barbiturate and alcohol addicts because these three forms of addiction are basically similar.[153]

In the United Kingdom drug addiction is considered a medical rather than a legal problem, and authorized physicians may prescribe drugs at low cost. The addict is therefore not regarded by the British public as a criminal. He does not have to steal or sell drugs to secure some source of supply for himself and a woman does not have to turn to prostitution. Addicts are, consequently, relatively noncriminal in that country.[154]

There are now several experimental programs involving methadone maintenance by which this chemical substitute is legally provided on a daily basis at an outpatient clinic to heroin addicts. In this way addicts can resume a normal life of work or education without being concerned about their supplies. The emphasis is on drawing the individual out of the drug subculture.

In the early 1970s the penalties for possession of marijuana in the United States were generally severe. The legalization of marijuana was a subject of extensive debate.[155] Evidence was cited on the one hand that the drug is injurious and, on the other, that it is harmless and should be made legal. A National Commission on Marijuana and Drug Abuse was appointed by the President and its recommendations were made in 1972. The Commission gathered information on its use, conducted extensive hearings and more than fifty research projects, and studied the effects on long-term users in countries where it has been widely used for many years—Jamaica, Greece, India, and Afghanistan. At that time they found that 24,000,000 persons in the United States admitted having tried marijuana. They also found that the use of marijuana had tripled in two and a half years. Of this number, 8,300,000 generally used it less than once a week, while there were 500,000 "heavy users," those who used it more than once a day. The Commission concluded that "From what is now known about the effects of marijuana, its use at the present level does not constitute a major threat to public health." They found little or no evidence that marijuana can cause addiction, brain damage, or lead to crime or violence or necessarily to the use of more powerful drugs such as heroin. It did find that its use while driving could be a threat to public safety. The recommendations of the commission were:

1. Elimination of fines and jail terms for smoking marijuana in private or possessing one ounce or less.
2. Retention of felony penalties for growing marijuana, selling it for profit, or possessing it with intent to sell.
3. Fines up to $100 for smoking in public, public possession of more than one ounce, or not-for-profit distribution of small amounts in public.
4. Jail terms of up to 60 days and a $100 fine for disorderly conduct linked to public marijuana use or intoxication.
5. Penalties of up to a year in jail, a $1000 fine and suspension of operator's permit for driving a vehicle or operating any dangerous instrument while under the influence of marijuana.
6. Classification of marijuana as contraband that could be confiscated by police wherever found outside the home, even if the possessor were not liable for criminal penalties.

NOTES

[1] Edwin H. Sutherland and Donald R. Cressey, *Principles of Criminology*, 8th ed. (Philadelphia: J. B. Lippincott Company, 1970), p. 18.
[2] Edwin M. Schur, *Crimes without Victims* (Englewood Cliffs, N. J.: Prentice-Hall, 1965), pp. 169–170.

³ For an account of prostitution in London written originally in the 1850s see William Acton, *Prostitution* (New York: Frederick A. Praeger, 1969).

⁴ For a discussion of various drugs and some of the often contradictory research on their effects see Oliver E. Byrd, *Medical Readings on Drug Abuse* (Reading, Mass.: Addison-Wesley Publishing Company, 1970) and Harold Kalant and Oriana Josseau Kalant, *Drugs, Society and Personal Choice* (Ontario: General Publishing Company, Ltd., 1971).

⁵ John A. O'Donnell and John C. Ball, *Narcotic Addiction* (Englewood Cliffs, N.J.: Prentice-Hall, 1965), and Marshall B. Clinard, *Sociology of Deviant Behavior*, rev. ed. (New York: Holt, Rinehart and Winston, 1968), Chap. 11.

⁶ Erich Goode, ed., *Marijuana* (New York: Atherton Press, 1969), p. 46.

⁷ *Task Force Report: Narcotics and Drug Abuse.* The President's Commission on Law Enforcement and Administration of Justice (Washington: D.C.: U. S. Government Printing Office, 1967), pp. 13–14.

⁸ *Ibid.*, p. 13. See also David Solomon, ed., *The Marihuana Papers* (New York: Signet Books, Bobbs-Merrill Company, 1966), and the concluding section of this chapter.

⁹ For a discussion of various effects, see Donald D. Pet and John C. Ball, "Marihuana Smoking in the United States," *Federal Probation*, **32** (September 1968), pp. 8–15. See also Goode, *Marijuana*.

¹⁰ Howard S. Becker, *Outsiders: Studies in the Sociology of Deviance* (New York: The Free Press, Macmillan Company, 1963), pp. 138–139.

¹¹ Edwin M. Lemert, *Social Pathology: A Systematic Approach to the Theory of Sociopathic Behavior* (New York: McGraw-Hill Book Company, 1951), p. 270.

¹² This is, of course, not always the case. For the story of a middle-class, college educated call girl prostitute, see Virginia McManus, *Not for Love* (New York: G. P. Putnam's Sons, 1960).

¹³ James H. Bryan, "Apprenticeships in Prostitution," *Social Problems*, **12** (Winter 1965), pp. 287–296.

¹⁴ *Ibid.*

¹⁵ *Ibid.*, p. 294. Also see Bryan, "Occupational Ideologies of Call Girls," *Social Problems*, **13** (Spring 1966), pp. 441–450.

¹⁶ Bryan, "Apprenticeships in Prostitution," p. 296.

¹⁷ Shlomo Shoham and Giora Rahav, "Social Stigma and Prostitution," *Annales Internationales de Criminologie*, **6** (1967), pp. 479–513.

¹⁸ *Ibid.*, p. 504.

¹⁹ John H. Gagnon, "Prostitution," *International Encyclopedia of the Social Sciences* (New York: The Macmillan Company, 1968), Vol. 12, p. 594.

²⁰ Walter C. Reckless, *The Crime Problem*, 3d ed. (New York: Appleton-Century-Crofts, 1961), pp. 276–277.

²¹ High earnings are also a leading motivation for those girls who go in for "stripping" in night clubs and other places. See James K. Skipper, Jr., and Charles H. McCaghy, "Stripteasers: The Anatomy and Career Contingencies of a Deviant Occupation," *Social Problems*, **17** (Winter 1970), pp. 391–404.

²² Kingsley Davis, "Sexual Behavior," in Robert K. Merton and Robert A. Nisbet, eds., *Contemporary Social Problems*, 2d ed. (New York: Harcourt, Brace, Jovanovich, 1966), p. 361.

²³ Norman R. Jackman, Richard O'Toole, and Gilbert Geis, "The Self-Image of the Prostitute," *Sociological Quarterly*, **4** (Spring 1963), pp. 150–161.

²⁴ Bryan, "Occupational Ideologies of Call Girls."

²⁵ David B. Lynn, "A Note on Sex Differences in the Development of Masculine and Feminine Identification," *Psychological Review*, **66** (1959), pp. 126–135. Also see Laud Humphreys, "New Styles in Homosexual Manliness," in Jo-

seph A. McCaffrey, ed., *The Homosexual Dialectic* (Englewood Cliffs, N.J.: Prentice-Hall, 1972), pp. 65–84. For a discussion of the female homosexual, see Jack H. Hedblom, "The Female Homosexual: Social and Attitudinal Dimensions," in McCaffrey, *The Homosexual Dialectic*, pp. 31–65.

26 Maurice Leznoff and William Westley, "The Homosexual Community," *Social Problems*, 3 (1956), pp. 257–263.

27 Evelyn Hooker, "The Adjustment of the Male Overt Homosexual," in Hendrik Ruitenbeek, ed., *The Problem of Homosexuality in Modern Society* (New York: E. P. Dutton & Co., 1963), pp. 141–161.

28 David Ward and Gene Kassebaum, "Homosexuality: A Mode of Adaptation in a Prison for Women," *Social Problems*, 12 (1964), pp. 159–177.

29 Lemert, *Social Pathology*, Chap. 4.

30 Erving Goffman, *Stigma: Notes on the Management of Spoiled Identity* (Englewood Cliffs, N.J.: Prentice-Hall, 1965), pp. 143–144.

31 Michael Schofield, *Sociological Aspects of Homosexuality: A Comparative Study of Three Types of Homosexuals* (Boston: Little, Brown & Company, 1965), p. 4. Also reprinted by permission of Longman Group Limited.

32 Barry Dank, "Coming Out in the Gay World," *Psychiatry*, 34 (May 1971), pp. 180–197.

33 Schofield, *Sociological Aspects of Homosexuality*, p. 181.

34 For a discussion of the role of public places in the lives of homosexuals, see Martin Hoffman, *The Gay World: Male Homosexuality and the Social Creation of Evil* (New York: Basic Books, 1968), Chap. 3.

35 Laud Humphreys, *Tearoom Trade: Impersonal Act in Public Places* (Chicago: Aldine Publishing Co., 1970). Also see article with the same title in *Transaction*, 7 (January 1970), pp. 10–25.

36 Schur, *Crimes without Victims*, p. 89.

37 Albert J. Reiss, Jr., "The Social Integration of Queers and Peers," *Social Problems*, 9 (Fall 1961), pp. 102–120, and Schofield, *Sociological Aspects of Homosexuality*, pp. 12–13.

38 Humphreys, *Tearoom Trade*.

39 Schofield, *Sociological Aspects of Homosexuality*, pp. 100–143.

40 D. J. West, *Homosexuality* (Chicago: Aldine Publishing Co., 1967), p. 58.

41 Martin S. Weinberg, "The Male Homosexual: Age-Related Variations in Social and Psychological Characteristics," *Social Problems*, 17 (Spring 1970), pp. 527–537.

42 Leon A. Greenberg, "Intoxication and Alcoholism: Physiological Factors," *The Annals*, 315 (January 1958), p. 27.

43 Clinard, *Sociology of Deviant Behavior*, p. 413.

44 Expert Committee on Mental Health, "Second Report of the Alcoholism Sub-Committee" (Geneva: World Health Organization, 1952), Technical Report No. 48.

45 David J. Pittman and Duff G. Gillespie, "Social Policy as Deviancy Reinforcement: The Case of the Public Intoxication Offender," in David J. Pittman, ed., *Alcoholism* (New York: Harper & Row, Publishers, 1967), pp. 106–124. Also see David Pittman and C. Wayne Gordon, *Revolving Door: A Study of the Chronic Police Case Inebriate* (New York: The Free Press, Macmillan Company, 1958).

46 David J. Pittman, "Public Intoxication and the Alcoholic Offender in American Society," *Task Force Report: Drunkenness*, The President's Commission on Law Enforcement and Administration of Justice (Washington, D.C.: U. S. Government Printing Office, 1967), p. 10.

47 Pittman and Gordon, *Revolving Door*.

48 John A. Clausen, "Social and Psychological Factors in Narcotics Addiction," *Law and Contemporary Problems,* **22** (1957), pp. 38–39.
49 Alfred R. Lindesmith, *Addiction and Opiates* (Chicago: Aldine Publishing Co., 1968), p. 64.
50 Clinard, *Sociology of Deviant Behavior,* p. 305.
51 Lindesmith, *Addiction and Opiates,* pp. 95–96.
52 James T. Carey, *The College Drug Scene* (Englewood Cliffs, N.J.: Prentice-Hall, 1968).
53 *Ibid.,* p. 52. Also see John H. McGrath and Frank R. Scarpitti, *Youth and Drugs* (Glenview, Ill.: Scott, Foresman and Company, 1970).
54 Harold Alksne, Louis Lieberman, and Leon Brill, "A Conceptual Model of the Life Cycle of Addiction," *International Journal of the Addictions,* **2** (Fall 1967), pp. 221–240.
55 Lindesmith, *Addiction and Opiates,* p. 63.
56 Goode, *Marijuana,* p. 16.
57 Howard S. Becker, "Becoming a Marihuana User," *American Journal of Sociology,* **59** (1953), pp. 235–242.
58 Goode, *Marijuana,* p. 62.
59 Erich Goode, "Multiple Drug Use among Marijuana Smokers," *Social Problems,* **17** (Summer 1969), pp. 48–63. Also see his *The Marijuana Smokers* (New York: Basic Books, 1970).
60 Carey, *The College Drug Scene.*
61 Goode, *Marijuana,* p. 63.
62 John C. Ball, Carl D. Chambers, and Marion J. Ball, "The Association of Marihuana Smoking with Opiate Addiction in the United States," *Journal of Criminal Law, Criminology and Police Science,* **59** (June 1968), pp. 171–182.
63 Alfred R. Lindesmith and John Gagnon, "Anomie and Drug Addiction," in Marshall B. Clinard, ed., *Anomie and Deviant Behavior: A Discussion and Critique* (New York: The Free Press, Macmillan Company, 1964), p. 170; and Charles Winick, "Physician Narcotic Addicts," *Social Problems,* **9** (Fall 1961), pp. 174–186.
64 Charles Winick, "The Use of Drugs by Jazz Musicians," *Social Problems,* **7** (Winter 1959–1960), pp. 240–254.
65 For a general discussion of prostitution today see T. C. Esselstyn, "Prostitution in the United States," *The Annals,* **376** (March 1968), pp. 123–135.
66 Paul Cressey, *Taxi-Dance Hall* (Chicago: University of Chicago Press, 1932).
67 David Mauer, "Prostitutes and Criminal Argots," *American Journal of Sociology,* **44** (January 1939), pp. 546–550.
68 Schofield, *Sociological Aspects of Homosexuality,* p. 135.
69 *Ibid.,* p. 82.
70 Gordon Westwood, *A Minority: A Report on the Life of the Male Homosexual in Great Britain* (London: Longmans, Green & Co., 1960), pp. 24–39.
71 Paul H. Gebhard, John H. Gagnon, Wardell B. Pomeroy, and Cornelia V. Christenson, *Sex Offenders: An Analysis of Types* (New York: Harper & Row, Publishers, 1965), p. 329.
72 Leznoff and Westley, "The Homosexual Community," p. 263.
73 Donald W. Cory, *The Homosexual in America* (New York: Greenberg, Publisher, 1951), p. 90. Also see D. J. Mercer, *They Walk in the Shadow* (New York: Comet Press, 1959).
74 For discussion, see Gordon Westwood, *Society and the Homosexual* (New York: E. P. Dutton & Co. 1953), Chaps. 19–21 and Cory, *The Homosexual in America,* p. 90. Also see Westwood, *A Minority,* pp. 68–77.

[75] Westwood, *A Minority*, pp. 83–86. Also see Gebhard, *et al.*, *Sex Offenders*, p. 348.

[76] Schofield, *Sociological Aspects of Homosexuality*, p. 183.

[77] Evelyn Hooker, "The Homosexual Community," in John H. Gagnon and William Simon, eds., *Sexual Deviance* (New York: Harper & Row, Publishers, 1967), pp. 180–181. Also reprinted in *Perspectives in Psychopathology* (Munksgaard Publishing, Copenhagen).

[78] See Nancy Achilles, "The Development of the Homosexual Bar as an Institution," in Gagnon and Simon, eds., *Sexual Deviance*, pp. 228–244.

[79] Hooker, "The Homosexual Community," pp. 178–179.

[80] *Alcohol Problems: A Report to the Nation*. Cooperative Commission on the Study of Alcoholism, prepared by Thomas F. A. Plaut (London: Oxford University Press, 1967).

[81] For a detailed discussion of the effect of these variables see Clinard, *Sociology of Deviant Behavior*, pp. 421–443.

[82] "Alcohol Project of the Emory University Department of Psychiatry," *Task Force Report: Drunkenness*, Appendix G, p. 90.

[83] John L. Haer, "Drinking Patterns and the Influence of Friends and Family," *Quarterly Journal of Studies on Alcohol*, 16 (1955), pp 178–185.

[84] Harrison M. Trice, "Identifying the Problem Drinker on the Job," *Personnel Magazine*, 33 (1957), pp. 527–533.

[85] Pittman and Gordon, *Revolving Door*, p. 67.

[86] Howard M. Bahr, "Institutional Life, Drinking, and Disaffiliation," *Social Problems*, 16 (Winter 1969), pp. 365–375.

[87] For a survey of the literature see Muriel W. Sterne, "Drinking Patterns and Alcoholism among American Negroes," in Pittman, *Alcoholism*, pp. 71–74.

[88] Earl Rubington, "The Chronic Drunkenness Offender," *The Annals*, 315 (January 1958), pp. 65–72; W. Jack Peterson and Milton A. Maxwell, "The Skid Row 'Wino'," *Social Problems*, 5 (Spring 1958), pp. 308–316; Joan K. Kackson and Ralph Connor, "The Skid Row Alcoholic," *Quarterly Journal of Studies on Alcohol*, 14 (September 1953), p. 475; and Donald Bogue, *Skid Row* (Chicago: University of Chicago Press, 1963).

[89] Bahr, "Institutional Life, Drinking, and Disaffiliation."

[90] Pittman and Gordon, *Revolving Door*.

[91] Rubington, "The Chronic Drunkenness Offender," p. 71.

[92] Samuel E. Wallace, "The Road to Skid Row," *Social Problems*, 16 (Summer 1968), pp. 102–103.

[93] For a discussion of the subculture of drug use in a college setting, see Carey, *The College Drug Scene*.

[94] John A. O'Donnell and Judith P. Jones, "Diffusion of the Intravenous Technique among Narcotic Addicts in the United States," *Journal of Health and Social Behavior*, 9 (June 1968), pp. 120–130.

[95] Isidor Chein and Eva Rosenfeld, "Juvenile Narcotics Use," *Law and Contemporary Problems*, 22 (1957), p. 58.

[96] Goode, "Multiple Drug Use among Marijuana Smokers," p. 54. Also see his *The Marijuana Smokers*.

[97] *Ibid.*

[98] Irit Friedman and Ilana Peer, "Drug Addiction among Pimps and Prostitutes, Israel 1967," *The International Journal of the Addictions*, 3 (Fall 1968), pp. 271–300.

[99] Lindesmith and Gagnon, "Anomie and Drug Addiction," in Clinard, ed., *Anomie and Deviant Behavior*, p. 172.

[100] Lawrence J. Redlinger and Jerry B. Michel, "Ecological Variations in Heroin Abuse," *The Sociological Quarterly*, 11 (Spring 1970), pp. 219–227.

[101] John A. O'Donnell, *Narcotic Addicts in Kentucky* (Chevy Chase, Maryland: Department of Health, Education, and Welfare, National Institute of Mental Health, 1969); and John C. Ball, "Two Patterns of Narcotic Drug Addiction in the United States," *Journal of Criminal Law, Criminology and Police Science*, 56 (1965), p. 211.

[102] Harold Finestone, "Cats, Kicks, and Color," *Social Problems*, 5 (July 1957), pp. 3–14.

[103] Isidor Chein, Donald L. Gerard, Robert S. Lee, and Eva Rosenfeld, *The Road to H* (New York: Basic Books, 1964), Chap. 6.

[104] Seymour Fiddle, "The Addict Culture and Movement into and out of Hospitals," as reprinted in Senate Committee on the Judiciary, Subcommittee to Investigate Juvenile Delinquency, *Hearings*, Pt. 13, New York City, September 20–21 (Washington, D.C.: U. S. Government Printing Office, 1963), p. 3156.

[105] Fiddle, "The Addict Culture and Movement into and out of Hospitals."

[106] Earl Rubington, "Drug Addiction as a Deviant Career," *International Journal of the Addictions*, 2 (1960), pp. 3–20.

[107] These and other reasons for relapse are discussed in Lindesmith, *Addiction and Opiates*, pp. 129–155. Also see Richard Stephens and Emily Cottrell, "A Follow-up Study of 200 Narcotic Addicts Committed for Treatment under the Narcotic Addict Rehabilitation Act (NARA)," *British Journal of Addiction*, 67 (1972), pp. 45–53.

[108] John C. Pollard, "Some Comments on Nonnarcotic Drug Abuse." Paper presented at the Nonnarcotic Drug Institute, Southern Illinois University, Edwardsville, Illinois, June 1967. Also see Carl D. Chambers and Leon Brill, "Some Considerations for the Treatment of Non-Narcotic Drug Abusers," in Leon Brill and Louis Lieberman, eds., *The Treatment of Drug Addiction and Drug Abuse* (Boston: Little, Brown & Company, 1970).

[109] Hugh Parry, "Tranquilizer Users," *Wayfarers Magazine*, February 1969. For a discussion of the widespread prescription of drugs by medical doctors to redefine everyday human experiences as medical problems for which drugs are the answer and the role of the pharmaceutical industry indirectly encouraging it, see Henry L. Lennard, Leon J. Epstein, Arnold Bernstein, and Donald C. Ransom, *Mystification and Drug Misuse: Hazards in Using Psychoactive Drugs* (San Francisco: Jossey-Bass, Inc., 1971).

[110] George B. Vold, *Theoretical Criminology* (New York: Oxford University Press, 1958), pp. 151–154.

[111] Edwin H. Lemert, *Social Pathology*, p. 246.

[112] Irwin Deutscher, "The Petty Offender: A Sociological Alien," *Journal of Criminal Law, Criminology and Police Science*, 44 (January–February 1954), p. 59.

[113] Vold, *Theoretical Criminology*, p. 148.

[114] *Ibid.*, p. 156. He does not refer to homosexual behavior in this statement.

[115] Davis, "Sexual Behavior," p. 532.

[116] Wayne R. LaFave, *Arrest: The Decision to Take a Suspect into Custody* (Boston: Little, Brown & Company, 1965), pp. 457–463.

[117] For a discussion of police harassment of prostitutes, see Paul Chevigny, *Police Power: Police Abuses in New York City* (New York: Vintage Books, Random House, 1969).

[118] Jerome H. Skolnick, *Justice without Trial: Law Enforcement in Democratic Society* (New York: John Wiley & Sons, 1966), p. 104.

[119] *Ibid.*, p. 112.

[120] *The Wolfenden Report*. Report of the Committee on Homosexual Offenses and Prostitution (New York: Stein and Day, 1963), pp. 143–144.

[121] Pamela A. Roby, "Politics and Criminal Law: Revision of the New York State Penal Law on Prostitution," *Social Problems,* 17 (Summer 1969), pp. 83–109.

[122] *Ibid.,* p. 99.

[123] *The Wolfenden Report,* p. 132.

[124] David S. Bailey, *Homosexuality and the Western Christian Tradition* (New York: David McKay Company, 1955).

[125] See John I. Kitsuse, "Societal Reaction to Deviant Behavior: Problems of Theory and Method," in Howard S. Becker, *The Other Side: Perspectives on Deviance* (New York: The Free Press, Macmillan Company, 1964), pp. 87–102.

[126] LaFave, *Arrest,* pp. 465–466.

[127] Wayland Young, "Prostitution," in Gagnon and Simon, *Sexual Deviance,* p. 235.

[128] Chevigny, *Police Power,* pp. 121–128.

[129] J. H. Gallo, "The Consenting Adult Homosexual and the Law," *U.C.L.A. Law Review,* Los Angeles, 13 (March 1966), pp. 657–685.

[130] Gallo *et al.,* "The Consenting Adult Homosexual and the Law," pp. 707–708. Also see Martin Hoffman, *The Gay World: Male Homosexuality and the Social Creation of Evil* (New York: Basic Books, 1968), pp. 79–99.

[131] West, *Homosexuality,* p. 91.

[132] LaFave, *Arrest,* pp. 108–110.

[133] *Task Force Report: Drunkenness,* p. 2.

[134] Pittman and Gordon, *Revolving Door.*

[135] Elizabeth Benz, *Man on the Periphery* (Rochester, N.Y.: Rochester Bureau of Municipal Research, 1964).

[136] James P. Spradley, *You Owe Yourself a Drunk: An Ethnography of Urban Nomads* (Boston: Little, Brown & Company, 1970). Also see James P. Spradley, "The Moral Career of a Bum," *Transaction,* 7 (May 1970), pp. 17–29.

[137] *Task Force Report: Drunkenness,* p. 2.

[138] *Ibid.,* p. 9.

[139] Spradley, "The Moral Career of a Bum," pp. 21, 24.

[140] *Task Force Report: Drunkenness,* p. 3.

[141] *Ibid.,* p. 73.

[142] Alfred R. Lindesmith, *The Addict and the Law* (Bloomington, Ind.: Indiana University Press, 1965), p. 80.

[143] Lindesmith, *Addiction and Opiates,* p. 222.

[144] Lois B. DeFleur, John C. Ball, and Richard W. Snarr, "The Long-Term Social Correlates of Opiate Addiction," *Social Problems,* 17 (Fall 1969), p. 233.

[145] Chevigny, *Police Power,* pp. 180–218.

[146] For a discussion of the informant in the narcotics enforcement pattern see Skolnick, *Justice without Trial,* pp. 139–163.

[147] Two books by professors of criminal law are Norval Morris and Gordon Hawkins, *An Honest Politician's Guide to Crime Control* (Chicago: University of Chicago Press, 1970); and Herbert Packer, *The Limits of the Criminal Sanction* (Stanford: Stanford University Press, 1968).

[148] Morris and Hawkins, *The Honest Politician's Guide to Crime Control,* p. 5.

[149] *Ibid.,* p. 20.

[150] *Ibid.,* p. 6.

[151] "Drunkenness Offenses," *The Challenge of Crime in a Free Society.* A Report of the President's Commission on Law Enforcement and Administration of Justice (Washington, D.C.: U. S. Government Printing Office, 1967), p. 236.

[152] Raymond T. Nimmer, *Two Million Unnecessary Arrests: Removing a Social Service Concern from the Criminal Justice System* (Chicago: American Bar Foundation, 1971).

[153] Lindesmith, *The Addict and the Law*, p. 270. Also see *Drug Addiction: Crime or Disease*. Interim and Final Reports of the Joint Committee of the American Bar Association and the American Medical Association on Narcotic Drugs (Bloomington, Ind.: Indiana University Press, 1960); and Troy Duster, *The Legislation of Morality: Law, Drugs, and Moral Judgment* (New York: The Free Press, 1970).

[154] Edwin M. Schur, *Narcotic Addiction in Britain and America: The Impact of Public Policy* (Bloomington, Ind.: Indiana University Press, 1962). Because of an increase in drug addiction, measures were recently adopted to create a degree of centralization in issuing prescriptions to drug users through hospital psychiatrists. Previously, any general physician could prescribe drugs.

[155] Erich Goode, ed., *Marijuana* (New York: Atherton Press, 1969), particularly Chap. 6, "The Question of Legalization." Also see Lester Grinspoon, *Marihuana Reconsidered* (Cambridge: Harvard University Press, 1971); and John Kaplan, *Marijuana—The New Prohibition* (New York: World Publishing Co., 1970).

SELECTED BIBLIOGRAPHY

Allen, David D., *The Nature of Gambling*. New York: Coward-McCann, 1952.

Bailey, David S., *Homosexuality and the Western Christian Tradition*. New York: David McKay Company, 1955.

Becker, Howard S., "Becoming a Marijuana User." *American Journal of Sociology*, **59** (November 1953), pp. 235–242.

Bogue, Donald, *Skid Row*. Chicago: University of Chicago Press, 1963.

Bryan, James H., "Apprenticeships in Prostitution." *Social Problems*, **12** (Winter 1965), pp. 287–296.

———, "Occupational Ideologies of Call Girls." *Social Problems*, **13** (Spring 1966), pp. 441–450.

Carey, James T., *The College Drug Scene*. Englewood Cliffs, N.J.: Prentice-Hall, 1968.

Chambliss, William J., "A Sociological Analysis of the Law of Vagrancy." *Social Problems*, **12** (Summer 1964), pp. 67–77.

Chein, Isidor, Gerard, Donald L., Lee, Robert S., and Rosenfield, Eva, with the collaboration of Daniel M. Wilner, *The Road to H*. New York: Basic Books, 1964.

Clinard, Marshall B., *Sociology of Deviant Behavior*, 3d ed. New York: Holt, Rinehart and Winston, 1968, chaps. 9, 10, and 11.

Duster, Troy, *The Legislation of Morality: Laws, Drugs, and Moral Judgment*. New York: The Free Press, 1970.

Esselstyn, T. C. "Prostitution in the United States." *The Annals*, **376** (March 1968), pp. 123–135.

Finestone, Harold, "Narcotics and Criminality." *Law and Contemporary Problems*, **22** (Winter 1957), pp. 69–85.

Gebhard, Paul H., Gagnon, John H., Pomeroy, Wardell B., and Christenson,

Cornelia V., *Sex Offenders: An Analysis of Types*. New York: Harper & Row, 1965.

Goode, Erich, *The Marijuana Smokers*. New York: Basic Books, 1970.

Grinspoon, Lester, *Marihuana Reconsidered*. Cambridge: Harvard University Press, 1971.

Hoffman, Martin, *The Gay World: Male Homosexuality and the Social Creation of Evil*. New York: Basic Books, 1968.

Hooker, Evelyn, "The Homosexual Community," *Perspectives in Psychopathology*. New York: Oxford University Press, 1965.

Humphreys, Laud, *Tearoom Trade: Impersonal Sex in Public Places*. Chicago: Aldine Publishing Co., 1970.

Jackman, Norman R., O'Toole, Richard, and Geis, Gilbert, "The Self-Image of the Prostitute." *Sociological Quarterly*, 4 (Spring 1963), pp. 150–161.

Kitsuse, John I., "Societal Reaction to Deviant Behavior: Problems of Theory and Method." In Howard S. Becker, *The Other Side: Perspectives on Deviance*. New York: The Free Press, Macmillan Company, 1964, pp. 87–102.

LaFave, Wayne R., *Arrest: The Decision to Take a Suspect into Custody*. Boston: Little, Brown & Company, 1965, pp. 457–463.

Leznoff, Maurice, and Westley, William A., "The Homosexual Community." *Social Problems*, 3 (April 1956), pp. 257–263.

Lindesmith, Alfred R., *Addiction and Opiates*. Chicago: Aldine Publishing Co., 1968.

McCaffrey, Joseph A., ed., *The Homosexual Dialectic*. Englewood Cliffs, N. J.: Prentice-Hall, Inc., 1972.

McGrath, John H. and Scarpitti, Frank R., *Youth and Drugs*. Glenview, Ill.: Scott, Foresman and Company, 1970.

Murtagh, John M., and Harris, Sara, *Cast the First Stone*. New York: McGraw-Hill Book Company, 1957.

Nimmer, Raymond T., *Two Million Unnecessary Arrests: Removing a Social Service Concern from the Criminal Justice System*. Chicago: American Bar Foundation, 1971.

O'Donnell, John A., *Narcotic Addicts in Kentucky*. Chevy Chase, Maryland: National Institute of Mental Health, 1969.

———, and Ball, John C., eds., *Narcotic Addiction*. New York: Harper & Row, 1966.

Packer, Herbert, *The Limits of the Criminal Sanction*. Stanford: Stanford University Press, 1968.

Pittman, David J., and Gordon, C. Wayne, *Revolving Door*. New York: The Free Press, Macmillan Company, 1958.

President's Commission on Law Enforcement and Administration of Justice, *Task Force Report: Crime and Its Impact—An Assessment; Task Force Report: Drunkenness; Task Force Report: Narcotics and Drug Abuse; The Challenge of Crime in a Free Society*. Washington, D.C.: U. S. Government Printing Office, 1967.

Roby, Pamela A., "Politics and Criminal Law: Revision of the New York State Penal Law on Prostitution." *Social Problems* 17 (Summer 1969), pp. 83–109.

Ross, H. Lawrence, "Traffic Law Violation: A Folk Crime." *Social Problems,* 8 (Winter 1960–1961), pp. 231–241.

Rubington, Earl, "The Chronic Drunkenness Offender." *The Annals,* 315 (January 1958), pp. 65–72.

Schofield, Michael, *Sociological Aspects of Homosexuality; A Comparative Study of Three Types of Homosexuals.* Boston: Little, Brown & Company, 1965.

Schur, Edwin M., *Crimes without Victims.* Englewood Cliffs, N. J.: Prentice-Hall, 1965.

———, *Narcotic Addiction in Britain and America: The Impact of Public Policy.* Bloomington, Ind.: Indiana University Press, 1962.

Skolnick, Jerome H., *Justice without Trial: Law Enforcement in Democratic Society.* New York: John Wiley & Sons, 1966.

West, D. J., *Homosexuality.* Chicago: Aldine Publishing Co., 1967.

Westwood, Gordon, *A Minority: A Report on the Life of the Male Homosexual in Great Britain.* London: Longmans, Green & Co., 1960.

Wheeler, Stanton, "Sex Offenses: A Sociological Critique." *Law and Contemporary Problems,* 25 (Spring 1960), pp. 258–292.

Willett, T. C., *Criminal on the Road: A Study of Serious Motoring Offenses and Those Who Commit Them.* London: Tavistock Publications, 1964.

Winick, Charles, "Physician Narcotic Addicts." *Social Problems,* 7 (Winter 1959–1960), pp. 240–254.

———, "The Use of Drugs by Jazz Musicians." *Social Problems,* 7 (Winter 1959–1960), pp. 240–254.

The Wolfenden Report: Report on the Committee on Homosexual Offenses and Prostitution. New York: Stein and Day, 1963.

Zola, Irving K., "Gambling in a Lower-Class Setting." *Social Problems,* 10 (Spring 1963), pp. 353–361.

Conventional Criminal Behavior | 5

Three types of criminal behavior systems can be broadly categorized: conventional, organized, and professional. Career criminals differ markedly from noncareer criminals who have been discussed thus far. While the types of career criminal behavior differ, they have several characteristics in common.[1]

First, persons engaged in career crime usually pursue crimes of gain, mostly property crimes. Career criminals either supplement an income through property crime or, as with organized criminals and professional criminals, make a living from criminal activity. In comparison to persons in legitimate occupations, career criminals make part or all of their living by pursuing activities that have been defined as illegal. One of the occupational hazards for the career criminal, however, is the risk of being arrested and convicted. Since only about 20 percent of all property offenses (and only those that are *known* by the police) are cleared by arrest, the risks are not exceptionally high. For many career criminals, the often-quoted adage that "crime does not pay" is a fiction, a myth maintained by and for law-abiding members of society.

Second, criminal activity is a part of the way of life of the career offender. A career in crime involves a life organization of roles built around criminal activities, which includes identification with crime, a conception of the self as a criminal, and extensive association with other criminals.[2] In career crime there is a progression in crime which includes the acquisition of more complex techniques, more frequent offenses, and, ultimately, dependence on crime as a partial or sole means of livelihood.

Third, persons in career crime tend either to develop a pattern of property violations or in some cases to specialize in a particular kind of offense. A professional criminal, for example, will specialize in one of a number of violations, such as picking pockets, sneak thieving, passing illegal checks, or shoplifting. Career criminals also develop over a period of time special skills and techniques for committing offenses.

Fourth, career criminals are engaged in systematic behavior that requires both personal and social organization. In contrast to noncareer crime, the violations of career criminals are not the result of personal conflicts and immediate circumstances. Career criminals commit their offenses only through awareness of the situation and after planning the offense. Career criminals depend upon the assistance of other criminals and may be involved in an organization of criminals. Because of the involvement of career criminals in crime, there is the prospect of a lifetime career in crime with increased isolation from the legitimate work patterns of society.

Conventional crime as a behavior system is at the bottom of the scale of career crime. The degree of development of conventional criminals and their sophistication in crime is much less than that found among organized and professional criminals. Compared to the other career criminals, conventional property criminals are less skillful in committing offenses and are not as well organized to avoid arrest and conviction. Conventional offenders often begin their illegal activities as juveniles, and many terminate their careers before they reach the age of thirty.

LEGAL ASPECTS OF SELECTED OFFENSES

Conventional criminals are those who commit the "conventional" common kinds of crime such as larceny, burglary, and robbery which have been regarded as crime for centuries. Burglary alone, for example, in 1970 accounted for 39 percent of the total crime index offenses in the United States.

Offenses against property were among the first to be punished under legal systems. Because the importance of various forms of property, however, have changed with developments in society, such as the introduction of autos and power interests, the penalties for crimes against property have also changed. Theft is the term encompassing all property crimes, but the basic theft offense in English common law was larceny. This act consists of taking and carrying away goods from the possession of another without the owner's consent. Originally the goods had to be in possession, but later this concept was enlarged to cope with the problems of an industrial and commercial society with the addition in the eighteenth century of embezzlement and obtaining money under false pretenses. Other additions have included receiving stolen property. Shoplifting is a form of larceny.

Other property crimes that involve theft and larceny with a long history under the common law are burglary and robbery. Burglary under the old common law was breaking and entering a dwelling house of another at night with intent to steal. Now this has been enlarged to include buildings other than houses and the night element has been eliminated. Robbery is regarded as aggravated larceny and consists of taking property from another with an element of force, placing the victim in some sort of fear.

CRIMINAL CAREER OF THE OFFENDER

Conventional criminals begin their careers early in life as juvenile delinquents. In the United States those from fifteen to seventeen years of age are the most arrested group for burglaries, larcenies, and auto theft. In the United States in 1970, 22.9 percent of those arrested for burglary were under fifteen, and 52.0 percent under eighteen; in auto theft 15.1 percent were under fifteen and 56.1 percent under eighteen. Comparable figures for robbery were 11.1 percent under fifteen and 33.4 percent under eighteen.[3] A Philadelphia study found that the highest age-specific rates in terms of population for arrests for robbery were 15–19 and 20–24.[4]

Their early life histories are likely to show a pattern of truancy, destruction of property, street fighting, and delinquent gang membership. By the time they are young adults, they have an extensive history of contact with the law, and possibly have had some experience in an institution.

> Life histories of persons who in young adult life became robbers and burglars show that criminality proceeds from trivial to serious, from occasional to frequent, from sport to business, and from crimes committed by isolated individuals, or by very loosely organized groups to crimes committed by rather tightly organized groups. This process in crimes of violence reaches its height when the offender is about nineteen years of age and then remains constant for five or ten years, when it either changes into crimes which require less agility and daring, or into the kind of criminal behavior connected with politics, gambling, liquor, and usury, or is abandoned entirely.[5]

Conventional criminals usually begin their careers in gangs in association with juveniles of similar social origins. As juveniles they become involved in a culture that is either neutral or opposed to the law of legitimate society. Their acts are not isolated and personal, but rather are often part of the way of life and norms of a local slum community.[6] At an early age they learn to commit illegal acts and find group support for their behavior. From early experience in such a setting they readily progress to adult criminal behavior in which thefts are more frequent, substantial, and sophisticated.[7] A Philadelphia study of twenty-seven black gangs with a total membership of 918, with a median age of 17.6 years, showed that 711 had police records.[8] The mean number of delinquency charges was 6.2 with 20 percent being charged with 10 or more offenses. Moreover, this study revealed that 41 percent of gang members who were adults had acquired criminal records. "The analysis of police delinquencies of gang members and inspection of criminal records of those juveniles who became adult offenders have made it clear that these individuals were persistent and dangerous offenders and have shown that a larger proportion of them became even more serious offenders."[9]

The progression from early juvenile gang delinquency to adult conventional crime is shown in a study of black armed robbers. Their criminal career histories were as follows:

> An early patterning of stealing from their parents, from school, and on the street; truancy, and suspension or expulsion from school; street

fighting, association with older delinquents, and juvenile delinquent gang memberships, all were usually evident in their social backgrounds. When compared with the men in the other criminal categories, it was found that there was more destruction of property in their delinquent activities, and there were more frequent fights with schoolmates, male teachers, and delinquent companions. There was a higher incidence of "mugging" and purse snatching. They had more often been the leaders of delinquent gangs, and, they claimed they were leaders because of their superior size and physical strength.[10]

A similar background in gang delinquency has been noted for the conventional career criminal in what Gibbons has called the "semiprofessional property criminal." He observed that these offenders represent the usual outcome of patterns of gang delinquency and, in turn, that "many juvenile gang offenders continue in criminality as semiprofessionals."[11]

As juvenile offenders progress into conventional career crime, they become more committed to crime as a way of life and develop a criminal self-conception. Because of repeated offenses, and because of subsequent arrests and convictions, conventional offenders eventually identify with crime. For occasional property offenders who pursue criminal activity only sporadically, there is vacillation in self-conception. But for conventional criminals who regularly commit offenses and who are continually isolated from law-abiding segments of society, a criminal self-conception is virtually inescapable. In addition, because property offenders are dealt with rather severely before the law, through arrest and sentencing, such offenders readily come to regard themselves as criminals. The criminal record is a constant reminder that the person has been stigmatized by the society. The record may provide a vicious circle whereby the offender, once stigmatized, often cannot enter into law-abiding society and must continue in a life of crime.

Most of the offenses included in conventional crime, whether juvenile or adult, are related to property and other material possessions in one way or another. Within the boundary of property offenses, conventional property criminals are likely to have a diversified offense record. These offenders commit a series of offenses which may include theft, larceny, robbery, and burglary. The amount of money involved in each offense is relatively small. As a result the offenses provide a part of the offenders' livelihood and they must be repeated regularly. Persons arrested for robbery, for example, tend to have previous records in theft rather than in acts of violence. A Boston study of robbery suspects apprehended during the first six months of 1968 found that among juveniles five times as many had been previously arrested for theft as for violent crimes.[12] National figures show that for suspects under seventeen the ratio is about 7 to 1. Similarly, a Philadelphia study of 1972 persons arrested for robbery reported:

Using different types of indexes of prior police arrest record, our study reveals that when an offender has a previous record, he is much more likely to have a criminal profile of offenses against property than against the person. For example, only 4 percent of the offenders have a past profile of assault, but 45 percent have a pattern of robbery, larceny or burglary. There is no significant difference between Negro and white offenders in this respect; neither is there a difference in criminal background between the violent and non-violent robbers of our study. Robbers, thus, are not a special class, but are primarily thieves who occasionally, though rarely, use force to achieve their objects. The display of violence in this context is on the whole an isolated episode. It is general persistence in crime, not a widespread specialization in crimes of violence, which is the main characteristic of robbers.[13]

Thus, because of the relative lack of skill and organization, conventional criminals, in comparison to organized and professional criminals, are more likely to be eventually arrested and imprisoned. Consequently, conventional offenders constitute a large portion of the prison population. Perhaps as many as half of all prison inmates are conventional offenders.[14] With similar offenders in mind, the following remarks were made by Gibbons in reference to the career of semiprofessional criminals: "Many semiprofessionals spend a considerable part of their early adult years in penal institutions where they are likely to be identified as 'right guys' or antiadministration inmates. It does not appear that conventional treatment efforts are successful in deflecting many of these persons away from continuation in crime. On the other hand, many of them ultimately do withdraw from crime careers upon reaching the early middle-age period."[15]

Some indication of the typical effects of processing by conventional institutions of conventional offenders is a follow-up study of Chicago boys committed to the Illinois State Training School for Boys in 1930 where

> 60.5 percent were found to have been committed to penal institutions, 68.5 percent were found to have been convicted, and 76.1 percent were found to have been arrested. When the adult careers of this group were examined for only the 5-year period following release, 52.9 percent were found to have been committed to penal institutions, while 61.2 percent had acquired records of convictions and 68.8 percent had been arrested. It is noteworthy that the addition of 10 years to the period of follow-up raised the incidence of recidivism only a few percentage points. This indicates that recidivism develops principally during the first 5 years following release from the training school.[16]

When crime is pursued as a way of life, as it is with conventional career criminals, other ways of living are not readily observed, understood, or desired by the offenders. Furthermore, the excitement and notoriety of a criminal career may seem more rewarding to the criminal than the prospects of hard work, responsibility, mediocrity, and monotony provided by a respectable, law-abiding career. A group consciousness among criminals makes movement to a law-abiding life less comprehensible and desirable. By the time of their early thirties, most conventional offenders, however, feel that a law-abiding career holds greater possibility than a criminal career that has not been particularly successful. There is a relatively small number who continue on to make professional careers of armed robbery, although some of those who become professional robbers do not have a background of gang delinquency, the career rather growing out of other later criminal associations.[17]

While some juvenile gang delinquents continue to engage in illegal activities as adults, particularly as adult conventional career criminals, it is unclear why a large number of them discontinue criminal behavior in their mid-twenties or early thirties. Reckless has pointed out that "it is much easier to determine why offenders continue in criminal careers than it is to understand what makes them quit."[18] It has been suggested that, except for certain types of crime, as a person grows older, he tends to lose touch with deviant and criminal associates because of marriage and family responsibilities. Such a change in life style is more important in breaking a criminal pattern than are most present attempts at rehabilitation in correctional institutions.

The movement from gang delinquent to adult criminal is not a uniform one and is affected by the opportunities available to him and his conception of the future. In a sense he moves from primary to secondary deviance with the development of a more established criminal career, with a criminal role and self-concept.

Once a gang boy gets beyond the age of 18, moreover, his situation changes rather dramatically. Whether he likes it or not, he now has a choice to make about what identity system to enter. He could get married, get a job, and assume the status of a full-fledged "adult"; he could decide to postpone this decision in legitimate ways such as joining the Army and going to school at night; or he could decide to remain for a few more years as an elder statesman on the streets, in which case he will continue to make use of the identity materials available to youth.

The decision he makes at this point in his career will depend in part on his situation. If he managed to graduate from high school, he may well decide to go on to college; but if he was expelled from high school, he may feel either bitter or reluctant about going back to night school to get the high school degree. He knows that he has been administratively reborn in the eyes of the law, and thus the risks he takes by staying in the streets increase considerably since he now may be processed by the courts as an adult. On the other hand, if his status in the gang world is still high, he may not want to trade it right away for a low-paying blue-collar job; and he knows he will be rejected by the Army if he has a jail record of any kind.

In short, it is at this point in his career that the "opportunities" available to him will affect his behavior, his attitudes, and the decisions he makes about his life. If there are no legitimate options open to him, options that at best would not make him suffer a sudden decrease in status and at worst would allow him not to face his ultimately dismal status-fate as an adult, then he may well decide to stay on the streets, despite the greater consequences involved in taking risks. He may adopt a "hustle," and he may also adopt a full-blown ideology along with it. Since he now views the conventional world as a place he is expected to enter, he tends to develop a "position" on it. Jobs become "slaves"; going to school becomes "serving time"; and in some cases the assumptions about marriage and getting a conventional job are replaced by fantasies about the quick and big "score." . . . They have an answer to everything, and they always "know the score."

After a few years of this existence, these boys are really at the end of their "delinquent" careers. Some get jobs, some go to jail, some get killed, and some simply fade into an older underground of pool rooms and petty thefts. Most cannot avoid ending up with conventional jobs, however, largely because the "illegitimate opportunities" available simply are not that good.[19]

GROUP SUPPORT OF CRIMINAL BEHAVIOR

The conventional offender is generally a product of the slums where pronounced juvenile gangs abound. Some indication of this is the fact that the fifty-seven largest cities with a population of over 250,000 account for nearly three out of four robberies committed annually in the United States. Not only violent personal offenders come out of these areas, but offenders who commit robbery and burglary. As one government report has concluded: "Study after study in city after city in all regions of the country have traced the variations in the rates for these crimes. The results, with monotonous regularity, show that the *offenses*, the *victims*, and the *offenders* are found most frequently in the poorest, and most deteriorated and socially disorganized areas of cities."[20] Rates of crime and delinquency tend to vary inversely with distance from the center of the city.[21] A Chicago follow-up study of offenders who had appeared before the juvenile court in 1920 revealed that 58.3 percent were arrested as adults. The highest proportion (65.5 percent) of those subsequently arrested came from slum areas of high delinquency. The conclusion of the study was that

the criminal career is frequently the result of a gradual process of habituation to forms of illegal behavior. It does not, of course, indicate that proportion of adult criminals developed by this process, but since more than 60 percent of all juvenile delinquents have adult criminal records, and since a large proportion of these are known to have engaged in serious offenses, this group, in the aggregate, must constitute a large part of the criminal population.[22]

A study of slum areas in three cities has concluded:

> When a teenager flatly asserts that, "Everyone on my block steals," he is overstating the case which must be hedged and qualified, but not by very much. Nearly every youngster on the slum block, whether in New York, Washington, or Chicago (with few but conspicuous exceptions) does develop some kind of a "larceny sense." In all probability, while still quite young, he will learn to steal and he will learn what the risks are— including when, where, and how not to go too far. Just as experimentation with sex approaches universality, so with theft.[23]

Slum areas are generally characterized as being overcrowded and congested, having bad and run-down housing, and being deficient in all amenities. Although slums do vary considerably from one type to another, these general patterns of living conditions are almost universal; and although these general patterns of physical characteristics are almost without exception typical of slums, it would be a serious mistake to view slums only in these terms.[24] The slum actually is far more than this; it is a way of life. Sociologically, it represents a subculture with its own set of norms and values, which is reflected in poor sanitation and health practices, often a lack of interest in formal education, deviant behavior, and characteristic attributes of apathy and social isolation. In this sense "slums" with extensive delinquency and crime may exist in areas of reasonably good physical facilities such as slum clearance projects. Slum residents have become isolated from the general power structure of the community and are looked upon as being inferior; in turn, they reflect, in their living and in their behavior, their own suspicions toward the world that they regard as the "outside."

Support for illegal behavior begins for many conventional offenders at an early age. Thrasher noted some time ago in his classic study of juvenile and youth gangs that adolescents in play groups, in the course of fun and adventure, engage in a variety of activities that are both legal and illegal in nature.[25] The extent to which these groups engage in illegal behavior depends upon such factors as the organization of the neighborhood, family characteristics, community values, and community reaction to gang activity. In some residential areas delinquency may be the principal means of adjusting to the problems of growing up. One delinquent described his illegal activity in relation to his social experiences as follows:

> My neighborhood was filled with rackets of all kinds, from stealing pennies from news stands to stick-ups. The little fellows begin by stealing little things and bumming from school. They drive around in swell cars and strut their stuff and have a swell broad on the string. No kid wants to be in a piker's racket very long and steal coal and junk, because he sees bigger money in the stick-up game, and if you make a hit with the right mob, you're all set.[26]

The activities which become most important to the gang may be in violation of the law. The illegal activities of the gangs are at first relatively minor. The members engage in a variety of conventional property offenses, such as stealing from stores, empty houses, drunks, and other sources of property. Gradually the offenses become more like those engaged in by adults, such as burglary, armed robbery, and grand larceny. As gangs increase in organization and tradition, they may come in conflict with other gangs in the vicinity. Personal offenses and violence of various forms may then become common.

This role of gangs in delinquent and criminal behavior is well documented. One national survey concluded that "the typical delinquent operates in the company of his peers, and delinquency thrives on group support. It has been estimated that between 60 and 90 percent of all delinquent acts are committed with companions. That fact alone makes youth groups of central concern in consideration of delinquency prevention."[27] Most delinquents are arrested in company with others, and it can be safely assumed that those who had no companions at the time of their arrest had at least one in the beginning of their delinquency. In one study of 5480 Chicago delinquents Shaw found that 81.8 percent of those brought into juvenile court had one or more companions.[28] Considering those with one or more companions, he found that 30.3 percent had one companion, 27.7 percent had two, 10.8 percent had three, 7.1 percent had four, and 5.9 percent had five or more.

Most juveniles engaged in robbery operate in gangs, particularly those in strong-arm robberies. In one study of crimes of violence which involved youth groups or gangs in seventeen cities in 1967, the Task Force on Individual Acts of Violence found that youth groups and gangs were involved in a significant percentage of all robberies. An analysis of major crimes cleared by arrests showed that 9.5 percent of youth groups or gangs were involved in armed robbery and 6.8 percent in unarmed robbery. In the case of groups or gangs where the majority of offenders were juveniles, the percentage involved in armed robbery was 14.1 percent and 18.6 percent in unarmed robbery.[29]

Some delinquent gangs are of short duration, while some last over a long period of time. Those that have some consistency may furnish excellent training in criminal techniques. New members learn from gangs how to burglarize, "roll" drunks, open freight cars, shoplift, steal autos, sell stolen goods, and even to "fix" or otherwise bribe policemen. One learns to acquire social status in the group by the skill one develops in these illegal activities. In a gang robbery, for example, one of the most important roles is that of "wheel man," the person who must steal a getaway auto, plan the escape route, and drive away from the robbery scene.[30] Some consider this to be the most important part in a robbery since quick escape is essential. The wheel man may also function as a lookout and on occasion participate in a robbery.

Delinquent gangs have a degree of group integration, are structured, and are conflict groups, whether with similar groups or the police.[31] The effectiveness of delinquent gangs in disseminating knowledge about crime lies in the fact that the group nature and common participation of gang activities make stealing an attractive alternative to the individual. Moreover, each gang is a social system with common symbols and common activities with each of its members assigned a social status or position. The position or social status of gang members is measured by display of courage and skill in the commission of a crime, in having a long record of delinquencies and arrests, and, most of all, by having been in a correctional institution. Some gangs involve common ties of ethnic background or race and are in conflict with another group. Common rationalizations and techniques of neutralization are extremely important in justifying illegal behavior. Through participation in gang behavior its members develop fairly uniform attitudes toward "opposition to authority, contempt for the traitor, recognition and prestige through delinquency, hero-worship, stigma of petty stealing, and control of the gang over its members."[32]

The group nature of conventional offense behavior has been illustrated in the case studies compiled by Shaw and McKay. One study described five brothers whose criminal careers began at around the age of five, when they started begging, and progressed to truancy and petty stealing, then to stealing more valuable objects.[33] They were arrested by the police many times, appeared frequently in court, and served periods of confinement in correctional and penal institutions, besides being placed on probation and parole several times. They began their delinquency in the company of a gang of boys. The more experienced and older delinquents encouraged the younger and less experienced to engage in more serious thefts. In a study of one delinquent in particular, Shaw described the group nature of delinquency as follows:

> The next step in the development of Sidney's delinquent trend, perhaps the most important, was his participation in the shoplifting activities of his play group. This type of delinquency was obviously an accepted tradition of the group, as indicated by the fact that three of its members had been involved in a number of instances of shoplifting prior to Sidney's initial contact with the group. It may be assumed that Sidney not only acquired the shoplifting techniques and moral code prevailing in this delinquent group, but that through his numerous experiences in shoplifting his delinquent attitudes and interests were more clearly defined and he became more closely identified with the criminal world.[34]

Patterns of social interaction develop in each juvenile gang. Group solidarity and tradition develop in the course of the common experience of the members. The gang may become of such importance to the members that they participate very little in the social and youth institutions of conventional society. Gang boys become dependent upon each other for a large share of their interpersonal gratifications. Nevertheless, the gang is less than satisfactory as a source of complete personal gratification. While important friendships and loyalties develop within the gang, "the unstable gang context, serving as an arena in which status threats are played out, tends to undermine these friendships and loyalties and makes them shorter lived and less binding."[35] The social roles, traditions, values, and location of the gang may remain relatively intact as members grow out of delinquency into adult crime and as new members become active. Gangs are not dependent upon their present membership for existence. Juvenile gangs are able to continue in spite of the necessary fluctuations in personnel.

In his research on gang delinquency, Short has documented several specific group processes and mechanisms that are involved in delinquency episodes. These are reactions to status threats, the gamble of status versus punishment risk, and the discharge of group obligations. They have been thus described:

(1) *Reactions to status threats.* When gang boys perceive threats to some valued status, delinquency often follows. This mechanism has been found to operate in response to perceived threats to leadership status, to a boy's status as a male, as a member of a particular gang, as an aspiring adult. It may operate individually or collectively, though the delinquent solution characteristically involves other members of the group. Why status threats should produce delinquency episodes doubtless is a very complex matter, but we have observed several characteristics of gang boys and their social worlds which apparently are related to this mechanism. There is, first of all, the lack among gangs of formal structure which lends itself to group continuity and stability. There is further the lack of institutionalized support in adversity which characterizes more formal organizations such as voluntary associations, schools, churches, businesses, and governments. At a more individual level leaders are able to control few resources of crucial value to the group and so their own ability to dominate the group by internally directed aggression is severely restricted. Gang members tend to lack social skills which might permit them to meet status threats in more creative, less delinquent ways. At the group level, delinquent actions often are acceptable, if not generally prescribed by, group norms. They constitute a sort of "least common denominator" around which members can rally. Finally, externally directed delinquency, particularly of an aggressive nature, serves to unify these loosely structured groups in common cause. Indeed, the latter appears to operate not only in conjunction with status threats, but independently, as a basic mechanism accounting for delinquency involvement by these youngsters. The point will be further developed at a later point in the chapter.

(2) *The gamble of status v. punishment risk.* In the calculus of decision making, status rewards within the group often tip the scales to-

ward "joining the action," and therefore becoming involved in delinquency, when the chief *risk* in such behavior appears to be the probability of punishment at the hands of a society which seems disinterested in one's personal fate. Episodes which seem to reflect simply a hedonistic orientation to life thus may be seen to involve a rational assessment of probabilities with the resultant decision to risk the consequences of joining the action, going along with the boys, and so on. The decision is understandable in view of the low risk of serious consequences associated with most delinquency episodes, and the somewhat higher probability of associated group rewards consequent to joining the action—the affirmation of friendship bonds, status accruals from performance in an episode, personal satisfaction derived from demonstration of toughness, masculinity and the like.

(3) *The discharge of group role obligations.* As obvious examples, a leader may be *required* to "join the action," or even to precipitate it, given a situation involving *group threat;* a "war counselor" is required to perform when gang conflict appears imminent or is engaged. Centrality in the group, or striving toward this goal, exposes one to involvement in situations with a high "delinquency potential," by means of the previously discussed mechanisms, including those associated with specific roles in the group. Thus, an apparent paradox in our self-concept data may be resolved. As reported elsewhere, boys who describe themselves in "scoutlike" terms (loyal, polite, helpful, religious, obedient) are *more* involved in conflict behavior than are boys who describe themselves as "cool aggressives" (mean, tough, troublesome, and cool). Our interpretation rests upon the connotation of *responsibility* in personal relations and recognition of their implied obligations, characteristic of the scout terms; this, in contrast with cool aggressive terms, each of which carries overtones of disruption or disregard of obligations to associates, or to convention, and of a type of detachment which is the antithesis of reciprocity in personal relations. The scouts, we believe, facilitate cohesive relations and reduce interpersonal tensions in these loosely structured groups. This, in turn, enhances their centrality in the group and so exposes them to situations in which role expectations, status threats, and potential rewards associated with joining the action make more likely their involvement in episodes of aggression.[36]

CORRESPONDENCE BETWEEN CRIMINAL AND LEGITIMATE BEHAVIOR

Conventional offenders are only partially committed to legitimate society. When there is commitment, it is usually sporadic and temporary. A fluctuation in commitment to legitimate society, outside a delinquent or criminal subculture, is evident in much of juvenile delinquency. Sykes and Matza have suggested that delinquents do not completely reject the dominant values and norms of the larger society but only neutralize the values and norms in the course of violating the law. In addition, such delinquents make use of the "subterranean values" of the dominant society, allowing these values to serve as a code of behavior rather than reserving them for only leisure-time activities.[37] Similarly, in a participant observation study of middle-class gangs, another study concluded that middle-class gang delinquency is in part an extension of values held by most members of society.[38] But it appears that delinquents are not fully committed to any particular value system. Matza has suggested that in being uncommitted the delinquent "drifts" between a delinquent and a nondelinquent way of life.

> Drift stands midway between freedom and control. Its basis is an area of the social structure in which control has been loosened, coupled with the abortiveness of adolescent endeavor to organize an autonomous subculture, and thus an independent source of control, around illegal action. The delinquent transiently exists in a limbo between convention and crime, responding in turn to the demands of each, flirting now with one, now the other, but postponing commitment, evading decision. Thus, he drifts between criminal and conventional action.[39]

Various theories have been advanced to explain delinquent gang behavior that leads to adult crime, a problem that is crucial in understanding the conventional type of criminal behavior.[40] Nearly all of them have sought to view gang behavior within the general patterns of behavior of legitimate society. Some of these delinquent gang theories have been provocative but have revealed serious limitations and, therefore, will not be discussed here.[41] Unfortunately, nearly all gang theories are limited to explaining lower class urban gang delinquency, despite the fact that gang delinquency also occurs in the middle class and appears to be increasing.

The most likely explanation appears to be one that combines the value of the local adult slum community with status striving within the gang. A delinquent gang is patterned and influenced as part of a larger social order; it is a functioning part of the neighborhood social system of which it is a part.[42] To some, gang delinquency is a product of the values of the hard core lower-class slum culture. Miller has identified these lower-class adult focal concerns as trouble, toughness, smartness, excitement, fate, and autonomy.[43] First there is concern over "trouble," with some attempts to avoid it and others to seek it. Second, there is concern for *"toughness"* as lower-class men often feel a need to show their physical powers, "masculinity," and bravery. "Smartness" centers on the capacity to outsmart, outfox, outwit, dupe, "take," or "con" another, as well as on the ability to avoid being "taken" oneself. "Excitement" and the search for thrills characterize many features of lower-class life; examples include the use of alcohol and often narcotics, gambling, and the recurrent practice of taking a "night on the town." Much emphasis is put on "fate" or luck by many who believe they have little control over forces affecting their lives. "Autonomy" is the final concern of the lower-class culture. External controls and restrictions on behavior and authority that seem coercive and unjust are bitterly denounced, although often actually they are desired. In a study of 350 gang members, Miller claims that his hypothesis is upheld as an explanation of frequent theft—"being male, being in middle adolescence and of lower status."[44] In fact, in his study, contrary to several others, whites were somewhat more likely to be involved in theft than blacks, indicating that lower social status was greater than other differentiating factors. Cloward and Ohlin have stressed much the same theme that in integrated slum areas adult criminal patterns serve as models and available illegitimate means for gangs to engage in theft and similar activities to achieve status and illegal income.[45] Their theory, however, also includes the idea that gang behavior arises where opportunities to achieve the monetary, occupational, and educational goals of society are blocked;[46] this part of the theory has been severely criticized.

An additional factor appears to be status striving within the gang itself. Short and Strodtbeck reported that they found delinquent gang behavior to be the result of status strivings within the gang rather than the product of class mobility limitation.[47] Of great importance was the delinquent boy's self-concept in the context of the group. In fact, some delinquent acts were status-maintaining functions, as seen in the attempts of the gang leader to maintain his status when threatened. He accomplishes this by getting the gang to commit delinquent acts. Gang behavior is thus a rational balancing of immediate loss of status within the group and the risk of punishment.

There is evidence that gang delinquency results from failure to achieve status within the context of the adult, middle-class-dominated institutions, such as the school, church, and economic and political institutions. The formation of the delinquent subculture involves the establishment of new groups with new rules and regulations by which members may compete successfully to obtain status. The solutions for lower-class boys provided by delinquent subcultures are primarily status rewarding, rather than economically rewarding, as suggested by the differential opportunity explanation. Frequently gang boys want money to buy status rewards within the group, for example, "sharp" clothes and for "kicks," alcoholic beverages, and drugs.

The importance of youth status is not confined to the delinquent gang for gang behavior appears to arise in general as an attempt by adolescents to gain status that is denied them by adults because of their age.[48] Delinquency problems result when a society does not provide meaningful functions for adolescents.[49] Fyvel has seen the increase of gang delinquency in Great Britain, and in other "affluent" societies, as the failure to provide meaningful symbols for adjustment and fulfillment in place of the symbols once provided by a class-dominated society.[50]

Other writers also emphasize the relevance of the age transition hypothesis of gang delinquency. In separate works, Erikson and Friedenberg have argued that adolescence is a time for experimentation, a period for establishing an identity prior to the adoption of adult roles.[51] Problems of identity appear to be particularly pressing in contemporary society. Gang delinquency may be one of the attempts to achieve identity and meaningfulness. The question is why does gang delinquency serve this function for some youths while other social arrangements serve this function for other youths. The answer is probably related to the location of the youth in the general structure of the society.

Most theories of gang behavior have attempted to provide a central framework for explaining delinquency in terms of basic concepts such as social class, role, and status aspirations. In general they are attempts to explain the reasons for gang delinquency in lower-class areas in large urban areas of the United States. There is some question as to their value in adequately explaining delinquency in the middle-class, small cities, or rural areas in this country, or the delinquency in those countries that have different class structures and values.[52] In summary, the lack of communication among the various age peer groups that has arisen with pronounced urbanism, may more accurately explain the development of adolescent delinquent subcultures, together with the acquisition of deviant norms as forms of status and excitement, particularly in slum areas.

SOCIETAL REACTION AND LEGAL PROCESSING

The severe reaction against persons who engage in conventional offenses, both in penalties and the likelihood of conviction, is a reflection of the power of those in the middle and upper classes to see that such offenses of the lower class are punished much more severely than are occupational or white collar property offenses. It is also influenced by the value placed on private property in American and in many other societies. In general, the differential punishment for certain criminal behavior, through the formulation and administration of criminal law, is the domain or groups in positions of power.[53] In the case of laws on property crime, "legislation will tend to erect the most formidable barriers against vulnerable segments of the society which attempt to usurp the properties of the entrenched elements."[54] An understanding of who defines behavior as criminal is as essential in the study of conventional crime as it is in the study of criminal behavior in general.

Many gang delinquents drift into adult criminality because they were arrested at an early age and encounter increasing rejection by the larger society.

Conceivably, one of the contingencies which influences the development of delinquent careers on the part of working class boys is the experience of early apprehension by the police, often an almost chance happening. . . . We may well find that, as boys get caught up in flirtations with deviant behavior, they encounter societal rejection which then impairs their adjustment to school and other social institutions, so they are driven further into delinquent conduct.[55]

The official processing of conventional criminal offenders results in the end in a lengthy series of arrests and convictions. The type of offenses they commit, often with not a great degree of skill, may lead to a considerable risk of apprehension and a high risk of conviction and incarceration in penal institutions. In this regard they are quite different from professional criminals. Many spend a considerable part of their lives in correctional institutions, possibly withdrawing from crime in their late thirties or early forties. Since society generally holds against a man his imprisonment rather than what he did, they are among the most stigmatized of all offenders.

According to national figures for the United States, less than one out of every five burglaries and auto thefts is cleared by arrest, but about 85 percent of all stolen autos are recovered. Most autos are stolen for "joyriding"; about one-fourth of autos are stolen for resale, stripping of parts, or use in another crime. From one-fourth to one-third of robberies are solved by arrest. Most offenders arrested for robbery are picked up at or near the scene soon after a robbery takes place.[56] Few robberies lead to arrest after a few days, indicating the importance of getting rapidly away from the scene.

The chance of being arrested and prosecuted for robbery is only about 25 percent, according to a Boston study, and approximately five out of nine persons arrested for robbery are convicted, many for a reduced charge.[57] Whether a suspect gets convicted or not depends on such factors as "the type of lawyer who defends him, his ability to get released on bail, the way he is arrested, and the type of robbery he is accused of committing."[58] Of the cases handled by the superior courts in 1968 nearly two-thirds (59.3 percent) were sent to prison. In a Philadelphia study of 1722 persons arrested for robbery, a 10 percent sample from 1960–1966, two-thirds of those taken into police custody and over three-fourths of those who experienced a court trial were convicted.[59] Blacks were convicted only slightly more frequently than were whites.

Of the convicted Philadelphia offenders, 44.9 percent received a penitentiary sentence (11.7 percent received 5 years or more, 8.1 percent from 3 to 5 years, 9.0 percent from 2 to 3 years, and 16.1 percent from 1 to 2 years); 31.0 percent received a prison sentence (3 to 11 months); and 24.1 percent received a nonimprisonment sentence (11.3 percent had a short-term jail sentence of less than 3 months, 10.3 percent had probation, 2.5 percent had a suspended sentence, and only one individual was fined).[60]

An analysis of the severity of sentences by selected social and legal variables indicated that the following variables were significantly associated with higher court severity: male offender, armed robbery, guilty on two or more bills of indictment, and a prior conviction record for robbery or felony against the person. Although not statistically significant, a young offender (under 21 years of age), a stolen money amount of less than 50 dollars, and an offense with no accomplice and which was not violent, are variables associated with less severe penalties. The most influential element, however, is the number and type of prior criminal conviction.[61]

In the administration of the law, conventional offenders are handled according to certain preconceived notions about their characteristics and behavior. Conventional offenders are among those offenders who usually do not reach the trial stage of the judicial process because their cases are settled by a plea of guilty. The prosecuting attorney and defense attorney through "bargaining" often alter the charge in order to avoid a trial. Since the penal code does not provide instructions for making decisions on complaint alterations, other guides must be devised by the attorneys. According to Sudnow, attorneys place concrete cases into more general categories of behavioral events.[62] For example, rather than referring to the statutory definition of burglary, reference is made to a nonstatutorily defined class of "burglaries," which Sudnow terms *normal burglaries*. On the basis of a characterization of a normal or typical burglary, attorneys are able to agree upon an appropriate reduction from the original charge, such as reducing a "typical" burglary to petty theft. Thus, an abstract behavioral type is used by those who officially react to conventional crime, as well as by those who study crime.

The programs used in the treatment and prevention of conventional crime are generally based on a conservative ideology. The approaches to juvenile delinquency, for example, have usually consisted of custody, rehabilitation, or redirection of individuals and families, overlooking the relation of offenders to more basic social conditions. "None of these efforts aims at social change conceived of in broad terms. They take the side of discipline, law and order, and rehabilitation, but not of social reform."[63] In general, little effort is made to change a local community, such as a slum, by enlisting large-scale citizen participation and developing indigenous leadership and self-help to overcome norms, values, and situations which contribute to delinquency and crime.[64]

By nature of the function they are asked to fulfill, and the methods by which they are expected to fulfill it, most agencies aimed at curbing delinquency tend to be conservative. By public definition, they are caring for youths who have deviated from the expected values or behavior of the established community and they are seeking to train youths to maintain a greater degree of conformity. In doing this, juvenile courts, psychiatric clinics, training schools, and similar agencies act to conserve the accepted values and behavior patterns of the community. They are a force for the preservation of the *status quo*. Traditionally, then, such agencies have either provided custodial care for the delinquent or sought to change the character of the delinquent. They have given very little attention to the nature of the social institutions from which their cases have deviated.[65]

Only recently have a considerable number of programs been instituted that go beyond the conservative ideology that has long dominated the social reaction to crime and in particular the crimes of conventional offenders.

NOTES

[1] Walter C. Reckless, *The Crime Problem*, 3d ed. (New York: Appleton-Century-Crofts, 1961), pp. 159–161.

[2] Marshall B. Clinard, *Sociology of Deviant Behavior*, 3d ed. (New York: Holt, Rinehart and Winston, 1968), pp. 256–258.

[3] *Crime in the United States.* Uniform Crime Reports—1970 (Washington, D.C.: U. S. Government Printing Office, 1971).

[4] André Normandeau, "Violence and Robbery: A Case Study," *Acta Criminologica*, 5 (1972), p. 77.

[5] Edwin H. Sutherland and Donald R. Cressey, *Criminology*, 8th ed. (Philadelphia: J. B. Lippincott Company, 1970).

[6] Marshall B. Clinard, *Slums and Community Development: Experiments in Self-Help* (New York: The Free Press, Macmillan Company, 1966).

[7] See Harold S. Frum, "Adult Criminal Offense Trends Following Juvenile Delinquency," *Journal of Criminal Law, Criminology and Police Science*, 49 (May–June 1958), pp. 29–49.

[8] Gerald D. Robin, "Gang Delinquency in Philadelphia," in Malcolm W. Klein, ed., *Juvenile Gangs in Context: Theory, Research, and Action* (Englewood-Cliffs, N.J.: Prentice-Hall, 1967).

[9] *Ibid.*, p. 24.

[10] Julian B. Roebuck and Mervyn L. Cadwallader, "The Negro Armed Robber as a Criminal Type: The Construction and Application of a Typology," *Pacific Sociological Review*, 4 (Spring 1961), p. 24.

[11] Don C. Gibbons, *Changing the Lawbreaker: The Treatment of Delinquents and Criminals*, © 1965, Prentice-Hall, Inc., Englewood Cliffs, N.J., p. 105.

[12] John E. Conklin, *Robbery and the Criminal Justice System* (Philadelphia: J. B. Lippincott Company, 1972), pp. 103–105.

[13] Normandeau, "Violence and Robbery," p. 83.

[14] A similar estimation is made in Russell R. Dynes, Alfred C. Clarke, Simon Dinitz, and Iwao Ishino, *Social Problems: Dissensus and Deviation in an Industrial Society* (New York: Oxford University Press, 1964), p. 543.

[15] Gibbons, *Changing the Lawbreaker*, p. 105.

[16] Henry D. McKay, "Report on the Criminal Careers of Male Delinquents in Chicago," *Task Force Report: Juvenile Delinquency and Youth Crime*. The

President's Commission on Law Enforcement and Administration of Justice (Washington, D.C.: U. S. Government Printing Office, 1967), p. 111.

17 Werner J. Einstadter, "The Social Organization of Armed Robbery," *Social Problems*, 17 (Summer 1969), pp. 64–82.

18 Reckless, *The Crime Problem*, p. 164.

19 Carl Werthman, "The Function of Social Definitions in the Development of Delinquency Career," *Task Force Report: Juvenile Delinquency and Youth Crime*, p. 170.

20 *The Challenge of Crime in a Free Society.* President's Commission on Law Enforcement and Administration of Justice (Washington, D.C.: U. S. Government Printing Office, 1967), p. 35. Authors' italics.

21 Clifford R. Shaw and Henry D. McKay, *Juvenile Delinquency and Urban Areas*, rev. ed. (Chicago: University of Chicago Press, 1969). Also see *Task Force Report: Crime and Its Impact*, Chap. 4.

22 *Task Force Report: Juvenile Delinquency and Youth Crime*, p. 110.

23 Bernard Rosenberg and Harry Silverstein, *The Varieties of Delinquent Experience* (Waltham, Mass.: Blaisdell Publishing Company, Ginn and Company, 1969), p. 97.

24 Clinard, *Slums and Community Development.* Also see Gerald D. Suttles, *The Social Order of the Slum: Ethnicity and Territory in the Inner City* (Chicago: University of Chicago Press, 1968). Even when the physical conditions, as in slum rehousing projects, are changed the slum way of life persists. See William Moore, Jr., *The Vertical Ghetto: Everyday Life in an Urban Project* (New York: Random House, 1969) and Lee Rainwater, *Behind Ghetto Walls: Black Families in a Federal Slum* (Chicago: Aldine Publishing Company, 1970). The slum way of life is often associated with blacks who are more likely to be the present residents of slums in the United States. Formerly at various times, immigrants from Sweden, Poland, and Italy were primarily slum area residents. Today many are white southerners from Appalachia. See Todd Gitlin and Nanci Hollander, *Uptown: Poor Whites in Chicago* (New York: Harper & Row, Publishers, 1970).

25 Frederick M. Thrasher, *The Gang* (Chicago: University of Chicago Press, 1927).

26 Clifford R. Shaw and Henry D. McKay, "Social Factors in Juvenile Delinquency," *The Causes of Crime.* National Commission on Law Observance and Enforcement (Washington, D.C.: U. S. Government Printing Office, 1931), Report no. 13, Vol. 2. Also see William F. Whyte, *Street Corner Society* (Chicago: University of Chicago Press, 1943).

27 *The Challenge of Crime in a Free Society*, p. 66. For a survey of various findings, see Thomas G. Eynon and Walter C. Reckless, "Companionship at Delinquency Onset," *British Journal of Criminology*, 2 (1961), pp. 162–170.

28 Shaw and McKay, "Social Factors in Juvenile Delinquency," *Report on the Causes of Crime*, 262–285.

29 Donald J. Mulvihill and Melvin Tumin, *Crimes of Violence.* National Commission on the Causes and Prevention of Violence, Staff Report Series, (Washington, D.C.: U. S. Government Printing Office, 1970), Vol. 12, p. 610.

30 Conklin, *Robbery*, p. 99.

31 William R. Arnold, "The Concept of Gang," *The Sociological Quarterly*, 7 (Winter 1966), pp. 59–75.

32 "Juvenile Delinquency," monograph of the Institute for Juvenile Research and the Chicago Area Project, Chicago, 1953, p. 5. For a discussion of recent research on group cohesion and member interaction in delinquent gangs, see

LaMar T. Empey, "Delinquency Theory and Recent Research," *Journal of Research in Crime and Delinquency*, 4 (1967), pp. 28–42.

33 Clifford R. Shaw, Henry D. McKay, and James F. McDonald, *Brothers in Crime* (Chicago: University of Chicago Press, 1938).

34 Clifford R. Shaw, *The Natural History of a Delinquent Career* (Chicago: University of Chicago Press, 1931), pp. 230–231.

35 James F. Short, Jr., and Fred L. Strodtbeck, *Group Process and Gang Delinquency* (Chicago: University of Chicago Press, 1965), p. 283.

36 James F. Short, Jr., "Social Structure and Group Processes in Gang Delinquency." Reprinted from Muzafer Sherif and Carolyn W. Sherif, editors, *Problems of Youth: Transition to Adulthood in a Changing World* (Chicago: Aldine Publishing Company, 1965); copyright © 1965 by Muzafer Sherif and Carolyn W. Sherif. Reprinted by permission of the authors and Aldine-Atherton, Inc. Also see Short and Strodtbeck, *Group Process and Gang Delinquency*.

37 Gresham M. Sykes and David Matza, "Techniques of Neutralization: A Theory of Delinquency," *American Sociological Review*, 22 (December 1957), pp. 664–670; and David Matza and Gresham M. Sykes, "Juvenile Delinquency and Subterranean Values," *American Sociological Review*, 26 (October 1961), pp. 712–719.

38 Harold L. Myerhoff and Barbara G. Myerhoff, "Field Observations of Middle Class 'Gangs,'" *Social Forces*, 42 (March 1964), pp. 328–336. Also see Ralph W. England, Jr., "A Theory of Middle Class Juvenile Delinquency," *Journal of Criminal Law, Criminology and Police Science*, 50 (March–April 1960), pp. 535–540.

39 David Matza, *Delinquency and Drift* (New York: John Wiley & Sons, 1964), p. 28.

40 This is quite a different problem from delinquent gang behavior in general. Such behavior occurs in the middle class but is unlikely to continue for any length of time or to develop a career pattern. Edmund W. Vaz, ed., *Middle-Class Juvenile Delinquency* (New York: Harper & Row, Publishers, 1967).

41 Cohen, for example, has suggested that gang behavior is a product of lower-class hostility to middle-class standards of behavior, such as school insistence on ambition, postponement of immediate satisfactions, respect for property, good manners, and so forth. Albert K. Cohen, *Delinquent Boys: The Culture of the Gang* (New York: The Free Press, Macmillan Company, 1955). This theory has been severely criticized. See, for example, David J. Bordua, "Delinquent Subcultures: Sociological Interpretations of Gang Delinquency," *The Annals*, 338 (November 1961), pp. 119–136; and J. I. Kitsuse and D. C. Dietrick, "Delinquent Boys: A Critique," *American Sociological Review*, 24 (1959), pp. 211–212.

42 Albert S. Alissi, "Delinquent Subcultures in Neighborhood Settings: A Social System Perspective," *Journal of Research in Crime and Delinquency*, 7 (January 1970), pp. 46–57.

43 Walter B. Miller, "Lower Class Culture as a Generating Milieu of Gang Delinquency," *Journal of Social Issues*, 14 (1958), No. 3, pp. 5–19.

44 Walter B. Miller, "Theft Behavior in City Gangs," in Malcolm W. Klein, ed., *Juvenile Gangs in Context: Theory, Research, and Action* (Englewood Cliffs, N.J.: Prentice-Hall, 1967), p. 37.

45 Richard A. Cloward and Lloyd E. Ohlin, *Delinquency and Opportunity: A Theory of Delinquent Gangs* (New York: The Free Press, Macmillan Company, 1960).

46 For a criticism of this theory and that of Cohen see Bordua, "Delinquent Subcultures."

[47] Short and Strodtbeck, *Group Process and Gang Delinquency.*
[48] Herbert A. Bloch and Arthur Niederhoffer, *The Gang: A Study of Adolescent Behavior* (New York: Philosophical Library, 1948). This approach finds support in S. N. Eisenstadt, *From Generation to Generation* (New York: The Free Press, Macmillan Company, 1956); also in Gerald Marwell, "Adolescent Powerlessness and Delinquency," *Social Problems,* **14** (1966), pp. 35–47.
[49] Paul Goodman, *Growing Up Absurd* (New York: Random House, 1960).
[50] T. R. Fyvel, *Troublemakers: Rebellious Youth in an Affluent Society* (New York: Schocken Books, 1961).
[51] Eric H. Erikson, *Childhood and Society* (New York: W. W. Norton Publishing Company, 1950); and Edgar Z. Friedenberg, *The Vanishing Adolescent* (New York: Dell & Company, 1962).
[52] A study of small city gangs concluded that there were many more similarities than differences between small city and metropolitan city gangs, but that no theoretical system explains adequately the gang dynamics in such areas. See Dale G. Hardman, "Small Town Gangs," *Journal of Criminal Law, Criminology and Police Science,* **60** (June 1969), pp. 173–181.
[53] Thorsten Sellin, *Culture Conflict and Crime* (New York: Social Science Research Council, 1938), Chap. 2; and Richard Quinney, "Crime in Political Perspective," *American Behavioral Scientist,* **8** (December 1964), pp. 19–22; and Richard Quinney, *The Social Reality of Crime* (Boston: Little, Brown and Company), 1970.
[54] Herbert A. Bloch and Gilbert Geis, *Man, Crime, and Society* (New York: Random House, 1962), p. 316.
[55] Don C. Gibbons, *Society, Crime, and Criminal Careers: In Introduction to Criminology* (Englewood Cliffs, N. J.: Prentice-Hall, 1968), p. 280.
[56] Conklin, *Robbery,* p. 183.
[57] *Ibid.,* p. 184.
[58] Normandeau, "Violence and Robbery," p. 83.
[59] *Ibid.*
[60] *Ibid.,* p. 59.
[61] *Ibid.,* p. 83.
[62] David Sudnow, "Normal Crimes: Sociological Features of the Penal Code in a Public Defender Office," *Social Problems,* **12** (Winter 1965), pp. 255–276. Also see William R. Arnold, "The Concept of Gang," *The Sociological Quarterly,* **7** (Winter 1966), pp. 59–75.
[63] John M. Martin and Joseph P. Fitzpatrick, *Delinquent Behavior: A Redefinition of the Problem* (New York: Random House, 1964), p. 37. Also see Alissi, "Delinquent Subcultures in Neighborhood Settings."
[64] Clinard, *Slums and Community Development.*
[65] Martin and Fitzpatrick, *Delinquent Behavior,* pp. 10–11.

SELECTED BIBLIOGRAPHY

Bloch, Herbert A., and Niederhoffer, Arthur, *The Gang: A Study in Adolescent Behavior.* New York: Philosophical Library, 1958.
Bordua, David J., "A Critique of Sociological Interpretations of Gang Delinquency." *The Annals,* **338** (November 1961), pp. 119–136.
Clinard, Marshall B., *Slums and Community Development.* New York: The Free Press, Macmillan Company, 1966.

Cloward, Richard A., and Ohlin, Lloyd E., *Delinquency and Opportunity: A Theory of Delinquent Gangs.* New York: The Free Press, Macmillan Company, 1960.

Conklin, John E., *Robbery and the Criminal Justice System.* Philadelphia: J. P. Lippincott Company, 1972.

Einstadter, Werner J., "The Social Organization of Armed Robbery," *Social Problems,* **17** (Summer 1969), pp. 64–82.

Empey, LaMar T., "Delinquency Theory and Recent Research." *Journal of Research in Crime and Delinquency,* **4** (1967). pp. 28–42.

Gibbons, Don C., *Changing the Lawbreaker.* Englewood Cliffs, N.J.: Prentice-Hall, 1965.

Klein, Malcolm W., ed., *Juvenile Gangs in Context: Theory, Research, and Action.* Englewood Cliffs, N. J.: Prentice-Hall, 1967.

Kobrin, Solomon, "The Conflict of Values in Delinquency Areas." *American Sociological Review,* **16** (October 1951), pp. 653–661.

McClintock, F. H., and Gibson, Evelyn, *Robbery in London: An Enquiry by the Cambridge Institute of Criminology.* London: Macmillan & Co., 1961.

Matza, David, *Delinquency and Drift.* New York: John Wiley & Sons, 1964.

———, and Sykes, Gresham, M., "Juvenile Delinquency and Subterranean Values." *American Sociological Review,* **26** (October 1961), pp. 712–719.

Miller, Walter B., "Lower Class Culture as a Generating Milieu of Gang Delinquency." *Journal of Social Issues,* **14** (1958), No. 3, pp. 5–19.

Normandeau, André, "Violence and Robbery: A Case Study," *Acta Criminologica,* **5** (1972), pp. 11–107.

President's Commission on Law Enforcement and Administration of Justice, *Task Force Report: Juvenile Delinquency and Youth Crime.* Washington, D.C.: U. S. Government Printing Office, 1967.

Roebuck, Julian B., and Cadwallader, Mervyn L., "The Negro Armed Robber as a Criminal Type: The Contruction and Application of a Typology." *Pacific Sociological Review,* **4** (Spring 1961), pp. 21–26.

Roebuck, Julian B., and Johnson, Ronald, "The Jack-of-All Trades Offender." *Crime and Delinquency,* **8** (April 1962), pp. 172–181.

Rosenberg, Bernard, and Silverstein, Harry, *The Varieties of Delinquent Experience.* Waltham, Mass.: Blaisdell Publishing Company, Ginn and Company, 1969.

Scott, Peter, "Gangs and Delinquent Groups in London." *British Journal of Delinquency,* **7** (July 1956), pp. 4–26.

Shaw, Clifford R., *The Jack Roller.* Chicago: University of Chicago Press, 1930.

———, and McKay, Henry D., *Juvenile Delinquency and Urban Areas,* rev. ed. Chicago: University of Chicago Press, 1969.

Short, James F. Jr., "Social Structure and Group Processes in Gang Delinquency," in Muzafer Sherif and Carolyn W. Sherif, eds., *Problems of Youth: Transition to Adulthood in a Changing World.* Chicago: Aldine Publishing Company, 1965.

———, and Strodtbeck, Fred L., *Group Process and Gang Delinquency.* Chicago: University of Chicago Press, 1965.

Spergel, Irving, *Racketville, Slumtown, Haulburg: An Exploratory Study of Delinquent Subcultures.* Chicago: University of Chicago Press, 1964.

Suttles, Gerald D., *The Social Order of the Slum: Ethnicity and Territory in the Inner City.* Chicago: University of Chicago Press, 1968.

Sykes, Gresham M., and Matza, David, "Techniques of Neutralization: A Theory of Delinquency." *American Sociological Review,* **22** (December 1957), pp. 664–670.

Thrasher, Frederick M., *The Gang: A Study of 1313 Gangs in Chicago.* abr. ed., Chicago: University of Chicago Press, 1963.

Vaz, Edmund W., "Juvenile Gang Delinquency in Paris." *Social Problems,* **10** (Summer 1962), pp. 23–31.

————, ed. *Middle-Class Juvenile Delinquency.* New York: Harper & Row, Publishers, 1967.

Political 6
Criminal Behavior

Law is a political instrument of government. Governments use the law to legitimate and perpetuate their control. Political crime exists whenever the state invokes its laws to punish those who present a threat to the government. But it is also true that governments violate the law. The crimes by government are usually committed for alleged reasons of state.

Thus, in a discussion of political crime, a distinction must be made between two kinds of criminal behavior: crimes against government and crimes by government. The first form of political crime is familiar to most criminologists, while the latter is usually ignored. Crime against government is recognized in attempts to protest, express beliefs about, or alter in some way the existing social structure. The violations—be they in violation of laws created for the suppression of such behavior or for other purposes (such as loitering and parading without a permit) but enforced for political reasons—are regarded by political authorities as detrimental to the state as it exists. Included in political crime is a wide range of behaviors: treason, sedition, sabotage, assassination, violation of military draft regulations, civil rights violations, student protest violations, violations resulting from the advocacy and support of "radical" ideas and actions, and failure to conform to certain laws because of religious beliefs.

On the other hand, crime by government consists of the criminal violations by governments themselves, or more particularly, by the agents of the government. Governmental crime can be further divided into: (1) violations of the civil liberties and rights of the citizens, as in the violation of constitutional guarantees and civil rights legislation by various government officials; (2) criminal acts committed in the course of enforcing the laws of the state, as in the example of assault and murder by police and prison guards; and (3) violations of higher laws by governments, particularly the violation of the international laws of warfare. In attempting to preserve a particular social and political order, therefore, governments and their officials violate laws which exist to protect the citizen from the abuses of government. That governments do not usually choose to prosecute themselves when these laws are broken does not make the violations any less criminal.

LEGAL ASPECTS OF SELECTED OFFENSES

Crime against Government

Political freedom is always qualified. The history of America is replete with laws that have been enacted and enforced in order to contain apparent threats to the status quo. Freedom of speech has been abridged, for example, by the Sedition Act of 1798, which provided for the punishment of anyone who uttered or published statements against the government, and by the strengthening of the Espionage Act in 1918.[1] Legal controls relating to security as well as to economic matters have been established during the emergencies of war,[2] and concern over native communism has occurred during postwar instability and unrest.[3]

The federal statutes are filled with other antisubversive provisions enacted during national crises. To name only a few, the Voorhis Act of 1940 restricted the registration of persons and organizations who acted as agents of foreign powers; the Smith Act of 1940 forbade the advocacy of the overthrow of the government; the Internal Security Act of 1950 (McCarran Act) required the registration of Communist and Communist-front organizations as well as strengthened other legislation on subversion; the Immigration and Nationality Act of 1952 (McCarran-Walter Act) provided for the deportation of resident aliens because of "disloyal" beliefs and associates; and the Communist Control Act of 1954 required the registration of Communist party members with the Attorney General. In addition to such legislation, loyalty and security programs have been initiated and black-list procedures have been established.[4]

While political freedom is a delicate and dubious matter in all political democracies, it is a particular problem in the United States. It seems apparent that Americans, as compared to other peoples in representative governments, are especially intolerant of social and political differences.[5] This intolerance is expressed in the denial of various civil rights to certain social and political minority groups, religious groups, racial and ethnic groups, and political dissenters. Numerous criminal laws and rulings have been formulated to handle these differences. Certain behaviors by political minorities committed out of conscience have been made illegal. In addition to the numerous acts that have been defined as subversive (by the groups in power), attempts to express dissatisfaction with nuclear testing, civil defense, racial discrimination, and war have been subject to criminal action. A host of previously existing laws have been used in the suppression of dissent and protest. Demonstrators for racial civil rights and other causes have been arrested on such charges as disorderly conduct, breach of peace, parading without a permit, trespassing, loitering, and violation of fire ordinances. Under other laws, persons have been arrested for refusing to pay income taxes used for military purposes, for picketing military bases, for engaging in student protests, and for refusing to register for the draft. All of these behaviors share the common element that the offenders are pursuing values out of conscience and conviction, but the values are different from those of the groups that are formulating and administering the criminal law. The result is that some persons are being defined as criminals.

The criminal laws that have been established to control perceived threats to the state are patently political. They make no apologies for their direct political intent. The existing political regime is to be honored and protected from any internal or external dangers. The purpose of the law is to uphold the state and to protect its ruling class. Even when certain procedural guarantees are recognized, such as due process and the right of civil disobedience, the law can be qualified at every point in order to maintain the status quo.

In respect to the instrumental functioning of the state, nowhere is this qualification of law better illustrated than in the military conscription laws. The involvement of the United States in Southeast Asia is recent years has brought new light to this matter. Those persons of draft age who can show an absolute pacifism on religious grounds can avoid military servitude. For the government that wages a war and needs men for the military, this provision does not hamper its functions. But suppose a significant number of men refused to fight on the legal ground of the right not to kill, that is, on the basis of selective conscientious objection to a particular war. There might well then be a military manpower shortage. Up to the present time the government has successfully thwarted efforts to change the draft laws. Yet, there may well be constitutional grounds to support selective conscientious objection.[6] But until the time such a right is legally recognized, those who claim this right will be defined as criminal.

Conspiracy and related laws are among the best examples of the government's attempt to assure its own survival. Legal cases in recent years, especially the cases of the Boston Five (regarding a "conspiracy" to aid the violation of the Selective Service law) and the Chicago Eight (associated with the demonstrations during the 1968 Democratic Convention), have shown the extent to which the government will politically use the law to ward off any apparent dangers. In these cases the most dubious charges have been made, the most questionable being that of "conspiracy." As a political weapon, the conspiracy law requires that the prosecution merely show that the defendants conspired, or rather, communicated in some way regarding a demonstration, draft resistance, or whatever. The prosecution need not show that the defendants actually engaged in particular overt acts, but merely that they said something. Among other things, whether or not the defendants are convicted, the conspiracy law is an effective form of political harassment whereby those who threaten the system can be detained for long periods of time at great personal expense.

The so-called antiriot laws also accomplish similar objectives for the state. Six of the eight Chicago defendants were prosecuted under 18 U.S.

Code 2101 and 2102, the newest federal antiriot act. The act makes it a felony to travel in interstate commerce with the intent to incite or participate in a riot. "Riot" is defined in the statute as any assemblage of three or more persons, in which at least one person threatens injury to another person or property, or actually does injure another person or property. The act was conceived in response to the ghetto riots of the 1960s. Speaking for an earlier version of the law, a statement by a congressman from Georgia illustrates that the act was a simplistic attempt to solve urban disorders by striking at the "outside agitators" who supposedly were behind the outbreaks of civil disorder:

> There is impressive evidence that many of the riots which have been plaguing our cities have been incited by persons who have been traveling from one city to another, deliberately stirring up trouble. We have all heard that in so many instances, preceding a riot, an outside agitator has appeared in the community to harangue an audience concerning the grievances. Sometimes those grievances have been real, sometimes they have not. But real or not, often the speeches of these agitators have been criminally inflammatory, and often in clear violation of our laws against inciting to riot.[7]

On the basis of such thinking, laws of consequence are enacted.

However, the most insidious, yet blatant, tactic used by the government against its citizens (including its political offenders) is the refusal to publicly and legally recognize the concept of political crime. Why is this? The reason seems to lie in the Anglo-American doctrine of legalism: that obedience to the existing law is a moral absolute.

> The situation in English and American society is often viewed as if all members of these societies had agreed to disagree on matters of morals and politics (we may doubt, however, how deep this disagreement has ever been), but agreed that all would respect the law because the law protected the right of each to his own separate opinion and a certain freedom in the expression of it. It is on a spirit of compromise and limited struggle within the legal rules of the game that the stability of English and American political institutions depends, and it is commonly felt that there would be anarchy without it.[8]

Since opposition to the government could not be legally *and* morally recognized, political crime as a concept could not be incorporated into the law. Political offenders have usually been dealt with under "nonpolitical" laws. The political offender has been officially handled in the same way as the conventional offender. To admit the concept of political crime into domestic jurisprudence would be to recognize the limitations of liberal democracy (that is, democratic elitism). Those in power, according to the present legal system, can effectively use the law to their own advantage.

Crime by Government

Criminologists, like most persons, have been reluctant to face the possibility that government can act criminally.[9] Following a classic image of government, we have tended to regard governments as being above the law. Since governments supposedly have sovereignty over the people, governments are to control the citizenry—not to regulate themselves. Only in the more radical tradition is government regarded as an artificial institution created by the people to serve their needs. But as long as the classic tradition is followed—with government having complete sovereignty—the immunity of government from the law is tacitly accepted.

When a radical conception of democracy is held, however, it readily becomes apparent that governments as the principal makers and enforcers of law are also lawbreakers. If the law is to some extent an institution of the citizenry, then the law can be used to protect the people from harms committed against them by those who act in the name of the government. It need not be paradoxical that those who make and enforce the law are lawbreakers.

What we have tended to adopt in the past, then, is a double standard toward crime. The major emphasis has been on crimes against the government (or "society") to the almost total neglect of crimes committed by the government against the people. One standard of legality and appropriate conduct has been maintained for one order of events while another standard has been used for the other. A case in point is the way we view violence by the state in comparison to violence by individual citizens:

> The American creed enshrines the concept of law (a government of laws, not of men) but has failed to realize that the law itself can be an oppressive instrument used by those in power to justify the status quo. An ethical dilemma is created when violence is used to support, as well as attack, the democratic system, when a double standard is used to judge violence: the violence of the State (police, military) has been approved and legitimated, whereas the private violence of individuals and groups has been condemned. Undoubtedly, the increasing virulence of dissent today is due to a growing awareness that this double standard is no longer tenable. Even when overt physical violence *is* deplored the more subtle, covert forms of violence inherent in the very system itself are ignored or glossed over.[10]

While individual violence, or even collective violence, has usually been viewed as criminal, similar acts by the government have not been regarded as acts of violence, or at most as instances of "legitimate violence."

Yet with the events of recent years, the existence of crimes by government has been increasingly realized. Governmental crime has become a fact in several areas of contemporary life. The civil rights movement, especially, illustrated the extent to which some local officials will violate the law in order to maintain a particular system. Several Supreme Court decisions and iegislative acts have made certain kinds of behavior—even when committed by government officials—illegal.

Similarly, we have come to realize that many of our civil liberties are being violated by those who are supposed to guarantee these rights. In the name of "law and order," legal agents have violated laws that are to protect such rights as the right of free speech, our right of privacy, and our right of due process. Federal agents have violated the law in the course of surveillance and through the gaining of evidence for criminal prosecution. Moreover, local police have blatantly violated basic human rights as well as the conventional laws of murder and assault in the course of enforcing other laws.[11]

Most recently the criminality of government has become obvious in the war crime allegations against the United States regarding its military conduct in Southeast Asia. An elaborate law of warfare exists to regulate nations in the course of war and to prosecute any violators. And as several writers have recently shown, these laws are applicable to the United States in general and to the Vietnam war in particular.[12] The Nuremberg war crimes trial set a precedent that has come back to haunt Americans: "If certain acts and violations of treaties are crimes," the Chief Prosecutor at Nuremberg observed, "they are crimes whether the United States does them or whether Germany does them."

As with all governmental crimes, however, governments are not inclined to prosecute themselves. While an international law of war crimes is of ancient origin, few nations have ever instituted proceedings to declare their own wartime actions criminal. It is the *victor* who initiates a war crimes trial—against the defeated. Hence, it was the German command that was tried after World War II, rather than American generals. The Anglo-American bombing of the civilian population of Dresden (resulting in the killing of thousands of civilians) was not considered at Nuremberg, but similar activities by the Germans were. To the victors belong not only the spoils, but also the right to prosecute the other side for committing war crimes.

Yet in the case of war crimes, as with all governmental crimes, acts in violation of the law may be observed and studied as criminal offenses. And there are those instances where the legal apparatus rises above the narrow interests of government. Gradually the crimes of government are being recorded into legal history.

CRIMINAL CAREER OF THE OFFENDER

Crime against Government

Political behaviors that may be defined as criminal by the state are many and varied. Nevertheless, political offenders share some general characteristics. First, political offenders do not usually conceive of themselves as criminals and do not identify with crime. However, when the government continues to define these persons as outlaws, they may begin to conceive of themselves as criminals against the state. In fact, to do so may become a part of the radical life.

Second, for most political offenders violation of the law is in itself not the objective. The law may be violated only incidentally. Or better, perhaps, the government decides what it wants to regard as law-violating behavior. At any rate, the political offender violates the law when such violations either make a political point or have the potential of bringing about other changes. In these instances, violation of the law can actually be a political tactic.

And third, the goals of the political offender are not personal, but are deemed desirable for the larger society. The actions are usually public rather than private. The political offender regards his behavior as important for a larger purpose. Political offenders carry on their activities in pursuit of an ideal.

There has been only a limited attempt to describe the more specific personal and social characteristics of persons who engage in political behavior that may be defined as criminal. However, we know that such characteristics as age, sex, ethnicity, and social class do not differentiate political offenders as a whole from the population in general.[13] Political offenders differ more from one another according to the type of political crime than they differ from the noncriminal population. For example, in regard to social class, persons in the IWW (Industrial Workers of the World), some of whom were defined by the United States government as criminal, were of the laboring class, while the members of many other radical political organizations have been from the middle class. Likewise, in respect to ethnicity, politically oriented movements have differed greatly from one another in their ethnic composition, with some movements drawing from the population at large. It appears that the crucial factors in the career of the political offender are not personal and social characteristics per se but the values of the offender and the value systems to which he is actively responding.

War resisters, for example, may differ considerably from one another in personal and social characteristics but share the same value system. Writing about resisters to the Indochina war, Wildeman has noted:

> Violation of Selective Service law, then, does not seem to be a criminally defined behavior that is typical of any one particular segment of our society with the notable exception of age and sex structures. Resistance to the arbitrary domination of power on the part of those held in subjection to that power is as ubiquitous and extensive as is that power itself. As the power of the government reaches across the void deeply into the lives of all the people, holding them in subjection to its criminal war policies, so too resistance and opposition to this incredible domination is found in every segment of the social structure.[14]

Political criminals are usually committed to some form of social order. The social order they have in mind, however, may differ from the existing order. It is because of their commitment to something beyond themselves and conventional society that they are willing to engage in criminal behavior. Persons who occasionally engage in political crime are interested in their society, but at times find it lacking in important ways. They may then sever their commitment to the society in place of a social order that could exist. The social order to which they are committed may be a modification of the one that exists or may possibly be an entirely new one. Nevertheless, the existing society always serves as a reference point for political offenders.

The traitor and the spy provide the classic examples of the political offender who is committed to another social order. The traitor is guilty of treason in giving aid to another government making war against his own government, or adhering to enemies of the state. The spy, on the other hand, is more often a citizen of another country and in the course of espionage obtains secret information, often of a valuable military nature, for a foreign power. He is committed to his own country but is anything but attached to the country from which he secures the information, the country in which he is regarded as a political criminal. The entire career of such an offender may be devoted to spying. For both the traitor and the spy, there is a commitment to a larger social order beyond their own self-interest (with the exception of the professional spy to whom spying is merely a "dirty business"). The conscientious adherence by traitors and spies to the principles of some society has been characterized as follows:

Although some political offenders are persons without integrity who have yielded to the extensive bribes paid either by foreign powers or by local groups, the vast majority are conscientious adherents to a political philosophy which threatens the existence of the government they are opposing. This was true of the attempts to wrest power from a tyrannical monarch and is equally true of those who aim to overthrow our own government or that of any foreign power today. Political offenders thus represent a paradox for they are criminals who carry on their illegal activities in pursuit of their ideals. They are not imbued with sordid schemes for extracting vast sums of money from unsuspecting victims, nor are they motivated by basic desires to destroy or kill, although these crimes may be necessary in the pursuit of their ideals. They are generally idealists devoted to a cause (however mistaken it may be) which they place higher than patriotism or personal safety. In most cases of treason the traitors place this cause higher than the existence of their own government. In cases of espionage the spies may be loyal agents of their own country and place its survival above that of the country whose national interests they would destroy—or whose secret papers they would secure. Or they may be hired agents of a foreign power and thus are guilty of treason. All spies are heroes, then, to their native land or the country whose cause they are espousing, while they are arch enemies to those governments whose secrets they secure.[15]

While possibly not as dramatic, the source of commitment is crucial in all forms of political crime.

The nature of the self-conceptions, morality, and rationality of political offenders is obvious in the many recent statements by various political offenders. For example, a war resister, in prison, expressed his beliefs in the following way:

> I believe in brotherhood and loving people. I suppose that on an individual basis it's a natural thing for a man to protect himself as a matter of self-defense, but it becomes a different thing, even for self-defense, when it's institutionalized. I think that military institutions have disunited and separated men, and that is contrary to a basic belief of mine. I couldn't take a life just for that. That other man might be my brother. I don't think any war is ever justified. While I do believe that I'm against war in general, this one particularly, just doesn't have anything to do with anything I believe in. I think all war is an expression of the sickness of mankind, part of that sickness which he should try to overcome. I just don't look at it as being a natural thing—like some people do. I just don't understand people who can think of war as a part of the way of life. I feel this is not me, and I can't participate in something like a war which seems crazy merely because some agency says I should. Basically, I'm just not a violent person.[16]

Similarly, one of the twenty-seven defendants in the San Francisco Presidio mutiny case of 1968 expressed his feelings about war:

> I believe that a man who knowingly aids, encourages, or makes it easier for another man to commit a crime, is guilty of that crime himself. If I support the armed forces, I would not only be advocating the use of force by my participation, but would be guilty by supporting the troops who actually do fight, of what I feel are the crimes of violence and murder. I alone must answer to my conscience; what I ought to do, I must do.[17]

His beliefs and subsequent actions led to a mutiny trial.

Some of the best verbalizations of the careers of political offenders have been given by the defendants in the conspiracy trial of the Chicago Eight. Referring to his own career, Lee Weiner has written:

> I never wanted to be a doctor, but after a while I accumulated a bunch of university degrees, and now I'm going to get another that will mean terrorized freshmen will call me "Doctor" on their bad days. It makes my mother happy. . . . During all of that time I talked, listened, hallucinated, and harangued at different places at different times. Some of it anybody would consider political. Now I'm thirty, have a beard, a wife, a two-year-old son who scares me sometimes, a color TV, and a tattoo on my forehead that says "Government Certified Radical." If I stay in touch with myself and continue to act free, the government has promised to additionally tattoo "Bomb Maker and Evil Man." It makes me happy.[18]

And one of the witnesses for the defense expressed the radical's position. When the prosecutor asked Linda Morse, "And the more you realize our system is sick, the more you want to tear it limb from limb, isn't that right?" she responded:

The more that I see the horrors that are perpetuated by this government, the more that I read about things like troop trains full of nerve gas traveling across the country where one accident could wipe out thousands and thousands of people, the more that I see things like companies just pouring waste into lakes and into rivers and just destroying them, the more I see things like the oil fields in the ocean off Santa Barbara where the Secretary of the Interior and the oil companies got together and agreed to continue producing oil from the off-shore oil fields and ruined a whole section of the coast, the more that I see things like an educational system which teaches black people and Puerto Rican people and Mexican-American people that they are only fit to be domestics and dishwashers, it that, the more I see a system that teaches middle-class whites like me to continue producing CBW warfare, to continue working on computers and things like that to learn how to control people better, yes, the more I want to see that system torn down and replaced by a totally different one—one that cares about people learning; that cares about children being fed breakfast before they go to school; one that cares about people going to college for free; one that cares about people living adult lives that are responsible, fulfilled adult lives, not just drudgery, day after day going to a job; one that gives people a chance to express themselves artistically and politically and religiously and philosophically. That is the kind of system I want to see in its stead.[19]

The career of the radical could have gone in many other directions. Abbie Hoffman, upon being sentenced in Chicago, told Judge Julius Hoffman about himself and the Cook County jail: "There's no light. It's not a nice place for a Jewish boy to be, with a college education."[20] Rennie Davis, upon receiving his prison sentence, spoke to the prosecutors, among them Tom Foran: "When I come out of prison it will be to move next door to Tom Foran. I am going to be the boy next door. The boy that could have been a judge, the boy that could have been a prosecutor, could have been a college professor, is going to move next door to organize his kids into the revolution. We are going to turn the sons and daughters of the ruling class in this country into Viet Cong."[21]

It is clear from all of this that an understanding of the political offender requires a conception of man that is quite different from the one usually employed by criminologists. The view that the criminal is produced by a variety of impersonal forces beyond his control is inadequate for the study of the political offender. The introspective nature of man is obvious in the career of the political offender. Man alone is capable of considering alternative actions, of breaking from the established order. A purposive, voluntaristic conception of man and his behavior is thus essential to the study of human behavior in general and political crime in particular.[22]

For the most part criminologists have concentrated their attention on the conventional (supposedly pathological) offender to the virtual neglect of the offender who challenges the existing system. That a criminal could have a moral conscience has not been seriously entertained by students of crime. No longer, however, is such a narrow view of crime possible. Indeed, the underlying character of much criminal behavior is political in nature, rather than being merely deviant or pathological. So it is today:

> The actions of the criminally defined are not so much the result of inadequate socialization and personality problems as they are conscientious actions taken against something. For many persons, behaviors that can readily be labeled as criminal may be the only appropriate means for expressing certain thoughts and feelings—and the only possibilities for bringing about social changes. The traditional channels of the political process may be inappropriate or may be insensitive for the grievances of much of the population.[23]

Crime by Government

The police have traditionally been the most obvious governmental offenders. Police brutality and other misconduct—much of it illegal—has been documented throughout the history of policing American communities. Recently a study of police operations in the slums of three cities (Washington, Boston, and Chicago) reported that "27 percent of all the officers were either observed in misconduct situations or admitted to observers that they had engaged in misconduct."[24] The forms of misconduct (which could be classified as felonies or misdemeanors) included shaking down traffic violators, accepting payoffs to alter sworn testimony, stealing from burglarized establishments, and planting weapons on suspects. Beyond the scope of the study, but documented elsewhere, was the violence committed by the police in the course of their standard operations.

Crimes by the police must be understood in the context of their careers. The police recruit, during his training, adopts a particular outlook on his work and develops a justification for using certain procedures in the line of "duty." He learns an ideology that later affects his work. Writing about the use of violence by the police, Westley has observed:

> The policeman finds his most pressing problem in his relationships to the public. His is a service occupation but of an incongruous kind, since he must discipline those whom he serves. He is regarded as corrupt and inefficient by, and meets with hostility and criticism from, the public. He regards the public as his enemy, feels his occupation to be in conflict with the community, and regards himself to be a pariah. The experience and the feeling give rise to a collective emphasis on secrecy, an attempt to coerce respect from the public, and a belief that almost any

means are legitimate in completing an important arrest. These are for the policeman basic occupational values. They arise from his experience, take precedence over his legal responsibilities, are central to an understanding of his conduct, and form the occupational concepts within which violence gains its meaning.[25]

Thus, because of the nature of policework, learned and experienced by each policeman, a rationale exists among the police for the use of harsh and oftentimes illegal methods. It is the fate of policework that a certain amount of criminality is built into the career of each policeman.

The careers of government policymakers and military men who commit war crimes in the course of their routine careers can be similarly understood. Well-meaning men, devoted to their careers, have made a series of decisions that result in day-to-day violation of international laws. The chief architects of the war in Vietnam—Dean Rusk, Walt Rostow, Robert McNamara, McGeorge Bundy, Alexis Johnson—made a series of decisions that depended on the defense of their past decisions. As a former White House aide (James C. Thomson, Jr.) has written:

> Men who have participated in a decision develop a stake in that decision. As they participate in further, related decisions, their stake increases. It might have been possible to dissuade a man of strong self-confidence at an early stage of the ladder of decision; but it is infinitely harder at later stages since a change of mind there usually involves implicit or explicit repudiation of a chain of previous decisions. To put it bluntly; at the heart of the Vietnam calamity is a group of able, dedicated men who have been regularly and repeatedly wrong—and whose standing with their contemporaries, and more important, with history, depends, as they see it, on being proven right. These are not men who can be asked to extricate themselves from error.[26]

Crimes by government officials are thus built on reputations. Military men have similar career contingencies. Field commanders in Vietnam (such as William Westmoreland and Creighton Abrams) have made reputations for themselves on the basis of war. Even the combatant has been able to use the war to further a career in the military. The tragedy, of course, is that war crimes have been committed as a basic part of career enhancement.

On a more general level, United States war crimes in Southeast Asia can be understood in terms of the development of the United States itself. The war in Vietnam and the crimes associated with it are not merely incidental occurrences; rather they are the logical consequences of American development and relations with the rest of the world.[27] The intervention of the United States in Southeast Asia is but the latest attempt to preserve its own interests. These interests have been the interests of the corporate rulers who, in order to assure the expansion of economic markets, have attempted to control the rest of the world. American foreign policy has therefore been imperialistic, extending American institutions abroad and determining the development of other nations, especially Third World nations. All of this has been cloaked in an ideology of manifest destiny, anticommunism, and preservation of the American way of life. It is in this context that individuals make policies that are criminal.

Anyone who engages in criminal acts constructs rationalizations to justify their actions and to provide appropriate self-conceptions. Governmental criminals do the same. To the policeman, he is just "doing his job," or possibly doing what is "expected" of him. The war criminal suggests that he is protecting national interests. Given the public belief in submission to sovereignty, such rationalizations are quite valid; certainly they are effective in perpetuating illegal law enforcement and crimes of war.

GROUP SUPPORT OF CRIMINAL BEHAVIOR

Crime against Government

The assumption in liberal democratic theory is that most groups in the society can make themselves heard at some crucial point in the decision-making process. If we cannot directly enter into decision making, the assumption is that our representatives will care for our needs. These assumptions, however, are by no means borne out by experience. Instead, many individuals and groups are either excluded from the traditional processes or are unsuccessful in being represented in the policy decision. And when the traditional processes fail, the only recourse may be to engage in nontraditional procedures. The use of these procedures may easily result in criminal behavior. That is to say, those in power will define as criminal those who resort to illegitimate politics.

A uniform conception of what is legitimate politics does not exist in any society. Individuals are socialized into politics on the basis of their particular social experiences.[28] In the course of political socialization and concrete experience, individuals and groups develop a conception regarding the relative legitimacy of existing political institutions. A political system is regarded as legitimate when the authority of those in control is respected and the available procedures in the political process are believed to be appropriate. Groups generally regard a political system as legitimate or illegitimate according to the way in which the values of the system correspond to their own values. The acceptance of particular societal values tends to maximize the legitimacy of the existing system. Groups that do not share these values are more likely to question the legitimacy of the system at certain times and are likely to engage in political behaviors ("extremist politics") which may be defined as criminal. To do otherwise is to be completely alienated from contemporary life.

The pursuit of illegal political behavior is not regarded as a serious matter for some persons. After all, selective obedience to the law is a common phenomenon in other social situations. Laws are obeyed according to a person's beliefs. The evasion of a criminal law most likely represents the following of an alternative norm. The political criminal may actually be following an ideal or utopian norm, a norm held by most people but rarely realized in actual behavior.[29] The conscientious objector, for example, refuses to have qualification placed on the moral injunction against killing another human being, feeling that the situation is no different in war from what it is in peace. The person who is disloyal to his country is nevertheless being true to higher loyalties. The traitor is not disloyal in his own eyes but is loyal to something he regards as more worthy of allegiance.[30] Such criminals are conscientiously following a set of norms and values that differs from that of the ruling class.

The fact that crime against government has group support is illustrated in the case of conscientious objectors during World War II. The overwhelming majority of persons convicted during the period were members of the "historic peace churches," including Jehovah's Witnesses, the Society of Friends, the Mennonites, and the Church of the Brethren, all of which are committed to the opposition of war by their fundamental doctrines.[31] The philosophical objectors, those not basing their objections on religious grounds, also found group support for their behavior. They were united often with religious objectors, through such organizations as the Pacifist Research Bureau, the War Resisters League, and the National Council Against Conscription.

The group nature of political crime varies, of course, from one kind of political crime to another. Some political criminals receive less group support than others. Also, the groups to which political offenders may belong differ greatly in their ideologies. In addition, the social organization of groups supporting political crime varies with the size of the group, cohesiveness of the group, formality of organization, duration of the group, geographical dispersion of the members, and patterns of leadership. Finally, groups differ in the techniques and tactics used by members in the course of committing offenses. Techniques and tactics include such diverse forms as oratory, face-to-face persuasion, writing and propaganda, nonviolent coercion, passive resistance, demonstrations, marches, strikes, suicide, street fighting, and guerrilla warfare.

Recent cases of political crime demonstrate the extent to which criminally defined political behavior receives group support. In a study of civil strife during the 1960s, conducted for the Violence Commission, it was shown that most of the activity (ranging from antiwar protests, to riots, to guerrilla warfare) was of a collective nature. Moreover, group cohesiveness played an important part in many of the actions that officials defined as criminal.

> Random crowds seldom initiate civil strife. We also can examine differences and similarities among nations in the kinds of organizations that provide the cohesion that is necessary for collective action. Group

cohesion may be provided by communal organization, or simply by people's awareness that they belong to the same ethnic, religious, or territorial community. Group contexts for action may also be provided by economic organizations, such as trade unions and cooperatives; by legal political organizations, such as political parties and issue-oriented groups like antiwar organizations; by clandestine groups like guerrilla and terrorist movements; and by the governmental hierarchy itself, including the civil service and military establishment.[32]

Similarly, the ghetto riots of the 1960s occurred in large part through shared experiences and group support. Grievances that had accumulated for years finally were raised to the level of group consciousness. Whole groups of the population became aware that the ghetto grievances of economic deprivation, discrimination, poor housing, and consumer exploitation could be (and should be) attacked. What became defined as violence by the government was for many blacks a means of achieving just demands and basic human rights. Summarizing the events of the 1960s, Fogelson writes:

> Reasons may be obscure, but results are clear. The blacks—or at any rate a substantial minority of them—refuse to tolerate racial discrimination, economic deprivation, consumer exploitation, and involuntary residential segregation any longer. Instead they intend to call attention to their grievances, to share in the benefits of affluent America, to even the score with white merchants, and ultimately to gain control over their communities. They have long tried to do so through elections, demonstrations, education, training, and other conventional channels; and they will probably continue to do so. But the riots made it quite clear that where the blacks find these channels obstructed they will not be confined by them. Nor will they be bound by the fear of arrest, the concern for personal safety, the commitment to orderly social change, the trauma of white racism, and the other restraints on rioting in the United States. Under these circumstances it is not remarkable that a significant minority of the blacks are now prepared, even determined, to resort to violence until their grievances are redressed.[33]

In the indictment of the Boston Five, the defendants were charged with conspiring "with each other, and with diverse other persons, some known and others unknown to the Grand Jury," with counseling, aiding, and abetting violations of the Selective Service law and with hindering the administration of the draft.[34] Thus, even in legal terms, group support of alleged illegal activity has been recognized. In particular, two of the defendants, Reverend William Coffin and Dr. Benjamin Spock, were charged with the overt act of distributing a statement entitled "A Call to Resist Illegitimate Authority." The document was signed by hundreds of people, a sure sign of group support—a nationwide conspiracy; but only two were tried for the crime as examples to the rest. All signers proclaimed in the statement: "We will continue to lend our support to those who undertake resistance to this war. We will raise funds to organize draft resistance unions, to supply legal defense and bail, to support families and otherwise aid resistance to the war in whatever ways may seem appropriate." To resist immoral authority did not seem to be a crime to the signers. But it was this same authority that controlled the legal system.

Finally, the pervasiveness of group support for political crime is illustrated in the conspiracy trial of the Chicago Eight. As the defense showed, the eight did not exist as a concrete group; this occurred only as a *result* of the trial. The defendants were quite different from one another, which led Abbie Hoffman to remark, "Conspire, hell, we couldn't agree on lunch." Instead the defendants represented an emerging life style, one shared by thousands of others. To resist repression was the binding element, but this was a threat to the established government. As Tom Hayden wrote later: "Our crime was that we were beginning to live a new and contagious life style without official authorization. We were tried for being out of control."[35] He added, "Our crime was our identity."

Crime by Government

The governmental offender, in most instances, receives support from his fellow workers. A major reason for this is that the illegal activity that he engages in is usually an integral part of governing. For example, the policeman who breaks the law is probably following the norms of his group. Likewise, when the police are involved in political encounters they are already disposed to act in ways that are in violation of the law. And, regarding the highest levels of government, those who formulate and execute criminal war policies work jointly to accomplish their objectives. However criminal their policies, support can be expected from their colleagues.

Many of the illegal activities of the ordinary policeman are prescribed and supported by group norms. Hence, it has been found in research that criminal practices of police are patterned through as informal "code." Furthermore, "It was found that the new recruits were socialized into 'code' participation by 'old timers' and group acceptance was withheld from those who attempted to remain completely honest and not be implicated. When formal police regulations were in conflict with 'code' demands among its practitioners, the latter took precedence."[36]

In fact, the policeman may give little consideration to the legality of his own actions in the course of enforcing other laws. The law that exists to protect the citizen from the abuses of government authorities is more likely to be regarded by the policeman as an obstacle to law enforcement. "For him, due process of law is, therefore, not merely a set of constitutional guarantees for the defendant, but also a set of working conditions which, under increasingly liberal opinions by the courts, are likewise becoming increasingly arduous."[37] From the viewpoint of the police, the civil liberties of the public impede the performance of the policeman's job. In such a context of group support, laws are broken by the enforcers of law.

The opportunity for unlawful behavior among the police is especially acute in the black community and in situations of political protest. In these cases, the police already have their own group norms that both prescribe a certain amount of illegal behavior and provide support for this behavior. As several studies have shown, the majority of policemen are hostile and prejudiced toward blacks.[38] Such attitudes impair the ability of the police to always engage in lawful behavior. In the ghetto riots of the late 1960s, police violence was not an unusual occurrence.

Similarly, the police handling of political protesters has often been violent and illegal. The police response to the demonstrations at the 1968 Democratic National Convention in Chicago, for example, has been described as "unrestrained and indiscriminate police violence."[39] Criminal violence by the police in these confrontations occurs in large part because of the views the police share regarding protesters. That is, "organized protest tends to be viewed as the conspiratorial product of authoritarian agitators—usually 'Communists'—who mislead otherwise contented people."[40] Such views, combined with frustration and anger, provide a ready support for harsh and illegal actions by the police. And since the police regard most people they encounter in these situations as already guilty, they think their own methods of control and apprehension are appropriate—no matter how criminal these methods may be.

CORRESPONDENCE BETWEEN CRIMINAL AND LEGITIMATE BEHAVIOR

Crime against Government

The behavior associated with crime against government in American society is initially consistent with the democratic principle of the right of expression and dissent. The right of petition and association is guaranteed in the First Amendment of the United States Constitution, which states that Congress shall make no law abridging "the right of the people peaceably to assemble, and to petition the Government for a redress of grievances." Yet, especially through state constitutions, the rights of the citizen are qualified.[41] While religious freedom is also a constitutional guarantee, religious freedom cannot be regarded as an absolute. In a complex society there are many competing interests and values which in operation often place limits on religious freedom.

The most familiar illustrations of the limits of religious freedom are found in situations where the peace, safety, and good order of the community impose them. It is clear that however large the area of religious freedom may be, and however reluctant the courts may be to set limits to that freedom, there are countervailing interests which are regarded as so vital to society that they serve as justification for some limitations. These interests include the protection of public morals and public health, the care of children, national defense, general welfare, and public order.[42]

Thus it may be seen that in practice there are limits to the freedom of expression. Although the behaviors included in political crime may correspond in principle to the democratic values of American society, the actual commission of the acts is restricted to what is regarded as politically legitimate.

The boundaries and definitions of political freedom are by no means constant within any political democracy. The latitude of dissent that may still be regarded as legitimate varies from one time to another. During some periods a considerable amount and degree of dissent may be tolerated, while in other periods dissent may be suppressed, particularly by means of the criminal law. In other words, political legitimacy is a concept that is manipulated by those in control of the state. And when threats to the state are exerted by those outside the power structure, the boundaries of political legitimacy can be severely restricted.

It is this tension between human freedom and state control that pervades modern democracies. While democratic theory guarantees the right to protest and even to revolt, administration of the right is in the hands of the authorities. This is the paradox of civil liberties: They are always in terms of the government's interests rather than the interests of the people. Our freedoms are to be regulated by others. In spite of the liberal rhetoric, actual freedoms are wanting in modern democracy.

> We are in a condition in which the First Amendment freedoms do not work effectively. Citizens have the right to speak, assemble, and protest freely until their actions begin to have a subversive effect on unresponsive authorities. It can be expressed as an axiom: at the point at which protest becomes effective, the state becomes repressive. Constitutional rights become primarily rhetorical. They are not extended to those who might use them to make basic structural change, to those who represent the beginning of a new society.[43]

Thus, abstract freedoms may flourish with ease. But when protests and actions become effective, civil liberties can be withdrawn. And not only may civil liberties be abridged, but repressive laws may be used to suppress potentially effective action.

> Hence the dissenter has the freedom to become a victim in the social process and history, and a battery of sedition, espionage, criminal anarchy, or labor laws exist in readiness for the appropriate moment of social tension and the breakdown in the social and ideological consensus which exists during periods of peace and stability. The celebrants of

American freedom rarely confront the concepts of order that underlie the large body of law for suppression that always exists in reserve.[44]

It is with these realizations that many individuals and groups in American society are engaging in actions that threaten the existing social and political arrangements. Many realize today that human rights are not being fulfilled and that they have the right to create a society that promotes these basic human rights. Thus we are aware today that many actions are political, and in so being are often illegal. But what is happening is basically consistent with the legitimate patterns that have been with us for ages. What is defined as criminal may actually be the fulfillment of basic human rights. Crime against government in such times expresses these rights.

Crime by Government

The correspondence between the crimes of government and legitimate behavior patterns is fairly simple and direct: They tend to be the same. That is, those who legislate and enforce the law—and determine what is to be regarded as legitimate—are in the position of violating the laws themselves without being criminally defined. True, there may be behavior patterns beyond the positive law that stipulate the illegitimacy of certain governmental actions; but as far as the official interpretation is concerned, what government does is legal. It is when the law on occasion is invoked against government authorities that the incongruity between their criminality and a higher morality is made clear.

The civil rights movement of the last ten years perhaps best illustrates the conflict between patterns of behavior. While the United States Supreme Court defined various forms of discrimination as being criminal, local communities, supported by their elected or appointed officials, held that the traditional patterns of discrimination were legitimate. Thus, Mouledoux has argued that southern history is characterized by governmental crime.

> This survey has examined the politically criminal nature of southern political power. It has shown that the South, by denying political identity to its Negro population, has violated the basic constitutional presuppositions of political community; that is, the right of all to live under law and to participate in the making and executing of that law. By developing this pattern of "exclusive" politics, the South has created a police state rather than a political community; the Negro has been forced to accept his subservient social status by techniques of extralegal violence supported by police power. And thus the South has moved frighteningly close to a totalitarian political order.[45]

Government authorities, as well as community members, responded to the civil rights movement by committing various criminal offenses. Blacks who attempted to vote in primaries were assaulted and beaten; homes were bombed and blacks were murdered. Three civil rights workers

(Michael Schwerner, Andrew Goodman, and James Chaney) were murdered in Mississippi by the local police and other members of the community. More recently, as the civil rights movement has turned into a movement for black power, members of the Black Panther party in northern cities have been murdered in their homes by law enforcement agents.[46] Thus government officials have been among the leaders in the attempt to uphold white supremacy—through criminal means when necessary.

Crime by the officials who guard and "correct" those who violate the law is another irony of the legal system. Ordinary criminals are to serve time, be punished, and treated for their transgressions. Yet the personnel who perform these functions may violate criminal laws in the course of their duties. Their crimes correspond closely to the objectives of security and punishment. Prison guards, in particular, are to do whatever is necessary in order to maintain security in the prison. The result is sometimes governmental crime by these legal agents.

These crimes are documented only in crisis situations. Several incidences of crimes by correctional workers, for example, became known to the public following the 1970 prison riots in several New York City jails.[47] The inmates were responding to the regularly harsh conditions in the jails, including excessive bail, overcrowding, and months of being confined without an indictment or a trial. After one of the revolts had ended peacefully, through negotiations between the inmates and the Mayor's office, several correctional officers began to systematically beat the prisoners in the courtyard of the jail. The beatings were recorded in photographs and eye-witness accounts. A reporter for the *Daily News* described what he saw:

> It was a gruesome scene. About 250 prisoners were sitting on the grass. Behind them, 30 Correction Department guards were lined up, all of them holding weapons—ax handles, baseball bats, and night sticks. One inmate was dragged out a doorway onto a loading platform and five guards attacked him with their clubs. They battered his head and blood flowed over his face and body. He was kicked off the platform and several other guards pounded him again with their clubs. His limp form then was lifted off the ground and thrown into a bus as another prisoner was hauled out and belted across the back with a club. Then more clubs rained down on him until he was motionless and bloodsoaked. He too was thrown into the bus. Another man was pushed out, his hands above his head. A bat caught him in the stomach and he doubled over. More clubs came down on his spine. Eight guards were slugging away at one time. A fourth prisoner emerged but the guards seemed to let go of him. He began running but the guards caught him and one put a knee into his groin. He toppled over and more guards kicked him over and over. Some more prisoners got the same treatment.[48]

And true to governmental crime, three weeks after the beatings the Queens District Attorney announced the indictment of eight inmates, exonerating all the guards. And the process continues, manifesting itself dramatically at Attica in 1971 with the killing of more than forty inmates and guards by New York state troopers following executive orders.

Another example of the correspondence between the crimes of government and the activities the government regards as legitimate is in respect to surveillance by the government. The United States Constitution guarantees certain rights that are not to be infringed upon. The act of governmental surveillance, according to a series of Supreme Court rulings, is illegal in most situations. Such techniques as unreasonable search and seizure, interrogation, wiretapping, and various forms of electronic surveillance have been declared unconstitutional except in a very few cases. Nevertheless, government agents continue to engage in these forms of surveillance. This was dramatically brought to public attention by the disclosure that the Army had been obtaining information through surveillance techniques affecting 18,000 civilians.[49] While the operation is undoubtedly unconstitutional, as the American Civil Liberties Union contends, it is problematical whether any of the Army agents or their superiors will be prosecuted. But the lesson is that government officials can commit criminal acts in the name of law and order.

Finally, correspondence between what the government regards as legitimate behavior and its own criminality is brought into sharp focus in the war crimes committed by the United States government in Vietnam. The massacre of over 500 civilians in My Lai on March 16, 1968, brought to public attention the fact that such incidences were occurring as a basic part of military policy in Southeast Asia.[50] The murder of civilians, the destruction of nonmilitary targets, and the murder of prisoners of war (all of these offenses being criminal violations of the laws of warfare) resulted from a military strategy that relied on these procedures as a matter of standard policy. Crime was not merely incidental to the American involvement in Vietnam; rather, it was an essential part of the way the United States decided to conduct that war. The Vietnam war and crime by the United States government had become one.

SOCIETAL REACTION AND LEGAL PROCESSING

Crime against Government

By definition the political offender is regarded as a threat and danger to the existing society. Those so regarded are not dealt with lightly. Reaction to the behavior of the political offender is also severe because the offender's loyalty to the state is in question, loyalty being regarded as a requirement for the members of a society. In addition, crime against government is treated harshly because of the composition of the groups that react officially. Conservative segments of society usually dominate the power structure of the state. Official action in regard to political crime usually represents the attempt to preserve the status quo. The political offender is punished with the hope that similar political behavior will not occur or will at least remain at a minimum.

Public reaction to activity regarded as threatening to political authority has taken many diverse forms. In the United States a stereotyped conception of the political radical has predominated as a very general form of reaction:

> The stereotyped ideas about radicals which lurk in the consciousness of the masses of people are easily provoked in experimental free-association reactions to the term, embracing such associations as "red," alien," "dirty," soapbox agitation," "Godless," "free lover," "bewhiskered," "bombs," and "sabotage." Stereotypes such as these, circulated in newspapers, fiction, and artistic representations, have been highly colored by the beliefs which grew up around anarchism in the nineteenth century and the IWW in the twentieth. Reports of assassinations by Russian revolutionaries and by anarchists in European countries, the assassination of President Garfield by an anarchist, along with the Haymarket riots in Chicago and IWW violence at Homestead, Pennsylvania, and elsewhere, did much to shape the American fixed notions of the radical. Not only has this older anarchistic stereotype remained alive, but it tends to be applied indiscriminately to socialists, Communists, pacifists, and other radicals, as well as to progressive or moderate reformers.[51]

While social disorders of various kinds can be interpreted by the public as legitimate protests, criminal conceptions are more easily and readily drawn. It is simpler to regard a public demonstration or a disturbance as a crime or rebellion rather than to search for the motives and the grievances behind the actions. The labels thus tend to be simplistic and derogatory.

The public conception of antiwar activities in recent years has tended to be quite negative. Not only have war protesters been adversely defined, but opposing actions have been taken against peaceful demonstrations.

> Insults are common: at one march in New York City, onlookers yelled "traitors" and "kill a commie for Christ!" At a demonstration in Chicago the jeers were "chicken . . . scum . . . commies . . . cowards . . . sissies . . . punks . . . weirdos." Some spectators have grabbed signs and banners from marchers opposing the war. In Madison, Wisconsin, a local paper reported that police "stood by without interfering when counter-pickets kicked in the paper coffin" being carried by the opponents of the war. Eggs, beer cans, rocks, and red paint are now regularly thrown at demonstrators who march in large cities. At a march in Boston, the protesters were harassed by leather-jacketed motorcyclists who zigzagged their cycles through the line of march. Some witnessing antiwar events have attempted to beat those who participated; some have succeeded. For example, during a march in Berkeley, California, on October 16, 1965, sixteen members of the Hell's Angels motorcycle club ran through a police line and attempted to seize the lead banner; according to the

San Francisco Chronicle, a "melee" followed. In Boston, a group of pacifists held a demonstration on the steps of a courthouse, and four burned draft cards. Twenty-five high school students then attacked, kicked, and pummelled the demonstrators, knocking at least seven of them to the ground. In perhaps the most extreme case, forty New York City patrolmen were required to rescue one opponent of the war who had been knocked to the ground, kicked, and stripped of his clothing. Several of the attackers were shouting "kill him" and "string him up."[52]

Public officials have often set the pace for reactions to the political offender. For example, after World War I, when some persons were calling for the release of radicals and pacifists from prison, the then Senator Warren Harding declared:

> No true American will argue that our laws should not be enforced. I refer to laws, no matter of what nature, whether they be those which deal with ordinary crimes and misdemeanors, or those which deal with acts of treason to the United States, threatening the Constitution and the fabric of social organization.
>
> I wish no one to misunderstand me, and therefore, I will say as plainly as I can that for my part I can see no essential difference between ordinary crimes on the one hand and political crimes and political prisoners on the other hand. If there is a distinction, surely it is not a distinction which favors political crimes or political prisoners. The thief, or ordinary criminal, is surely less of a menace to those things which we hold dear then the man or woman who conspires to destroy our American institutions.[53]

It has not been common for public officials to recognize the moral character of the political offender. To group them with, or even below, the conventional criminal has been the usual policy. In recent times protesters have been publicly called "thugs" and "terrorists" by the President, "misfits" and "garbage" by the Vice President. Playing up a public demonstration at one of his public appearances, President Nixon said in 1970: "Let me add one personal note. The terrorists of the far left would like nothing better than to make the President of the United States a prisoner in the White House. Let me set them straight: As long as I am President, no band of violent thugs is going to keep me from going out and speaking with the American people wherever they want to hear me and wherever I want to go. This is a free country, and I fully intend to share that freedom with my fellow citizens."[54]

Opposition of citizens to governmental policies is used by government officials as a political tool. Officials are thus in a position to shape the public's conception of the political offender. A particular image of the offender is created by those in power in order to secure their own position. An official reality is created. This is illustrated in a discussion of the reaction to the war resister:

We may conclude this discussion of the manner in which others react to the criminally defined resister with a reference to the intense struggle to create a stereotype image of him in the mind of the general public. The arena in which this battle takes place is the mass media and the contenders are political leaders and others among the power elite who command access to the media. The prize is the satisfaction and security on the part of the rulers in government that they have successfully instilled their particular values and ideologies in the minds of the masses. It is in reality a power struggle, the result of which is the creation of a specific social reality of the resister. The ritual of much publicized exchanges takes place between political officials who, perhaps sincerely responding to their constituencies, perhaps seeking political exposure, praise these young men as heroes and true Americans. The majority, however, attack them viciously as cowards, criminals , and outcasts. The stereotype of the resister in the mind of the public, whether it be as criminal or hero, is a social creation, the result of the ongoing struggle between the powerful segments of society for control over the definition of reality in the minds of the people.[55]

The legal reactions to political crime have been particularly severe. For example, during World War II the average sentence for conscientious objectors was more stringent than for many other convicted criminals. Nearly 90 percent of the convicted conscientious objectors were sentenced to prison, with over 30 percent receiving a four- to five-year term. For the entire period only a little over 4 percent of the cases were granted probation.[56]

Jailing and deportation have been used in the United States as means of controlling radicalism. The most dramatic use occurred in November 1919 and January 1920 when federal agents, under the direction of Attorney General A. Mitchell Palmer, staged a series of nationwide dragnet raids and detained for deportation several thousand alien members of the Union of Russian Workers, the Communist Labor party, and the Communist party. In this instance no criminal proceedings were involved. Attorney General Palmer did not try to prosecute actual crimes of radicals against the United States because this would have required an indictment and a trial by jury. Rather, he relied on an administrative process for the apprehension and deportation of radical aliens and thereby circumvented normal legal procedures.[57]

More direct and immediate reactions have taken place, as in the intentional killings by police in such disturbances as the Haymarket riot of 1886 and the Pullman strike of 1894. Police intimidation and brutality have been evident in more recent times in the handling of "race riots." Some of the violence that has occurred in such disorders has been prompted by the police.[58]

The nature of police reaction to political protest was dramatically brought to public attention in the events that occurred during the 1968 Democratic

Convention in Chicago. During that week in August, the Chicago police, in the course of arresting 668 demonstrators, committed numerous violent acts against them. A report of the events, sponsored by the National Commission on the Causes and Prevention of Violence, concluded that the police response to the demonstrators was unrestrained and indiscriminate. Furthermore, "that violence was made all the more shocking by the fact that it was often inflicted upon persons who had broken no law, disobeyed no order, made no threat. These included peaceful demonstrators, onlookers, and large numbers of residents who were simply passing through, or happened to live in, the areas where confrontations were occurring."[59]

For some types of political offenders, quasi-judicial procedures are used in their prosecution. In the case of conscientious objectors and war resisters, for example, local draft boards play an important role in the administration of draft laws. And it is in this process that we find great variations in legal interpretation from one local draft board to another. Differential administration of the draft law is affected by a number of factors:

> It is, of course, just one more dimension of the tired, but so troubling, problems of inequities in the law between the rich and the poor, between the uneducated and the educated. And, once again, the chance of birth, of geographical location, of background, will in great part determine whether man is to be classified a felon or not—whether he will spend three to five years of his life in jail or not. In its interpretation of the law, in its use of a broad or narrow standard in defining a conscientious objector, the draft board makes its bias felt.[60]

Also important in processing the individual is the way in which the draft board perceives the individual's credibility as a conscientious objector. Out of such stuff criminals are created.

Furthermore, the national policy toward the prosecution of conscientious objectors varies from one time to another. In general, the rate of prosecution increases with the extent to which war resistance threatens the interests of the government. Since 1965, with the escalation of the war in Southeast Asia, the number of prosecutions relating to draft laws has increased ten times.[61] In 1965 there were 369 draft evasion cases; in 1970 the figure had risen to 2950 cases. But most sobering of all, is the fact that once individuals are sentenced their chances of a just appeal are very limited.[62] The appeal mechanisms are not effective and the appeal board members, like the local draft board members, are subject to many biasing factors. Through such processes the fate of the war resister is decided.

Judicial proceedings have served to define and limit other types of political crime. The courts have been used by most governments in behalf of political goals. Kirchheimer, in an analysis of the court's role in the control of opposing political viewpoints and actions, has noted that three types of political trials have been used to accomplish the goals of the political authority:

A. The trial involving a common crime committed for political purposes and conducted with a view to the political benefits which might ultimately accrue from successful prosecution.

B. The classic political trial: a regime's attempt to incriminate its foe's public behavior with a view to evicting him from the political scene.

C. The derivative political trial, where the weapons of defamation, perjury, and contempt are manipulated in an effort to bring disrepute upon a political foe.[63]

Through political procedures such as these, political foes are eliminated from political competition.

The United States has a rich history of political trials. While there have been few dramatic state trials for such offenses as treason, the courts have been used by the government on numerous occasions for political purposes. "In the furious game of politics, the legal system offers a tempting opportunity for those in power to damage enemies, tarnish their image, and isolate them from potential allies by casting them as criminals."[64] The judicial system has thus played a prominent role in recent years as a response to a range of activities. In responding to social change and unrest, including the antiwar protests, student demonstrations, and black militancy, the courts have been largely repressive.[65] They certainly have not shown a strong capacity to uphold democratic values and protect civil liberties.

The politicality of the courts has been drawn to public attention in the course of several recent trials, especially in the trial of Black Panthers and the Chicago conspiracy case. In fact, in the Chicago trial, the defendants explicitly attempted to show how the court was being political. Hence, they refused to observe the traditional decorum of the courtroom. The severe contempt charges that followed the Chicago trial indicated the court's reaction to the defendants' political use of the trial. However, the court refused to admit that the government itself had initially decided to make the trial a political one.

Political crime is thus an integral part of contemporary life. As long as governments regard certain persons as threats to their functioning and to their existence, the criminal law will be used for political purposes. And as long as people have the will to oppose oppressive governments, there will be behaviors that will be defined as criminal.

Crime by Government

Public reaction to governmental crime is not usually strong, at least not to begin with. The major reason for this is that the public has been led to believe that whatever the government does is right—and that whatever the government does must by definition be legal. By equating government and law, citizens have tended to give license to government to do whatever it pleases. What we have forgotten is that government, in its true sense, is a process of rule by the people, not a process or entity beyond the people.

Most people find it difficult to believe that their government engages in criminal behavior. The reactions to the massacre at My Lai were typical of how the public responds to governmental crime.[66] Some people simply refused to admit that the massacre had occurred: A man, when presented with the news, observed, "Our boys wouldn't do this. Something else is behind it." Some simply approved: "It was good. What do they give soldiers bullets for—to put in their pockets?" A woman defended the shooting of children: "It sounds terrible to say we ought to kill kids, but many of our boys being killed over there are just kids, too." Some said the massacre was only to be expected: "It just seems to be one of the outcomes of war."

It is difficult for the public to form intelligent opinions about governmental crime. The problem is twofold. First, the news that the public gets is either censored, as in the case of military news from Vietnam, or a particular conception of reality is presented in the mass media.[67] What the public gets, then, is a one-sided account of what the government is doing.

The second problem in reference to public opinion about governmental crime is the way in which the government forces its consensus on the public. The public is inclined to believe its leaders, and the rulers are able to manipulate the conceptions that are presented to the public. And the ultimate irony is that those who rule continue their policies even when public opinion rises against them.

> That the voluntaristic basis of consensus usually justifies the actions of the men of power is less consequential than that, as we see today in the case of the American public and Vietnam, the policy continues when mass agreement withers away and even disappears. For consensus is identifiable with class goals and needs, suitably wrapped in a vague ideology of American nationalism and its global responsibility. These class goals and interests prevail even when the consensus disappears, and it is at this very point we see that administrators base policy on the control of power and interests rather than society's sanction or consent.[68]

What happens in terms of legal processing when governmental crimes are detected? The results are usually predictable: The charges are dropped, the defendants are cleared, or, at most, an official may be dismissed from his former responsibilities. Thus, although three students were killed and several more injured at Orangeburg State College in 1968, the South Carolina highway patrolmen who fired the shots were cleared of any wrongdoing. Similar events and results were to occur later at Jackson State College in Mississippi.

Likewise, at Kent State University in 1970, National Guardsmen killed four students and then were exonerated of any blame. Instead, a state grand jury indicted twenty-five persons in connection with campus protests. The grand jury did not indict any guardsmen because they "fired their weapons in the honest and sincere belief and under circumstances which would have logically caused them to believe that they would suffer serious bodily injury had they not done so." (No evidence of sniper fire could be found.) The "major responsibility" for the events at Kent State, the grand jury continued, "rests clearly with those persons who are charged with the administration of the university." The university administration, the report asserted, had fostered "an attitude of laxity, over-indulgence and permissiveness," and faculty members had placed an "over-emphasis" on "the right to dissent."[69] That is, the fact that the government could be at fault was never seriously entertained.

Although there are other legal means available, such as a national or international court, the prosecution of United States war crimes in Vietnam has been restricted to court martial proceedings.[70] By so doing, responsibility for war crimes has been attributed to the ordinary soldier, or at most to his unit commander. In other words, by means of the court martial, those who have made criminal war policies at the highest levels have been excluded from criminal responsibility. Court martial cases (such as that of Lieutenant William Calley) have ignored the responsibility at higher levels of government.

When the government fails to legally regulate itself the public sometimes reacts by morally questioning the acts of the government. This has happened in the case of United States war crimes. Several citizens' groups have been established to publicize the criminality of American war policies, particularly the National Committee for a Citizens' Commission of Inquiry on U.S. War Crimes in Vietnam, and the National Veterans' Inquiry into U.S. War Crimes. These efforts were preceded by what has become the classic example of an organized response to governmental crime—the Bertrand Russell International War Crimes Tribunal.[71] While the Russell Tribunal was not taken seriously by a majority of citizens at its inception, it has since set the moral tone for a public reaction to the crimes of government. When the law ceases to be for and by the people, when it is primarily a tool of a government beyond the people, the only recourse open to the public is a moral one.

NOTES

[1] Herbert L. Packer, "Offenses against the State," *The Annals*, **339** (January 1962), pp. 77–89.

[2] Edgar C. McVoy, "Wartime Controls in a Democratic Society," *American Sociological Review*, **11** (February 1946), pp. 85–89; and Howard Woolston, "Free Speech in War Time," *American Sociological Review*, **7** (April 1942), pp. 185–193.

[3] Robert K. Murray, *Red Scare: A Study in National Hysteria, 1919–1920* (Minneapolis: University of Minneapolis Press, 1955).

[4] Ralph S. Brown, *Loyalty and Security* (New Haven, Conn.: Yale University Press, 1958).

[5] Herbert H. Hyman, "England and America: Climates of Tolerance and Intol-

erance," in Daniel Bell, ed., *The Radical Right* (New York: Doubleday & Company, 1963), pp. 227–257.

6 See John Wildeman, "War Resistance and the Governmental Process," manuscript, Department of Sociology, Hofstra University, 1971; and Norman Redlich and Kenneth R. Feinberg, "Individual Conscience and the Selective Conscientious Objector: The Right Not to Kill," *New York University Law Review*, **44** (November 1969), pp. 875–900.

7 Peter and Deborah Babcox and Bob Abel, eds., *The Conspiracy* (New York: Dell Publishing Company, 1969), pp. 28–29.

8 B. L. Ingraham and Kazuhiko Tokoro, "Political Crime in the United States and Japan: A Comparative Study," *Issues in Criminology*, 4 (Spring 1969), pp. 145–170.

9 For an exception, see Joseph C. Mouledoux, "Political Crime and the Negro Revolution," in Marshall B. Clinard and Richard Quinney, *Criminal Behavior Systems: A Typology* (New York: Holt, Rinehart and Winston, 1967), pp. 217–231.

10 Lynne B. Iglitzin, "Violence and American Democracy," *Journal of Social Issues*, **26** (Winter 1970), pp. 165–166.

11 See Paul Chevigny, *Police Power: Police Abuses in New York City* (New York: Pantheon Books, 1969).

12 Anthony A. D'Amato, Harvey L. Gould, and Larry D. Woods, "War Crimes and Vietnam: The 'Nuremberg Defense' and the Military Service Resister," *California Law Review*, **57** (November 1969), pp. 1055–1110; Richard A. Falk, "War Crimes and Individual Responsibility: A Legal Memorandum, *Transaction*, **7** (January 1970), pp. 33–40; Telford Taylor, *Nuremberg and Vietnam: An American Tragedy* (Chicago: Quadrangle Books, 1970).

13 See Edwin M. Lemert, *Social Pathology* (New York: McGraw-Hill Book Company, 1951), pp. 180–187.

14 Wildeman, "War Resistance and the Governmental Process," p. 27.

15 Mabel A. Elliott, *Crime in Modern Society* (New York: Harper & Row, Publishers, 1951), p. 180.

16 Willard Gaylin, *In the Service of Their Country: War Resisters in Prison* (New York: Grosset & Dunlap, 1970), p. 278.

17 Fred Gardner, *The Unlawful Concert: An Account of the Presidio Mutiny Case* (New York: The Viking Press, 1970), p. 228.

18 Lee Weiner, "The Political Trial of a People's Insurrection," in Babcox and Abel, eds., *The Conspiracy*, p. 193.

19 J. Anthony Lukas, *The Barnyard Epithet and Other Obscenities: Notes on the Chicago Conspiracy Trial* (New York: Harper & Row, Publishers, 1970), pp. 81–83.

20 Jason Epstein, *The Great Conspiracy Trial: An Essay on Law, Liberty and the Constitution* (New York: Random House, 1970), p. 429.

21 Lukas, *The Barnyard Epithet*, p. 15.

22 See Richard Quinney, "A Conception of Man and Society for Criminology," *Sociological Quarterly*, 6 (Spring 1965), pp. 119–127.

23 Richard Quinney, *The Problem of Crime* (New York: Dodd, Mead & Company, 1970), p. 180.

24 *The New York Times* (July 5, 1968), p. 1.

25 William A. Westley, "Violence and the Police," *American Journal of Sociology*, **59** (July 1953), p. 35.

26 Committee of Concerned Asian Scholars, *The Indochina Story* (New York: Bantam Books, 1970), pp. 250–251.

27 Richard Quinney, "U.S. War Crimes in Southeast Asia," manuscript, Department of Sociology, New York University, 1971.

28 Herbert H. Hyman, *Political Socialization* (New York: The Free Press, 1959); and Robert E. Lane, *Political Life: Why People Get Involved in Politics* (New York: The Free Press, 1959).

29 Robert M. Williams, Jr., *American Society* (New York: Alfred A. Knopf, 1960), pp. 379–380.

30 Morton Grodzins, *The Loyal and Disloyal: Social Boundaries of Patriotism and Treason* (Chicago: University of Chicago Press, 1956).

31 Mulford Q. Sibley and Ada Wardlaw, *Conscientious Objectors in Prison, 1940– 1945* (Ithaca, N.Y.: Pacifist Research Bureau, 1945), Chap. 1.

32 Ted Robert Gurr, "A Comparative Study of Civil Strife," in Hugh Davis Graham and Ted Robert Gurr, eds., *Violence in America: Historical and Comparative Perspectives* (New York: Bantam Books, 1969), p. 586.

33 Robert M. Fogelson, "Violence and Grievances: Reflections on the 1960s Riots," *Journal of Social Issues*, 26 (Winter 1970), p. 160.

34 Jessica Mitford, *The Trial of Dr. Spock* (New York: Alfred A. Knopf, 1969), p. 4.

35 Tom Hayden, *Trial* (New York: Holt, Rinehart and Winston, 1970), p. 33.

36 Ellwyn R. Stoddard, "The Informal 'Code' of Police Deviancy: A Group Approach to 'Blue-Coat Crime,'" *Journal of Criminal Law, Criminology and Police Science*, 59 (June 1968), p. 212.

37 Jerome H. Skolnick, *Justice without Trial: Law Enforcements in Democratic Society* (New York: John Wiley & Sons, 1966), p. 202.

38 See Donald J. Black and Albert J. Reiss, Jr., "Patterns of Behavior in Police and Citizen Transactions," *Studies in Crime and Law Enforcement in Major Metropolitan Areas*. The President's Commission on Law Enforcement and Administration of Justice (Washington, D.C.: U. S. Government Printing Office, 1967), Vol. 2, Field Survey III, pp. 132–139.

39 The Walker Report to the National Commission on the Causes and Prevention of Violence, *Rights in Conflict* (New York: Bantam Books, 1968), p. 1.

40 Jerome H. Skolnick, *The Politics of Protest* (New York: Ballantine Books, 1969).

41 David Fellman, *The Constitutional Right of Association* (Chicago: University of Chicago Press, 1963).

42 David Fellman, *The Limits of Freedom* (New Brunswick, N.J.: Rutgers University Press, 1959), p. 25.

43 Hayden, *Trial*, pp. 44–45.

44 Gabriel Kolko, *The Roots of American Foreign Policy* (Boston: Beacon Press, 1969), p. 8.

45 Mouledoux, "Political Crime and the Negro Revolution," p. 219.

46 See *The New York Times* (October 26, 1970), pp. 1 and 31.

47 *The New York Times* (October 15, 1970), pp. 1 and 32.

48 Jack Newfield, "The Law is an Outlaw," *The Village Voice* (December 17, 1970), p. 1.

49 Richard Halloran, "Army Spied on 18,000 Civilians in 2-Year Operation," *The New York Times* (January 18, 1971), pp. 1 and 22.

50 Quinney, "U.S. War Crimes in Southeast Asia."

51 Lemert, *Social Pathology*, p. 200.

52 Ted Finman and Stewart Macaulay, "Freedom to Dissent: The Vietnam Protests and the Words of Public Officials," *Wisconsin Law Review*, 1966 (Summer 1966), pp. 41–42.

[53]Ingraham and Tokoro, "Political Crime in the United States and Japan," pp. 162–163.

[54] *The New York Times* (November 1, 1970), p. 66.

[55] Wildeman, "War Resistance and the Governmental Process," pp. 542–543.

[56] Lemert, *Social Pathology*, pp. 203–204.

[57] William Preston, Jr., *Aliens and Dissenters: Federal Suppression of Radicals 1903–1933* (Cambridge, Mass.: Harvard University Press, 1963), Chaps. 7 and 8.

[58] Allen D. Grimshaw, "Government and Social Violence: The Complexity of Guilt," *Minnesota Review*, 3 (Winter 1963), pp. 236–245; Grimshaw, "Actions of Police and the Military in American Race Riots," *Phylon*, 24 (Fall 1963), pp. 271–289.

[59] The Walker Report to the National Commission on the Causes and Prevention of Violence, *Rights in Conflict*, p. 1.

[60] Gaylin, *In the Service of Their Country*, p. 320.

[61] *The New York Times* (August 30, 1970), p. 24.

[62] Robert L. Rabin, "Do You Believe in a Supreme Being—The Administration of the Conscientious Objector Exemption," *Wisconsin Law Review*, **1967** (Summer 1967), pp. 673–675.

[63] Otto Kirchheimer, *Political Justice: The Use of Legal Procedure for Political Ends* (Princeton, N.J.: Princeton University Press, 1961), p. 46.

[64] Leon Friedman, "Political Power and Legal Legitimacy: A Short History of Political Trials," *The Antioch Review*, 30 (Summer 1970), p. 157.

[65] Skolnick, *The Politics of Protest*, pp. 293–326.

[66] Seymour M. Hersh, *My Lai 4: A Report on the Massacre and Its Aftermath* (New York: Vintage Books, 1970), pp. 151–170; Edward M. Opton, Jr., Erwin Knoll, and Judith Nies McFadden, eds., *War Crimes and the American Conscience* (New York: Holt, Rinehart and Winston, 1970), pp. 111–127.

[67] Committee of Concerned Asian Scholars, *The Indochina Story*, pp. 153–156.

[68] Kolko, *The Roots of American Foreign Policy*, p. xiii.

[69] *The New York Times* (October 17, 1970), pp. 1 and 22.

[70] See Robert Sherrill, *Military Justice is to Justice as Military Music is to Music* (New York: Harper & Row, Publishers, 1970).

[71] Proceedings of the Russell International War Crimes Tribunal, *Against the Crime of Silence* (Flanders, N.J.: O'Hare Books, 1968).

SELECTED BIBLIOGRAPHY

Chapin, Bradley, *The American Law of Treason*. Seattle: University of Washington Press, 1964.

Chevigny, Paul, *Police Power: Police Abuses in New York City*. New York: Pantheon Books, 1969.

D'Amato, Anthony A., Gould, Harvey L., and Woods, Larry D., "War Crimes and Vietnam: The 'Nuremberg Defense' and the Military Service Resister." *California Law Review*, 57 (November 1969), pp. 1055–1110.

Dunham, Barrows, *Heroes and Heretics: A Social History of Dissent*. New York: Alfred A. Knopf, 1964.

Epstein, Jason, *The Great Conspiracy Trial: An Essay on Law, Liberty and the Constitution.* New York: Random House, 1970.

Falk, Richard A., "War Crimes and Individual Responsibility: A Legal Memorandum." *Transaction,* 7 (January 1970), pp. 33–40.

Fellman, David, *The Limits of Freedom.* New Brunswick, N.J.: Rutgers University Press, 1959.

Fogelson, Robert M. "Violence and Grievances: Reflections on the 1960s Riots." *Journal of Social Issues,* 26 (Winter 1970), pp. 141–163.

Friedman, Leon, "Political Power and Legal Legitimacy: A Short History of Political Trials." *The Antioch Review,* 30 (Summer 1970), pp. 157–170.

Gardner, Fred, *The Unlawful Concert: An Account of the Presidio Mutiny Case.* New York: The Viking Press, 1970.

Gaylin, Willard, *In the Service of Their Country: War Resisters in Prison.* New York: Grosset & Dunlap, 1970.

Gellhorn, Walter, *Individual Freedom and Governmental Restraints.* Baton Rouge, La.: Louisiana State University Press, 1956.

Grodzins, Morton, *The Loyal and the Disloyal.* Chicago: University of Chicago Press, 1956.

Hayden, Tom, *Trial.* New York: Holt, Rinehart and Winston, 1970.

Hersh, Seymour M., *My Lai 4: A Report on the Massacre and Its Aftermath.* New York: Vintage Books, 1970.

Iglitzin, Lynne B., "Violence and American Democracy." *Journal of Social Issues,* 26 (Winter 1970), pp. 165–186.

Kirchheimer, Otto, *Political Justice: The Use of Legal Procedure for Political Ends.* Princeton, N.J.: Princeton University Press, 1961.

Knoll, Erwin, and McFadden, Judith Nies, eds., *War Crimes and the American Conscience.* New York: Holt, Rinehart and Winston, 1970.

Lukas, J. Anthony, *The Barnyard Epithet and Other Obscenities: Notes on the Chicago Conspiracy Trial.* New York: Harper & Row, Publishers, 1970.

Manwaring, David, *Render unto Caesar: The Flag-Salute Controversy.* Chicago: University of Chicago Press, 1962.

Marx, Gary T., "Civil Disorder and the Agents of Social Control." *Journal of Social Issues,* 26 (Winter 1970), pp. 19–57.

Mitford, *The Trial of Dr. Spock.* New York: Alfred A. Knopf, 1969.

Mouledoux, Joseph C., "Political Crime and the Negro Revolution," in Marshall B. Clinard and Richard Quinney, *Criminal Behavior Systems: A Typology,* New York: Holt, Rinehart and Winston, 1967, pp. 217–231.

Murray, Robert K., *Red Scare: A Study in National Hysteria, 1919–1920.* Minneapolis: University of Minnesota Press, 1965.

Packer, Herbert L., "Offenses against the State." *The Annals,* 339 (January 1962), pp. 77–89.

Preston, William, Jr., *Aliens and Dissenters: Federal Suppression of Radicals, 1903–1933.* Cambridge, Mass.: Harvard University Press, 1963.

Proceedings of the Russell International War Crimes Tribunal, *Against the Crime of Silence.* Flanders, N. J.: O'Hare Books, 1968.

Quinney, Richard, "U. S. War Crimes in Southeast Asia." Manuscript, Department of Sociology, New York University, 1971.

Schafer, Stephen, "The Concept of the Political Criminal." *Journal of Criminal Law, Criminology and Police Science,* **62** (September 1971), pp. 280–287.

Schwartz, Herman, "The Legitimation of Electronic Eavesdropping: The Politics of Law and Order." *Michigan Law Review,* **67** (January 1969), pp. 455–510.

Sherrill, Robert, *Military Justice is to Justice as Military Music is to Music.* New York: Harper & Row, Publishers, 1970.

Sibley, Mulford Q., and Jacob, Philip E., *Conscription of Conscience.* Ithaca, N.Y.: Cornell University Press, 1952.

Skolnick, Jerome H., *The Politics of Protest.* New York: Ballantine Books, 1969.

Stoddard, Ellwyn R., "The Informal 'Code' of Police Deviancy: A Group Approach to 'Blue-Coat Crime.'" *Journal of Criminal Law, Criminology and Police Science,* **59** (June 1968), pp. 201–213.

Taylor, Telford, *Nuremberg and Vietnam: An American Tragedy.* Chicago: Quadrangle Books, 1970.

Walker Report to the National Commission on the Causes and Prevention of Violence, *Rights in Conflict.* New York: Bantam Books, 1968.

Westley, William A., "Violence and the Police." *American Journal of Sociology,* **59** (July 1953), pp. 34–41.

Wildeman, John, "War Resistance and the Governmental Process." Manuscript, Department of Sociology, Hofstra University, 1971.

Wolfgang, Marvin, "Political Crimes and Punishment in Renaissance Florence." *Journal of Criminal Law, Criminology and Police Science,* **44** (January–February 1954), pp. 555–581.

Occupational 7
Criminal Behavior

The concept of white collar crime was introduced in 1939 by Edwin H. Sutherland in his presidential address to the American Sociological Society.[1] In his original formulation, Sutherland used the term to refer to violation of legal codes in the course of occupational activity by persons who are "respectable" and "of high social status." The concept turned the attention of criminologists to the study of offenses which had not been included within the scope of criminology. Traditionally criminologists had studied the conventional offenses, such as murder, robbery, and larceny, largely to the exclusion of those offenses in violation of the laws that regulate the numerous occupations.

The realization that middle- and upper-class persons commit their own forms of crime was by no means limited to Sutherland.[2] Earlier sociologists had criticized unscrupulous behaviors that occurred in the course of achieving the American dream. E. A. Ross, in particular, directed his attention to "criminaloids," a term that predated white collar crime by over thirty years. During the 1930s, the criminologist Albert Morris called attention to "criminals of the upperworld." But it was with Sutherland's work that such crime began to be taken seriously by a number of criminologists.

The concept of white collar crime has altered our picture of crime. The stereotype of the criminal as necessarily lower class and pathological had to be changed.[3] But more than this, the concept of white collar crime turned the attention of criminologists to a consideration of the relation of crime to the pursual of one's legitimate occupation. Gradually the concept was expanded to include the violations that occur in all occupations, irrespective of social class. Newman in his critique of white collar crime, for example, suggested that "farmers, repairmen, and others in essentially nonwhite collar occupations, could through such illegalities as watering milk for public consumption, making unnecessary 'repairs' on television sets, and so forth, be classified as white collar violators."[4] In his research on wartime black market violations, Clinard included all gasoline station operators and anyone who rented property, irrespective of their social status.[5] Consequently, Quinney suggested that an expansion of the concept of white collar crime to include all violations that occur in the course of occupational activity—regardless of the social status of the offender—would increase the utility of the concept.[6] Thus, occupational crime can be defined as violation of the criminal law in the course of activity in a legitimate occupation.

The concept of white collar crime is, however, in need of further reformulation. Even when Sutherland's concept is expanded by considering all occupations, there remains the question of the larger context of the violations and the nature of the violator. Sutherland added considerable ambiguity to the concept by referring to occupational activity but then engaging in research on the violations that take place in large corporations. Furthermore, rather than regarding the corporations as violators, he studied the policy-making officials of corporations. Realizing these problems in the concept of white collar crime, Bloch and Geis have divided the concept into a number of subtypes:

> One of the major shortcomings of studies of white-collar crime, as noted earlier, has been the failure to delineate clearly homogeneous types of offenses in terms of such things as *modus operandi*, legal categories, characteristics of the perpetrators, impact on particular victims, or the social context in which the offenses arose. As a starting point, it might be desirable to distinguish among offenses committed (1) by individuals as individuals (e.g., lawyers, doctors, and so forth), (2) by employees against the corporation or business (e.g., embezzlers), (3) by policy-making officials for the corporation (e.g., in antitrust cases), (4) by agents of the corporation against the general public, (e.g., in advertising fraud), and (5) by merchants against customers (e.g., in consumer frauds).[7]

For the purpose of our typology of criminal behavior systems, we are dividing white collar crime into two distinct types: occupational crime and corporate crime. Occupational crime consists of offenses committed by individuals for themselves in the course of their occupations and the offenses of employees against their employers. Corporate crime consists of the offenses committed by corporate officials for their corporation and the offenses of the corporation itself. The general public or the consumer may be exploited in the course of both occupational and corporate crime. When consumer fraud is committed by the individual businessman or the professional, such crime will be included in occupational crime; when consumer fraud is committed by the corporation or the corporate official, it will be included in corporate crime.

The discussion in this chapter will be limited to occupational crime. Corporate crime will be defined and discussed in the next chapter.

LEGAL ASPECTS OF SELECTED OFFENSES

Lawbreaking is often divided into two categories: the traditional crimes, such as larceny, burglary, and robbery, which are usually punished under the criminal law; and those violations of law (occupational crimes) which are not usually punished through the use of the criminal law but rather through civil law and administrative law. Punishment by the government through the civil law includes injunctions, treble damage suits, and license suspension suits. Administrative actions include license suspensions, seizure of illegal commodities, monetary payments, and so on.

Research on occupational crime has concentrated on offenses committed by businessmen, politicians, government employees, labor union officials, doctors, and lawyers. Such violations include infringements of law by businessmen and business employers, restraint of trade (through monopoly, illegal rebates, infringements of patents, trademarks, and copyrights), misrepresentation in advertising, unfair labor practices, financial manipulations, and wartime crimes such as black marketeering. Embezzlement is a common form of occupational crime committed by businessmen of various kinds, especially bankers. In developing countries violations by businessmen of the income tax laws, import and export regulations, and currency control measures are often common.

Politicians and government employees commit various occupational offenses, including direct misappropriation of public funds or the illegal acquisition of these funds through padded payrolls, illegally placing relatives on the payroll, or monetary payments from appointees. Their illegal activities are usually more subtle, however. Politicians and government employees may gain financially by furnishing favors to business firms, such as illegal commissions on public contracts, issuance of fraudulent licenses or certificates, and tax exemptions or lower tax evaluations. Labor union officials may engage in such criminal activities as misappropriating or misapplying union funds, defying the government by failure to enforce laws affecting their unions, entering into collusion with employers to the disadvantage of their own union members, or using fraudulent means to maintain control over the union. Doctors may illegally prescribe narcotics, perform illegal abortions, make fraudulent reports or give false testimony in accident cases, and split fees. Fee splitting, wherein a doctor gives part of his fee to the doctor referring the case to him, is illegal in many places in the United States because of the danger that such referrals might be based on the fee rather than on the practitioner's ability. Lawyers engage in such illegal activities as misappropriating funds in receiverships, securing perjured testimony from witnesses, and "ambulance chasing" in various forms, usually to collect fraudulent damage claims arising from an accident. Members of other occupations may also violate the law in various ways.

Legal regulation of occupations has a long and varied history. The beginnings are to be found in the development of licensure practices among the medieval guilds. These practices sought to protect the economic interests of the members and to protect the community from harmful economic and trade activities. By the beginning of the nineteenth century, the tradition of professional and occupational licensing was well established in America, especially in the case of law and medicine. Later in the century the laws were greatly modified, and in many instances repealed, following the laissez-faire philosophy. But with the eventual founding of national and state occupational associations, regulations were once again established.

The founding of these associations was largely for the purpose of promoting the interests of the particular occupations. Often the purpose was to protect one occupation from the encroachment of another. Akers, in research on the regulation of health professions, writes:

> The foundings of state associations were often for the express purpose of promoting occupational legislation, sometimes in a defensive move to prevent other, already established, professions from regulating them. The New Jersey Pharmaceutical Association (1870), for instance, was formed only after steps were undertaken by the medical society of New Jersey to force legislative measures on "all dispensers of medicines" in the state. Within a week of the formation of the New York Optical Society (1896), a bill to regulate the practice of refracting opticians (the early denotation of optometrists) was introduced in the New York legislature. Securing passage of a medical practice act was one of the main reasons for the organization of the Virginia Medical Society. The initial organization of each of the five professions in Kentucky was shortly followed by the enactment of a practice act. Since its organization, each association has been the driving force in legislation regulating practice in its own field.[8]

By 1900 all the established professions had laws, due to the pressure from their respective associations. Hence, the occupational associations, not the general public, have been responsible for the laws that regulate the occupations. To this day, the statutes and administrative codes that regulate occupations and professions are made by the occupations and professions themselves, representing their own parochial interests.

Occupations and professions, especially through their associations, thus have a virtual monopoly on the lawmaking that affects their operations.

> The state association, in conjunction with the examining board, initiates moves for legislation, decides what provisions should be added, deleted, or changed, drafts preliminary and final proposed bills, persuades a legislator to introduce the bill, and works for its passage throughout the time it is being considered. If proposed practice legislation comes from any other direction, the association will oppose it and work for its defeat.[9]

Moreover, each occupation attempts to protect itself from the competition of other occupations. Looking at the relation between five health professions in one state, the following situation was observed:

> The general picture of the context of conflict among the five professions in Kentucky can be summarized as follows: Chiropractic and optometry generally do not oppose one another but have not made any apparent efforts to cooperate with and support one another. Medicine, dentistry,

and pharmacy in recent times have not actively opposed one another and, in fact, are members of an allied group of health professions. Medicine and chiropractic consistently oppose each other, and sometimes optometry and medicine engage in political combat. Medicine, dentistry, and pharmacy occasionally all oppose certain aspects of chiropractic's legislation. Secondarily, they may be politically opposed to optometry. Medicine and dentistry seem to cooperate more closely than any other two groups, and they seldom oppose pharmaceutical legislation, although not always wholeheartedly supporting it. Finally, each profession experiences conflict with additional groups besides the other four health professions.[10]

It was also found that those professions that have the greatest organizational resources and cohesive structures are the most successful in gaining legislation that favors their own interests. The power of certain occupations to overwhelm other occupations and groups is a basic fact of legislative politics. All this passes under the guise of maintaining high standards of service for the public good.

CRIMINAL CAREER OF THE OFFENDER

A major characteristic of occupational crime is the way in which the offender conceives of himself. Since the offenses take place in connection with a legitimate occupation and the offender generally regards himself as a respectable citizen, he does not regard himself as a criminal. At most, he regards himself as a "lawbreaker." In this sense his attitude is similar to that of offenders who are convicted of such crimes as statutory rape, nonsupport, or drunken driving. Because the offender is a member of a legitimate occupation, it is difficult for the general public, while not condoning his activities, to conceive of him as being a real criminal. This attitude is, in turn, reflected in the conception that occupational offenders have of themselves. Although some writers have felt for this reason that occupational criminals are not real criminals, the lack of self-concept as a criminal in criminological studies of lawbreakers can be as significant as the presence of such a self-concept.

The maintenance of a noncriminal self-concept by the offender is one of the essential elements in the process leading to occupational crime. Cressey, in his study of 133 persons imprisoned for violations of trust, found that three interrelated steps were present in all the cases: (1) a nonsharable financial problem, (2) knowledge of how to violate and an awareness that the problem could be secretly resolved by violating their position of trust, and (3) rationalizations about the violations.[11] The violators were able to apply to their own conduct verbalizations which allowed them to adjust their concepts of themselves as trusted persons with their concepts of themselves as users of entrusted funds or property. Potential trust violators defined the situation through rationalizations in terms which enabled them to regard the criminal behavior as essentially noncriminal. It was rationalized that the behavior was merely "borrowing," that it was justified, that it was part of the "general irresponsibility" for which they were not completely accountable, or that it was due to unusual circumstances.

Occupational offenders are thus able to appropriately rationalize their law-violating behaviors. In some cases their justifications are in terms of attitudes toward the law itself. For example, in a study of rent control violations among landlords, it was found that the violations were related to the offender's conception of the fairness of the particular law.

> Now one may assume that, insofar as a landlord has a concept of a fair rent which exceeded the legal maximum for some accomodation, he is persistently motivated to seek to reduce the discrepancy. Perhaps this is not sufficient in itself to induce a landlord to violate his ceiling. But it would certainly enter the mind of any landlord who, for whatever reasons, "needs" more money, or serve as reason enough for any landlord who simply "wants" his "fair return" or whatever he originally anticipated from his rental business.[12]

Among the violators, over 90 percent regarded the rent ceilings as unfair. Such attitudes are probably as much a rationale for violation among such offenders as a subsequent rationalization for their criminal behavior.

A similar instance of rationality in the violations of occupational offenders is found in a study of "blue collar theft."[13] Workers in an electronics assembly plant would on occasion remove company or personal property from the plant for their own use. Horning discovered that the workers were highly selective about the property they would steal from the plant, based primarily on their conception of who owned the property and the certainty of that ownership. They avoided labeling their acts as "theft." Pilfering was rationalized in terms of such verbalizations as "the Company expects it" or "the Company doesn't mind."

Finally, the life organization of the occupational offender is not built around a criminal role. He plays a variety of roles, the most prominent one being that of respected citizen. The reputations of occupational offenders have been observed in several studies. In an examination of the most flagrant cases of price and rationing violations during World War II, those in which criminal prosecution was instituted, it was noted that less than one violator in ten was reported to have had any criminal record.[14] In studies of other occupational offenders, it has been found that the overwhelming majority of the offenders reside in the most desirable areas of the city.[15] In terms of career life style, the occupational offender can hardly be distinguished from the nonoffender.

GROUP SUPPORT OF CRIMINAL BEHAVIOR

When Sutherland introduced the concept of white collar crime, he noted the importance of the interpersonal associations of the offender in becoming a white collar criminal. Indeed, he argued, most forms of criminal behavior can be understood according to the same process.

> The hypothesis which is here suggested as a substitute for the conventional theories is that white-collar criminality, just as other systematic criminality, is learned; that it is learned in direct or indirect association with those who already practice the behavior; and that those who learn this criminal behavior are segregated from frequent and intimate contacts with law-abiding behavior. Whether a person becomes a criminal or not is determined largely by the comparative frequency and intimacy of his contacts with the two types of behavior. This may be called the "process of differential association." It is a genetic explanation both of white-collar criminals and lower-class criminality. Those who become white-collar criminals generally start their careers in good neighborhoods and good homes, graduate from college with idealism, and, with little selection on their part, get into particular business situations in which criminality is practically a folkway, becoming inducted into that system of behavior just as into any other folkway. The lower-class criminals generally start their careers in deteriorated neighborhoods and families, find delinquents at hand from whom they acquire the attitudes toward, and the techniques of, crime through association with delinquents and through partial segregation from law-abiding people. The essentials of the process are the same for the two classes of criminals.[16]

Sutherland then added:

> This is not entirely a process of assimilation, for inventions are frequently made, perhaps more frequently in white-collar crime than in lower-class crime. The inventive geniuses for the lower-class criminals are generally professional criminals, while the inventive geniuses for many kinds of white-collar crime are generally lawyers.

Since the time that Sutherland introduced the concept of white collar crime, most of the studies of occupational crime have viewed the behavior in terms of the group attachments of the offender. Occupational crimes have been explained according to the principle of differential association, whereby criminal behavior is learned from others who define the behavior favorably and in isolation from those who do not.

In some occupations members may even learn specific techniques by which the law can be violated, and build up such rationalizations as "business is business," or "good business demands it." This diffusion of illegal practices is spread from a person already in the occupation to new persons, and from one business establishment, political machine, or white collar group to another. The majority of World War II black market violations in the United States by businessmen appear to have had their origins in behavior learned in association with others. Unethical and illegal practices were circulated in the trade as part of a definition of the situation, and rationalizations to support these violations of law were transmitted by this differential association. Types of violations were picked up from conversations with businessmen and descriptions of violations in trade journals and the press.

Although many forms of occupational crime can be satisfactorily explained by a theory of differential association (it would seem obvious where there has been continuous and intimate association with unethical and illegal norms and isolation from other norms), this theory as an explanation for *all* cases has several limitations. Many individuals do not engage in these practices, even though they are familiar with the techniques and rationalizations of violation and frequently associate with persons similarly familiar. A businessman could hardly remain in a business any length of time without acquiring a rather complete knowledge of the illegalities involved. Persons appear to accept or reject opportunities for occupational crime according to their orientations toward their roles and their attitudes toward general social values. Some of these factors are negative attitudes toward other persons in general, the relative importance attached to a status symbol of money as compared with law obedience, and the relative importance attached to personal, family, or business reputations.

Each occupational or work situation seems to contain its own set of group norms concerning the possibility of illegal behavior. This has been born out in the study of theft in the electronics assembly plant. It was found that the work group subculture contains a set of norms which prescribes the kinds of property that may be pilfered, the conditions under which pilfering may occur, and the situations in which the workers can expect the support of their fellow workers. The work group provides two broad guidelines for the pilferer:

> The first sets the limit by indicating that pilfering should be confined to the "valueless" property of uncertain ownership. The second indicates that pilfering should be limited to that which is needed for personal use. To exceed these limits was viewed as a threat to the entire system. Those who exceeded the limits were no longer granted the tacit support of the work group, which includes the right to neutralize one's guilt feelings and deny oneself the definition of one's acts as theft.[17]

Some forms of occupational crime are related to the structure of the occupation in which the offender is engaged and to the roles played by the offender within the occupation. The importance of the occupational structure and occupational roles of the offender has been shown in a study of prescription violation among retail pharmacists.[18] Because the occupation of retail pharmacy consists of two divergent occupational role expectations, professional and business, pharmacists experience the problem of adapting to one of several "occupational role organizations." The types of occupational role organizations, in turn, differ in the extent to which they produce tendencies toward prescription violation. Pharmacists with an occupational role organization that includes an orientation to the professional role are bound by a system of occupational control that includes guides for the compounding and dispensing of prescriptions. Pharmacists who lack the professional orientation to pharmacy are not bound by the occupational controls. The business-oriented pharmacists are interested in the general business goal of monetary gain. They subscribe to the popular belief in business that self-employment carries with it independence and freedom from control. The professional norms, as incorporated in the prescription laws, exercise little control over the occupational behavior of the pharmacists who are oriented to the business role.

In the study of prescription violation it was found that violations occur more frequently among business pharmacists and least often among professional pharmacists, with professional-business pharmacists and indifferent pharmacists (those not oriented to either role) being intermediate in frequency of violations. It was concluded that prescription violation is related to the structure of the occupation and the "differential orientation" of retail pharmacists to the roles within the occupation. Thus, group support for occupational crime can be in the form of diffuse and subtle processes. Each occupation likely contains its own supports both for and against the violation of occupational laws.

CORRESPONDENCE BETWEEN CRIMINAL AND LEGITIMATE BEHAVIOR

Occupational crime cannot be fully understood without reference to the structure and values of society. The values involved in the regulation of commercial transactions may conflict with those of free enterprise, individualism, or supply and demand. Attitude toward selective obedience to a "good" or "bad" law becomes the key to compliance. "The demand of law arises out of the conflicts in cultures, and because there is conflict in cultures, the law is not effective as a deterrent upon other groups that did not at first demand the law."[19]

One of the most important reasons for the high degree of correspondence between some forms of occupational crime and patterns of legitimate behavior is that many of the activities were not defined as criminal until recent years. Gradually public opinion is defining these behaviors as criminal. Yet many occupational crimes are violations of laws that are not part of the values of some segments of society.[20] The concern among criminologists for the study of occupational crime brings into focus a long-neglected relationship between criminal behavior, criminal law, penal sanctions, and social structure.[21] In a highly differentiated society the ambivalence of average citizens, businessmen, and lawyers reflects structured conflicts in social roles and the larger social system. Additional studies should give us some idea of the conditions that lead to the definition of behavior as criminal and of the way in which legal norms intersect and are integrated with the norms of other institutional structures. Values, norms, and other aspects of middle- and upper-class cultures may help explain occupational crime in much the same way that knowledge of the culture of the lower class is necessary to understand conventional crimes.

The extent of correspondence between some occupational crime and legitimate patterns is indicated in our everyday language. This language can easily provide the offender with appropriate verbalizations. Furthermore, these verbalizations may actually be "vocabularies of motive" for the offender. As in the case of embezzlers:

> Vocabularies of motive are not something invented by embezzlers (or anyone else) on the spur of the moment. Before they can be taken over by an individual, these verbalizations exist as group definitions in which the behavior in question, even crime, is in a sense *appropriate*. There are any number of popular ideologies that sanction crime in our culture: "Honesty is the best policy, but business is business"; "It is all right to steal a loaf of bread when you are starving"; "All people steal when they get in a tight spot." Once these verbalizations have been assimilated and internalized by individuals, they take a form such as: "I'm only going to use the money temporarily, so I am borrowing, not stealing," or "I have tried to live an honest life but I've had nothing but troubles, so to hell with it."[22]

A symbiotic relation exists between occupational crime and the very organization of legitimate society. This has recently been brought to our attention by the discovery that doctors are committing offenses in reference to our medical insurance system.[23] Not only are doctors obtaining excessive and probably illegal amounts of money for services supposedly rendered, but they are violating income tax laws in the course of doing this. A Treasury official told Congress that more than one doctor out of every three who receives substantial income from treating patients under the Medicare and Medicaid programs is cheating on his income tax. The figures on the extent of this tax evasion by doctors emerged from an investigation of the tax returns of 11,000 doctors who received $25,000 or more in Medicare and Medicaid payments in 1968. Since about 65 percent of all income received by doctors in the United States (an estimated total of $11.6 billion in 1968) comes from health plans, the violations amount to a sizable sum. Needless to say, without the health plans doctors would have to find money elsewhere if they wanted to maintain their large incomes. No wonder the American Medical Association lobbies for such programs rather than supporting an extensive medical program that would assure care to everyone possibly at the expense of reducing the yearly income of the doctor.

Further evidence of the correspondence between criminal behavior and legitimate behavior is found in the relation between the automobile manufacture industry and the automobile dealer. The market structure of the auto industry dramatically indicates the criminal character of much of legitimate society. Fraudulent behavior by the auto dealer is in large measure a result of the forces placed on him by the auto manufacturer. The basic relation that sets up the possibility of criminal behavior has been described as follows:

> While only four domestic manufacturers of cars remain, their products are distributed through 30,000 dealers with facilities scattered throughout the United States. Technically, the dealer is an independent businessman. Rarely, however, does he have the capital to acquire more than a fraction of the value of property involved in the dealership. The rest is supplied by the manufacturer, and although the dealer may increase his ownership, rising costs of real estate, equipment and facilities, plus expansion of the dealership, may keep him dependent on the manufacturer for a long time. Further, he operates under restrictive agreement, terms of which are set by the manufacturer.[24]

On the basis of this relation, the auto dealer must meet minimum sales responsibilities, which often leads to fraudulent warranties. In addition, he engages in unscrupulous sales tactics and other behaviors of questionable legality, including high financing, parts pushing, service gouging, the forcing of accessories, and phony repairs. The following case illustrates the fraudulent nature of repair charges:

> An Amarillo, Texas man drove his car into a shop for a small repair. The mechanic turned in a ticket for 80 cents, with no charge for labor. Next day the mechanic spied the car still in the shop and found that his original ticket had been replaced by one for $60. When he asked why, the shop foreman told him that the shop could not make money on 80-cent items, that the owner had been called and "expected" to pay for service to his car, and that was the reason for keeping the car an extra day and for padding the repair bill.[25]

Hence, in automobile sales and repairs, the franchise system which is controlled by the large auto manufacturers sets the terms for the daily operation of auto dealers. The American market structure is closely associated with—and is a force in—the occupational crimes that occur at other levels of the system.

Thus it can be seen that occupational crime is not far removed from the legitimate realm of American society. In discussing "our criminal society," Schur describes the relation between criminal behavior and certain values, drawing upon Taft's insightful notion of the "criminogenic" character of American society:

> Of course, this undercurrent of values conducive to business crimes and related offenses is not surprising, given the extensive influence of the

"business spirit" in our society. Indeed, certain of the values that help promote criminality in America are far from being subterranean in character. Thus, sociologist Donald Taft has cited the following "characteristics of American society" as having possible significance in the causation of crime: "its dynamic quality, complexity, materialism, growing impersonality, individualism, insistence upon the importance of status, restricted group loyalties, survivals of frontier traditions, race discrimination, lack of scientific orientation in the social field, tolerance of political corruption, general faith in law, disrespect for some law, and acceptance of quasi-criminal exploitation." While this list is something of a hodgepodge (including some subterranean values, some more dominant ones, and also a few behaviors that are more a result of certain values than values in their own right), the first few items—dynamism, complexity, materialism, impersonality, and individualism—may be especially noteworthy. These are clearly dominant values or characteristics of American life, and they seem in some sense to have very real bearing on at least some types of criminality.[26]

No need to look for individual pathologies when parts of the American dream can help us understand crime.

SOCIETAL REACTION AND LEGAL PROCESSING

Occupational crime differs from other crime not only in its unique form of activity but in the toleration and support it receives from the public. In particular, punishments given for occupational offenses almost without exception differ from the punishments given for other offenses. Among the reasons for the public's toleration of occupational crime is the fact that occupational crime is usually more complex and often diffused over a longer period of time than is the case with ordinary crimes, and this fact obscures the essential criminality of the acts. Furthermore, the type of publicity given occupational crimes, as contrasted to the more overt crimes like burglary or larceny, seldom creates much public resentment.

In the laws directed at the behavior of businessmen and other occupational members there has been a strong tendency to enact lenient statutes and to enforce them in a similar fashion, showing favoritism to offenders of high social status. Many of these laws provide no criminal sanctions, and where sanctions are included, they have been used hesitantly. Thus, the laws outlawing occupational offenses differ from conventional laws of crime not only in their origin, but in philosophy, in the determination of responsibility or intent, in enforcement and prosecution procedures, and in the sanctions used to punish the violators.

The enforcement and administration of occupational laws depend largely on especially created agencies rather than on police and prosecutors. The administrative process of hearing cases, rather than trial procedures, closely approximates juvenile court procedures. The actions are more often remedial in nature, as in the use of injunctions, rather than direct punishment of the offender through fine or imprisonment. All of this becomes apparent when one considers that an apprehended burglar or robber is punished by a jail sentence, a fine, or probation, whereas a doctor may be punished through the revocation of his license, a lawyer by disbarment, or a businessman by a government warning or injunction, the levying of civil damages, or the suspension of his license to do business.

Regulation of the medical profession provides an excellent example of the way in which occupational laws are enforced and administered. A special administrative agency exists in most states for regulating medical practice laws. In New York, for instance, a board of examiners is appointed by the Regents of the state. Moreover, the board is composed of medical practitioners, appointed by the governor with the consent of the state senate. The board issues licenses and has the responsibility of disciplining members, which may consist of revoking licenses after a hearing. Only as a last resort are cases turned over to the state's Attorney General for criminal prosecution.

All of this is to say that the physician is virtually a free agent. Once he has a license he has a lifetime certificate to practice largely at his own discretion. When violations of medical practices laws are detected, the state board is not fast to act. Thus, self-discipline among doctors is more illusory than real.

> Within the profession itself the disciplining of colleagues has little support; physicians do not like to police their fellows, and this reluctance is reflected at every level of organized medicine. At that, the strongest penalty a medical society or hospital staff can levy is expulsion. But removal from a society or hospital has no bearing on the doctor's license; though unacceptable to his peers, the offender retains his legal privilege to treat patients. Moreover, just as the profession is slow to prosecute violators within its ranks, so also is it loath to pursue the cause of more effective laws. As a result, the inadequate statutes currently on the books are likely to remain unamended for the foreseeable future.[27]

Yet malpractice suits and other cases do arise in the medical profession and sometimes reach the courts. In the case of malpractice, at least 2000 professional-liability claims are brought against doctors each year in the United States. The Law Department of the American Medical Association estimates that at least one malpractice claim has been filed against 18 percent of all doctors in private practice. And the judgments and settlements in malpractice cases total about $50 million each year.[28]

But the malpractice plaintiff meets with considerable resistance when he takes his case before the court.[29] Many courts actually obstruct the plaintiff by requiring the testimony of medical witnesses. The problem with this procedure is that the doctors who testify are very likely to sympathize with their fellow doctors. Furthermore, doctors and hospital staffs are known to tamper with medical records, if such tampering will reflect favorably on the defendant's case. Just as false or biased testimony may be given in malpractice suits, so too may records be altered.

Of those malpractice cases that are successfully prosecuted, the question arises as to their effect on malpracticing doctors. Ironically, as one study reports, the practice of such doctors actually *increased* after the suit.[30] One of the losers in court commented, "I guess all the doctors in town felt sorry for me because new patients started coming in from doctors who had not sent me patients previously." Once again, almost by definition, a profession has a way of protecting itself from public scrutiny. It is able to minimize the harm that might come to its members, irrespective of the harm that its members inflict on the public.

Other characteristics of societal reaction and legal processing of occupational offenders are found in the case of employee thieves. In a study of the judicial disposition of employee thieves in three different department stores, it was found that stores vary in their handling of detected offenders.[31] In one store only 2 percent of its offenders were prosecuted, in another 8 percent were prosecuted, and in the other 34 percent of the offenders were prosecuted. The courses of action open to each store consisted of dismissal of the employee without criminal prosecution, dismissal and criminal prosecution, or retention of the employee.

A major reason for not prosecuting the employee thieves was the desire on the part of the department stores to avoid publicity.

> Although the company's reason for not prosecuting is often stated to be fear of suit by the employee for false arrest or malicious prosecution, fear of reprisal is a minor influence in the decisional process. Its influence is negligible compared with much more potent considerations. A much more direct influence is the employer's desire to avoid publicity about staff dishonesty, perhaps feeling that trust violators reflect upon his ability to select honest and loyal workers. The image of a business, particularly a sizable one, is hardly improved by leaving itself open to the charge of persecuting defenseless employees who, through circumstances beyond their control, found it necessary to steal from the boss.[32]

And as to what determined if a store would prosecute, Robin concluded that

> (1) the recovery characteristics were much less important determinants of disposition than the absolute size-of-theft; (2) regardless of the proportion of the amount stolen that was recovered, if an employee stole at least 100 dollars and if Company A [the company that prosecuted most often] believed a conviction could be obtained, his chances of being prosecuted were better than even; and (3) assuming there was sufficient evidence, an employee's chances of being prosecuted increased

directly with the amount pilfered, and he was virtually assured of prosecution when a large amount was stolen and complete reparation was not obtained.[33]

The sentences administered by the courts to the 256 convicted employee thieves (99 percent of those prosecuted) provides an indication of societal reaction to theft by department store employees.

The offender was fined in 73 of the 256 cases. The average fine imposed was 72 dollars for those receiving any fine and 20 dollars for all convicted offenders; one-quarter of the fines were 100 dollars or more. The offender was ordered to make restitution in 44 percent of the cases, the average amount being 637 dollars in this group and 286 dollars for all offenders. Among those ordered to make restitution, the amount was under 100 dollars in 27 percent of the cases and 500 dollars or more in 29 percent of the cases. The offender was both fined and ordered to make restitution in 27 percent of the cases. The offender's sentence was suspended in 55 percent of the 256 cases. Among those given any suspended sentence, the average length was 11 months, with two-thirds given less than 1 year and only 9 percent 3 years or more. Fifteen percent of the offenders were given a definite suspended sentence and ordered to make restitution only. The offender was put on probation in 46 percent of the 256 cases. The average length of probation was 17 months; one-third were placed on probation for more than 1 year. Almost one-quarter were given a suspended sentence and placed on probation only; one-third were either given a suspended sentence or placed on probation only; and 30 percent were placed on probation and ordered to make restitution only.[34]

In other words, only 5 percent of the convicted violators were sentenced to prison. Nonpunitive sentences were given in 95 percent of the cases. And of the nonpunitive sentences, most were nominal, representing minimal judicial action. Employee thieves, obviously, are among the least stigmatized offenders in American society.

One final form of societal reaction and legal processing may be observed: the case of criminal tax fraud. The majority of prosecutions for income tax violations are directed against self-employed persons. The major portion of these persons are in the occupations of medicine, law, and accounting, followed by persons in real estate, building, construction trades, and farming. They are all prosecuted for violating the federal income tax law in filing tax forms of income made in their occupational activities.

To induce compliance to tax laws, a scale of sanctions has been devised, ranging from interests on unpaid tax liability, to statutory additions to tax, to civil and criminal penalties. Further, compliance is insidiously planned by the conception that everyone honestly pays his taxes, combined with the image that violations are always detected and prosecuted. An element of fear hangs over the whole process.

The selection of tax cases for investigation is done by the district offices of the Internal Revenue Service. Most investigations begin as a result of auditing tax returns, although leads also come from the IRS's data processing centers, other government units, informants, and other intelligence sources. The culmination of an investigation may be the decision to prosecute for criminal fraud. In recent times the yearly number of full-scale investigations has been around 2000. Of this number, 600 to 700 end up in district courts for criminal prosecution.

The sanctions for criminal tax fraud indicate the nature of societal reaction to the offense. What characterizes the reaction to criminal tax fraud is ambivalence. The sentencing practices consequently vary greatly from one juridsiction to another.

> Sentencing practices for defendants convicted of income tax evasion vary widely from district to district and judge to judge. When 54 Federal judges were polled to determine what sentence they would impose on a hypothetical defendant convicted of income tax evasion, they divided almost evenly between incarceration, on the one hand, and probation or fine, on the other. An Internal Revenue Service study of sentencing for income tax fraud for the years 1946 through 1963 shows that the percentage of prison sentences to convictions ranged from zero in South Dakota and 3 percent in the Western District of Virginia to 88 percent in the Western District of Washington and 93 percent in the Western District of Tennessee. In all districts during that period, imprisonment was imposed in only 38 percent of the cases. And of the 593 defendants convicted of criminal income tax fraud in 1966, 40 percent received prison terms. Terms of less than one year were imposed on 80 percent of those imprisoned.[35]

The Tax Division of the United States Department of Justice has presented the rationale for such practices:

> Some of the traditional purposes of sentencing— isolation, rehabilitation—have little application to the typical individual convicted of income tax evasion. Most offenders have no prior record of conviction and do not require isolation from society for its protection. Moreover, severe sentences are not required to rehabilitate the offender. Statistics of the Department of Justice suggest that there is a negligible amount of recidivism. Of the 1,186 persons convicted of criminal tax fraud in 1963 and 1964, only two persons were repeat offenders. The ignominy of indictment, prosecution and conviction rather than the particular type of sentence imposed discourages the ordinary defendant from repeating his crime.[36]

The sanctions for income tax violation are designed to deter others from committing the offense. Likely the same objective holds for other occupational offenses as well. Societal reaction, including legal processing, is to be of sufficient nature and extent to provide instructive example to others.

NOTES

[1] Edwin H. Sutherland, "White-Collar Criminality," *American Sociological Review*, 5 (February 1940), pp. 1–12.

[2] See Gilbert Geis, ed., *White-Collar Criminal: The Offender in Business and the Professions* (New York: Atherton Press, 1968), pp. 1–19.

[3] Frank E. Hartung, "White Collar Crime: Its Significance for Theory and Practice," *Federal Probation*, 17 (June 1953), pp. 31–36.

[4] Donald J. Newman, "White-Collar Crime," *Law and Contemporary Problems*, 23 (Autumn 1958), p. 737.

[5] Marshall B. Clinard, *The Black Market: A Study of White Collar Crime* (New York: Holt, Rinehart and Winston, 1952).

[6] Richard Quinney, "The Study of White Collar Crime: Toward a Reorientation in Theory and Research," *Journal of Criminal Law, Criminology and Police Science*, 55 (June 1964), pp. 208–214.

[7] Herbert A. Bloch and Gilbert Geis, *Man, Crime, and Society*, 2d ed. (New York: Random House, 1970), p. 307.

[8] Ronald L. Akers, "The Professional Association and the Legal Regulation of Practice," *Law and Society Review*, 2 (May 1968), p. 465. *Law and Society Review* is the official publication of The Law and Society Association.

[9] *Ibid.*, p. 467.

[10] *Ibid.*, p. 476. Also see Ronald L. Akers, "Professional Organization, Political Power, and Occupational Laws," unpublished Ph.D. dissertation, University of Kentucky, 1966.

[11] Donald R. Cressey, *Other People's Money* (New York: The Free Press, 1953).

[12] Harry V. Ball, "Social Structure and Rent-Control Violations," *American Journal of Sociology*, 65 (May 1960), p. 603.

[13] Donald N. M. Horning, "Blue-Collar Theft: Conceptions of Property, Attitudes toward Pilfering, and Work Group Norms in a Modern Industrial Plant," in Erwin O. Smigel and H. Laurence Ross, eds., *Crimes against Bureaucracy* (New York: Van Nostrand Reinhold Company, 1970), pp. 46–64.

[14] Clinard, *The Black Market*, p. 295.

[15] Frank E. Hartung, "A Study in Law and Social Differentiation, as Exemplified in Violations of the Emergency Price Control Act in the Detroit Wholesale Meat Industry," unpublished Ph.D. dissertation, University of Michigan, 1949, p. 221; and Richard Quinney, "Retail Pharmacy as a Marginal Occupation: A Study of Prescription Violation," unpublished Ph.D. dissertation, University of Wisconsin, 1962, p. 261.

[16] Sutherland, "White-Collar Criminality," p. 11.

[17] Horning, "Blue-Collar Theft," p. 62.

[18] Richard Quinney, "Occupational Structure and Criminal Behavior: Prescription Violation by Retail Pharmacists," *Social Problems*, 11 (Fall 1963), pp. 179–185.

[19] Albert K. Cohen, Alfred Lindesmith, and Karl Schuessler eds., *The Sutherland Papers* (Bloomington, Ind.: Indiana University Press, 1956), p. 102.

[20] Richard C. Fuller, "Morals and the Criminal Law," *Journal of Criminal Law, Criminology and Police Science*, 32 (March–April 1942), pp. 624–630; Richard Quinney, "Is Criminal Behavior Deviant Behavior?" *British Journal of Criminology*, 5 (April 1965), pp. 132–142.

[21] Vilhelm Aubert, "White Collar Crime and Social Structure," *American Journal of Sociology*, 58 (November 1952), pp. 263–271.

[22] Donald R. Cressey, "The Respectable Criminal," *Transaction*, 3 (March–April 1965).

[23] *The New York Times* (September 22, 1970), p. 1.
[24] William N. Leonard and Marvin Glenn Weber, "Automakers and Dealers: A Study of Criminogenic Market Forces," *Law and Society Review*, 4 (February 1970), p. 411.
[25] *Ibid.*, p. 417.
[26] Edwin M. Schur, *Our Criminal Society: The Social and Legal Sources of Crime in America*, © 1969, pp. 185–186. By permission of Prentice-Hall, Inc., Englewood Cliffs, N.J.
[27] Howard R. and Martha E. Lewis, *The Medical Offenders* (New York: Simon and Schuster, 1970), p. 21.
[28] *Ibid.*, p. 24. For related research on disbarment of lawyers, see Kenneth J. Reichstein, "Ambulance Chasing: A Case Study of Deviation and Control within the Legal Profession," *Social Problems*, 13 (Summer 1965), pp. 3–17.
[29] Lewis, *The Medical Offenders*, pp. 312–320.
[30] Richard D. Schwartz and Jerome H. Skolnick, "Two Studies of Legal Stigma," *Social Problems*, 10 (Fall 1962), pp. 133–142.
[31] Gerald D. Robin, "The Corporate and Judicial Disposition of Employee Thieves," *Wisconsin Law Review*, 1967 (Summer 1967), pp. 685–702.
[32] *Ibid.*, p. 692.
[33] *Ibid.*, p. 696.
[34] *Ibid.*, p. 697.
[35] *Crime and Its Impact—An Assessment*. President's Commission on Law Enforcement and Administration of Justice (Washington, D.C.: U. S. Government Printing Office, 1967), pp. 114–115.
[36] *Ibid.*, p. 115.

SELECTED BIBLIOGRAPHY

Akers, Ronald L., "The Professional Association and the Legal Regulation of Practice." *Law and Society Review,* 2 (May 1968), pp. 463–482.

Aubert, Vilhelm, "White Collar Crime and Social Structure." *American Journal of Sociology,* 58 (November 1952), pp. 263–271.

Ball, Harry V., "Social Structure and Rent-Control Violations." *American Journal of Sociology,* 65 (May 1960), pp. 598–604.

Clinard, Marshall B., *The Black Market: A Study of White Collar Crime.* New York: Holt, Rinehart and Winston, 1952.

Cressey, Donald R., *Other People's Money.* New York: The Free Press, 1953.

Geis, Gilbert, ed., *White-Collar Criminal: The Offender in Business and the Professions.* New York: Atherton Press, 1968.

Groves, Harold M., "An Empirical Study of Income-Tax Compliance." *National Tax Journal,* 6 (December 1958), pp. 241–301.

Hartung, Frank E., "White Collar Crime: Its Significance for Theory and Practice." *Federal Probation,* 17 (June 1953), pp. 31–36.

——, "White Collar Offenses in the Wholesale Meat Industry in Detroit." *American Journal of Sociology,* 56 (July 1950), pp. 25–32.

Horning, Donald N. M., "Blue-Collar Theft: Conceptions of Property, Attitudes toward Pilfering, and Work Group Norms in a Modern Industrial Plant," in Erwin O. Smigel and H. Laurence Ross, eds., *Crimes against*

Bureaucracy. New York: Van Nostrand Reinhold Company, 1970, pp. 46–64.

Leonard, William M., and Weber, Marvin Glenn, "Automakers and Dealers: A Study of Criminogenic Market Forces." *Law and Society Review*, 4 (February 1970), pp. 407–424.

Lewis, Howard R. and Martha E., *The Medical Offenders*. New York: Simon and Schuster, 1970.

Newman, Donald J., "White-Collar Crime." *Law and Contemporary Problems*, 23 (Autumn 1957), pp. 228–232.

Quinney, Richard, "Occupational Structure and Criminal Behavior: Prescription Violation by Retail Pharmacists." *Social Problems*, 11 (Fall 1963), pp. 179–185.

———, "The Study of White Collar Crime: Toward a Reorientation in Theory and Research." *Journal of Criminal Law, Criminology and Police Science*, 55 (June 1964), pp. 208–214.

Reichstein, Kenneth J., "Ambulance Chasing: A Case Study of Deviation and Control within the Legal Profession." *Social Problems*, 13 (Summer 1965), pp. 3–17.

Robin, Gerald D., "The Corporate and Judicial Disposition of Employee Thieves." *Wisconsin Law Review*, 1967 (Summer 1967), pp. 685–702.

Spencer, John C., "White Collar Crime," in T. Grygier, H. Jones, and John Spencer eds., *Criminology in Transition*. London: Routledge & Kegan Paul, Ltd., 1965, pp. 233–266.

Sutherland, Edwin H., "Is White-Collar Crime Crime?" *American Sociological Review*, 10 (April 1945), pp. 132–139.

———, "White-Collar Criminality," *American Sociological Review*, 5 (February 1940), pp. 1–12.

Corporate 8
Criminal Behavior

The concept of corporate crime presents a problem both to lawyers and criminologists. Lawyers have been uncertain as to whether a corporation can be defined and prosecuted as a criminal. For criminologists the problem has been who or what is to be the object of study. Today the problems of lawyers and criminologists are becoming one. The common question arises: What is to be meant by "corporate crime"?

Although Sutherland termed his concept "white collar crime," what he had in mind, among other things, were the offenses committed by corporate officials. Yet, in his argument, he condemned corporations for the crime they seemed to engender. In 1948, after introducing the concept of white collar crime, Sutherland presented a paper, "Crime of Corporations,"[1] in which he provided materials that were to be part of the book he published the next year. But he titled the book *White Collar Crime*.[2]

Sutherland obviously had difficulty distinguishing between corporations and officials of corporations. Who was the criminal, the corporation or the corporate official? Geis states the problem precisely:

> The major difficulty in *White Collar Crime* as criminological research lies in Sutherland's striking inability to differentiate between the corporations themselves and their executive and management personnel. Corporations are, of course, legal entities which can be and are subjected to criminal processes. There is today little restriction on the range of crimes for which a corporation may be held responsible, though it cannot, for obvious reasons, be imprisoned. For the purpose of criminological analysis, however, corporations cannot be considered persons, except by recourse to the same type of extrapolatory fiction that once brought about the punishment of inanimate objects. Sutherland attempted to resolve this obvious dilemma by maintaining, not without some acerbity, that the crimes of corporations are precisely the crimes of their executives and managers.[3]

Today the problem is especially urgent. For some time corporations have been legal entities, subject to criminal prosecution. But today many new laws are being created which make the corporation itself criminally liable for a range of social harms. We have discovered that our environment has been victimized by corporations. We realize, as well, that injustices are being committed against the consumer by corporations. So today the corporation, as well as officials of the corporation, is being defined as criminal. For the criminologist, the study of corporate crime—including crimes by the corporation and crimes by corporate officials—is a pressing concern.

LEGAL ASPECTS OF SELECTED OFFENSES

Not until the beginning of the nineteenth century were certain business activities made illegal in the United States. Gradually such activities as the following were punished in one form or another by the state: restraint of trade, false advertising, insolvency of banks due to fraud or negligence of officials, sale of fraudulent securities, misuse of trademarks, manufacture of unsafe foods and drugs, and pollution of the environment.

Previously, the philosophy of laissez-faire and caveat emptor (let the buyer beware) dominated the general social, political, and economic thinking in the Western World, prohibiting the development of certain needed legal restrictions on business activity. The new legislation grew out of industrialization, the replacement of the entrepreneur by the corporation, and the development of large-scale labor unions. Old conventional colonial laws often were not applicable and in their place regulatory and administrative laws emerged that were directed chiefly at the new forms of economic enterprise.

Toward the end of the nineteenth century, an antimonopoly movement emerged in response to these new economic forces. This movement was accompanied by the belief that the problem of monopoly could be solved only through government intervention. The result was the creation of a new kind of criminal law, an administrative law, which not only protected private property but also assisted in maintaining a particular kind of national economy. American capitalism was thus secured, rather than threatened, by the new legal restrictions.

Antitrust law was soon enacted in the Sherman Act of 1890. To combine in restraint of trade and to monopolize became public offenses. The federal government was now empowered to proceed against violations of the law by criminal actions.

Such controls were further strengthened by legislation and rulings during the "progressive era," the first fifteen or twenty years of this century. But what happened was the establishment of laws that protected business itself. The period, with the aid of new laws, marks the triumph of big business.

> There were any number of options involving government and economics abstractly available to national political leaders during the period 1900–1916, and in virtually every case they chose those solutions to problems advocated by the representatives of concerned business and financial interests. Such proposals were motivated by the needs of the interested businesses, and political intervention into the economy was frequently merely a response to the demands of particular businessmen.

In brief, conservative solutions to the emerging problems of an industrial society were almost uniformly applied. The result was a conservative triumph in the sense that there was an effort to preserve the basic social and economic relations essential to a capitalist society, an effort that was frequently consciously as well as functionally conservative.[4]

The crowning achievement for corporate business was the creation of the Federal Trade Commission, which ruled out "unfair methods of competition." Business and politics became one. "The business community knew what it wanted from the commission, and what it wanted was almost precisely what the commission sought to do. No distinction between government and business was possible simply because the commission absorbed and reflected the predominant values of the business community."[5]

The legislation of the New Deal further protected the capitalist system. Rather than being an enemy of capitalism, Franklin D. Roosevelt preserved the system. His administration "saved the system by ridding it of its grosser abuses and forcing it to accommodate itself to larger public interests. History may eventually record Franklin D. Roosevelt as the greatest American conservative since Hamilton."[6]

The attack upon business, then, beginning in the latter part of the nineteenth century and continuing to the present, has not been against corporate enterprise but has been inspired and led by corporate interests. Antitrust legislation was established for the interests of capitalist economics.

Recognizing that businessmen have been responsible for their own regulation, Sutherland went on to investigate the extent to which corporate officials violate their own laws.[7] What he found was that businessmen would have it both ways: they want to eliminate unfair competition from their competitors, but they will violate the law to their own advantage. In his study, Sutherland thus found that among the seventy largest industrial and mercantile corporations in the United States, courts and commissions had made 547 adverse decisions against them. An average of 7.8 decisions had been taken against each corporation, with each corporation having at least one adverse decision. The laws that the corporations violated were, in addition to antitrust, those that sanctioned false advertising, certain labor relations, and infringement of patents and trademarks. Sutherland argued that all of these violations were crimes since they were socially injurious and penalties were provided in the laws.

The legal processes involved in the supposed protection of the public's health are similar to those found in corporate legislation. Government has come to play an increasing role in establishing controls on the manufacture and sale of food and drugs.[8] Criminal laws and commissions have been created to protect our health. However, the interests of the food and drug industry receive more protection from these controls than does the public interest.

Gradually the public became aware of dangers in the foods and drugs they were consuming. Many measures were proposed. The first legislation, true to form, was gained by those business interests desiring to protect their respective products from what they regarded as unfair competition. Finally in 1906, after over 150 pure food and drug bills had been introduced in Congress, the Federal Food and Drug Act was passed. The act declared it unlawful to manufacture or introduce any adulterated or misbranded food and drug. Offending products were to be seized, and criminal penalties were provided for violations of the act.

The Food and Drug Act, however, suffered from many deficiencies as far as protection of the public was concerned. Some were overcome in the passage of the Federal Food, Drug and Cosmetic Act of 1938. The act required, among other things, more effective methods for the control of false labeling and advertising. Further abuses were considered in legislation during the 1960s. Nevertheless, pharmaceutical interests, especially manufacturers and dispensers of drugs, and food manufacturers have a wide latitude in their activities. The principal regulatory agency, the Food and Drug Administration, is more closely tied to the interests of the food and drug industry than to those of the general public.[9]

Only recently have we realized the extent to which corporations are polluting the environment. In the minds of the people, the nation's corporations are committing crimes against the environment. Ralph Nader strongly presents the case, writing particularly about air pollution:

> Air pollution (and its fallout on soil and water) is a form of domestic chemical and biological warfare. The efflux from motor vehicles, plants, and incinerators of sulfur oxides, hydrocarbons, carbon monoxide, oxides of nitrogen, particulates, and many more contaminants amounts to compulsory consumption of violence by most Americans. There is no full escape from such violent ingestions, for breathing is required. This damage, perpetuated increasingly in direct violation of local, state, and federal law, shatters people's health and safety but still escapes inclusion in the crime statistics. "Smogging" a city or town has taken on the proportions of a massive crime wave, yet federal and state statistical compilations of crime pay attention to muggers and ignore "smoggers." As a nation which purports to apply law for preserving health, safety, and property, there is a curious permissiveness toward passing and enforcing laws against the primary polluters who harm our society's most valued rights. In testament to the power of corporations and their retained attorneys, enforcement scarely exists. Violators are openly flouting the laws and an Administration allegedly dedicated to law and order sits on its duties.[10]

Considerable legislation for the express purpose of pollution control has been enacted. For example, a federal Air Quality Act was enacted in 1967. The shortcomings of the law are similar to those found in other environmental legislation. Namely, the act favors the interests of the corporate polluters. The act is primarily a delaying device, whereby corporations can continue to pollute. The act thus shifts the burden of proving adverse health effects from the polluter to the public, establishes that industry has a right to pollute up to a certain level, and transforms what should be political decisions into esoteric scientific jargon.[11]

Passage of the Air Quality Act of 1967 was a success for several interest groups. Only the general public was excluded.

> On November 21, 1967, President Johnson proudly affixed his signature to the Air Quality Act of 1967. Each faction had won something, except for the public. Lyndon Johnson got a law whose title he could claim as his own. Jennings Randolph had made a good showing for the coal industry. Edmund Muskie won the real battle to determine the direction of the federal air pollution control program for the next several years, and he did so without creating enemies, especially within the ranks of industry. Industry was happy to have a law it could live with without changing its plans.[12]

And there is little reason to believe that the National Air Quality Standards Act of 1970 is any further removed from similar vested interests. Such is likely to be the fate of "public law" as long as it is out of the hands of the people. To be sure, some violations will be detected and prosecuted. But this may be little more than a façade, behind which coporations are polluting the environment at their own discretion for their own profit.

CRIMINAL CAREER OF THE OFFENDER

What is most clearly apparent in the career of the offending corporate official is his respectable social status. Yet, a contradiction continues to exist:

> There is an obvious and basic incongruity involved in the proposition that a community's leaders and more responsible elements are also its criminals. Business leaders and corporation executives by and large play important roles in civic and community affairs. They more often than not constitute an important source of imaginative leadership for community enterprises of all kinds. The very fact of reputable community standing is therefore one of the more confusing and inconsistent aspects of the concept "white collar crime," as the term has been elaborated in American studies.[13]

So the corporate official's respectability, even when he is a violator, exists almost by definition. Corporate officials are typically drawn from the middle class; and if not, they are highly regarded in the community by the mere fact of being a corporate executive.

The respectability of corporate offenders has been observed by a reporter who described the defendants in the 1961 antitrust case in the heavy electrical equipment industry as "middle-class men in Ivy League suits—typical businessmen in appearance, men who would never be taken for lawbreakers." One of the defendants, a General Electric vice-president who was later sentenced to prison, was earning $135,000 a year. His background has been summarized as follows:

> He had been born in Atlanta and was 46-years-old at the time he was sentenced to jail. He had graduated with a degree in electrical engineering from Georgia Tech, and received an honorary doctorate degree from Sienna College in 1958, was married, and the father of three children. He had served in the Navy during the Second World War, rising to the rank of lieutenant commander, was a director of the Schenectady Boys Club, on the board of trustees of Miss Hall's School, and not without some irony, was a member of Governor Rockefeller's Temporary State Committee on Economic Expansion.[14]

When corporate officials violate the law, they have the appropriate rationalizations to view their conduct. In the process, they maintain a non-criminal self-conception. The testimony of a Westinghouse executive, at the electrical equipment antitrust hearing, illustrates this point:

> *Committee Attorney*: Did you know that these meetings with competitors were illegal?
> *Witness*: Illegal? Yes, but not criminal. I didn't find that out until I read the indictment. . . . I assumed that criminal action meant damaging someone, and we did not do that. . . . I thought that we were more or less working on a survival basis in order to try to make enough to keep our plant and our employees.[15]

Also, such offenders believe that they have not caused harm to anyone. An official of the Ingersoll-Rand Corporation noted, "It is against the law." But he added, "I do not know that it is against public welfare because I am not certain that the consumer was actually injured by this operation."

After considering the testimony of the corporate offenders involved in the electrical equipment antitrust cases, Geis offers an explanation that says much about the rational character of the offenders and their decision to violate the law:

> For the conspirators there had necessarily to be a conjunction of factors before they could participate in the violations. First, of course, they had to perceive that there would be gains accruing from their behavior. Such gains might be personal and professional, in terms of corporate advancement toward prestige and power, and they might be vocational, in terms of a more expedient and secure method of carrying out assigned tasks. The offenders also apparently had to be able to neutralize or rationalize their behavior in a manner in keeping with their image of themselves as law-abiding, decent, and respectable persons. The ebb and flow of the price-fixing conspiracy also clearly indicates the relationship, often overlooked in explanations of criminal behavior, be-

tween extrinsic conditions and illegal acts. When the market behaved in a manner the executives thought satisfactory, or when enforcement agencies seemed particularly threatening, the conspiracy desisted. When market conditions deteriorated, while corporate pressures for achieving attractive profit-and-loss statements remained constant, and enforcement activity abated, the price-fixing agreements flourished.[16]

As crimes against the environment are now being taken more seriously, the character of the corporation itself as an offender is being understood. What becomes obvious is that the nation's leading corporations are committing destructive acts against man and nature. Specifically, all of this is being done systematically and repeatedly, rather than randomly and occasionally. The crimes are being committed as a standard operating procedure. In order to insure profits at a minimum of expense, these corporations are willfully engaging in crime. The corporations themselves as legal entities, as well as some of the corporate officials who make specific decisions, are criminal. And what is most frightening is that once these systematic crimes become normal operating procedure, they are not the responsibility of any one individual in the corporation. Rather, they are corporate crimes, in the sense that the corporation itself is the criminal.

That such crime is no accident, carried out by disreputable businesses, is made clear in the indictments recently brought against several of the largest corporations for dumping mercury into lakes and rivers.[17] The dangers of mercury to animal and human life have been known for some time. A very small trace of mercury will cause neurological disorders such as blindness, paralysis, irreparable damage to internal organs, and certainly death. Once in the waters, mercury can affect the whole biological cycle.

The disastrous consequences of mercury contamination could not escape the attention of corporate officials. Moreover, policy-making officials were certainly aware that their industries were discharging mercury into the waters. One corporation alone, Dow Chemical Company, was casually discharging 200 pounds of mercury a day into Lake St. Clair.

The responses of the spokesmen for the polluting corporations are most instructive. They all showed surprise and indignation, and tried to prove that they were concerned about the problem. The Penwalt Corporation issued the following statement: "At our Calvert City, Ky., plant, which uses mercury cells, we have been and are working on the subject of continuing compliance with the applicable state standards."[18] Allied Chemical said in a statement that it had made substantial progress in eliminating mercury pollution and that it was continuing to work on the problem. The vice-president of the Olin Chemical Corporation said that the company was working on a "crash program."

Imagine how far a traditional offender, a murderer for example, would get if he argued, after committing his act, that he was working on his problem or that he was making considerable progress in finding ways to control his behavior. The violent offender has no right to show surprise that his conduct is being questioned. The criminal corporation seems to have this right. This right comes, however, only after years of becoming engrained in the economic structure. That the corporation has a "normal" career in American economic history, has given it a special privilege to destroy at will.

GROUP SUPPORT OF CRIMINAL BEHAVIOR

Crime by corporations or corporate officials receives considerable support from similar, even competing, individuals and businesses. Lawbreaking can become a normative pattern within certain corporations, and violation norms may be shared between corporations and their executives. Corporate officials learn the necessary values, motives, rationalizations, and techniques favorable to particular kinds of crime. Many businessmen may even, for a considerable part of their day, be isolated from law-abiding definitions of business conduct. Further, businessmen are often shielded from criticism, and may find some support for their activities in the mass media. In addition, business executives associate chiefly with other businessmen, both at work and in their social activities, so that the implications of corporate crime are removed from personal scrutiny.

Corporate crime involves considerable organization among the participants. The degree of organization may range from the comparatively simple reciprocal relationships involved in a business transaction to the more complex procedures involved in the illegal activities of several large corporations. In the latter case, the violations may not only include another corporation, but may extend to many corporations and subsidiaries. The organization of the illegal activity may be quite informal, as in false advertising, it may be simply organized, although deliberate, as in the case of black market activities, or it may be complex and involved, as in the case of antitrust violations.

The group support that corporate officials receive from one another in relation to their criminal activities is shown in a study of the violation of labor relations and trade practices laws.[19] Lane investigated the violations of these laws among shoe manufacturers in eight New England communities. He found that there were wide variations in the number of firms violating the laws in each community. For example, in Haverhill, Massachusetts, 7 percent of the companies violated the laws, while in Auburn, Maine, 44 percent violated them. In some of the communities none of the shoe firms violated the laws, whereas in other communities almost half of the firms had gotten into legal trouble. The author concluded from this that "one of the reasons is the difference in attitude toward the law, the government, and the morality of illegality."

Lane then suggested that those shoe manufacturers who associate with men whose attitudes favor violation are more likely to break the law;

whereas the manufacturers who are isolated from these attitudes are less likely to break the law. The findings seemed to support this position. Furthermore, Lane found that the violations of the firms located in small communities received some support from local newspapers. The small town atmosphere appeared to provide a rationale for such violations.

Considerable group support for violation was found in the antitrust cases of the electrical equipment companies. There were even *plans* drawn up for violating antitrust laws.

> The offenders hid behind a camouflage of fictitious names and conspiratorial codes. The attendance roster for the meetings was known as the "Christmas card list" and the gatherings, interestingly enough, as "choir practice." The offenders used public telephones for much of their communication, and they met either at trade association conventions, where their relationship would appear reasonable, or at sites selected for their anonymity. It is quite noteworthy, in this respect, that while some of the men filed false travel claims, so as to mislead their superiors regarding the city they had visited, they never asked for expense money to places more distant than those they had actually gone to—on the theory, apparently, that whatever else was occurring, it would not do to cheat the company.[20]

The corporate officials would even draw lots to determine who would submit the pricing bids. Promotions within the corporation depended upon the willingness of officials to go along with these schemes.

Price-fixing, in other words, had become an established way of corporate life. Part of the job assignment was to engage in price-fixing arrangements. The judge in the electrical equipment antitrust case made the crucial observation:

> I am convinced that in the great number of cases, the defendants were torn between conscience and an approved corporate policy, with the rewarding objectives of promotions, comfortable security and large salaries—in short, the organization or company man, the conformist who goes along with his superiors and finds balm for his conscience in additional comforts and the security of his place in the corporate set-up.[21]

The operations of the food industry, finally, dramatically illustrate the extent of group support given to dubious and illegal practices.[22] The food industry is the largest retail industry in the United States. Further, the corporations within the industry are moving toward monopoly of particular products. For instance, 95 percent of all prepared soups are sold by Campbell Soup, and 85 percent of American breakfast food is produced by four firms (Kellogg, General Foods, General Mills, Quaker Oats). Other large corporations are becoming a part of the food conglomerates: the Greyhound Corporation is taking over Armour Foods, International Telephone and Telegraph has taken over Continental Bakery, and so forth. The food business, in other words, is a giant industry whose goal is profit-making rather than the health of the consumer. And the governmental agency, the Food and Drug Administration, is more of a defender of the industry's interests than an advocate for the public.

What this means is that the food industry is relatively free to engage in wholesale deception, misrepresentation of advertising, misbranding, and the sale of dangerous foods. Hazardous chemicals can be added to foods without sufficient research as to their effects. Food preservatives and additives are used to enhance the profits of the industry at the expense of the consumer's health.

Group support of criminal behavior? When there is a monopoly, with few restrictions and little surveillance, group support is raised to the level of standard operating procedure that pervades the entire industry. Support for dangerous and illegal practices is built into the normative structure of the industry.

CORRESPONDENCE BETWEEN CRIMINAL AND LEGITIMATE BEHAVIOR

In America we have taken our survival for granted. Our ethic has consisted of a firm belief that technology is the surest way to progress, that production and consumption can achieve unlimited proportions, and that the natural environment is to be used indiscriminately by man. Many of today's crimes, especially corporate crime, are related to this ethic. Indeed, a great deal of such crime corresponds closely to legitimate behavior patterns.

The overemphasis on technology, on production for its own sake, and on unnecessary consumption has apparently given us the right to commit crimes against man and the environment. An increasing gross national product is the index of the standard of American life. In the meantime, the quality of our lives has no measure.

Much of the destruction around us is supported by one of our basic traditions, the Judeo-Christian religious tradition. That tradition, enhanced by Western science, has been one of "man against nature." In Genesis we read man is to "have dominion over the fish of the sea and over the birds of the air and over every living thing that moves upon the earth." From this has followed practices that range from pollution of the air and waters, to defoliation, to nuclear warfare. Large American corporations have been given religious license to commit crimes against the environment (and sometimes against man) in the course of achieving increased production and control.

For these reasons the government itself has been insensitive to protecting the environment. The governmental agencies that supposedly regulate destructive enterprises engage in outright collusion with the enterprises. One only has to look to the experiences of Storm King Mountain, the Hudson

River Highway, Marble Canyon, the deals of the Interior Department and the Army Corps of Engineers, the California Water Plan, and the offshore oil and gas developments. A government that would protect us from destructive business practices is actually a part of the practices.

And now there is a governmental and corporate drive to control pollution. True to the American way of doing things, however, those who would control pollution are the ones who are producing the pollution *and* the pollution control devices. An article in *Ramparts* states the problem:

> The pollution control industry is really an extension of both the technological capabilities and the marketing patterns of the capital goods sector of the economy. Most of the companies involved in pollution control are not only polluters themselves but are the same firms which supply the chemicals, machines, plant fuels and parts for even bigger polluters, such as General Motors, U. S. Steel, Boeing, Standard Oil, Philco-Ford, American Can Co. and Consolidated Edison. For many of these firms, pollution control is merely one aspect of a program of "environmental diversification," which is generally accompanied by heavy investment and aggressive acquisition programs.[23]

In precise terms, the article continues, "Pollution control as conceived by the pollution control industry is merely an extension of the same pattern of profit-seeking exploitation and market economics which is at the root of the environmental crisis itself." Thus, the activities of corporations, including crimes against the environment, are closely tied to what has always been regarded as sound business.

This correspondence between criminal behavior and legitimate patterns is by no means limited to corporate crimes against the environment. Basic to the antitrust cases of price-fixing between large corporations is the attempt on their part to attain a secure economic market situation. In the electrical equipment cases, "The elimination of competition meant the avoidance of uncertainty, the formalization and predictability of outcome, the minimization of risks."[24] Crime, from the standpoint of the corporation, is a minor affair when the higher stakes involve a secure economic arrangement and an expanding market.

Correspondence between the criminality of corporate activity and legitimate patterns in our society is especially obvious in the ways in which corporations advertise their products. Such advertising is one of the most sophisticated forms of fraud, committed in this case against the consumer. Fraudulent advertising is an integral part of our system of production and consumption.

> . . . any sensitive observer of the American scene recognizes that modern mass advertising at its heart represents a kind of institutionalization of deception and misrepresentation. Indeed many perceptive social critics insist it is nothing less than an enormous swindle—albeit a somewhat genteel one. We are all too familiar with advertising's appeal to the emo-

tions, its play on (and to some extent creation of) status anxieties, its continuous use of techniques of symbol-manipulation that in other contexts would be called the devices of "propaganda," its relentless insistence on the individual's ever-expanding consumption "needs"— whether related to real need and usefulness or not. American advertising has perfected, perhaps to a degree not yet attained elsewhere, great skill in "creating" commodity obsolescence. It has also made ingenious (though basically exploitative) use of some psychological and social scientific knowledge about man's basic impulses as a grounding for advertising and marketing campaigns—through the so-called "motivation research" that Vance Packard vigorously exposed in his book *The Hidden Persuaders*. Overall, it has demonstrated a thoroughgoing commitment to and promotion of the values of "conspicuous consumption" and "pecuniary emulation" so trenchantly commented upon by Thorstein Veblen in his classic *Theory of the Leisure Class*.[25]

Cases of fraudulent advertising are fast accumulating. (Not that fraudulent advertising is a new occurrence, but existing laws on advertising are now occasionally being invoked.) For example, the chief of the Food and Drug Administration has charged that a third of the nation's manufacturers of prescription drugs are violating federal laws prohibiting false and misleading advertising.[26] He observed, in addition, that the drug companies spend approximately $2.4 billion producing drugs and between $600 million to $800 million on advertising and promotion. Among the violations noted were extension or distortion of the claims for usefulness beyond that approved in the product's final printed labeling; a quote from a study used to imply improperly that the study represents a much larger and general experience with the drug; data from papers that report no side effects while contrary evidence from much better research is ignored; and ads constructed from data once valid but rendered obsolete or false by more recent research.

Similarly, the Food and Drug Administration has recently notified the manufacturers of several brands of mouthwash to stop advertising that their products "effectively destroy bacteria that cause bad breath in the mouth," "combat cold symptoms and minor throat irritations," and provide "temporary relief of minor sore throat and mouth irritations."[27] The mouthwashes, to the contrary, were found to be ineffective for preventive or therapeutic claims. The manufacturers were given thirty days to reply to the notice, otherwise the FDA would order the products off store shelves. (Certainly not a strong sanction for years of fraudulent advertising.)

Other cases in recent years involve legal actions against the manufacturers of Excedrin for "false, misleading and deceptive advertising," against automobile tire manufacturers for misleading safety representations, against toothpaste companies for false claims, against the Geritol Company for deceptive advertising, against the manufacturers of detergents, and so on.[28] In these and many other cases, not only is the advertising fraudulent but the health and safety of the consumer are often endangered. Use of many American products, as even prescribed in the advertisements, results in thousands of injuries and deaths to consumers each year.[29]

One does not need to look to the streets for violence when it can be so easily found in the products used in the home. Such crimes cannot be understood apart from the legitimate way of life.

SOCIETAL REACTION AND LEGAL PROCESSING

Strong legal actions are not usually taken against corporations or their officers. When legal actions do occur, usually initiated by administrative agencies, they do not present a significant problem to the corporation. For even after long litigation often the only result is a modest fine against the corporation or an insignificant sentence for an official. But even before such measures are taken, companies are usually given considerable advance notice of their violations. They may be asked simply to modify their advertising claims, or to alter or withdraw their product. Court action may be taken only as a last resort.

Until recent times, public reaction to corporate crime has been rather mild. Consumer consciousness has been very weak. A study in the 1950s of consumer attitudes toward such pure food violations as adulteration and misbranding found that the sample of consumers tended to view the violations as more comparable to traffic offenses than to burglary.[30] The respondents viewed the violators as "law breakers" rather than as "criminals." Yet, the sentences that they would give to the violators were more stringent than those actually imposed by the courts for the same cases of food adulteration and misbranding. In terms of the administration of the law, court decisions in pure food violations did not represent the will of the majority of the consumers. But today with the increasing awareness of corporate crimes against the environment and the consumer, public reaction to such crimes has increased even more. There is reason to believe that the public itself will be playing a more important role in checking the abuses of corporate power.

Part of the lack of public reaction to consumer fraud in the past has been because the public has not been informed. The agency that should provide such information, the Food and Drug Administration, has been negligent in its task. The FDA maintains a benign attitude toward the public: "that the public is primarily an ignorant and hysterical mob from whom any suggestions of danger must be kept at all cost."[31] The attitude tends, in turn, to lull the public into a false sense of security. Finally, the FDA's attitude toward the public is perpetuated by its "public hearings."

Allegedly called to protect the public interest by allowing controversial questions of food regulation to be resolved by careful public fact-finding procedures, the public hearings have become a gigantic maze through which the FDA tries to sneak its predetermined set of facts unscathed. Rather than using the public hearing to try to determine the magnitude of a possible problem and then propose a method for solving it, the FDA arrives at its conclusions behind closed doors and then convenes a public hearing only when forced to seek endorsement for its position.[32]

Not only does the Food and Drug Administration maintain a particular position regarding the public, but it also has a position in reference to the food industry. That position, one of general faith in the food industry, prevents the public from getting accurate information about food safety, quality, and cost. The FDA assumes that the food industry voluntarily insures the safety and quality of food it produces and distributes. Because of this mistaken belief, the FDA is not able to advance the interest of the public.

> In the place of sustained action to advance health by helping to improve the American diet, the FDA substitutes a naive faith that the way American food is produced, preserved, and distributed is exceptionally fine. It maintains this faith in the face of increasing scientific evidence that chemical additives can be extremely dangerous, that the vitamin content of the American diet is deteriorating, that saturated fat in food may be a contributing factor to more than 70 percent of all American deaths, and that American food is getting filthier. Faith has a way of withstanding fact. But while the FDA goes through the ritualistic exercise that it passes off as regulation, it is the food consumer who is injured.[33]

In other words, the FDA is not able to effectively enforce the laws on consumer protection. Not only does it lack the inclination to enforce the laws, but it does not have the knowledge and techniques to detect and enforce violations. The FDA is far behind the advances made by the food industry.

> As a result, between 1950 and 1965 the food industry went through its period of fastest growth almost completely unmonitored. In that time a brand new series of problems—including the hazards involved with the chemical environment through the use of food additives, the threat of food contamination becoming nationwide through a modern mass-distribution system, the monitoring of dangerous pesticide residues in widely distributed foods, the introduction of brand new synthetic foods made up entirely of chemicals—developed without serious and effective attention from the FDA.[34]

The agency charged with protecting the American consumer from dangerous products and false advertising, the Federal Trade Commission, is not doing any better in enforcing existing criminal laws. Ralph Nader's group of investigators have noted, and then documented, that the FTC has failed in its job as consumer protector in four specific regards:

1. The FTC has failed to detect violations systematically.
2. The FTC has failed to establish efficient priorities for its enforcement energy.

3. The FTC has failed to enforce the powers it has with energy and speed.
4. The FTC has failed to seek sufficient statutory authority to make its work effective.[35]

And a major reason for these failures and thus for the lack of effectiveness, they contend, is that the FTC is more a representative of the corporate producer than it is of the public interest. The FTC protects the interests of those it is supposed to regulate.

The control of air and water pollution suffers from the same problems. And the situation is compounded by an insufficient system of detection, a problem which the federal government is not able to solve either.

> Control agencies, by and large, have been unable to exploit the technology that exists. Most rely almost exclusively on a crude armory of sticky papers, pickle jars, "candles," and plastic buckets. Many with more sophisticated equipment fail to use it effectively. Five or six years ago, for example, the city of Cleveland purchased a fifty-thousand-dollar mobile air monitor which has been sitting in one spot ever since. Some agencies, intoxicated with science, pour most of their manpower and money into monitoring to the neglect of their enforcement responsibilities. The Washington State Office of Air Quality, for example, has assigned twenty-one of its twenty-three employees the task of setting up a sampling network. The allocation stems in part from state law, which places most of the burden of control on local agencies. Nonetheless it is doubtful whether two engineers will be able to discharge the important residual enforcement responsibility of the state. The survey and study syndrome has already established itself in many agencies. Federal emphasis on ambient air standards promises to spread the cancer.[36]

For these reasons consumer protection is now being sought in the courts. Citizens are seeking judicial relief because government agencies are so ineffective in the enforcement of product and environmental standards. Recently, for example, a law was passed in Michigan which permits any person to file suit to protect the air, water, and other natural resources.[37] Prior to this precedent, a citizen could only sue for personal damages. Now protection of the environment is recognized as a right in itself. The courts have been granted the power to issue injunctions, impose conditions, and direct government agencies to upgrade standards.

But it is becoming clear that the criminal law cannot by itself prevent the prevalent and wide-ranging corporate crimes. The Antitrust Division of the Department of Justice has reached a similar conclusion on the limitations of legal controls. These controls are inadequate for a number of reasons:

> Present statutory maximums often make criminal fines trivial for corporations in proportion both to their ability to pay and to the profits resulting from the criminal violations; in a number of States corporate executives may be lawfully reimbursed by the corporation for fines im-

posed on them; and since discovery of criminal violations of the anti-trust laws is very difficult, even substantial civil penalties may not constitute adequate deterrents.[38]

Legal scholars are presenting similar arguments, questioning the utility of applying criminal sanctions to such offenses.[39]

Criminal law alone simply does not assure compliance as long as those corporations that are controlled exercise political control and influence over regulatory agencies and courts. What is needed is greater political control by the public over the corporations and their power and influence in the political economy. And only with basic changes in the culture and structure of American society will there be a solution to corporate crime.

NOTES

[1] Edwin H. Sutherland, "Crime of Corporations," in Albert K. Cohen, Alfred R. Lindesmith, and Karl F. Schuessler, eds., *The Sutherland Papers* (Bloomington, Ind.: Indiana University Press, 1956), pp. 78–96.

[2] Edwin H. Sutherland, *White Collar Crime* (New York: Holt, Rinehart and Winston), 1949.

[3] Gilbert Geis, "Toward a Delineation of White-Collar Offenses," *Sociological Inquiry*, **32** (Spring 1962), p. 162.

[4] Gabriel Kolko, *The Triumph of Conservatism: A Reinterpretation of American History, 1900–1916* (New York: The Free Press, 1963), p. 2.

[5] *Ibid.*, p. 278.

[6] Samuel Eliot Morison and Henry Steele Commager, *The Growth of the American Republic* (New York: Oxford University Press, 1950), p. 630.

[7] Sutherland, *White Collar Crime*.

[8] See Richard Quinney, *The Social Reality of Crime* (Boston: Little, Brown and Company, 1970), pp. 77–82.

[9] From *Chemical Feast* by James S. Turner. Copyright © 1970 by The Center for Study of Responsive Law. All rights reserved. Reprinted by permission of Grossman Publishers.

[10] Ralph Nader, "Foreword," from *Vanishing Air* by John C. Esposito. Copyright © 1970 by The Center for Study of Responsive Law. All rights reserved. Reprinted by permission of Grossman Publishers.

[11] Esposito, *Vanishing Air*, p. 260.

[12] *Ibid.*, pp. 278–279.

[13] George B. Vold, *Theoretical Criminology* (New York: Oxford University Press, 1958), pp. 253–254.

[14] Gilbert Geis, "The Heavy Electrical Equipment Antitrust Cases of 1961," in Marshall B. Clinard and Richard Quinney, *Criminal Behavior Systems: A Typology* (New York: Holt, Rinehart and Winston, 1967), pp. 139–151.

[15] *Ibid.*, p. 144.

[16] *Ibid.*, pp. 150–151.

[17] *The New York Times* (July 25, 1970), p. 1. Also see *The New York Times* (September 11, 1970), p. 1.

[18] *The New York Times* (July 25, 1970), p. 1.

[19] Robert A. Lane, "Why Business Men Violate the Law," *Journal of Criminal Law, Criminology and Police Science*, **44** (August 1953), pp. 151–165.

[20] Geis, "The Heavy Electrical Equipment Antitrust Cases of 1961," p. 143.
[21] Quoted in Herbert A. Bloch and Gilbert Geis, *Man, Crime, and Society*, 2d ed. (New York: Random House, 1970), p. 311.
[22] Turner, *The Chemical Feast*, pp. 82–106.
[23] Martin Gellen, "The Making of a Pollution-Industrial Complex," *Ramparts* (May 1970), pp. 22–23. Also see James Ridgeway, *The Politics of Ecology* (New York: E. P. Dutton Co., 1970).
[24] Geis, "The Heavy Electrical Equipment Antitrust Cases of 1961," p. 150.
[25] Edwin M. Schur, *Our Criminal Society: The Social and Legal Sources of Crime in America*, © 1969, pp. 168–169. By permission of Prentice-Hall, Inc., Englewood Cliffs, N.J.
[26] *The New York Times* (May 26, 1966), p. 1.
[27] *The New York Times* (August 4, 1970), p. 20.
[28] Edward R. Cox, Robert C. Fellmeth, and John E. Schulz, *Nader's Raiders: Report on the Federal Trade Commission* (New York: Grove Press, 1969), pp. 20–28.
[29] Morton Mintz, "There's No Bloody Place Like Home," *The Progressive*, **34** (September 1970), pp. 22–24.
[30] Donald J. Newman, "Public Attitudes toward a Form of White Collar Crime," *Social Problems*, **4** (January 1957), pp. 228–232.
[31] Turner, *The Chemical Feast*, p. 209.
[32] *Ibid.*, p. 210.
[33] *Ibid.*, p. 81.
[34] *Ibid.*, p. 43.
[35] Cox, Fellmeth, and Schulz, *Nader's Raiders*, p. 39.
[36] Esposito, *Vanishing Air*, p. 178.
[37] *The New York Times* (July 29, 1970), p. 2.
[38] *Crime and Its Impact—An Assessment*. President's Commission on Law Enforcement and Administration of Justice (Washington, D.C.: U. S. Government Printing Office, p. 105).
[39] Sanford H. Kadish, "Some Observations on the Use of Criminal Sanctions in Enforcing Economic Regulations," *University of Chicago Law Review*, **30** (Spring 1963), pp. 423–449. Also see Harry V. Ball and Lawrence M. Friedman, "The Use of Criminal Sanctions in the Enforcement of Economic Legislation: A Sociological View," *Stanford Law Review*, **17** (January 1965), pp. 197–223.

SELECTED BIBLIOGRAPHY

Ball, Harry V., and Friedman, Lawrence M., "The Use of Criminal Sanctions in the Enforcement of Economic Legislation: A Sociological View." *Stanford Law Review*, 17 (January 1965), pp. 197–223.

Cox, Edward R., Fellmeth, Robert C., and Schulz, John E., *Nader's Raiders: Report on the Federal Trade Commission*. New York: Grove Press, 1969.

Edelhertz, Herbert, *The Nature, Impact and Prosecution of White-Collar Crime*. U. S. Department of Justice, Law Enforcement Assistance Administration. Washington, D.C.: U. S. Government Printing Office, 1970.

Esposito, John C., *Vanishing Air*. New York: Grossman Publishers, 1970.

Geis, Gilbert, "The Heavy Electrical Equipment Antitrust Cases of 1961,"

in Marshall B. Clinard and Richard Quinney, *Criminal Behavior Systems: A Typology.* New York: Holt, Rinehart and Winston, 1967, pp. 139–151.
————, "Toward a Delineation of White-Collar Offenses." *Sociological Inquiry,* 32 (Spring 1962), pp. 159–171.

Herling, John, *The Great Price Conspiracy: The Story of the Antitrust Violations in the Electrical Industry.* Washington, D.C.: Robert B. Luce, 1962.

Kadish, Sanford H., "Some Observations on the Use of Criminal Sanctions in Enforcing Economic Regulations." *University of Chicago Law Review,* 30 (Spring 1963), pp. 423–449.

Lane, Robert A., "Why Business Men Violate the Law." *Journal of Criminal Law, Criminology and Police Science,* 44 (August 1953), pp. 151–165.

Newman, Donald J., "Public Attitudes toward a Form of White Collar Crime." *Social Problems,* 4 (January 1957), pp. 228–232.

Ridgeway, James, *The Politics of Ecology.* New York: E. P. Dutton & Co., 1970.

Sutherland, Edwin H., *White Collar Crime.* New York: Holt, Rinehart and Winston, 1949.

Turner, James S., *The Chemical Feast.* New York: Grossman Publishers, 1970.

Organized 9
Criminal Behavior

Organized crime, as understood by criminologists today, refers to business enterprises organized for the purpose of making economic gain through illegal activities.[1] A Presidential Commission has defined it as involving "thousands of criminals, working within structures as complex as those of any large corporation, subject to laws more rigidly enforced than those of legitimate governments. Its actions are not impulsive but rather the results of intricate conspiracies, carried on over many years and aimed at gaining control over whole fields of activity in order to amass huge profits."[2]

LEGAL ASPECTS OF SELECTED OFFENSES

Currently, organized crime is one of the major forms of crime in American society, although numerically it does not involve a large proportion of criminal offenders. Large-scale organized crime did not exist in the United States prior to this century.[3] During the frontier period in American history, a number of outlawed activities were carried out on a modest scale by roving criminal groups. In cities, various adult criminal groups gained control of illegal activities in their localities, such as gambling, prostitution, distribution of beer and liquor, and various rackets. These gangs prospered because of the desired, although illegal, services they provided for the public and their connection with local politics.

After the turn of the century organized crime expanded into a wider range of activities and extended over larger geographical areas. The single event that brought about the greatest change in organized crime was Prohibition, forbidding by law the sale and distribution of alcoholic beverages. Because of the Eighteenth Amendment, adopted in 1920, and the supporting Volstead Act, organized crime was able to provide the illegal services and commodities demanded by millions of citizens. Conflict between organized adult gangs and widespread use of violence were inevitable as rival groups competed to serve the public. A number of the strongest gangs finally dominated the scene. These organized groups, because of the large sums of money they amassed and the elaborate organization they achieved, continued in illegal activity after Prohibition was repealed.[4]

The modern era of organized crime is represented by the crime syndicate. Organized crime has been expanded to the point where leaders coordinate illegal activities over state and regional boundaries. This new era is also represented by the extension of organized crime into an increasing number of legitimate businesses and occupational activities. The characteristic features of modern organized crime can be summarized as follows:

1. hierarchical structure involving a system of specifically defined relationships with mutual obligations and privileges
2. monopolistic control or establishment of spheres of influence among different organizations and over geographic areas
3. dependence upon the potential use of force and violence to maintain internal discipline and restrain competition
4. maintenance of permanent immunity from interference from law enforcement and other agencies of government
5. large financial gains secured through specialization in one or more combinations of enterprises

Organized crime can be distinguished from other criminal behavior by the elements of "corruption" and "enforcement."

> There are at least two aspects of organized crime that characterize it as a unique form of criminal activity. The first is the element of corruption. The second is the element of enforcement, which is necessary for the maintenance of both internal discipline and the regularity of business transactions. In the hierarchy of organized crime there are positions for people fulfilling both of these functions. But neither is essential to the long-term operation of other types of criminal groups. . . . Organized-crime groups . . . are believed to contain one or more fixed positions for "enforcers," whose duty it is to maintain organizational integrity by arranging for the maiming and killing of recalcitrant members. And there is a position for a "corrupter," whose function is to establish relationships with those public officials and other influential persons whose assistance is necessary to achieve the organization's goals. By including these positions within its organization, each criminal cartel, or "family," becomes a government as well as a business.[5]

Organized crime itself actually consists of a number of different types of individual crimes. The following general classification can be used to include most forms of organized crime: (1) control of illegal activities, (2) control of legitimate business, and (3) racketeering.

Control of Illegal Activities

Much organized crime traditionally has been found in areas of illicit behavior, such as gambling, loan sharking, narcotics, and prostitution. One study of organized crime found that its members "control all but a tiny part of illegal gambling in the United States. They are the principal loan sharks.

They are the principal importers and wholesalers of narcotics."[6] In these areas, public sentiment is divided over the actual immorality of such behavior. Organized crime, thus, finds limited opposition from the public when it controls these illegal activities. Furthermore, organized crime provides a service for sections of the public when it assures access to these activities.

Gambling is the largest source of revenue for organized crime. It includes lotteries, off-track horse-betting, numbers games, large dice games, and illegal casinos. Few organized gambling operations in large cities are not tied to such operations. Bets may vary from a quarter to very large sums and the profits for organized crime are enormous, ranging into the hundreds of millions of dollars. Gambling operations are highly complex.

> Most large-city gambling is established or controlled by organized crime members through elaborate hierarchies. Money is filtered from the small operator who takes the customer's bet, through persons who pick up money and slips, to second-echelon figures in charge of particular districts, and then into one of several main offices. The profits that eventually accrue to organization leaders move through channels so complex that even persons who work in the betting operation do not know or cannot prove the identity of the leader. Increasing use of the telephone for lottery and sports betting has facilitated systems in which the bookmaker may not know the identity of the second-echelon person to whom he calls in the day's bets. Organization not only creates greater efficiency and enlarges markets, it also provides a systematized method of corrupting the law enforcement process by centralizing procedures for the payment of graft.[7]

Loan sharking, the lending of money at higher rates than the legally prescribed limit (they may charge 1 to 150 percent a week interest), is probably second only to gambling as an area of profit. Much of the lending money comes from gambling operations. Loans are made to small businessmen whose channels of credit are closed, gamblers, narcotic users, politicians, and other persons who need money to cover their expenses or debts.

Narcotic sales are organized like a legitimate importing-retailing business involving the distribution of drugs through several levels to the street peddler. Because of severe penalties organized crime is less involved at the retail level, leaving this aspect to individual pushers.

> The large amounts of cash and the international connections necessary for large, long-term heroin supplies can be provided only by organized crime. Conservative estimates of the number of addicts in the nation and the average daily expenditure for heroin indicate that the gross heroin trade is $350 million annually, of which $21 million are probably profits to the importer and distributor. Most of this profit goes to organized crime groups in those few cities in which almost all heroin consumption occurs.[8]

Control of Legitimate Business

In addition to the control of illegal activities, organized crime has infiltrated legitimate businesses. This has been accomplished by employing illegal means and by investing large financial resources. Organized crime has at times, of course, used legitimate business as a front for other criminal activities. More recently, however, organized crime has used legitimate business as a major source of income. Organized crime has a vested monopoly in some legitimate enterprises, such as cigarette vending machines and juke boxes. They are owners of a wide variety of enterprises, such as real estate, retail firms, restaurants and bars, hotels, automobile agencies, trucking concerns, food companies, linen supply outlets, garbage collection routes, and other such services. A United States Chamber of Commerce "Deskbook on Organized Crime" states that in 1970, Cosa Nostra controlled one of the nation's largest hotel chains and a bank with assets of more than 70 million dollars. The Kefauver Committee found that organized crime had infiltrated approximately fifty areas of legitimate business, including advertising, the amusement industry, the automobile industry, banking, insurance, juke box distribution, the liquor industry, loan businesses, the oil industry, radio stations, real estate, and scrap surplus sales.[9]

Organized crime invests the profits it has derived from illegal services in legitimate businesses and these funds serve to establish a legitimate source of profits for income taxes and also help to avoid prosecution. The business organizational arrangement involves business consultants, accountants, and attorneys who work full time. The control of business concerns is secured through (1) investing concealed profits acquired from gambling and other illegal activities, (2) accepting business interests in payment of the owner's gambling debts, (3) foreclosing on usurious loans, and (4) using various forms of extortions. A favorite operation is to place a concern it has acquired into fraudulent bankruptcy after milking its assets.[10]

Somewhat related to the control of legitimate business is the infiltration of organized crime into politics. Political graft and corruption are usually mentioned as forms of organized crime. Few groups of organized criminals, however, become involved in politics for the sole purpose of economic gain. Such infiltration is usually for the purpose of protection from legal interference in other criminal activities of organized crime. The liaison with public officials is actually a method of achieving immunity from the law, and should be so considered rather than regarded as a separate type of organized crime.

All available data indicate that organized crime flourishes only where it has corrupted local officials. As the scope and variety of organized crime's activities have expanded, its need to involve public officials at every level of local government has grown. And as government regulation expands into more and more areas of private and business activity, the power to corrupt likewise affords the corrupter more control over matters affecting the everyday life of each citizen. Contrast, for example, the way governmental action in contract procurement or zoning functions today with the way it functioned only a few years ago. The potential harm of corruption is greater today if only because the scope of governmental activity is greater. In different places at different times, organized crime has corrupted police officials, prosecutors, legislators, judges, regulatory agency officials, mayors, councilmen, and other public officials, whose legitimate exercise of duties would block organized crime and whose illegal exercise of duties helps it.[11]

Racketeering

The third and final general type of organized crime is racketeering, the systematic extortion of money from persons or organizations. Its purpose is financial gain on a regularized basis. Racketeering operations are, of course, infinitely varied in terms of the methods of operation and the kinds of organizations victimized. For the most part, racketeering in the United States has been concentrated in organizations engaged in the distribution of services and commodities.

Powerful organized criminal groups may extend their operations to the control of many kinds of products and services. The wholesaling of perishable products, such as fruit, vegetables, and fish, is often another field of racketeering operations. Racketeering is prevalent in laundry businesses, cleaning establishments, trucking, loading businesses, and among such workers as motion picture operators, bartenders, waiters, truck drivers, and retail clerks. These organizations are especially vulnerable to the operation of rackets. One of the simplest forms of this type of racketeering is the protection racket in which persons or organizations are "protected," by payment of regular fees, for the privilege of operating without being injured, damaged, or destroyed by the organized criminals. This kind of operation is not exclusive of other forms of racketeering, but may be used as one means of maintaining control over various services and commodities.

Racketeering has operated successfully for a number of years in controlling some groups of organized labor. Various schemes are employed such as the infiltration of certain labor unions, extortion of money from employees for union cooperation, and cheating the members of the union through, for example, not paying them union wages or misuse of union welfare and pension funds. Workers may be forced to pay high fees and dues in order to find and hold jobs. Union leadership may be taken over by organized criminals. A considerable portion of the operating funds of unions may go to organized crime. Furthermore, money may be extorted from employers. Strikes are often threatened as a means of controlling employers. The building trades are particularly vulnerable to racketeering because of the importance of purchasing materials at crucial times and the need to complete projects by a certain date.

There are four fundamental operations when the syndicates of Cosa Nostra become labor brokers.[12]

1. Real unionization is often prevented by pretending, after the organization is paid, that the shops are really "unionized." A larger business concern, for example, may think it is cheap to pay $5000 for a nonunionized union shop. Such a company may be "unionized" but the employees do not get union wages and there is no "union trouble" for the employer.
2. Employees are made members of fictitious "paper locals," which are established partly to help the employer reduce his labor costs. Cosa Nostra members may even "sell" unions to one another.
3. Employers may be threatened with strikes or violence if they do not pay bribes to Cosa Nostra members leading the controlled unions.
4. Union funds are actually stolen or diverted illegally from pension or welfare funds.

CRIMINAL CAREER OF THE OFFENDER

As with any large-scale enterprise, organized crime requires a structure of positions with an accompanying hierarchy of command. It has been noted by Burgess that the hierarchical structure of organized crime represents a "feudal system."[13] At the top of the pyramid are powerful leaders, the "lords," who make the important decisions and run the organization. These leaders maintain a master-serf relationship over other persons in the feudal structure. A middle echelon of gangsters, henchmen, and lieutenants carry out the demands of the leaders. At the bottom of the structure are persons marginally associated with organized crime—narcotics peddlers, prostitutes, bookies, runners—who deal directly with the public. The structure is held together by a chain of command, personal loyalties, a moral code, alliances with rival groups, and hostility toward conventional society.

The hierarchical structure of organized crime makes generalization about the careers of its members difficult. Some have specialized training and are directly recruited from law and accounting, while others, as young men, are given university training with the idea that they will join the syndicate. "Cosa Nostra members occupying the higher echelons of organized crime are orienting their sons to the value of education, if only as a part of the general move toward respectability. . . . they are sending their sons to college to learn business skills, on the assumption that these sons will soon be eligible for 'family' membership."[14] Many organized criminals, especially those lower in the hierarchy, have careers similar to the conventional offender, in which there is association with young gang members and a long series of delinquencies and crimes. Instead of ending their careers in their early twenties, however, they continue their criminal activities in association with organized criminals.

Some who grow up in certain slum areas tend to emulate the older members of organized crime and generally aspire to a career in organized crime. In one study, eight out of the ten delinquents in an area said they would like to be associated with organized crime as the occupation they would most like to have in ten years.[15] Such boys stressed the need for connections such as belonging to the right club or having certain criminals as sponsors. In certain slum areas the relation of organized criminals and conventional businesses are mutually supportive. Organized crime uses a legitimate business as a front for various operations to the latter's profit. Organized criminals in such areas, operating in gambling, among unions, and in usury have considerable power and influence on the conventional social structure.

> Frankie, a young adult who still considered himself a member of a delinquent group, when speaking about the influence of the racketeers, said that they were known to everybody in the neighborhood. If you wanted to open up a legitimate business and needed additional capital, you could sometimes borrow money from the racketeers. If you were losing out in business, they might be helpful. If somebody got "busted," or arrested, a racketeer would put up bail money and, in an emergency, the racketeer could be called upon for a payoff, since he had the right contacts in the police department. Of course this was strictly business, and you had to repay the loans or favors.[16]

Delinquents are selected by organized criminals on the basis not of the technical knowledge they display but of attitudes such as being a real "stand-up guy," of being loyal, willing, and trustworthy. As one researcher has put it, organized crime is looking for boys with "brains," "heart," "connections," and "trust."[17] In neighborhoods where organized crime is important a boy might drive his uncle's car to pick up gambling receipts or he might be given other roles to prepare for an organized criminal career. The leaders may pay special attention to the behavior of a boy when he is jailed.

The attraction of organized crime for slum boys is primarily the easy money and connections, as the case of a young adult illustrates.

> Benny said that he would like to be a racketeer when he was a little older. The racketeers he knew made $1,500 to $2,000 a week. He'd like to make all that money. . . . He said that the important thing was to be smart, keep your mouth shut, and to have connections. He said that most of the fellows in his neighborhood did not have connections. Mainly they could become shoplifters and burglars. He looked down on them. That type of activity was "stupid." He said that he had already spent six months helping a particular bookmaker. . . . Bookmaking was really just like a business. The people in it were decent and honest. It was true they stuck together. He had no hesitation about getting involved. . . . It wasn't like being a gangster in the old sense. Now, it was like being in a clean business.[18]

The delinquent gang of the slum produces the adult gangster who uses strong-arm methods and is employed for this purpose by organized criminal groups. Gangsters usually come from large city slums, frequently have long criminal records of armed robberies, and have a conception of themselves as "tough." Those who are successful in organized crime sometimes later become its leaders.

In many instances organized criminal machines have called upon the services of gangsters for protective or offensive operations only to have the gangsters take over the operations themselves. In other instances gangsters have been content to be on the payroll of a prosperous organization and to get a considerable cut of the profits without assuming full control. Gangsters are usually recruited from the slums of American cities. They have come up through the sand lots of crime and have made crime their career. Most of them have been members of small boys' gangs and have graduated to larger boys' gangs and later to affiliation with organized crime and political machines. They have made themselves useful to both political machines and organized crime.[19]

Organized crime may thus provide a person with the opportunity for a lifetime career in crime. Selection of a career in organized crime, rather than one of the other criminal careers, is apparently dependent upon the existing social conditions of the area in which the person lives.[20] Little is known, however, of the specific mobility of the criminal from one position to another once he is a part of the hierarchy of organized crime. The career histories of organized criminals are not usually available because of the secrecy and nature of their work. There are indications, however, that as organized crime has moved from the bootlegging and prostitution rackets of the 1920s and 1930s into gambling, usury, and the control of legitimate businesses, there is more need for expertise in management operations and less for security and secrecy since the new operations are more in the open. Organized crime syndicates, therefore, are becoming more loose, flexible, and creative and, rather than punishing wrongdoers, they are rewarding those in the organization who display the ability to make profits. This contemporary skill is difficult to defeat.

For example, in about three months, New York Cosa Nostra members in the spring of 1965 organized and then operated a multimillion-dollar cigarette-smuggling operation which involved purchase of huge quantities of untaxed cigarettes in North Carolina, truck transportation of the cigarettes to New York, a network of warehouses and wholesalers, and a huge system of retail sellers, including milkmen, vending-machine servicemen, and union shop stewards. Managers of a legitimate firm dealing in legitimate merchandise could not have organized such an enterprise in less than three years. Cosa Nostra struck so quickly and efficiently that the police and other enforcement agencies were rather helpless.[21]

Except for some movement up the scale in the organization, there are indications that mobility varies with the type of position in the hierarchy, for example, making money or enforcing discipline.

One young man with the right connections and the right attitudes might be rewarded with a job as a collector of street-level bets, as a courier who picks up and delivers usury monies, or as a truck driver in a cigarette smuggling operation. If he is ambitious and talented, he may do all three. Another young man may be rewarded with an executioner position, such as "wheel man," "finger man," or "hit man." Both men are either salaried employees or behave as if they were, even if unpaid or paid on a piece-work basis. Neither has high status, and neither has necessarily been ad-mitted to membership in Cosa Nostra. But the career-development pattern for the first man is much clearer than the pattern for the second. If either man is admitted to membership, his initial position is likely to involve moneymaking, perhaps at a supervisory level such as book-maker, rather than discipline. On occasion, an executioner may be given a salaried position as bodyguard to his boss, but bodyguards do not ordinarily move up to supervisory positions oriented principally to dis-cipline, such as enforcer and buffer. Either of the two men may, after years of work as a soldier-bookmaker who shares his profits with his superiors, move up to lieutenant-enforcer, lieutenant-buffer, lieutenant-corrupter, or lieutenant-money mover. The four positions are listed in ascending order of status. The person occupying a high-status money-mover position is self-employed to a greater degree than is the corrupter and, in descending order, the buffer and enforcer. His frontiers of action are wider, and his income is greater.[22]

Progression into organized crime usually represents for the offender an increasing isolation from conventional society. While there are undoubtedly variations according to the location of the person within the hierarchy of organized crime, most organized criminals are committed to the world of crime. Their commitment to the larger society is concentrated on the goal of pecuniary success. The means of achieving such success are illegal. There is little or no interest on the part of organized criminals for the welfare of the larger society. A number of social conditions and forces in American society are conducive to the separation of the organized criminal from the larger society. In coming up through the ranks of street gangs, organized criminals have been nominally separated from the dominant culture.[23]

The leaders of organized crime are involved in activities that are in con-tinuous conflict with the law. A philosophy of justification allows them to carry out their illegal activities. They have contempt for the government, its officials, and the general public. The leaders of organized crime may, how-ever, choose to live segmented lives, retiring to the seclusion of respectabil-ity.[24] Their commitment, nevertheless, remains with the world of crime, where in detachment from the values of the larger society they receive their prestige, power, and a life style of luxury.

GROUP SUPPORT OF CRIMINAL BEHAVIOR

Persons involved in most levels of organized crime associate regularly with other criminals and receive group support for their criminal behavior. Since most persons in organized crime associate with a particular group of criminals, support and prescription of behavior come from a specific group of criminals. These groups are organized for the purpose of gaining monopolistic control over a sphere of activity. During Prohibition in the United States, for example, specific organized criminal groups competed in an attempt to control the manufacture and distribution of liquor. More recently organized criminal groups have attempted to gain monopolistic control of gambling, prostitution, drug traffic, and various rackets.

Monopolistic control of a criminal activity by criminal groups often entails an interlocking control over other illegal activities. Interlocking interests are found in organized crime in patterns similar to those in corporate business. Furthermore, in achieving monopolies, organized crime is not restricted by traditional political and geographical boundaries.

Organizational Structure

From an organizational standpoint, all of organized crime operates on a syndicated basis. That is, skilled persons with considerable capital resources are organized to establish and maintain a large-scale business enterprise devoted to the coordination and control of products or services. Illegal activity is involved in that the nature of the coordination and control may be illegal, and, also, the products and services may be illegal. However, given the syndicated pattern of organized crime, there are questions regarding the pervasiveness and geographical extensiveness of the organization of illegal activity. For example, in the United States are there a great number of criminal groups on a syndicated basis? Are some groups interlocked according to a plan? Or, is there a single crime syndicate in the United States that coordinates all the activities of organized crime?

Recent evidence throws some light on the structure of organized crime in this country. The meeting of over sixty known gang leaders in upstate New York in 1957, the so-called Appalachian Conference, suggests a periodic gathering of leaders in organized crime to discuss problems of mutual interest and concern.[25] The meeting also indicates the existence of a complex and differentiated system consisting of a number of criminal groups engaged in the business of organized crime. The 1963 testimony of Joseph Valachi, former organized criminal turned informer, before the McClellan Committee provides further clues to the syndicated nature of organized crime in the United States.[26] He named the Cosa Nostra as a group of "families" engaged in illegal economic gain. At the top of the "family" system is a commission which serves as a court to settle disputes and inflict

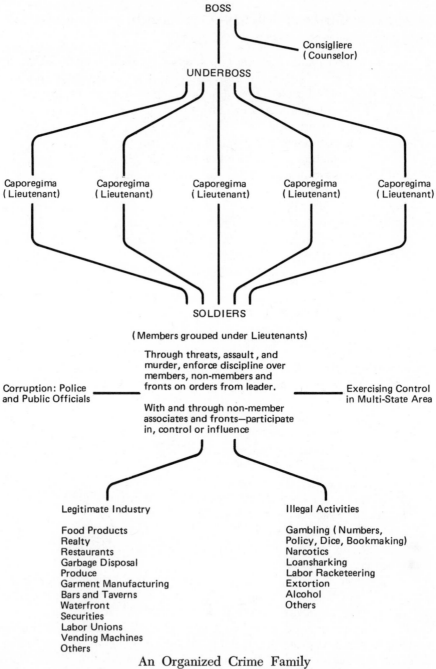

An Organized Crime Family

SOURCE: *The Challenge of Crime in a Free Society*. A Report of the President's Commission on Law Enforcement and Administration of Justice (Washington, D.C.: U. S. Government Printing Office, 1967), p. 194.

punishments. The Cosa Nostra apparently provides for the autonomous functioning of several organized criminal groups.

A full description of the structure of organized crime in the United States, often referred to as "Cosa Nostra," was reported in 1967 by the President's Commission on Law Enforcement and Administration of Justice. According to the report, the core of organized crime today consists of twenty-four groups (or "families," although many are not related), which operate as criminal cartels in large cities across the country. The top echelons of the families are all Italians and Sicilians or of Italian and Sicilian descent. While the scope and effect of the organized criminal operations vary from one area to another, the wealthiest and most influential groups operate in New York, New Jersey, Illinois, Florida, Louisiana, Nevada, Michigan, and Rhode Island. In terms of the internal structure of each of the twenty-four core groups, membership varies from as many as 700 men to as few as twenty, with a total membership of about 5000 persons. In addition, perhaps 10,000 or more persons are involved as bet collectors, runners, and so forth. Some authorities, however, have questioned the existence of a nationwide Cosa Nostra as being insufficiently documented and organized crime as being exclusively of Italian or Sicilian origin.[27]

Each family is headed by one man, the "boss," who maintains order and maximizes profits. Beneath each boss is an "underboss," who collects information for the boss, relays messages to him, and passes instructions down to underlings. On the same level as the underboss is the *consigliere*, who is a counselor or adviser to the boss. Below the level of the underboss are the *caporegime*, some of whom serve as buffers between upper- and lower-level personnel while others serve as chiefs of operating units. The lowest-level members are the *soldati*, the soldiers or "button" men who report to the *caporegime*. Outside the structure of the family are the large number of employees and agents who do most of the actual work in the various criminal enterprises. Finally, the President's Commission notes, the twenty-four families or criminal cartels are ruled by a "commission." This body is a combination legislature, supreme court, board of directors, and arbitration board but functions primarily as a judicial body. The commission is composed of the bosses of the most powerful families and varies from nine to twelve men. The balance of power of this nationwide council currently rests with the leaders of the five families of New York, which is considered the unofficial headquarters of the entire operation of organized crime in the United States.

From a historical perspective, it appears that organized crime has been undergoing organizational change in recent years. Thus, the old Mafia of Sicily, as a traditional type of organization, has developed into a highly complex organization in America. As the Cosa Nostra, it operates as a modern bureaucracy in terms of hierarchy of authority, specialization, a system of rules, and impersonality.[28]

Code of Conduct

To a certain extent all career criminals observe a code of behavior in not informing the police on another's activities. With organized crime the code of conduct is highly developed and extends into areas such as the maintenance of internal discipline and the power of leadership. It is very similar to the Sicilian Mafia's code and as effectively enforced. It involves "(1) *intense loyalty* to the organization and its governing elite, (2) *honesty* in relationships with members, (3) *secrecy* regarding the organization's structure and activities, and (4) *honorable behavior* which sets members off as morally superior to those outsiders who would govern them."[29] Loyalty, respect, honor, and absolute obedience are expected of all members. Compliance is helped by custom, material rewards, and violence either through beatings or execution. No subordinates should interfere with the leader's interests, they should not inform the police, and, if necessary, subordinates should go to prison to protect those in power in the organization.

> Although the code of organized criminals is purportedly for the protection of "the people," it is administered and enforced for the protection of each boss. Since the boss of a "family" has the most to lose if the organization is weakened through an attack by outsiders, he enthusiastically promotes the notion that an offense against one is an offense against all. Moreover, this same principle protects the boss from his own underlings. The principle gets transformed so that it deals with matters of safety rather than matters of offense—the safety of all depends upon the safety of each. Since each conforming member is guaranteed a livelihood without fear of encroachment by other members or by nonmembers, each member must be "protected." This transformation, of course, authorizes the boss to take extreme measures to insure his own safety by crushing any plot or potential plot against him by his underlings. The principle also encourages informing. Despite the code's admonition to be tight-lipped, one is guilty by association if he does not report that a member has injured him or another member. By promulgating the idea that "We are all equals in matters of defense," the boss makes lower-status workers his "boys," who henceforth are dependent upon his paternalism. Organized criminals frequently refer to some subordinate, who might be fifty years old, as "the kid." A boss who can establish that he will assist his followers when they have been offended or when they are in need has gained control over these men. They become indebted to him. They are obligated to reciprocate, in the name of "honor" and "loyalty," thus enhancing his privileged position. The saying is, "If you don't respect the boss, no one will respect you."
>
> Those aspects of the code which prohibit appealing to outside authorities for help and justice also serve to concentrate power in the hands of the few and, hence, to enable leaders to exploit followers. The ruler of an organized-crime unit, whether it be an entire Cosa Nostra "family" or a thirty-man lottery enterprise, has three classes of enemies—law-enforcement officers, outsiders who want his profits, and underlings. The code protects him from all of them.[30]

Force and Violence

Organized crime depends upon the use or threat of force and violence, plus intimidation and bribery, as methods of operation to ensure large economic gains, to control illegal activities, and to survive in competition with other criminal groups. The "gangster," who is usually associated with organized criminal enterprises, actually performs the violent acts. Continued slaying of rival gang members marks the existence of gangland warfare. Because of underground tactics, such killings are not usually cleared by arrest.

The St. Valentine's Day massacre of 1929 stands out as the archetype of gangland warfare. Al Capone and his gang had acquired control of the illegal liquor field in the Chicago area during the Prohibition era. Eventually other rivals attempted to "muscle in" and compete for the large profits. Capone eventually exhibited superiority over his principal rival gang with summary dispatch. On St. Valentine's Day, Capone's gunmen, disguised as police officers, lined seven members of the Bugs Moran gang against the wall of a garage and mowed them down with submachine guns. Although such a mass killing in organized crime has never been equaled, hundreds of slayings have occurred in the course of economic competition in organized crime.

A more recent use of violence in organized crime has been employed in racketeering. Since the 1930s organized crime has found a fertile field in "protecting" businessmen from possible harm. By means of intimidation organized criminals have been able to extort large sums of money from legitimate businesses. A classic illustration of how the racket works can be found in the laundry business. Laundry proprietors in particular cities have been visited by gang representatives who inform the proprietors that the laundry business is in "danger" and that protection will be provided. Failure on the part of laundrymen to subscribe to the protection plan has resulted in destruction of laundry equipment or personal violence. Such demonstrations of force, provided of course by those who would otherwise provide "protection," usually convinces laundry proprietors and other businessmen that protection is worth the money demanded for it.

A government study in 1969 has concluded, however, that the trend of murders and violence has diminished as the sophistication of organized crime has increased.[31] However, the threat of force and the creation of fear may well have increased as the power base and mode of operations of organized crime have changed.

Permanent Immunity

The existence of organized crime is dependent on the maintenance of permanent immunity from interference of law enforcement agencies.[32] Permanent immunity is achieved in several ways. First, the leaders of organized crime are not usually arrested and prosecuted because they stay behind the scenes of operation. Gangland activity cannot be readily traced to its leaders. Second, persons lower in the hierarchy of organized crime, if arrested, are likely to be released by action from their superiors. Such release and avoidance of prosecution and punishment are assured through what is popularly known as the "fix." For various reasons, persons not directly involved in criminal activity contribute to the protection of organized criminals. Law enforcement officials, judges, doctors, businessmen, and others may at times provide needed services for the protection of organized criminals.

A third way in which organized crime may acquire immunity is by gaining political power through contributions to political organizations. Elected officials may owe their election to organized criminals. Furthermore, regular "payoffs" to officials provide protection for organized crime. Thus, on a permanent basis, organized crime may be immune to law enforcement through political graft and corruption. Fourth, because organized crime provides the public with illicit and desired services, such as prostitution, gambling, and narcotics, a certain amount of immunity from arrest and prosecution results from public toleration of organized crime.

A fifth means of immunity is found in the functioning of the law itself. Existing laws and enforcement procedures have not been especially successful in coping with organized crime. The survival and continuance of organized crime is possible because legal action is kept at a minimum. Lack of effective legislation and weak law enforcement are, in turn, a reflection of public toleration of organized crime in the United States.

Finally, through the infiltration of legitimate business, organized crime is able to evade the law. Organized crime today often operates behind the façade of legitimate business, obscuring its operation and making its detection difficult. Also, in the case of racketeering, organized crime escapes the law because intimidated businessmen must contend with reprisal if a report is made. In addition, organized crime and legitimate business may mutually assist one another, as in the regulation of prices of given commodities or through the enforcement of labor contracts. As Vold has commented, the interdependence of the underworld of crime and the upperworld of business assures the maintenance of both systems.[33] Mutual assistance, accompanied by public espousal of the profit motive under almost any arrangement, provides considerable assurance of immunity for organized crime.

CORRESPONDENCE BETWEEN CRIMINAL AND LEGITIMATE BEHAVIOR

While many citizens strongly condemn a stereotyped picture of organized crime, they are often in favor of the economic enterprise that makes it possible and the services that it provides. As already indicated, a number of characteristics of American society give support to organized crime. In fact, it may be argued that organized crime is a result of the particular structure of our society. To begin with, the motives for organized crime are largely the same as those valued so highly in the free enterprise system.[34] Organized crime, like legitimate business, attempts to achieve maximum returns with a minimum of expenditure through efficient organization and skilled management. The difference is that legitimate business operates within the law (most of the time) and organized crime operates outside the law. From the standpoint of the problem of control, organized crime seems to be more significantly affected by economic facts of supply and demand, and the fads and foibles in consumer habits, than by legislation and sporadic attempts at formal control.

Gambling, as a major area of operation for organized crime, is a deeply ingrained aspect of American culture. As Bloch pointed out, gambling is a natural consequence of a culture that encourages success, skill, competition, and diversion.[35] The element of chance and the tendency to speculate in certain risks not only are found in illegal gambling but are a major part of investment and finance in the legitimate business world. It is little wonder that a large-scale business has developed in America to satisfy the demand for gambling. There is an increasing demand for drugs among segments of the American population, and borrowing money at interest is a common feature of modern life. Before it was bootlegging during the Prohibition era and prostitution, all of which provided needed services.

In one of the early writings on organized crime, Lindesmith stressed the social context of organized crime when he noted that organized crime is an integral part of our total culture.[36] He observed that such factors as the profit motive, indifference to public affairs, general disregard for law, laissez-faire economics, and questionable political practices have produced a fertile place for organized crime in our large cities. Similarly, Bell has indicated that the development of organized crime, and gambling in particular, is related to immigration patterns, ethnic groups, neighborhood politics, and the American economy.[37]

Organized crime receives a great deal of public toleration in the United States because of its close relation to legitimate business. As Vold concluded:

> One basic fact stands out from the details of this discussion, namely, that organized crime must be thought of as a natural growth, or as a developmental adjunct to our general system of private profit economy. Business, industry, and finance all are competitive enterprises within the area of legal operations. But there is also an area of genuine economic demand for things and services not permitted under our legal and social codes. Organized crime is the system of business functioning in the area. It, too, is competitive, and hence must organize for its self-protection and for control of the market.[38]

Organized crime thus provides illegal services and products to business and the public. It continues to exist without a great deal of public action against it because of a hypocrisy in which citizens try to prohibit illegal practices in which they often indulge. In this clash of values and interests, organized crime provides the illegal services that the public desires. This paradox has been described as follows:

> It would seem that the vast majority of Americans today would like to have their proverbial cake and eat it, too, by theoretically affirming values which they hold dear, and, at the same time, reserving for themselves a certain leeway in realizing wishes which may not always correspond to these values. As a result, law and a high degree of lawlessness exist side by side, and moralists and gangsters complement each other.[39]

SOCIETAL REACTION AND LEGAL PROCESSING

While creation of more effective laws and an attempt at better law enforcement may assist in the control of organized crime, the structured paradox of public indignation of illegal behavior, on the one hand, and toleration and approval of illegal behavior, on the other, provide American society with its most serious handicap in the control and prevention of organized crime. The absence of a strong public reaction to organized crime has been crucial to its growth in America. "Usually, when a crime is committed, the public calls the police, but the police have to ferret out even the existence of organized crime. The many Americans who are compliant 'victims' have no incentive to report the illicit operations. The millions of people who gamble illegally are willing customers who do not wish to see their supplier destroyed."[40] The President's Commission concluded that one of the major problems in combatting organized crime is the lack of public and political commitment to its control.

> The public demands action only sporadically, as intermittent, sensational disclosures reveal intolerable violence and corruption caused by organized crime. Without sustained public pressure, political office seekers and office holders have little incentive to address themselves to combatting organized crime. A drive against organized crime usually uncovers political corruption; this means that a crusading mayor or district attorney makes many political enemies. The vicious cycle perpetuates itself. Politicians will not act unless the public so demands; but much of the urban public wants the services provided by organized crime and does not wish to disrupt the system that provides those services. And much of the public does not see or understand the effects of organized crime in society.[41]

Organized crime, as has been pointed out, gets its profits primarily from gambling and usury. In addition, it engages in narcotics distribution, labor fraud and extortion, and the control of some legitimate businesses. The profits made from illegitimate businesses are then invested in legitimate businesses which creates respectability and makes detection of the illegal profits difficult. All of these activities are interrelated and consequently are confusing to the public. With no other criminal behavior pattern, except perhaps certain occupational and corporate crime, is there such a complexity and consequent confusion in public attitudes.

Efforts to control organized crime have not been successful. None of the syndicates have been successfully broken up and few of the hierarchy have ever been convicted or imprisoned. There are many serious technical problems in effectively dealing with this type of crime.[42] First, there are serious *difficulties in obtaining proof* because of the secrecy and complexity of operations, the difficulty of getting documentary evidence, and the use of intimidation against prosecution witnesses and to deter others from cooperating with the police. The code of conduct of its members makes successful prevention even more difficult.

> Street workers, who are not members of organized crime families, cannot prove the identities of the upper-level personnel. If workers are arrested for gambling or other illicit acitivites, the fear instilled in them by the code of nondisclosure prevents their telling even the little they may know. The organization provides money and food for families of incarcerated workers; this helps to keep the workers loyal. Lawyers provided by the cartels for arrested employees preserve the interests of the organization ahead of those of the particular defendant.[43]

Second, the *lack of adequate specialized state or local law enforcement resources* to deal with the peculiar nature of organized crime is a second serious problem. Effective investigation and prosecution of organized crime requires extensive experience. One major organized crime case may take two to three years to develop and several more years to take through prosecution and appeal. Third, there is generally a *total lack of coordination* in that local police are hampered by their limited geographical jurisdiction and coordination with other agencies. And, fourth, there is a lack of *strategic intelligence reports* to forecast the nature and the future direction of organized criminal activities.

Sanctions against organized criminal activities are available, but they are difficult to employ or the penalties are extremely light because of political influence or other reasons and in light of the lucrative returns.

> Gambling is the largest source of revenue for the criminal cartels, but the members of organized crime know they can operate free of significant punishment. Street workers have little reason to be deterred from joining the ranks of criminal organizations by fear of long jail sentences or large fines. Judges are reluctant to jail bookmakers and lottery operators. Even when offenders are convicted, the sentences are often very light. Fines are paid by the organization and considered a business expense. And in other organized crime activity, when management level figures are convicted, too frequently the sentences imposed are not commensurate with the status of the offender.[44]

There is evidence, however, that stricter enforcement of some laws now available might still be unsuccessful. If a leading member of a crime syndicate is sent to prison, the organizational structure is such that someone else is available to move into his place. Moreover, vigorous enforcement is likely to result in more clever evasive devices to get around the law. Only if something can be done about organized crime as an entity might prosecution be successful, but this would involve serious constitutional questions and those of due process under the law. Organized crime can be looked at as a behavior system; it is as yet not a legal entity.

> The fact is that "organized crime," as such, is not now against the law. It is not against the criminal law for an individual or group of individuals rationally to plan, establish, develop, and administer an organization designed for the perpetration of crime. Neither is it against the law for a person to participate in such an organization. What is against the law is bet-taking, usury, smuggling and selling narcotics and untaxed liquor, extortion, murder, and conspiracy to commit these and other specific crimes.[45]

The police and prosecutors are concerned with violations of specific criminal laws rather than with the complex behavior systems described here.

NOTES

[1] See Thorsten Sellin, "Organized Crime: A Business Enterprise," *The Annals,* 347(May 1963), pp. 12–19.

[2] *The Challenge of Crime in a Free Society.* A Report by the President's Commission on Law Enforcement and Administration of Justice (Washington, D.C.: U. S. Government Printing Office, 1967), p. 194.

[3] See Virgil W. Peterson, *Barbarians in Our Midst* (Boston: Little, Brown & Company, 1952); Harry Elmer Barnes and Negley K. Teeters, *New Horizons in Criminology,* 3d ed. (Englewood Cliffs, N.J.: Prentice-Hall, 1959), Chap. 2; Ruth Shonle Cavan, *Criminology,* 3d ed., (New York: Thomas Y. Crowell Company, 1962), Chap. 6.

[4] Andrew Sinclair, *Era of Excess: A Social History of the Prohibition Movement* (New York: Harper & Row, Publishers, 1964), especially Chaps. 10 and 11.

[5] *Task Force Report: Organized Crime.* Report of the President's Commission on Law Enforcement and Administration of Justice (Washington, D.C.: U. S. Government Printing Office, 1967), p. 8. In a later publication Cressey enlarged this to include the corruptee as well. "An organized crime is any crime committed by a person occupying, in an established division of labor, a position designed for the commission of crime, *providing* that such division of labor also includes at least one position for a corrupter, one position for a corruptee, and one position for an enforcer." "The Structural Skeleton" from *Theft of the Nation: The Structure and Operations of Organized Crime in America* by Donald R. Cressey. Copyright © 1969 by Donald R. Cressey. Reprinted by permission of Harper & Row, Publishers, Inc. Donald R. Cressey, "The Functions and Structure of Criminal Syndicates," *Task Force Report:*

Organized Crime, pp. 25–60 in Appendix A. This book is an extensive revision of a report originally prepared for the President's Commission on Law Enforcement and Administration of Justice.

[6] Cressey, *Theft of the Nation,* p. xi.

[7] *The Challenge of Crime in a Free Society,* p. 189.

[8] *Ibid.*

[9] *Third Interim Report.* U. S. Senate Special Committee to Investigate Organized Crime in Interstate Commerce, p. 171.

[10] Cressey, *Theft of the Nation,* pp. 99–107.

[11] *The Challenge of Crime in a Free Society,* p. 191. For a case study of the relation of organized gambling to political corruption in a community, see John A. Gardiner, with the assistance of David J. Olson, "Wincanton: The Politics of Corruption," *Task Force Report: Organized Crime,* pp. 61–79, Appendix B.

[12] Cressey, *Theft of the Nation,* pp. 95–99.

[13] Ernest W. Burgess, "Summary and Recommendations," *Illinois Crime Survey* (Chicago: Illinois Association for Criminal Justice, 1929), pp. 1092–1094.

[14] Cressey, *Theft of the Nation,* pp. 241–242.

[15] Irving Spergel, *Racketville, Slumtown, Haulburg: An Exploratory Study of Delinquent Subcultures* (Chicago: University of Chicago Press, 1964), p. 96.

[16] *Ibid.,* p. 18.

[17] *Ibid.,* pp. 159–163.

[18] *Ibid.,* p. 100.

[19] Walter C. Reckless, *The Crime Problem,* 3d ed. (New York: Appleton-Century-Crofts, 1961), p. 203.

[20] Solomon Kobrin, "The Conflict of Values in Delinquency Areas," *American Sociological Review,* 16 (October 1951), pp. 653–661.

[21] Cressey, *Theft of the Nation,* p. 245.

[22] *Ibid.,* pp. 243–244.

[23] Gus Tyler, "The Roots of Organized Crime," *Crime and Delinquency,* 8 (October 1962), p. 338.

[24] See Virgil W. Peterson, "The Career of a Syndicate Boss," *Crime and Delinquency,* 8 (October 1962), pp. 339–354.

[25] U. S. Senate Select Committee on Improper Activities in the Labor or Management Field, *Final Report,* Pt. 3.

[26] *Organized Crime and Illicit Traffic in Narcotics,* U. S. Senate Permanent Subcommittee on Investigations, 88th Cong., 1st Sess. (Washington, D.C.: U. S. Government Printing Office, 1963), Pt. 1.

[27] The claims for a Cosa Nostra and Italian exclusiveness in it are discussed in *The Challenge of Crime in a Free Society,* pp. 191–196. See also *Task Force Report: Organized Crime* and Cressey, *Theft of the Nation.* Morris and Hawkins believe that the existence of "Cosa Nostra," some of the supposed operations, and even the name is not sufficiently documented, despite government reports, and that it is even contradictory. See Norval Morris and Gordon Hawkins, *The Honest Politician's Guide to Crime Control* (Chicago: University of Chicago Press, 1970), pp. 203–225 and particularly p. 205. Also see J. L. Albani, *American Mafia—Genesis of a Legend* (New York: Appleton-Century-Crofts, 1971). An historian, Mark Haller, has pointed out that various ethnic groups and blacks have participated in organized crime and that it has served as a means of upward mobility for some of the Italian, Irish, Polish, and Jewish immigrants and for some of those of black ancestry. See Mark H. Haller, "Organized Crime in Urban Society: Chicago in the Twentieth Century," *Journal of Social History,* 5 (Winter, 1971–1972), pp. 210–234.

[28] Robert T. Anderson, "From Mafia to Cosa Nostra," *American Journal of Sociology,* **71** (November 1965), pp. 302–310.

[29] Cressey, *Theft of the Nation,* p. 171.

[30] *Ibid.,* pp. 186–187.

[31] *Crimes of Violence.* A Staff Report to the National Commission on the Causes and Prevention of Violence, prepared by Donald J. Mulvihill and Melvin M. Tumin, with Lynn A. Curtis (Washington, D.C.: U. S. Government Printing Office, 1969), Vol. 11, pp. 195–203. Also see Mark H. Furstenberg, "Violence and Organized Crime," *Crimes of Violence,* Vol. 13, pp. 911–939.

[32] Gardiner, "Wincanton," *Task Force Report: Organized Crime.*

[33] George B. Vold, *Theoretical Criminology* (New York: Oxford University Press, 1958), pp. 237–240.

[34] Donald R. Taft and Ralph W. England, Jr., *Criminology,* 4th ed. (New York: Crowell-Collier and Macmillan, 1964), Chaps. 12 and 16.

[35] Herbert A. Bloch, "The Sociology of Gambling," *American Journal of Sociology,* **57** (1951), pp. 215–221.

[36] Alfred R. Lindesmith, "Organized Crime," *The Annals,* **217** (September 1941), pp. 76–83.

[37] Daniel Bell, "Crime as an American Way of Life," *Antioch Review,* **13** (June 1953), pp. 131–154.

[38] Vold, p. 240. Also see Daniel P. Moynihan, "The Private Government of Crime," *Reporter,* (July 6, 1961), pp. 14–20.

[39] Robert K. Woetzel, "An Overview of Organized Crime: Mores Versus Morality," *The Annals,* **347** (May 1963), p. 8.

[40] *The Challenge of Crime in a Free Society,* p. 198.

[41] *Ibid.,* p. 200.

[42] *Ibid.,* pp. 198–199.

[43] *Ibid.,* p. 198.

[44] *Ibid.,* p. 199.

[45] Cressey, *Theft of the Nation,* p. 299.

SELECTED BIBLIOGRAPHY

Albani, J. L., *American Mafia—Genesis of a Legend.* New York: Appleton-Century-Crofts, 1971.

Anderson, Robert T., "From Mafia to Cosa Nostra." *American Journal of Sociology,* **71** (November 1965), pp. 302–210.

Bell, Daniel, "Crime as an American Way of Life," in Marvin E. Wolfgang, Leonard Savitz, and Norman Johnston, eds., *The Sociology of Crime and Delinquency,* 2d ed. New York: John Wiley & Sons, Inc., 1970, pp. 165–180.

Bloch, Herbert A., "The Gambling Business: An American Paradox." *Crime and Delinquency,* **8** (October 1962), pp. 355–364.

Bloch, Herbert A., and Geis, Gilbert, *Man, Crime and Society.* New York: Random House, 1962, Chap. 9.

Cressey, Donald R., *Theft of the Nation.* New York: Harper & Row, Publishers, 1969.

———, "Organized Crime and Inner City Youth." *Crime and Delinquency,* **16** (April 1970), pp. 129–139.

Gardiner, J., *The Politics of Corruption: Organized Crime in an American City*. New York: Russell Sage Foundation, 1970.

Johnson, Earl, Jr., "Organized Crime: Challenge to the American Legal System, Part I." *Journal of Criminal Law, Criminology and Police Science*, 53 (December 1962), pp. 399–425.

Kefauver, Estes, *Crime in America*. New York: Doubleday & Company, 1951.

Lawrence, Louis A., "Bookmaking." *The Annals*, 269 (May 1950), pp. 46–54.

Lewis, Norman, *The Honored Society*. New York: Dell Publishing Company, 1964.

Lindesmith, Alfred R., "Organized Crime." *The Annals*, 217 (September 1941), pp. 76–83.

Peterson, Virgil W., "The Career of a Syndicate Boss." *Crime and Delinquency*, 8 (October 1962), pp. 339–354.

President's Commission on Law Enforcement and Administration of Justice, *The Challenge of Crime in a Free Society*. Washington, D.C.: U. S. Government Printing Office, 1967.

———, *Task Force Report: Organized Crime*. Washington, D.C.: U. S. Government Printing Office, 1967.

Schiavo, Giovanni, *The Truth about the Mafia*. New York: Vigo Press, 1962.

Sellin, Thorsten, "Organized Crime: A Business Enterprise." *The Annals*, 347 (May 1963), pp. 12–19.

Thornton, Robert Y., "Organized Crime in the Field of Prostitution." *Journal of Criminal Law, Criminology and Police Science*, 46 (March–April 1956), pp. 775–779.

Tyler, Gus, *Organized Crime in America: A Book of Readings*. Ann Arbor: University of Michigan Press, 1962.

———, "The Roots of Organized Crime." *Crime and Delinquency*, 8 (October 1962), pp. 325–338.

Vold, George B., *Theoretical Criminology*. New York: Oxford University Press, 1958, Chap. 12.

Woetzel, Robert K., "An Overview of Organized Crime: Mores Versus Morality." *The Annals*, 347 (May 1963), pp. 1–11.

Professional Criminal Behavior | 10

Professional crime differs from conventional crime in several significant ways. First, the professional criminal engages in illegal behavior for the purpose of economic gain, or even economic livelihood. Second, the criminal career of the professional criminal is highly developed. Third, considerable skill is usually involved in the crimes of the professional criminal. Fourth, the professional criminal enjoys high status among criminals. And fifth, the professional criminal is usually able to avoid detection and is fairly successful in keeping out of prison.

Most of the illegal conventional activities, such as robbery and burglary, can be performed by professional criminals. Indeed, professional criminals are increasingly becoming involved in the conventional activities, but performed in a professional way. One observer of armed robbery has thus noted that a professionalized form of armed robbery ("the heist") is emerging in the United States.[1] It consists of finding a mark (the location for the holdup), getting together a team of specialists, planning the holdup, and executing the job.

Traditionally, however, professional crime has been limited to nonviolent forms of behavior and activities that do not require the use of strong-arm tactics. In this sense, criminal activities that involve the *theft* of large sums of money through the use of skillful, nonviolent methods best represent professional crime. As such, the varieties of professional theft have been divided by one professional thief into the following categories:

1. picking pockets (cannon)
2. sneak thieving from stores, banks, and offices (the heel)
3. shoplifting (the boost)
4. stealing from jewelry stores by substituting inferior jewelry for valuable jewelry (pennyweighting)
5. stealing from hotel rooms (hotel prowling)
6. confidence game (the con)
7. miscellaneous rackets such as passing illegal checks, money orders, and other papers (hanging paper)
8. extorting money from others engaged in or about to engage in illegal acts (the shake)[2]

Sutherland's model of professional theft has dominated criminologists' thinking about professional crime.[3] Today, however, with recent studies of other criminal activities, the concept of professional crime is expanding.[4] Moreover, professional crime as a behavior system is in the process of change, meeting the demands of a changing society.

Therefore, for our purposes, professional crime can be divided into six subtypes:

1. larceny (including shoplifting, pickpocketing, sneak thieving)
2. confidence games
3. robbery
4. burglary
5. forgery (including counterfeiting)
6. extortion

In all cases, the crimes differ from conventional crime in terms of the distinct behavior system of the professional criminal.

LEGAL ASPECTS OF SELECTED OFFENSES

Generally the character of professional crime is determined apart from the criminal law. That is, it is not the legal definition of the behavior that distinguishes professional crime from other crimes, but it is the way in which the crime is performed that determines the professional character of the behavior. For example, the criminal law is not of much help in defining the confidence game. Most jurisdictions do not even reserve a special statute for confidence game crimes. Instead, confidence game crimes are included under such general practices as fraud, embezzlement, forgery, gambling, and swindling.

What distinguishes such professional crimes as the confidence game from such legal categories as fraud, then, are the facts that are associated with the commission of the act. In the confidence game, the important factor is the way in which the victim is involved. The victim is never innocent, but is led into a scheme where he may benefit through his own dishonesty.

> The practices of swindling and forgery and the perpetration of various fraudulent schemes which prey upon the victim's innocence, ignorance, or gullibility are not classified as confidence. Such schemes merely seek to cheat someone because of his ignorance or naivete. Therefore, cheating little old ladies or amorous widows cannot be considered as confidence unless these ladies are led into some scheme they know to be dishonest— a scheme which they believe will help them achieve some gain. They, however, are "taken" themselves. The practice of confidence, then, is the manipulation of the victim through nonviolent methods into a situation of dishonesty in order to take advantage of the victim's dishonesty.[5]

Such a definition of the confidence game is not usually found in the criminal law. Professional crimes, for the most part, then, are sociological constructs rather than legal categories.

Most of the laws that are violated in the course of pursuing professional crime have thus been created to regulate conventional behaviors. This is nowhere better illustrated than in the case of the law of theft. For at one time the idea of theft, even in its most conventional forms, did not exist. It was with expanding production and trade that the law was established to protect the property of the propertied classes. Whether or not that property was taken by amateur, conventional, or professional criminals was not the issue. Rather, that the property of the merchant was to be protected from theft was the overriding issue.

The law of theft emerged out of the Carrier's Case in fifteenth-century England.[6] The legal problem in the case was that of precedent. That is, heretofore the common law held that anyone in possession of property could not technically steal that property. But in the Carrier's Case, property (probably wool or cloth) was taken by the person transporting the property, who did not own the property (the bailee). The judges, in order to meet the changing social and economic demands, departed from precedent, opening the door for the modern law of theft.

The social and economic conditions of the period were crucial forces behind the decision of the judges in the Carrier's Case. A new order, based on industry and trade, was developing. Even the Crown was heavily involved and, like all merchants, needed the protection of laws to successfully carry out trade. To assure the safe transport of their products, the law of theft was created. Eventually, with the growth of banking and the use of paper money, the law was expanded to include embezzlement by clerks, officers, and the like. Thus, the legal protection of property has always been to the interest of the propertied classes of society. How that property was taken, and by whom, was of less importance than the loss of the property.

Only in recent years have laws considered the nature of professionally executed offenses. The federal government, for example, now has the power to prosecute the confidence man if the victim has been induced to cross a state line in getting the money, provided the amount is over $5000. In addition, the United States Postal Service can have confidence men prosecuted when such offenses infringe upon using-the-mails-to-defraud laws. Tax laws regulate some of the activities in the confidence rackets, and increased regulation of the stock market controls to some extent the professional trade in fraudulent stocks.

But professional criminals are still able to operate around these laws. Such is the very nature of professional crime. Maurer, in his study of the big con, thus concludes:

> Confidence men trade upon certain weaknesses in human nature. Hence, until human nature changes perceptibly there is little possibility that there will be a shortage of marks for con games. And so long as there are marks with that fatal combination of larceny and money, the

law will find great difficulty in suppressing confidence games, even assuming a sincere interest on the part of local officials. Increased legal obstacles have, in the past, had little ultimate effect upon confidence men except, perhaps, to make them more wary and to force them to perfect their work to a still finer point. As long as the political boss—whether he be local, state, or national, foreign or of the home-grown variety—fosters a machine wherein graft and bribery are looked upon as a normal phase of government, and as long as juries, judges, and key enforcement officers can be had for a price, the confidence man will continue to live and thrive.[7]

CRIMINAL CAREER OF THE OFFENDER

Of all the criminal offenders, the professional criminal has the most highly developed criminal career; and as the word implies, professional criminals are accorded great prestige by other criminals. They engage in a variety of highly specialized crimes, all of which are directed toward economic gain. By means of skill and sometimes elaborate techniques, professional criminals are often able to acquire considerable sums of money without being arrested or prosecuted.

Professional criminals tend to come from better economic backgrounds than do conventional and organized criminals. Many, according to one professional thief, start in legitimate employment as salesmen, hotel clerks, waiters, or bellboys.[8] A person entering professional crime may continue to engage in his legitimate employment until he is successful in crime.

The professional criminal is also likely to begin his career at a relatively late age. Furthermore, once in professional crime, he tends to continue in it for the rest of his life. The life career of the confidence man has been summarized in the following way:

> The con man begins his special career at a much older age than other criminals, or perhaps it is better said that he continues his criminal career at a time when others may be relinquishing theirs. Unemployment occasioned by old age does not seem to be a problem of con men; age ripens their skills, insight, and wit, and it also increases the confidence they inspire in their victims. With age the con man may give up the position of the roper and shift to being an inside man, but even this may not be absolutely necessary. It is possible that cultural changes outmode the particular con games older men have been accustomed to playing and thereby decrease their earnings somewhat, but this seems unlikely. We know of one con man who is seventy years of age and has a bad heart, but he is still as effective as he ever was.[9]

The longevity in crime is attributable in part, of course, to the fact that very few professional criminals are ever arrested, brought to trial, convicted, or serve time in prison.

A significant characteristic of professional criminals is the philosophy of life they develop to justify their criminal careers. But, as Tannenbaum has noted, "the philosophy of criminals does not differ from that of any other group. So far as other men believe in a set of assumptions and use them to explain their conduct, so far they do no more and no less than the criminal does. Each uses his philosophy of life as a means of making his activities seem reasonable."[10] In his relations with persons of similar interest, the professional criminal acquires a philosophy which gives him answers to questions related to the worth of his activity and to his own self-image.

Basic to the professional criminal's philosophy of life is the belief that all men are actually dishonest and that the criminal is engaging in activity similar to that of other businessmen. The professional criminal also justifies his behavior by the belief that all noncriminals would commit crime if they could. As one successful confidence man, Joseph "Yellow Kid" Weil, said of himself:

> The men I fleeced were basically no more honest than I was. One of the motivating factors in my action was, of course, the desire to acquire money. The other motive was a lust for adventure. The men I swindled were also motivated by a desire to acquire money, and they didn't care at whose expense they got it. I was particular. I took money only from those who could afford it and were willing to go in with me in schemes they fancied would fleece others.[11]

The victim of the con game, after all, has been willing to participate in a crime in order to make money. The professional criminal can justify his own crime in terms of the behavior of the victim. Such justifications are, of course, shared and supported by professional criminals in their associations with one another.

There are, of course, distinct variations in the careers of the different types of professional criminals. Among confidence men alone, for instance, there is "a continuum ranging from the unsuccessful, bungling, frequently arrested short-con man (flimflammer), whose modus operandi is dated and pitched at a low level, to the highly successful, accomplished big-con man who is infrequently arrested and whose modus operandi is original and pitched at a high level."[12] Although short con men learn their "trade" from the big con, they lack the finesse, skill, and industry necessary to become successful in the big con games. They are able, nevertheless, to maintain a rationalization for their behavior, comparing it to other criminal behavior as well as to other occupations:

> You know how it goes in this dog-eat-dog world. You got to take the other guy before he takes you. You know, the real sharpie outwits the marks. Of course, it all depends on how you get ahead. My way was no different from, say, a lawyer or businessman. You know, a lawyer has a license to steal. The cops should lay off con men. We don't hurt nobody. You can't con an honest man. The mark has more larceny in his heart than we do. The cops should do their job and clear the streets of the

muggers, heist men, hop heads, and the rest. Why, it's dangerous for a decent man like me to walk down the street at night.[13]

Most professional criminals are extremely careful in selecting their victims. They believe that some people are more worthy of being victimized than others. The professional robber, for example, makes a conscious effort to choose victims that can well afford the loss, primarily large organizations such as a bank or supermarket.[14] The employee therefore is not regarded as the victim by the professional robber. In the robbery encounter, the employee is not a victim who will suffer a personal loss, but is merely an agent of the impersonal organization that is being victimized.

Bob is a twenty-five-year-old white man. His arrest record indicates no recent arrests. According to him, he and his accomplices had committed a series of seven or eight robberies of public utility offices in the months before they were arrested. He is now serving a ten-to-twenty year term for robbery in a state prison.

He became involved in this series of robberies at his brother's suggestion. The latter was out of jail on bail pending trial for another robbery and needed money to hire a lawyer. In the past, his brother had found that public utility offices were lucrative targets to rob, providing large sums of money and minimum resistance. Because Bob's brother was "hot," he stayed in the car during the robbery while Bob and another accomplice entered the office to get the money.

One of the rules observed during the series of holdups was that no customer who happened to be in the office was to be robbed. One reason for this was that such an act would be another charge of robbery if they were caught. More important was the feeling that since the customer would be parting with his own money, resistance was more likely. Such resistance might lead to injury to the victim or create a disturbance which would bring the police to the scene. Another reason for not robbing the customer was that the amount of money he was carrying was apt to be small when compared to the sum that would be taken from the public utility.

These robberies were spaced every two or three weeks over a six-month period. Experience with this crime meant that the gang knew they could get about $5000 to $10,000 each time they robbed, and that less planning was needed each time they robbed. They knew how roles would be allocated, how the money would be divided (equally among the partners), and what obstacles they might encounter inside the office. Mapping the escape route was the only thing that had to be done differently each time.[15]

The professional thief has similar rationalizations for his acts, based on considerable truth. He can easily hold that stealing is an honest way to make a living. Talking about his life style, a professional thief in San Quentin makes the following observations:

The way I see it a guy has several ways to go in this world. If he's not rich in front, he can stay honest and be a donkey. Only this way he works for someone else and gets fucked the rest of his life. They cheat him and break his back. But this guy is honest.

Now another way is he can start cheating and lying to people and maybe he can make himself a lot of money in business, legally I mean. But this guy isn't honest. If he's honest and tries to make it this way he won't get nowhere.

Another way he can make it and live a halfway decent life and still be honest is to steal. Now I don't mean sneaking around and taking money or personal property from assholes who don't have nothing. I mean going after big companies. To me this is perfectly honest, because these companies are cheating people anyway. When you go and just take it from them, you are actually more honest than they are. Most of the time, anyway, they are insured and make more money from the caper than you do.

Really, I think it is too bad it is this way. I mean it. I wish a guy could make a decent living working, which he can't do because those people who have it made got that way fucking the worker. And they are going to keep it that way. And all the crap about having to have laws protecting property. These are just laws set up by those people who got all the property and are going to make sure they keep it.[16]

The professional thief's comments on the nature of law and society could enlighten the work of most criminologists.

GROUP SUPPORT OF CRIMINAL BEHAVIOR

The social nature of professional theft has been summarized by Sutherland in his interpretation of an extensive document written by a professional thief.[17] Sutherland observed that professional theft is characterized by (1) *skill*—a complex of techniques exists for committing crime; (2) *status*—professional criminals have a position of high prestige in the world of crime; (3) *consensus*—professional criminals share common values, beliefs, and attitudes, with an *esprit de corps* among members; (4) *differential association*—association is with other professional criminals to the exclusion of law-abiding persons and other criminals; and (5) *organization*—activities are pursued in terms of common knowledge and through an informal information and assistance system. Related to these characteristics are several others which are also associated with the group support that underlies professional crime.

The recruitment of persons into professional theft is fairly well established. Recognition by other professional thieves, as Sutherland has noted, is the absolutely necessary and definitive characteristic of the professional thief.[18] Without such recognition, no amount of knowledge and experience can provide the criminal with the requirements for a successful career in professional crime.

Included in the process of acquiring recognition as a professional thief are the two necessary elements of selection and tutelage.[19] A person cannot acquire recognition until he has had tutelage or the necessary training, and tutelage is granted only to a few selected persons. Selection and tutelage are interrelated and continuous processes. A person is tentatively recognized and selected for limited training and in the course of tutelage advances to more certain stages of recognition.

Contact is, of course, a necessary requisite for selection and tutelage. Professional criminals may come in contact with prospective professionals through their limited association with other criminals (amateur thieves, burglars), with persons on the fringes of criminal activity (pimps, "fences"), or with persons engaged in legitimate occupations. The contacts may be made in places where professional criminals are working, in jails, or in places of leisure-time activities. Selection is reciprocal in that both professional thieves and prospective candidates must be in mutual agreement regarding the arrangement.

Tutelage involves the learning of skills, techniques, attitudes, and values through informal means. The neophyte, rather than receiving formal verbal instruction, learns while engaging in criminal activity. During the probationary period the neophyte assimilates standards of group morality, such as honesty among thieves and not informing on others; learns methods of stealing and disposing of goods; and becomes acquainted with other professional criminals. Gradually he is accepted as a professional thief. And as long as the recognition continues, whether he continues in criminal activity or not, he is regarded as a professional criminal by other professional thieves.

The social nature of other forms of professional crime is somewhat different from that of professional theft. Some professional criminals may work alone. And some professional criminals are self-taught, requiring little tutelage or recognition. Consider the example of two California bank robbers who decided to go into crime on their own, after researching the possibilities:

> So we decided to go into crime, and, in order to decide which branch we wanted to go into, since we were both inexperienced criminals at the time, we decided to do as much research as we could and find out which made the most money the fastest and that percentagewise was the safest. I think you'll find that every public library in a city has statistics on the number of crimes committed the previous year, how much money each crime was, and you could figure out, from the amount stolen, the number of crooks caught, and the number of convictions, what you wanted to know. We spent four days at the public library and we researched, and we came up with armed robbery as the most likely for us.[20]

In the case of fraudulent check writing, little training is necessary. The skills required are elementary. The learning of check writing by "Sam" has been described as follows:

He was first a check writer, which is a craft requiring little or no tutelage. It takes no great flash of wisdom to realize that people will give you money for a slice of paper or to realize that if you are going to depend on that for your livelihood, it might be more pleasant to use names other than your own. Highly skilled craft aspects, such as check raising, are now fairly rare. The problem in check passing is handling the person with the money you want, and that is dependent on personal style rather than technical skill. Check writing is a solitary profession, it is better done alone, it is one in which the worst thing that can happen is to become well-known. Check writers do not socialize very well; they may meet in jail, but they do not tend to hang around together outside.[21]

Check writing is not the only professional crime that can be successfully executed alone and without a great deal of training. Although professional shoplifters sometimes work in small troupes, many prefer to work alone.[22] Similarly, Lemert found in this study of check forgers that these offenders work alone, carefully avoiding contacts and interaction with other criminals. "Moreover, their preference for solitude and their secretiveness give every appearance of a highly generalized reaction; they avoid not only coopera- tive crime but also any other kinds of association with criminals. They are equally selective and cautious in their contacts and associations with the noncriminal population, preferring not to become involved in any enduring personal relationships."[23]

And in the case of armed robbery, when social organization does exist among career offenders, it is usually in the form of a partnership. Rather than the permanent association of offenders, group activity is on a smaller and more flexible basis.

Hence there is little evidence in the social organization of robbers of group cohesion during periods of stress in the manner described by Sutherland. The robber's organization is a more fluid arrangement taking into account existing conditions; it is not conceived by those involved as a permanent group but more or less a loose confederation of individuals joined together for a specific purpose on a short-term basis. Among certain types of robbers specific role relationships do develop; however, these always are assumed to be temporary by the robbery participants even though the association is of some duration. When this type of social organization exists no provision need be made for incapacitated mem- bers; each member considers himself on his own.[24]

Thus, many professional criminals today, especially the professional "heavy" criminals, form into groups only for specific purposes, disbanding when the need for assistance no longer exists.[25] Professional criminals are only loosely organized, and the degree of group activity varies according to the requirements of the situation.

A final way of looking at the social nature of professional crime is through the language of the offender. While many criminals tend to use a distinctive language, some types of professional criminals have an extensive and colorful argot. The hundreds of terms used by these professional offenders have developed over a considerable period of time; many were common in the seventeenth century. The language has grown out of the specialized activity of the professional criminal. The argot used reflects the attitudes of the professional toward the law, himself, the victim, other criminals, and society in general. As an example of this argot, Maurer, in an extensive analysis of the argot of the professional pickpocket, quotes a professional pickpocket who gave the following account of what happened to him in police court:

> *Judge*: Now you just tell the Court in your own way what you were doing.
> *Me*: Well, Judge, your honor, I was out gandering around for a soft mark and made a tip that was going to cop a short. I eased myself into the tip and just topped a leather in Mr. Bates' left prat when I blowed I was getting a jacket from these two honest bulls. So I kick the okus back in his kick and I'm clean. Just then this flatfoot nails me, so here I am on a bum rap. All I crave is justice, and I hope she ain't blind.[26]

Within professional crime, there are distinctive argots according to the various types of criminal activity. Some of the argots are closely related, while others are widely divergent. All real professionals are able to speak the one argot that is associated with their particular crime. Extensive knowledge of the argot is truly the mark of the professional; many years are required to use it effectively.

Why do argots develop? According to Maurer there are several reasons.[27] First, because professional criminals work outside the law, there are strong pressures to consolidate the criminal subculture. A common argot serves to develop group solidarity and provides a sense of camaraderie among members of the subculture. Second, specialized work requires and fosters the creation of a special language. Professional criminals within a particular racket, as craftsmen, are faced with identical problems which must be solved with certain known techniques. Third, many concepts exist for professional criminals for which there are no terms in the vocabulary of the ordinary citizen. It is necessary that professional criminals create, borrow, or adapt words to meet their unique needs. Finally, Maurer discredits the usually assumed reason for criminal argot, that is, that criminals develop a special language to confuse and deceive their victims. Maurer believes this form of argot usage is minimal and limited. Most professionals speak argot only among themselves, not in the presence of outsiders. It appears that secrecy and deception are very minor reasons for the formation and use of argot among professional criminals. The specialized language serves, rather, as a means of social support for the way of life of the professional criminal.

CORRESPONDENCE BETWEEN CRIMINAL
AND LEGITIMATE BEHAVIOR

A similarity exists between professional criminal behavior and the legitimate behavior patterns of conventional society in that the professional criminal is engaged in a full-time pursuit; he is self-employed. Also, normally law-abiding persons must serve as "accomplices" in order for some forms of professional crime to exist. The confidence game perhaps best illustrates the correspondence between professional criminal behavior and legitimate behavior patterns.

Of the types of professional theft, the confidence game is the most sophisticated and respected form. Furthermore, the "big con" is the aristocrat of professional crime and is granted the greatest prestige in the world of crime. Confidence men receive this deference not only because of their ability to gain large sums of money through skill, without the use of guns and violence, but also because of their cultural backgrounds, their dress and manners, and their general style of life.

Confidence games are generally divided roughly into big con and short con games. Short con games require only a short period of time to carry out and are limited to small amounts of money. Big con games require a longer period of time and involve larger sums of money. Short con games take place between one or two con men and their victim. Big con games generally require the abilities and planning of a number of persons. Big con games proceed through a series of steps. Maurer, who has extensively studied forms of the big con, such as the "wire" and the "pay-off" (racing swindles), and the "rag" (involving stocks and bonds), lists the following steps in a big con swindle:

1. locating and investigating a well-to-do victim (putting the mark up)
2. gaining the victim's confidence (playing the con for him)
3. steering him to meet the insideman (roping the mark)
4. permitting the insideman to show him how he can make a large amount of money dishonestly (telling him the tale)
5. allowing the victim to make a substantial profit (giving him the convincer)
6. determining exactly how much he will invest (giving him the breakdown)
7. sending him home for this amount of money (putting him on the send)
8. playing him against a big store and fleecing him (taking off the touch)
9. getting him out of the way as quickly as possible (blowing him off)
10. forestalling action by the law (putting in the fix)[28]

Thus, the first requirement for the operation of a con game is the willing participation of an accomplice. A prospective victim, the "mark," must be found who will enter into an illegal scheme. Such an alliance assures the con man a degree of protection and makes the victim a partner in the proceedings. The legitimate behavior patterns of our society are suggestive of, or at least neutral toward, participation in the confidence scheme. This is illustrated in a comment by one professional con man who noted the following: "It is hard to con an honest man, but there are so few truly honest men that the so-called con game can be successfully worked on the average person. A professional con man works on the assumption that 99 out of every 100 people are suckers."[29]

In his study of the big con, Maurer has observed that most marks come from the upper strata of society.[30] Included among marks are bankers, wealthy farmers, police officials, and professional men, especially doctors, lawyers, dentists, and an occasional college professor. Even respectable church trustees on occasion use church funds in order to play the con game. One church trustee, who was sentenced to prison for misappropriating church funds, received the following wry comment from his con man, ironically, who was acquitted: "He was a very religious man, but I guess the temptation for the dough was too much for his scruples." But, according to Maurer, it is the businessman that makes the best mark.

> Businessmen, active or retired, make fine marks for big-con games. In fact, probably the majority of marks fleeced by the big-time confidence men are businessmen. Their instincts are sound for the confidence game, they respond well to the magnetic personalities of roper and inside-man, and they have or can raise the necessary capital with which to plunge heavily.[31]

The confidence game, thus, can be best understood as a sociological phenomenon in relation to legitimate behavior patterns. As Schur has indicated, the confidence game appeals to the playful, sporting, and manipulative aspects of our society.[32] Confidence games, much like the games of the young, represent a form of pleasurable activity. Confidence game activity also appeals to the American value of successful salesmanship. The con man, as a successful businessman, is able to outwit members of the public who are willing to participate in illegal activity.

Another indication of the relation between professional crime and legitimate behavior is found in the "fence" who assists in the successful operation of professional theft. Since nearly all professional theft is undertaken for economic gain, the stolen merchandise must be sold in some way. The fence, often a clothing or appliance dealer, or a jewelry merchant, serves as the middleman between the thief and the sale of the merchandise. The professional thief thereby reduces the risk of being arrested with the goods in his possession and avoids the necessity of having to sell the goods on the open market. And the fence is able to supplement his legitimate business.

The close association between professional crime and legitimate society is finally evident in the patterns of professional crime, and the changes in these patterns. In a task force report by the President's Crime Commission, the following associations and changes were noted:

> As conditions in society change, certain criminal occupations become relatively unprofitable, and other opportunities develop. The nature of crime will tend to change accordingly. Criminal activity like legitimate business activity may respond to the market, to supply and demand curves, and to technological developments. Professional crime, guided by the profit motive, can be expected to be particularly responsive to such factors. One example is the reported decline in safecracking. This is apparently due in part to such factors as increased law enforcement surveillance and mobility, and improvements in the design of safes. Undoubtedly the fact that safes no longer play an important role has also contributed to the decline—modern economic transactions involve the transfer of credits much more than the transfer of cash. Thus it may have become both more difficult and riskier to rob safes, and also less profitable. At the same time, more promising opportunities for crime have arisen. One of these is check-passing. The Commission's study learned that nearly every burglar nowadays is also in the check business. One professional burglar said that in one period of several weeks between burglaries he passed over $20,000 of stolen checks. A generation ago burglars did not even look for checks to steal.[33]

Other changes in professional crime, influenced by social and economic changes, include crimes related to the automobile, such as auto theft, auto stripping, and stealing from parked cars. There has also been a rapid increase in frauds related to home improvement and insurance. In general, professional criminals are turning from picking pockets, confidence games, and bank robbery to other economic opportunities. Professional crime, like legitimate activities, must alter its enterprises, diversify, or reorganize in order to remain solvent.

SOCIETAL REACTION AND LEGAL PROCESSING

The relatively high status of professional criminals is indicated, not only by their relation to other types of offenders, but also by the special treatment they are accorded by the police, court officials, and others. Because of their favored position in crime, professional criminals are able to make arrangements with public officials that allow them to avoid conviction and punishment. The professional criminal may even be able to avoid arrest by regular payments to certain officials.

The professional criminal has the ability to fix cases because of the cooperation of certain members of society. One professional criminal described the involvement of others in the fix as follows:

In order to send a thief to the penitentiary, it is necessary to have the cooperation of the victim, witnesses, police, bailiffs, clerks, grand jury, jury, prosecutor, judge, and perhaps others. A weak link in this chain can practically always be found, and any of the links can be broken if you have pressure enough. There is no one who cannot be influenced if you go at it right and have sufficient backing, financially and politically. It is difficult if the victim is rich or important; it is more difficult in some places than in others. But it can practically always be done. It is just a question, if you have the backing, of using your head until you find the right way.[34]

A major point in the fix is the police department. Even before the arrest, provisions for a fix can be made by the professional criminal. As Sam the check writer has observed:

But about paying off, what we were talking about before: only once in a while can you do it, and the time to pay off is before you ever get arrested. If you got a policeman in town and you're going there—say he's chief of detectives or he's chief investigator for the service department or something like that—then before the case is ever even negotiated, before you've ever even done the crime, if you have given him a new hat or bought him a steak once in a while or taken him fishing or something like that, then you have a better chance. Then you can *talk* to him.[35]

Sam maintained a working relationship with the police department:

This same man who was in charge of the check department, I have had him call me numerous times wanting gals for the policemen and wanting to score for some grass or some pills. He'd get to partying and want to stay high. Or when I had my joint, he'd call me up and tell me that the chief wanted a case of liquor because he's going to have a party. And all this is accepted.[36]

The selection of a lawyer is also important to the professional criminal in providing for the fix. As the check writer notes:

When you want a lawyer, you don't want a trial lawyer, you want a fixer. You don't care how good he is in a courtroom, you want to fix it; you don't want to go to trial. You're hiring him *not* to go to trial. And if you *have* to go to trial, you're hiring him to get the least amount of time, you're hiring him so whenever you walk into the courtroom you already know what you're going to get because he's already dealt out what.[37]

And a different kind of lawyer is needed if the case goes to court:

But if you got to go to trial, then you don't want any one of these old fixers that doesn't know how to fight a case. You want a good trial lawyer. And most good trial lawyers are young lawyers that are right out of law school, because at law school they've practiced on this and they're actually better than some of your older lawyers.[38]

In other words, the professional criminal is able to escape conviction because of certain informal processes that operate in the administration of the law. Or to put it more directly, "no criminal subculture can operate continuously and professionally without the connivance of the law."[39]

Public toleration of professional crime results from a combination of factors, including the correspondence between some forms of professional crime and some legitimate behavior patterns, the involvement of the public as victims in illegal arrangements, and public apathy toward crimes that do not affect each person directly and concretely. Maurer has suggested also that the public tolerates professional crime because of a naïveness about crime and the relationship between the criminal and the law.

> The man in the street sees crime something like this: if a confidence man trims someone, he should be indicted and punished; first he must be caught; then he must be tried; then, if convicted, he should be sent to prison to serve his full term. The average citizen—if we ignore his tendency to wax sentimental about all criminals—can be generally counted upon to adopt the following assumptions: that the victim of the swindle is both honest and unfortunate; that the officers of the law want to catch the con men; that the court wishes to convict the criminals; that if the court frees the con men, they are *ipso facto* innocent; that if they are convicted, they will be put in the penitentiary where they belong to serve out their time at hard labor. If these assumptions even approximated fact, confidence men would have long ago found it impossible to operate.[40]

The myth that surrounds the operation of the legal process no doubt serves as a device for the public toleration of much crime.

But perhaps the greatest barrier to any form of societal reaction is the lack of social visibility enjoyed by professional criminals.[41] Because of the lack of social visibility, professional crime escapes strong reaction from the legal system, the victim, and society at large. The professional criminal is able to carry out his offenses without being detected. He is able to escape being reported by the victim because the victim is often involved in the offense. Furthermore, the acts of the professional criminal are usually attributed to conventional and amateur offenders. The result is the relative obscurity of the professional criminal, which also means the continuation of a low degree of social visibility.

Finally, everything seems to indicate that professional crime is changing as other changes are taking place in society. At the end of the last century, persons and organizations that were the victims of professional crime established a number of schemes that subsequently brought about a change in the organization and operation of professional crime.[42] The establishment of the bankers' associations, the creation of merchants' protective agencies, and improvements in police methods have made the risks for some forms of professional crime exceedingly great. Also important has been the increasingly widespread use of business and payroll checks as well as personal checks. Because of these reactions, the systematic check forger no longer has to resort to criminal associates or to employ the more complex procedures used in past decades. Thus, it can be seen that professional crime, as is true of other types of crime, is related to the structure of society. As society and the reaction to crime change, so do the organization and operation of the types of crime.

NOTES

1 Everett DeBaum, "The Heist: The Theory and Practice of Armed Robbery," *Harper's Magazine*, **200** (February 1950), pp. 69–77.
2 "Chic Conwell," in Edwin H. Sutherland, *The Professional Thief* (Chicago: University of Chicago Press, 1937), Chap. 3.
3 Sutherland, *The Professional Thief*, Chap. 9.
4 Especially Werner J. Einstadter, "The Social Organization of Armed Robbery," *Social Problems*, **17** (Summer 1969), pp. 64–83; Edwin M. Lemert, "The Behavior of the Systematic Check Forger," *Social Problems*, **6** (Fall 1958), pp. 141–149; and John E. Conklin, *Robbery and the Criminal Justice System* (Philadelphia: J. P. Lippincott Company, 1972), pp. 63–68.
5 Robert Louis Gasser, "The Confidence Game," *Federal Probation*, **27** (December 1963), p. 27.
6 Jerome Hall, *Theft, Law and Society*, 2d ed. (Indianapolis: Bobbs-Merrill Company, 1952).
7 From *The Big Con* (p. 256), copyright, 1940, R. 1968, by David W. Maurer, reprinted by permission of the publisher, The Bobbs-Merrill Company, Inc.
8 Sutherland, *The Professional Thief*, pp. 21–25.
9 Edwin M. Lemert, *Social Pathology* (New York: McGraw-Hill Book Company, 1951), pp. 323–324.
10 Frank Tannenbaum, *Crime and the Community* (New York: Columbia University Press, 1938), p. 177.
11 Joseph R. Weil and W. T. Brannon, *"Yellow Kid" Weil* (Chicago: Ziff-Davis Publishing Company, 1948), p. 293.
12 Julian B. Roebuck and Ronald C. Johnson, "The 'Short Con' Man," *Crime and Delinquency*, **10** (July 1964), p. 237.
13 *Ibid.*, p. 243.
14 Einstadter, "The Social Organization of Armed Robbery," p. 80.
15 Conklin, *Robbery*, pp. 66–67.
16 John Irwin, *The Felon* (Englewood Cliffs, N. J.: Prentice-Hall, 1970), p. 11.
17 Sutherland, *The Professional Thief*, Chap. 9.
18 *Ibid.*, p. 211.
19 *Ibid.*, pp. 211–215.
20 Reprinted with permission of The Macmillan Company from *A Thief's Primer*, p. 20, by Bruce Jackson. Copyright © 1969 by Bruce Jackson.
21 *Ibid.*, p. 23.
22 Mary Owen Cameron, *The Booster and the Snitch: Department Store Shoplifting* (New York: The Free Press, 1964), pp. 40–45.
23 Lemert, "The Behavior of the Systematic Check Forger," p. 143.
24 Einstadter, "The Social Organization of Armed Robbery," pp. 67–68.

[25] See Don C. Gibbons, *Society, Crime, and Criminal Careers* (Englewood Cliffs, N. J.: Prentice-Hall, 1968), pp. 255–257.
[26] David W. Maurer, *Whiz Mob* (New Haven, Conn.: College and University Press, 1964), p. 55.
[27] Maurer, *The Big Con*, pp. 228–229.
[28] *Ibid.*, pp. 15–16.
[29] Gasser, "The Confidence Game," p. 47.
[30] Maurer, *The Big Con*, Chap. 4.
[31] *Ibid.*, p. 94.
[32] Edwin H. Schur, "Sociological Analysis of Confidence Swindling," *Journal of Criminal Law, Criminology and Police Science*, 48 (September–October 1957), pp. 296–304.
[33] President's Commission on Law Enforcement and Administration of Justice, *Crime and Its Impact—An Assessment* (Washington, D.C.: U. S. Government Printing Office, 1967), pp. 98–99.
[34] Sutherland, *The Professional Thief*, pp. 82–83.
[35] Jackson, *A Thief's Primer*, p. 133.
[36] *Ibid.*, pp. 123–124.
[37] *Ibid.*, p. 130.
[38] *Ibid.*, p. 131.
[39] Maurer, *Whiz Mob*, p. 129.
[40] Maurer, *The Big Con*, p. 176.
[41] James A. Inciardi, "Visibility, Societal Reaction, and Criminal Behavior," *Criminology*, 10 (1972).
[42] Lemert, "The Behavior of the Systematic Check Forger," pp. 146–147.

SELECTED BIBLIOGRAPHY

Bloch, Herbert A., and Geis, Gilbert, "Professional Crime." *Man, Crime, and Society*, 2d ed. New York: Random House, 1970, pp. 167–189.
Cameron, Mary Owen, *The Booster and the Snitch: Department Store Shoplifting*. New York: The Free Press, 1964.
Einstadter, Werner J., "The Social Organization of Armed Robbery." *Social Problems*, 17 (Summer 1969), pp. 64–83.
Gasser, Robert Louis, "The Confidence Game." *Federal Probation*, 27 (December 1963), pp. 27–54.
Jackson, Bruce, *A Thief's Primer*. New York: The Macmillan Company, 1969.
Lemert, Edwin M., "The Behavior of the Systematic Check Forger." *Social Problems*, 6 (Fall 1958), pp. 141–149.
Maurer, David W., *The Big Con*. New York: Signet Books, 1962.
———, *Whiz Mob*. New Haven, Conn.: College and University Press, 1964.
Polsky, Ned, "The Hustler." *Social Problems*, 12 (Summer 1964), pp. 3–15.
Roebuck, Julian B., "The Negro Numbers Man as a Criminal Type: The Construction and Application of a Typology." *Journal of Criminal Law, Criminology and Police Science*, 54 (March 1963), pp. 48–60.
———, and Johnson, Ronald C., "The 'Short Con' Man." *Crime and Delinquency*, 10 (July 1964), pp. 235–248.

Schur, Edwin M., "Sociological Analysis of Confidence Swindling." *Journal of Criminal Law, Criminology and Police Science,* 48 (September–October 1957), pp. 296–304.

Sutherland, Edwin H., *The Professional Thief.* Chicago: University of Chicago Press, 1937.

Name Index

Subject Index

Theft, 24, 57, 58, 131, 132, 134, 138, 144, 194, 200
  auto, 18, 57, 59, 62, 63, 73, 132, 133, 139, 146, 258
  blue collar, 192
  by employees, 200–201
  professional criminals and, 246, 247, 251–253, 256, 257, 258
Trade, restraint of, 20, 189, 207
Trademarks, misuse of, 20, 189, 207, 208
Traffic offenses, 78
Traitors, 161
Treason, 154, 179
Trends in criminal typology, 14
Trespassing, 155
Types of criminal behavior, 1–21
Typologies, 2–21
  criminology and, 2–10
  empirical, 11
  ideal, 11
  individualistic, 5–7
  legalistic, 3–5
  social, 7–10

Usury, organized crime and, 240

Vagrancy, 78, 107, 117
Vandalism, 18, 24, 57–59, 61–74
Violence, 24–50
  collective, 24, 158
  crimes of, 24–56
  intraracial nature of, 39–40
  organized crime and, 237
  situational interaction and, 40–42
  subcultures of, 29–34
Violent personal criminal behavior, 16, 18, 24–56
  correspondence between legitimate behavior and, 18, 45–48
  criminal career of offenders, 18, 27–29
  group support of, 18, 29–45
  legal aspects of, 18, 25–27
  legal processing of, 18, 48–50
  societal reactions to, 18, 48–50
Volstead Act, 224
Voorhis Act, 155

War crimes, 159, 165, 166, 169, 174, 181
War Resisters League, 167
White collar crime, 187–202, 206